OXFORD WORLD'S CLASSICS

WILLIAM HAZLITT
SELECTED WRITINGS

WILLIAM HAZLITT was born in Maidstone in 1778, the second son of a radical, Unitarian minister. After a brief period in the United States, the family settled in Shropshire, where Hazlitt lived until he went to Hackney College in London in 1793. Here he came into contact with some of the leading radical thinkers of the period, and read widely in philosophy and literature. Between 1795, when he left Hackney College, and 1808 when he married and started a career as a professional writer, Hazlitt wrote philosophy, painted portraits, and met both Coleridge and Wordsworth. In 1812 he started work as a political reporter for the *Morning Chronicle*. During the next ten years he established a reputation as a journalist, drama reviewer, literary and art critic, lecturer, essayist, and champion of the radical cause in politics. From 1817 onwards he began regular publication of collections of his writings in book form. These included *The Round Table* and *Characters of Shakespeare's Plays* in 1817, *Political Essays* in 1819, *Table Talk* in 1821, and *The Spirit of the Age* in 1825.

In 1821 Hazlitt's infatuation with Sarah Walker began. This led him to divorce his wife in 1822, and, in the following year, he published *Liber Amoris*, a thinly fictionalized account of his disastrous love affair with Sarah. In 1824 he married Isabella Bridgewater, and the couple travelled in France and Italy. During this period Hazlitt met Stendhal, and started work on his biography of Napoleon which occupied him for the rest of his life. The marriage with Isabella broke up in 1827. In 1830 he died poverty stricken in a lodging-house in Frith Street, Soho.

JON COOK is Director of the Centre for Creative and Performing Arts and a Senior Lecturer in English Studies at the University of East Anglia. He is the co-author of *Romanticism and Ideology*, and a number of essays and articles on romanticism, contemporary poetry, and cultural studies.

D0898366

OXFORD WORLD'S CLASSICS

*For over 100 years Oxford World's Classics have brought
readers closer to the world's great literature. Now with over 700
titles—from the 4,000-year-old myths of Mesopotamia to the
twentieth century's greatest novels—the series makes available
lesser-known as well as celebrated writing.*

*The pocket-sized hardbacks of the early years contained
introductions by Virginia Woolf, T. S. Eliot, Graham Greene,
and other literary figures which enriched the experience of reading.
Today the series is recognized for its fine scholarship and
reliability in texts that span world literature, drama and poetry,
religion, philosophy and politics. Each edition includes perceptive
commentary and essential background information to meet the
changing needs of readers.*

OXFORD WORLD'S CLASSICS

WILLIAM HAZLITT

Selected Writings

Edited with an Introduction and Notes by
JON COOK

UNIVERSITY PRESS

OXFORD

UNIVERSITY PRESS

Great Clarendon Street, Oxford OX2 6DP

Oxford University Press is a department of the University of Oxford.
It furthers the University's objective of excellence in research, scholarship,
and education by publishing worldwide in

Oxford New York

Athens Auckland Bangkok Bogotá Buenos Aires Cape Town
Chennai Dar es Salaam Delhi Florence Hong Kong Istanbul Karachi
Kolkata Kuala Lumpur Madrid Melbourne Mexico City Mumbai Nairobi
Paris São Paulo Shanghai Singapore Taipei Tokyo Toronto Warsaw

with associated companies in Berlin Ibadan

Oxford is a registered trade mark of Oxford University Press
in the UK and in certain other countries

Published in the United States
by Oxford University Press Inc., New York

First published as a World's Classics paperback 1991
Reissued as an Oxford World's Classics paperback 1998
Reissued 2009

British Library Cataloguing in Publication Data

Data available

Library of Congress Cataloging in Publication Data

Hazlitt, William, 1778–1830.
William Hazlitt: selected writings/edited with an introduction by Jon Cook.
p.   cm.—(Oxford world's classics)
Includes bibliographical references.
I. Cook, Jon.   II. Title.   III. Series.
PR4771.C66   1991   824'.7—dc20   90–21481

ISBN 978–0–19–955252–8

6

Printed in Great Britain by
Clays Ltd, St Ives plc

ACKNOWLEDGEMENTS

I am indebted to the work of P. P. Howe whose edition of the *Complete Works of William Hazlitt* has been of great help in tracking down allusions and quotations.

I would also like to thank the following for advice and support: David Aers, Jean Clark, Alex Potts, Martin Hollis, David Punter, Raphael Samuel, Lorna Sage, Victor Sage, Roger Sales, Sita Narasimhan. Special thanks to Diane DeBell and Alice Cook, to Anne Bevan for help in preparing the typescript, and to Kim Scott Walwyn and Judith Luna for their patience.

CONTENTS

Introduction   ix
Note on the Text   xxxix
Select Bibliography   xl
A Chronology of William Hazlitt   xliii

SELECTED WRITINGS OF WILLIAM HAZLITT

POLITICS

What is the People?   3
On Consistency of Opinion   29
Illustrations of 'The Times' Newspaper   41
Character of Mr Burke   54
Malthus   67
The French Revolution   84

CULTURE

On Modern Comedy   101
Modern Tragedy   109
The Fight   117
The Indian Jugglers   128
On Public Opinion   142
On Fashion   148
Our National Theatres   155
English Characteristics   157
Brummelliana   158

THE SELF

Self-Love and Benevolence   165
Mind and Motive   183
On Personal Identity   190
Characteristics   202

HEROES

My First Acquaintance with Poets   211
from The Life of Napoleon   230

viii CONTENTS

Edmund Kean   242
from Liber Amoris: Conclusion   249

ART AND LITERATURE

Fragments on Art. Why the Arts are not Progressive?   257
Whether the Fine Arts are Promoted by Academies   262
On Gusto   266
Originality   270
On the Elgin Marbles   277
Hogarth   297
On Poetry in General   308
Shakespeare   323
Macbeth   335
Coriolanus   345
Mr Wordsworth   347

Explanatory Notes   359

INTRODUCTION

THERE are a number of reasons for wanting to read Hazlitt now. Some of these are historical, but only in that particular sense where enquiry into a past writer renews reflection on the present. The period of Hazlitt's life, from 1778 to 1830, was one of far-reaching changes in English cultural and political life. Hazlitt was deeply engaged by these changes, both as a writer trying to affect their direction, and as an analyst of their causes. We have learnt to name these changes in various ways: as romanticism, as the development of a particular form of conservatism which has become deeply embedded in English life. Hazlitt's writing is, amongst other things, involved in a dialogue with some of the principal protagonists of English romanticism and conservatism: Burke, Coleridge, and Wordsworth. Hazlitt's distinctive urbanity is that he could recognize the power of these writers while at the same time fiercely disputing the political and cultural tendencies they represented. As a result, in reading his work, we can discover an account of the purposes of writing and the status of the writer which is at odds with the definitions which were in preparation when he wrote and were to become influential. Another way of putting this is to claim that Hazlitt had what can now seem a distinctly un-English preoccupation with freedom. This makes reading him now an uneven experience: he can by turns seem both old-fashioned and startlingly modern.

In *The Life of Napoleon,* a work completed shortly before he died, we can discover something of Hazlitt's sense of the responsibilities of the writer from his account of the French Revolution, where he tells a story about the causes of the Revolution which brings together print, politics, and knowledge:

The French Revolution might be described as the remote but inevitable result of the invention of the art of printing. The gift of speech, or the communication of thought by words, is that which distinguishes men from other animals. But this faculty is limited and imperfect without the intervention of books, which render the knowledge possessed by everyone in the community accessible to all. There is no doubt that the press . . . is the great organ of intellectual improvement and civilization.

Print features as the hero of what may now seem a startlingly naïve and familiar story about enlightenment. Hazlitt proposes a mutually sustaining and progressive relationship between what he calls an art, what we would call a technology, and the development of culture. Culture progresses because print frees knowledge for a new, extensive circulation. The consequence is the creation of a new power and a new kind of community, one that Hazlitt commonly referred to as 'public opinion'. Within this community, knowledge is a central value and this is importantly so because print removes knowledge from the realm of the esoteric and makes it 'accessible to all'.

Hazlitt's idiom in this passage from *The Life of Napoleon* is fittingly rational. He traces a pattern of cause and effect that follows the invention of printing. Yet this rational pattern indicates a process so momentous that Hazlitt's language is drawn towards the resources of myth to register its significance. The causal process is the basis for something like a rebirth and a bringing to perfection of the human. Print perfects the 'gift of speech'. It gives what Hazlitt describes as a 'second breathing of understanding into the life of man'. And the process is inevitably political, involved in a struggle which Hazlitt variously regarded as the epic or tragic subject of his time:

From the moment that the press opens the eyes of the community beyond the actual sphere in which each moves, there is from that time inevitably formed the germ of a body of opinion directly at variance with the selfish and servile code that before reigned paramount.

The 'selfish and servile code' is tyranny, and tyranny in Hazlitt's work becomes an emblem for whatever thrives on secrecy, ignorance, and superstitious beliefs about the divine origin of political authority. It is a form of power which Hazlitt sometimes believed could not survive a widely dispersed knowledge of its operations. Where it does persist, as it did in eighteenth-century France, the result is political revolution.

Hazlitt's story about the causes of the French Revolution gives us one image of him as a writer. His self-definition as an intellectual opposed to tyranny indicates his affiliation to what Terry Eagleton has described as the founding moment of modern European criticism, 'born of a struggle against the absolutist state' in which a 'polite informed public opinion pits itself against the arbitrary diktats of authority.'[1] The struggle against tyranny informs Hazlitt's writing both as an explicit reference and as a more intractable compulsion which he must visit over and over again. Tyranny, that is, is both a fact about the political world, and, uneasily, a metaphor which engages with sadistic or masochistic impulses in a human nature, apparently indifferent to the guidance of reason.

To notice this ambivalence in Hazlitt's relation to tyranny is to notice, at the outset, a deceptiveness in the confidence with which Hazlitt writes about the onset of the French Revolution in *The Life of Napoleon*. The rational idiom can readily seem a calculated act of defiance. First published in 1828, Hazlitt's version of the Revolution in *The Life of Napoleon* is written against the horror-struck rhetoric of a number of his celebrated contemporaries for whom the Revolution was not the incarnation of enlightenment but a fundamental crime against social order and cultural continuity. Hazlitt's writing in *The Life of Napoleon* may re-enact the founding moment of European criticism's struggle against absolutism, but it is very much a *re-enactment*, the deliberate staging of a style whose confidence had been hollowed out, if not betrayed, by events after 1789.

The main source of betrayal was a powerful form of English cultural and political conservatism which used the French Revolution as an ideological gift-horse, a horror story which showed the necessity of obedience and the folly of freedom. What was betrayed was that putative community of readers and writers devoted to the pursuit of personal and political liberty. Indeed this new conservative formation surfaces in

[1] T. Eagleton, *The Function of Criticism* (Verso: London, 1984), 9.

Hazlitt's writing as the malign and perverted opponent of the community of enlightenment. It helps explain why he writes so often as if wounded by history. It helps explain, too, why his writing can often assume that public opinion has become treacherous, the community of plain speech and democratic principle radically diminished. Doubts about the condition of his audience can produce startling discrepancies in his manner of addressing them. *What is the People*, his remarkable polemic against the conservatism fathered by Edmund Burke, begins by turning on an imaginary addressee: 'And who are you that ask the question? One of the people. And yet you would be something! Then you would not have the People nothing.'

As readers we are invited to suspect a corrupt motive in asking the question in the first place, as though it proceeds from some snobbish contempt or scepticism about popular values. The dramatic opening of *What is the People* assumes an interlocutor with a curl in his lip, a figure who invokes the weight of Burkean conservatism which it is Hazlitt's task to refute. He does this by turning Burke's arguments and his rhetoric against him. Where Burke had invoked the authority of custom and tradition in defence of aristocratic and monarchical government, Hazlitt invokes the same authority in defence of popular rights. Where Burke had located the origins of culture in the exclusive 'spirit of a gentleman and the spirit of religion', Hazlitt finds its source in the democracy of 'our common nature'. And where Burke had seen 'a swinish multitude' threatening the continuity of culture, Hazlitt renames them 'the people' and sees the continuity of their claim to popular sovereignty threatened by the power of tyrannical government. It is as though Hazlitt had stepped into the cultural field of force established by Burke's rhetoric and deftly switched its direction so that it attacks what Burke intended it to defend.

What is the People, like other of Hazlitt's political writings, shows him in one of his preferred stances, that of a 'good hater'. Hazlitt had first used the phrase to describe Shylock in a piece he wrote on *The Merchant of Venice*. The words carry a hint of paradox: not just being good at hating but hating for the good. Prompted by Edmund Kean's sympathetic acting of Shylock, Hazlitt revalues an emotion usually classified as negative or ignoble. He can find in Shylock a resonant image for his own idea of himself as a social outcast and scapegoat for the hypocrisies of a dominant culture. Like Shylock, Hazlitt confronted his contemporaries with promises they preferred to forget. Amongst them, Wordsworth, Coleridge, and Southey were recurring targets for attack. Their careers were exemplary of a wider cultural transformation replete with discarded loyalties. By the mid-1790s, a literary sensibility which, in however limited a way, had promoted compassion for the poor and criticism of the privileged had fallen under political suspicion. Renouncing radical sympathies had become a hallmark of respectability. And, as Marilyn Butler has indicated, there was a consequent redirection of polite cultural activity:

the hitherto dominant public was transformed by political events in the 1790s into the prime object of fear, the people. The necessity to reconstitute the arts without the people became a driving force behind the creative endeavours in the post-revolutionary decade.[2]

This cultural necessity, had turned the Coleridge of 1795, who had invoked Christianity in his Bristol lectures as the authority for an attack on private property, into the Coleridge of 1798 who wrote to his elder brother that he had 'snapped my squeaking baby-trumpet of sedition, and the fragments lie in the lumber-room of Penitence'. Coleridge's language rehearses an influential myth of maturity which was launched at this time. Radical commitment is infantile, a matter of 'squeaking baby-trumpets'. Growth to maturity is a growth to conservatism. At the same time as Coleridge was nervously declaring himself an adult, Wordsworth was in the early stages of composing his autobiographical poem, *The Prelude*, which made disillusionment with political radicalism a key transition in his development to a chastened mature poet, attached to pieties of place and tradition. Thus the history of personal

[2] M. Butler, *Romantics, Rebels and Reactionaries* (Oxford University Press: Oxford, 1981), 36–8.

identity Wordsworth devised around 1800 came to echo the work that Burke had done for political and national identity some ten years earlier. Both had to expel the radical rationalist, whose demands for equality threatened the proper order of the political state and of the self.

Hazlitt refused this account of maturity, a fact that may well make him difficult to read for those who continue to live in its terms. What that refusal implied was a further disagreement between Hazlitt and the English conservative imagination about the nature of historical development, and the political forms that seemed to be guaranteed by the direction of history. Against the view that the French Revolution was an aberrant event, a violence done to the texture of historical continuity itself, Hazlitt argued that it was a further, momentous episode in a historical process characterized by the ever increasing spread of liberty. The American Revolution was another such episode, as was, in the context of English history, the abdication of James II in 1688. The constitutional significance of James's abdication was a subject of keen debate. For radicals like Hazlitt, it indicated that political sovereignty resided in the people, who could legitimately depose a monarch who threatened their freedom. It also indicated that England was a country where liberty was moving into the ascendent. This understanding is reflected in Hazlitt's response to some of his eighteenth-century forebears, notably Hogarth and Sterne. Their work was characterized by an individuality and assertiveness which itself indicated a more general tendency towards political and civil freedom. The battle against tyranny was by no means simply won, but at least it was moving in the right direction.

The subsequent reversal of a historical process which seemed to guarantee liberty was accompanied by the collapse of a more patriotic confidence that Britain was tending towards a state which guaranteed the freedom and equality of its subjects. For Hazlitt, this sacrifice of democratic potential had manifold consequences, including a cultural and political amnesia in the centres of the new conservative nation which could distort thinking that laid claim to the title of radicalism. In an 1816 review of Robert Owen's *New View of Society*, Hazlitt

took Owen to task for claiming that his 'view' was new at all.
It had all once been the common talk of the people:

> Does not Mr Owen know that the same scheme, the same principles,
> the same philosophy of motives and actions, of causes and consequen-
> ces, of knowledge and virtue, of virtue and happiness were rife in the
> year 1793, were noised abroad then, were spoken on the house-tops,
> were whispered in secret, were published in quarto and duodecimos,
> in political treatises, in plays, poems, songs and romances . . .

The 'year 1793' becomes Hazlitt's brief fantasy about England's lost democracy. As Hazlitt's list in the second half of his
sentence implies, this is not just to do with political doctrine:
one of the things that makes democracy democratic is its habit
of passionate and various communication. The ironies that
attend Owen's unconscious appropriation of popular ideas
accumulate. In forgetting the source of his ideas, he has also
forgotten the diversity of their transmission. What was shared
in 1793 has become an exclusive property in Owen's *New View*,
a work addressed by a conscientious industrialist to a ruling
élite about how best to manage the poor and the working
class. In the process, a discourse which the people once owned
has been turned anxiously upon them as an instrument of
regulation.

The point here is not to reach for a history book as though
that would guarantee the historical veracity of Hazlitt's account of 1793, but to note it as one example of a myth he
invents to sustain his own polemic. A parallel point could be
made about his use of the notoriously vague word, 'the
people'. Hazlitt does not write about 'the people' in the name
of some notional sociological clarity. The drama of his polemic
concerns issues of affiliation and belief. The purpose of a
piece like *What is the People* is to engage an audience in some
deliberation about where they stand in a momentous political
and cultural struggle. This is not done in the interests of a
particular party or faction; indeed Hazlitt presents himself as
proudly independent of political cliques. He writes with a
large engagement in mind, such that decisions made about
'the people', whether they be on the side of Burke and Malthus on the one hand or Hazlitt and Cobbett on the other,

will have considerable consequences for how individuals imagine the society they live in and where they locate within it the agencies of order and disorder. These issues were fiercely contested at the time Hazlitt was active as a political writer, and to write on the radical side was a matter of personal risk. Hazlitt's associates, the Hunt brothers, had been imprisoned in 1812 for a satire on the Prince Regent, and their persecution was just one example of a wider repression of the radical press orchestrated by Sidmouth, Home Secretary to the Government, and judges like Eldon and Ellenborough. At the risk, then, of legal restraint and social ostracism, Hazlitt opposed a discourse, variously derived from Burke, Malthus, and their followers, which identified 'the people' as the chief threat to social order and thereby helped justify measures for their surveillance and control.

Hazlitt's political writings are not attempts to soothe political turbulence with detached wisdom or theoretical certainty. In this respect he is unlike Tom Paine, a fellow radical with whom he shares some political ground. In *The Rights of Man*, the most widely read political work of the period, Paine refutes Burke's attack on the French Revolution by proving him wrong in matters of fact and of theory. He sustains his critique by developing a metaphor of politics as a theatre, but in Paine's argument it is exactly Burke's failure that he mistakes the theatre of politics for its reality, and so betrays through histrionic display the rationality proper to a clear understanding. Writing some twenty years after the first publication of *The Rights of Man*, and in a political atmosphere which had, amongst other things, forced Paine to leave England, Hazlitt's implied understanding of political life is by contrast thoroughly dramatic, even melodramatic, in its stance. Politics is the stage of a great struggle between tyranny and liberty. Hazlitt does not write with Paine's detached confidence, but provokes and defends with equal fierceness. With some reason, he believes that the cause of liberty is all but lost, or, that, at best, it has been driven into a marginal existence. The power of the opposition is powerfully felt in Hazlitt's style and this circumstance shifts it into a different register to Paine's, at once more aggressive and satirical and less confident of political success. Indeed, Hazlitt's style is itself a political message, the medium for a defence of liberty which connects the right of free speech to the courage to be outspoken. His political writings come to exemplify the freedoms they argue for in the very manner of their articulation.

This point about the political message carried by Hazlitt's style carries implications for his writings generally. Again, the comparison with Paine is relevant. Paine's capacity to indict the histrionic tendencies of Burke's writing depends upon a belief that language can be the transparent medium of rational demonstration, an instrument that can be used to know and name the world in such a way as to clearly distinguish the merely imagined from the properly real. According to Paine, if you know the facts that he knows and accept his theory about the origin of natural and civil rights, then the power of Burke's rhetoric simply dissolves. Hazlitt's relation to language is significantly different. He recognized that Burke's effectiveness as a writer had not been undermined by Paine's critique. What Paine dismissed as theatrical in Burke's style was, in Hazlitt's view, a crucial source of its power:

Burke was so far from being a gaudy or flowery writer, that he was one of the severest writers we have. His words are most like things; his style is the most strictly suited to the subject. He unites every extreme and every variety of composition; the lowest and the meanest words and descriptions with the highest. He exults in the display of power, in shewing the extent, the force and intensity of his ideas; he is led on by the mere impulse and vehemence of his fancy, not by the affectation of dazzling his readers by gaudy conceits or pompous images. He was completely carried away by his subject . . . Burke most frequently produced an effect . . . by the force of contrast, by the striking manner in which the most opposite and unpromising materials were harmoniously blended together . . . The florid style is a mixture of affectation and common-place. Burke's was a union of untameable vigour and originality.

Hazlitt's eulogy of Burke seems to be constructed out of a sense of mutually cancelling judgements. Burke is praised for his decorum—'his style is most suited to the subject'—and for his refusal of decorum: 'He unites the lowest and meanest words and descriptions with the highest.' His work evidences an egotistical demonstration—Burke 'exults in the display of power'—and a loss of self: 'he was completely carried away by his subject.' The effects of his writing are produced both by 'the force of contrast' and by the capacity to harmonize 'the most opposite and unpromising materials'. In this respect, Hazlitt's celebration of Burke's style echoes other eighteenth- and early nineteenth-century accounts of genius which are similarly drawn to paradoxical formulations or something which is, in effect, a variation on paradox: the idea that genius consists in the synthesis of contradictory qualities. Only by dealing in paradox can the critic hope to capture this quality.

Burke's 'display of power' is connected, in Hazlitt's account, with the capacity of his writing to be sublime. For Hazlitt, Burke is a sublime author in at least two senses. One echoes Longinus in his classical treatise on the sublime, in so far as Hazlitt, like Longinus, is concerned to give some critical account of qualities of greatness in literature that cannot be explained by an appeal to rule or method. The other is more specific to the eighteenth century and has to do with the favourite character of eighteenth-century philosophy, the mind. The drama of Burke's relation to language indicates sublimity of mind. This emerges in Hazlitt's defence of Burke against the charge that he was a verbose writer:

If he sometimes multiplies words, it is not for want of ideas, but because there are no words that fully express his ideas, and he tries to do it as well as he can by different ones. He had nothing of the *set* or formal style, the measured cadence, and stately phraseology of Johnson, and most of our modern writers . . .

Burke's writing, unlike that of 'Johnson and most of our modern writers', cannot be described as the transparent medium of fact and reason. It disturbs a standard eighteenth-century metaphor about the relations between language and the mind, that language is a picture of the mind in the sense that it can fully represent what the mind does when it thinks. Burke's writing indicates the presence of ideas that cannot be pictured by language in this way. His writing paradoxically indicates what cannot be written, thoughts that exceed language. These indications of the unrepresentable constitute the evidence of sublimity. What Hazlitt finds in Burke's style has numerous analogues in romantic poetry. Wordsworth's 'thoughts that lie too deep for tears' in the 'Ode on the Intimations of Immortality' the unrevivable 'symphony and song' in Coleridge's 'Kubla Khan', the 'mysterious tongue' that Shelley hears in the wilderness in his poem 'Mont Blanc', are just a few examples of a persistent doubleness in 'romantic writing', where the given and available language is haunted by its own inadequacy to deal with what it strives to represent. The distinctive power of Burke's writing for Hazlitt, and its deceptive histrionic display for Tom Paine, was its capacity to suggest a sublimity in the nature of political allegiance, a core value that could not be discerned or represented by the language of common sense or reason.

From a historical distance the sublime can seem the invention of a culture which wanted to feel more secure by frightening itself. It also helped promote a chronic ambivalence about power and its origins. If the sublime marked some manifestation of the mind's power, there was some equivocation about whether this power resided in a human or quasi-divine mind, or, as another possibility, in the representation of the divine in the human. In so far as the sublime was an aesthetic experience, it renewed the mystique of art, allocating to it the privilege and burden of expressing the inexpressible, at a time when there was considerable concern that art was losing its value by becoming a commodity in the market-place, subject to a commercial organization of production and consumption. Viewed more generally, the sublime gave a new legitimacy to forms of emotional turbulence which had, earlier in the eighteenth century, been regarded as signs of chaos by the rational man.

Hazlitt's writings responded to these differing emphases of the sublime, but in markedly different ways. His sympathy with the power of Burke's language did not inhibit his scepticism about the construction of metaphysical systems which drew on sublimity as one kind of evidence for the transcendental, divine origins of mind. For Hazlitt, Coleridge's later writings, in however wayward a fashion, exemplify this tendency. His reviews of them still bear the traces of Hazlitt's admiration and affection for Coleridge, but he thought most of the *Bio-graphia Literaria* 'a long-winding metaphysical march' and deplored Coleridge's admiration for German idealist philosophy. Hazlitt discerned the effect of Kant's thinking on Coleridge, and he judged the effect wholly corrupting, not least because it pretended to remove argument from the pressures of public debate and questioning:

He [Kant] has but one method of getting over difficulties:—when he is at a loss to account for anything, and cannot give a reason for it, he turns short round upon the enquirer, and says that it is self-evident. If he cannot make good an inference upon acknowledged premises, or known methods of reasoning, he coolly refers the whole to a new class of ideas, and the operation of some unknown faculty, which he has invented for the purpose, and which he assures you *must* exist—because there is no other proof of it.

Hazlitt's objections are those of a sceptical thinker who does not believe that the invention of a name necessarily proves the existence of what is named. But, alongside that, is another kind of objection to any intellectual system which claims truth as its exclusive property. Hazlitt's contrasting beliefs about the nature of the truth and knowledge are summarized in one of the aphorisms in his book, *Characteristics*, first published in 1823: 'Truth is not one, but many; and an observation may be true in itself that contradicts another equally true, according to the point-of-view from which we contemplate the subject.'

This commitment to relativism is one of many indications of Hazlitt's modernity. Any perspective may be contradicted by another because reality is so various that no single point of view will ever encompass it all. Knowledge is therefore necessarily dramatic, born out of the thinker's commitment to a process of debate which pits contradictory observations against each other. Whatever truths emerge will be provisional and in need of further refinement.

These intellectual commitments are at one with the characteristics of Hazlitt's style. The force of aphorism is a central feature here. In *The Advancement of Learning*, published some 200 years before Hazlitt's writing career started, one of his favourite authors, Francis Bacon, had recommended the aphoristic style as the most effective means of communicating knowledge. It was free from the laboured elaboration of the scholastic manner, and was indicative of a thinker who, according to Bacon, was 'solid and grounded'. If the aphorism was a stylistic sign of intellectual authenticity, it was a further measure of authenticity that the aphorism promoted rather than concluded enquiry. According to Bacon the aphorism represented 'a knowledge broken', and so invited 'men to inquire further'.

Hazlitt's commitment to an aphoristic style renewed Bacon's concern with open intellectual enquiry. But this was not a matter of simple imitation. Hazlitt had his own version of what his style indicated, and how it connected to cultural tendencies of the time. In his essay, *On the Causes of Popular Opinion*, he described his own writings as 'the thoughts of a metaphysician expressed by a painter. They are subtle and difficult problems translated into hieroglyphics.' This places writing at a mid-point, giving abstract thought the immediacy of the visual image, but also, as in a hieroglyph, moving the visual image from literal representation into code. The aphorism is relevant to this process because it condenses abstract thought into arresting statement, a verbal equivalent to the visual image in its power to command attention. The painterly expression of metaphysical thought indicates a fantasy about writing which will connect the language of abstract thought to a vividly realized image of the thinker. Writing becomes a speaking portrait. And this drew it into the orbit of another form which, according to Hazlitt powerfully expressed individual subjectivity, the art of drama: in his view the language of Shakespeare, the supreme dramatic intelligence, was 'hieroglyphical'. The aphoristic style moves writing in the direction of drama. It carries into print the afterglow of memorable dramatic occasions, when one utterance is pitted against another in passionate controversy.

This reminds us that Hazlitt's style was forged in theatres as well as art galleries. He was powerfully attracted to theatrical performance, whether this was taking place on stage or not. It constituted an ideal of expressive selfhood which Hazlitt opposed to the abstracting tendencies of modern civilization. His thinking on this subject is scattered throughout his work, in the letter *On Modern Comedy* written to the *Morning Chronicle* in 1817, in his discussions of Shakespeare, and in this survey of the theatre written in 1820:

> We participate in the general progress of intellect, and the large vicissitudes of human affairs; but the hugest private sorrow looks dwarfish and puerile.... In a word, literature and civilization have abstracted man from himself so far; and the press has been the ruin of the state unless, we are greatly deceived ...

Against this tendency to abstraction, Hazlitt opposed 'the circle of dramatic character and natural passion' in which 'each individual is to feel as keenly, as profoundly, as rapidly as possible, but he is not to feel beyond it for others or for the whole. Each character on the contrary, must be a kind of centre of repulsion to the rest.'

What Hazlitt writes here is a fierce elegy for the form of imaginative being necessary to tragedy. Effectively, his argument is that improvements brought by civilization bring with them a form of the self incapable of engaging with tragic passion. If moral altruism, the capacity to feel 'for others or for the whole', is a mark of civilized behaviour, then dramatic character is opposed to it. But Hazlitt is not using dramatic character to smuggle in a justification of self-interest. What appeals to him is a form of being which is pre-philosophical because it does not try to explain behaviour by appeal to abstract principles, whether such appeals are used to justify altruism or self-interest.

Hazlitt seems caught here in a familiar antithesis, where expressive power is threatened by the progress of an abstract and rational civilization. A sense of the constraining artificiality of civilization had fuelled projects for literary and political reform from the middle of the eighteenth century. Wordsworth's 1800 preface to the *Lyrical Ballads*, for example, makes proposals for the transformation of poetic language which carry a clear cultural criticism. His desire to make poetry out of 'a selection of language really used by men' leads him to a statement about the social conditions best suited to that language:

Low and rustic life was generally chosen because in that condition the essential passions of the heart find a better soil in which they can attain their maturity, are less under restraint, and speak a plainer and more emphatic language; because in that condition of life our elementary feelings co-exist in a state of greater simplicity, and consequently may be more accurately contemplated and more forcibly communicated . . .

Wordsworth is attracted to rural life because it is there that the common language of our nature, or, at least, of men's nature, can be discovered. This common language is connected to an ideal of expressiveness: in rural life 'the essential passions of the heart . . . speak a plainer and more emphatic language.' It is therefore the proper basis for the language of poetry both because it is expressive and because it addresses what Wordsworth wants us to believe we all share: 'the primary laws of our nature', 'our elementary feelings'. This basis is readily found in a rural life existing prior to those artificial distinctions of an urban civilization which divide one passion from another and inhibit any recognition of a common human nature.

Wordsworth was contributing to an established eighteenth-century argument about where to find a common language expressing a shared human nature in a society characterized by diverse regional dialects and by the specialized vocabularies of the trades and the professions. In such a society the language of literature should model itself on what was agreed as a common language because then it could supposedly address a humanity shared across social and linguistic barriers. But Wordsworth's preface, although clearly framed by the argument about common language, differs from an earlier, mid-eighteenth-century version of it in at least two ways. He finds his model of common language in 'low and rustic life' and not in the idiom of the gentleman who, John Barrell has argued, 'was believed to be the only member of society who spoke a language universally intelligible; his usage was "common", in the sense of being neither a local dialect nor infected

by the terms of any particular art'.[3] Secondly, Wordsworth
located the essence of human behaviour not in the exercise
of reason, but in the passions and their expression, especially
when 'we associate ideas in a state of excitement'.

Hazlitt agreed with Wordsworth about the passions but not
about rural life. The expressiveness of Hazlitt's 'dramatic character' is close to Wordsworth's 'state of excitement'; its value
based in the passions, feeling 'as keenly, as profoundly, as
rapidly as possible'.[4] But Hazlitt's prescriptions about the
social circumstances which promote dramatic character are
largely negative. If the abstract tendency of modern civilization discourages the expressiveness of dramatic character, so
too does country life. Hazlitt had no time for Wordsworth's
rural pieties. He writes about country people with the disdain
of the metropolitan critic. Far from producing a common
language of the passions, or providing examples of the association of ideas in 'states of excitement', Hazlitt believed that
rural life produced a stultifying self-absorption. In *The Round
Table*, he wrote that the egotism of country people 'becomes
more concentrated, as they are more insulated, and their
purposes more inveterate, as they have less competition to
struggle with. . . . Their minds become hard and cold, like
the rock, which they cultivate.'

There was, of course, and by contrast, the vivid incarnation
of dramatic character in Shakespeare's plays, but a major
point of Hazlitt's argument about Shakespeare is that Shakespeare's excellence is unrepeatable. We can discern here
something of Hazlitt's temperament as a writer, his devotion
to impossibility, failed projects, catastrophes, whatever resists
redemption. If he writes as the plain speaker, the figure of
independent and trustworthy judgement defying cultural and
political corruption, there is another aspect to him: the writer
as melancholy isolate, resigned to the inevitability of failure.
In Hazlitt's case, this condition has an urban cast. His writing

---

[3] J. Barrell, *English Literature in History 1730–80: An Equal, Wide Survey* (Hutchinson: London, 1983), 34.

[4] For an influential 18th-century discussion of the priority of the passions over
reason, see David Hume's *Treatise of Human Nature*, esp. Bk. II, section 3, 'Of the
influencing natures of the will'.

indicates a figure moving between theatres, art galleries, taverns, and lodging-houses, in search of some arresting spectacle which will momentarily suppress the solitary's awareness of his solitude. Any accommodation is temporary, including the country retreat. The genial sociability of tone, cultivated in that strand of Hazlitt's writing which includes essays like *The Indian Jugglers*, seems fabricated against the depressive silence of a distinctly urban solitude.

The point here is not to offer a psychological explanation of Hazlitt's work, but to identify his attraction to a form of writing which frames moments of energy or revelation in melancholic reflection. It indicates his affinity with Keats, another writer whose work is agitated by the pursuit of elusive ideals of expressive being. But if Hazlitt refuses to be like Wordsworth and describe the social conditions which favour expressiveness, this does not mean that his ideas about dramatic character have no bearing on the cultural politics of the period. His emphasis on expressiveness as dramatic pointedly contrasts with the ideals of lyric expressiveness variously at work in the writing of Wordsworth, Coleridge, Shelley, and Keats. This lyric ideal brings with it the assumption that solitude is the condition of the highest expressiveness; this is true even when Wordsworth in the 1800 preface to the *Lyrical Ballads* describes the social conditions favouring expressive being, because, as is evident in his poems and in his critical justifications of them, Wordsworth's society is composed of solitaries who occasionally bump into each other through the workings of chance or nature's law. Although the solitude that sustains expressiveness is viewed ambivalently, as both a blessing and a curse, a privilege and a constraint, the underlying ethos of romantic lyricism is that expression is fullest when the density and variousness of the social world falls away. The sound of other voices threatens lyrical existence.

Hazlitt opposed the expressiveness of dramatic character both to lyrical solitude and to an abstract civilization, but this did not mean opposing dramatic character to the idea of the social world as such. The 1820 theatre survey shows Hazlitt's sense of the doubly expressive nature of drama. 'Each individual is to feel as keenly, as profoundly, as rapidly as possible,' and this reveals a typically romantic kind of expressive intensity. But there is another dimension that comes from the conflict amongst individuals, what Hazlitt describes as 'their dire contention with each other'. He is clearly attracted to the energies generated by conflict, but it is not just that which gives drama its further dimension of expressiveness. Conflict induces a new level of excitement and intensity within dramatic character: the collision of different characters' 'hostile interests' must 'tug at their heart-strings and call forth every faculty of thought, of speech, of action'. Dramatic excitement, then, is not produced by the sheer existence of conflict, but in the manifestation of its psychological consequences. In particular, the process Hazlitt describes suggests a fascination with the way sympathy for the other side can arise out of the conflict between contending parties, 'the tug at their heart-strings' which, in turn, provokes further intensities of expression. But this interplay of hostility and sympathy is the way drama enacts the discovery that we are crucially social beings, defined by our dependencies and rivalries with others. Drama, for Hazlitt, is pre-eminently a social art, not just because it populates a stage and a theatre, but because it acts out a basic feature of the nature of social life itself.

The dramatic form that underlies Hazlitt's account in the 1820 survey of the theatre is tragedy. But, as the earlier letter *On Modern Comedy* makes clear, what is true of tragedy is true of other kinds of drama. Comedy is similarly threatened by the abstract tendency of modern civilization. 'We are become a nation of authors and readers,' Hazlitt lamented, 'and even this distinction is confounded by the mediation of reviewers.' The erosion of individual difference meant a decline in the stock of idiosyncratic folly which Hazlitt regarded as necessary for good comedy. What *On Modern Comedy* also makes clear is Hazlitt's view that drama is the highest of all the arts. It maximizes the resources of communication, combining the strengths of the other arts of writing and painting while dispensing with their limitations. Drama 'represents not only looks but motion and speech. The painter gives only the former, looks, without action or speech, and the mere writer only the latter, words without looks or action.'

As a model of vivid communication, drama militates against attempts to establish a single norm of good style. This is one of the many things that attracts him to Shakespeare, something exemplified in this comment from his 1818 lecture on Shakespeare and Milton:

By an art like that of the ventriloquist, he throws his imagination out of himself, and makes every word appear to proceed from the mouth of the person in whose name it is given. His plays alone are properly expressions of passion, not descriptions of them. His characters are real beings of flesh and blood; they speak like men, not like authors . . . The gusts of passion come and go like sounds of music borne on the wind. Nothing is made out by formal inference and analogy, by climax and antithesis: all comes, or seems to come, immediately from nature . . .

The antithesis between expressiveness and civilization is again at work. The language of Shakespeare's characters bears the imprint of their individuality. In doing this it is an 'expression' and not a 'description' of passion because Hazlitt believes that although our common nature is based in passion, the precise form of passion is idiosyncratic. These are so many signs that expression in Shakespeare 'comes, or seems to come, immediately from nature' and the contrast is with the predictable and rule-governed standard of civilized language where 'everything is made out by formal inference and analogy, by climax and antithesis'.

For Hazlitt, Shakespeare fulfils what Wordsworth aspires to in the preface to the *Lyrical Ballads*, a language that is expressive because natural, natural because expressive. A further difference between the two writers is that Shakespeare, unlike Wordsworth and his eighteenth-century forebears, does not identify an ideal form of language as the property of any particular social class, whether gentleman or peasant. One thing that Hazlitt finds impressive about Shakespeare is his indifference to rank: 'There was no respect of persons with him. His genius shone equally on the evil and on the good, on the wise and the foolish, the monarch and the beggar.'

This underlying neutrality did not make Shakespeare a political democrat in the modern sense. In his account of *Coriolanus*, Hazlitt discerned Shakespeare's fascination with

forms of individual ambition and power that were contemptuous of the will of the people. But this did not prevent
Shakespeare's plays from being a linguistic democracy: the
power to communicate did not depend on social or political
status. The intensity and unpredictability of communication
that Hazlitt discovered in Shakespeare's plays effectively dissolved eighteenth-century debates about a common language,
set above diversity of accent and idiom. What was common
about language could not be defined in a single style, but in
a dramatic action where one idiom encountered another.
Hazlitt distrusted the kinds of language which shy away from
dramatic engagement in order to secure group or individual
identity. His usual term to describe them is 'cant'.

The precedent of Shakespeare's diversity, unpredictability,
and the responsiveness of his language to the pressure of a
character's immediate circumstance, helped free Hazlitt from
the constraint of a uniform style. Hazlitt attempts dramatic
flexibility and excitement by variations in pitch, rhythm, and
sentence length, by sudden reversals of perspective, by the
refusal of conclusions. His writing incorporates an eclectic
range of different literary genres and popular idioms; hence,
for example, the shift from rational critique to popular, carni-
valesque mockery in his attack on Malthus, or the juxtaposition of sporting slang and polite style in his essay *The Fight*,
which was nearly banned as a result by its first editor because
he thought it 'a very vulgar thing'.

These experiments in style, were attempts to move prose
towards the ideal of dramatic expressiveness that Hazlitt
claimed for Shakespeare. And if an ideal of dramatic utterance
informs Hazlitt's style it also works as an underlying metaphor
for the act of writing itself, especially as that has to do with
the writer's capacity to witness and re-create those moments
when expression is suddenly freed from psychological, social,
or political constraint. Such moments are, in Hazlitt's view,
manifestations of power. They are the equivalent to what he
describes in his lecture on Shakespeare as 'the objects of
dramatic poetry' which 'affect us by their sympathy, by their
nearness to ourselves, as they take us by surprise, or force us
upon action'. The action enjoined upon Hazlitt is a kind of

writing which will respond with its own expressiveness to the evidence of expressiveness in others. The dramatic interplay created between writer and subject is necessarily unpredictable, confined to no particular artistic genre or social milieu. Hazlitt discovers it in the career of Napoleon, in Kean's acting of Shylock, his discovery of Renaissance painting in the Louvre, in the preaching of the young Coleridge, or in his encounter with the 'tall English yeoman', recorded in Hazlitt's essay *The Fight*, who talks as well as Cobbett writes. What these diverse occasions share is 'originality' in the complex meaning that term has for Hazlitt: expression is original when it discloses a self in its distinct individuality, when it reveals an aspect of nature hitherto unrealized or forgotten, and when it draws us to a scene where language is close to its original state before its incorporation into an artificial civilization.

These occasions of originality have an ambivalent status in Hazlitt's writing. They are often framed elegaically as though he is constrained to witness originality at a paradoxical point of emergence which is simultaneously a moment of loss. This, in turn, reflects the tension between an ideal of dramatic expression and Hazlitt's diagnosis of cultural modernity, whose characteristic medium, according to Hazlitt, is the press. If the press could be an agent of liberty for Hazlitt, it was also marked by a contradictory tendency to introduce a blandness and uniformity of opinion which he thought 'the ruin of the stage'. The constraints this imposes on modern authorship are made clear in Hazlitt's satirical commentaries on the literary world, as in this example from his *Lectures on the Age of Elizabeth*:

Modern authorship is become a species of stenography: we continue even to read by proxy. We skim the cream of prose without any trouble; we get at the quintessence of poetry without loss of time. The staple commodity, the coarse, heavy, dirty, unwieldy bullion of books is driven out of the market of learning, and the intercourse of the literary world is carried on, and the credit of the great capitalists sustained by the flimsy circulating medium of magazines.

The author as 'stenographer', working at second-hand, circulating the opinions of others, seems antithetical to the power Hazlitt discovers in Shakespeare's plays. Writers and readers collude in making life easy for themselves. Having opinions about books becomes a substitute for reading them, and, as the metaphors in this passage make clear, opinion is not grounded in any substantial commitment to learning or debate.

This diagnosis of modernity may be familiar, but Hazlitt gives it his own accent. His work certainly reveals the dilemmas of modern authorship. Hazlitt is the author as 'stenographer', recycling other people's opinions as well as his own. The constraint here is not so much cultural as economic. Hazlitt earned his living as a writer, and his living was precarious. The demand for copy was always threatening to outstrip supply— hence the requirement to recycle, to serve up old work in new guises. In these circumstances, Hazlitt's fascination with the expressive power of Shakespeare or Renaissance art can appear a consoling fiction, an impossible attempt to align modern authorship with an image of cultural authority and independence which will divert attention from Hazlitt's own economic dependency and marginal status.

In drawing our attention to dilemmas of this kind, Hazlitt dramatizes the pathos of his situation as an author. But it is characteristic of Hazlitt's work generally that the stark antithesis between dramatic expression and modern authorship does not become a stable dogma. The dramatic metaphor for writing has other implications, suggesting an analogy between the author and the professional actor skilled in routines which can momentarily command the attention of distracted and volatile audiences. Hazlitt cherished those skills, as his essay *The Indian Jugglers* makes clear. The extent of his care is indicated by the argument of the essay: Hazlitt begins by distinguishing between the technical skills of the jugglers from the apparently superior powers of original genius, only then to defer a final decision as to which he most values. Writing may well have seemed to him poised somewhere between the two.

The example of Shakespeare offered another kind of therapy. It could console the modern author by suggesting that his very lack of visibility and status was itself a condition of genius. Hazlitt develops the thought, which he shared with

Coleridge and Keats, that Shakespeare was the least egotistical of writers, that he was, in Hazlitt's words, 'nothing in himself; but he was all that others were, or that they could become.' The distinction of Shakespeare's genius consists of this absence of egotism, and it is this quality that, for Hazlitt, indicates his final superiority to other writers. What this in turn means is that Shakespeare's genius can be defined by humble as well as elevated analogies. His art does not need to be defined by equating it with social distinction:

> The poet may be said, for the time, to identify himself with the character he wishes to represent, and to pass from one to another, like the same soul successively animating different bodies. By an art like that of the ventriloquist, he throws his imagination out of himself, and makes every word appear to proceed from the mouth of the person in whose name it is given.

The simile of ventriloquism draws attention to a paradox of expression: Shakespeare expresses himself by imagining the expressions of others. This again finds an echo in Hazlitt's activity as a critic. The critic takes on the quality of a dramatic genius by becoming absorbed by a particular individuality seeking expression. This is what Hazlitt attempts when he writes what are called 'characters'. Character can mean what it usually does: the particular mark which distinguishes one individual from another. But its meaning is extended by Hazlitt to include what it is that distinguishes one work of art from another. Hence his Characters of Shakespeare's plays has a double sense, concerned both with the characters within them, and with the distinct character of the play itself. Bringing this out becomes the critic's main task, rather than assessing a work's conformity to the rules of genre or morality.

But ventriloquism carries another implication in Hazlitt's case: the attempt to animate various voices which will identify the writer himself. Hazlitt assumes language like an actor putting on a mask. The marks can vary: plain speaker, urbane critic, tribune of the people, melancholy isolate. The effect is to make the act of writing both dramatic and ironic: dramatic because of our awareness that Hazlitt assumes different roles as a writer, ironic because of the deceptive character of these roles, which appear to constrain as well as express the writer's personality. This contributes to the distinctive poise of Hazlitt's thought; at once passionately attached to certain ideals, but also aware of their possible limitations.

Hazlitt's manner of thinking about expressiveness and civilization applies to other recurrent ideas in his work, which can only be briefly discussed here. The critique of rational egotism which pervades his thought was the subject of his first published work, *An Essay on the Principles of Human Action*. Here Hazlitt attempted to turn the idiom of Hobbesian philosophy against one of its central axioms, that human action is motivated by self-interest even when it appears not to be. Hazlitt thought he had refuted this idea by an analysis of the mind's relation to time: we were inevitably selfish in relation to the past and present because we were incapable of directly experiencing another's memories or their present sensations. But this constraint did not hold for the future, which was inevitably the sphere of any deliberation about human action. The future was the province of imagination and nothing required us to imagine our future any more vividly than the futures of others. A habitual concern with the self and its interests might well inhibit this capacity, but, Hazlitt claimed, we were not automatically interested in our future selves in the way we were in our present and past selves.

Hazlitt prided himself on what he took to be a fundamental discovery in the philosophy of mind and action. In his personal mythology, he dated his identity as an original thinker from his refutation of egotistical accounts of motivation. What is characteristic of Hazlitt's war against egotism is the way he transposes it into different contexts, from the discourse of eighteenth-century philosophy into an account of Shakespeare's genius, and then again into essays reflecting on the nature of the self and action. The validity of an idea in Hazlitt's work consists as much in its capacity to survive such transpositions as in its logical coherence. It also indicates Hazlitt's willingness to offer his ideas to as diverse an audience as he could discover; he abandoned writing in the manner of Hume and Locke because its idiom came to seem too specialized and lacking in imaginative sympathy and, therefore, could not sustain Hazlitt's conviction that worthwhile ideas should be taken out into the world and tested in secular debate.

In the process, the critique of egotism set out in *An Essay on the Principles of Human Action* is modified. When drawn into the orbit of Hazlitt's cultural and literary criticism, egotism joins abstraction as one of the cardinal signs of modernity. This is the point where, for Hazlitt, a dominant tendency in modern philosophy and modern poetry meet. Both feed egotism; both are opposed to dramatic thinking. The tendency in philosophy is manifest in the work of Hobbes, Mandeville, Helvetius, and the Utilitarians. In poetry, the exemplary figure is Wordsworth, whose work provokes an ambivalent response in Hazlitt. He admires the poet's invention of language of feeling freed from the artificialities of eighteenth-century poetic style. He has reservations about the form of imagination which accompanies this: Wordsworth's 'devouring egotism' which reduces the range of human feeling to whatever Wordsworth can sanction as his own. The implication is that Wordsworth's claim to be representative is at odds with his withdrawal from those engagements with audiences and with other writers which would validate that claim. He is at once the most egotistical and the least dramatic of poets, and, for both these connected reasons, the antithesis of Shakespeare.

Hazlitt pitched the idiom of his essays against those modern forms of philosophy and imagination which, whatever their apparent antagonisms, colluded in giving legitimacy to egotism. He does not oppose these with an equally calculated altruism, but with disinterestedness. What he means by this is outlined in his essay *On Consistency of Opinion*:

I think that it is my sympathising *beforehand* with the different views and feelings that may be entertained on a subject, that prevents my retracting my judgement, and flinging myself into the contrary extreme afterwards. If you proscribe all opinion opposite to your own, and impertinently exclude all the evidence that does not make for you, it stares you in the face with double force when it breaks unexpectedly upon you. . . . But if you are aware from the first suggestion of a subject, either by subtlety of tact, or close attention, of the full force of what others possibly feel and think of it you are not exposed to the same vacillation of opinion . . .

This transposes Hazlitt's ideal of Shakespearean imagination into an ethic of intellectual life. Disinterestedness is the capacity to sympathize with 'different views and feelings' in the process of arriving at a judgement. In contrast with a later Arnoldian view of disinterestedness, Hazlitt's version does not elevate the critic above contention. What it does do is create the conditions for holding a belief truly, although that in itself is not a guarantee that the belief is true. As the context of the passage makes clear, 'vacillation of opinion' has a contemporary political referent for Hazlitt in the careers of Wordsworth and Coleridge. Both manifested a distinctively modern egotism in their inability to anticipate opposition to their early radical commitments. Once that opposition came, they lacked the dramatic flexibility to sustain those commitments, and could only denounce them in order to defend their conversion to conservatism.

On Consistency of Opinion has a corrupt establishment in view which it is the critic's duty to resist. A similar polemical force is at work in another of Hazlitt's critical preoccupations: his view that the arts were not progressive. The context of Hazlitt's thinking was a long-standing debate about the conditions that caused the arts and sciences to flourish or decline. One view, exemplified in the eighteenth century by Shaftsbury, held that political liberty was essential to the health of the arts and sciences. Another more pessimistic view, exemplified by Hume, maintained that whenever the arts and sciences flourished a process of decline would inevitably follow. But, whatever these differences in emphasis, the arts and sciences were held in a common frame, subject to the same conditions of progress or decline. Hazlitt broke this common frame by arguing that development in arts and science were subject to different and even antithetical logics:

Nothing is more contrary to the facts than the supposition that in what we may understand by the fine arts, as painting and poetry, relative perfection is only the result of repeated efforts, and that what has been well done leads to something better. . . . One chemical or mathematical discovery may be added to another, because the degree and sort of faculty required to apprehend and retain them, are in both cases the same; but no one can voluntarily add the colouring of

Rubens to the expression of Raphael, till he has the same eye for
colour as Rubens and for expression as Raphael. . . . In fact we judge
of science by the number of effects produced—of art by the energy
which produces them. The one is knowledge—the other power.

Once these distinctions between the arts and sciences are
expressed historically, Hazlitt argues that the arts, far from
progressing, are subject to a process of decline. He takes it as
self-evident that the highest achievements in the arts occurred
at a very early stage in their respective histories. Modern
practitioners work in the shadow of these unrepeatable
achievements.

Hazlitt's argument about the arts can be understood as the
basis for polemic, as a cultural diagnosis, and as a metaphor
for freedom. As polemic the argument fuelled his assault on
the British art establishment of the day. Hazlitt was deeply
suspicious of Joshua Reynolds's attempts to improve the
education of artists and their public through the institution
of the Royal Academy. Where Reynolds thought to dignify the
artist by turning art into a profession, Hazlitt regarded profes-
sionalism and genius as antithetical. The Royal Academy
provided a dignified cover story for turning art into a species
of commodity production. It was 'a mercantile body . . .
consisting chiefly of manufacturers of portraits' who pander
'to the personal vanity and ignorance of their sitters'.

Far from improving art and educating its public, the Royal
Academy hastened a process of decline which Hazlitt thought
was already inevitable. Hazlitt's polemic against Reynolds and
the Academy is suffused by a melancholy resistance to the idea
that art can be improved by becoming subject to an educa-
tional regime. Hazlitt makes the history of art speak against
this meliorism. One radical implication of this view of history,
and one which Hazlitt occasionally voices, is that there can be
no such thing as a beneficial tradition in the arts. The arts are
strongest at an early stage of their history because their expressiveness is not constrained by the accumulation of precedent. Artists were not obliged to be always looking over their
shoulder to see what others had done. They could be 'original'
in one of Hazlitt's primary senses, by representing in their art
some particular aspect of nature which had been uniquely

disclosed to them. By contrast, the opportunities for originality in modern conditions are limited not only by the accumulation of preceding work which stands between the artist and an original representation of nature, but also by the need to assert the distinction of any work against the claims of contemporary rivals; hence, the restrictive egotism which Hazlitt discerned in a number of his contemporaries, an egotism necessary for their survival in a crowded market.

Hazlitt's arguments about artistic decline may seem dictated by the perspectives of nostalgic thinking: the value of a work of art increases the further removed it is in time from the critic's first-hand knowledge of how it is produced. But, again, it is important to notice Hazlitt's flexibility in working through the implications of his critical beliefs. He announces that the arts are not progressive with the force of an imperative, but the idea is never applied dogmatically. Decline does not occur uniformly across the arts: a painter as recent as Hogarth represents to Hazlitt a major achievement in British art and one which only underlines its precipitate decline in the years following Hogarth's death. Hazlitt's intimations of decline may shadow his critical judgements, but that does not prevent him from responding positively to the aspects of originality he discovers in contemporary writers like Wordsworth or Scott. Moreover, Hazlitt's experience as a critic of various arts establishes a context for judgement which is not exclusively dictated by the criterion of decline. So, his impatience with contemporary British painting can be based upon a sense of the expressive limits of the medium of painting as such, its inability to produce the sublime effects that Hazlitt discovers in literature: thus, Benjamin West's picture, *Death on a Pale Horse*, was incapable of sublimity because the 'painter cannot make the general particular, the infinite and imaginary defined and palpable, that which is only believed and dreaded an object of sight.'

Once these flexibilities and variations are granted, however, nostalgia remains a strong presence in Hazlitt's relation to art and is at one with its status in his writing as a myth of freedom. In opposing the power of art to the knowledge of science, Hazlitt expresses a desire for a form of communication removed from the regulation of discourse and the normative power of institutions. He attempts to return our experience of art to a moment which Susan Sontag has described as 'before all theory, when art knew no need to justify itself, when one did not ask of a work of art what it said because one knew (or thought one knew) what it did.'[5] The attempt is essentially ironic, and self-defeating because in writing about art the critic returns it to the very realm of discourse from which he wants to defend it. Running alongside this is another kind of fantasy: art, in Hazlitt's writing, both in its creation and its reception, stands for the possibility of an unprecedented and unpredictable event. The career of Napoleon is the political correlative for Hazlitt's sense of this kind of freedom and power in art, and stands as a reminder of how much artistic genius meant to him as a form of ambition realized without the privilege of noble birth or professional status.

Hazlitt's beliefs about art illustrate his ambivalence towards the legacy of the eighteenth-century enlightenment, which in his *Life of Napoleon*, had figured as the cause of the French Revolution. If reason, and the circulation of ideas through the printing press, promoted new kinds of freedom, they also were in the service of new forms of centralization and standardization which seemed to diminish the possibilities of dramatic expression and debate. Similarly, if power figures in Hazlitt's work as the exercise of an unjustifiable domination which can be dispersed by rational analysis, it is also the subject of an intense imaginative fascination which reason cannot simply dispel. Hazlitt's value as a writer may well be in the thoroughness with which he registers such ambivalences and his corresponding refusal of the protection of intellectual systems or political establishments. As a dramatic thinker he can be volatile and unpredictable, a writer who resists critical framing. But this is at one with Hazlitt's sustained commitment to the values of freedom and dissent, something which sets him apart from a subsequent English tradition of critical thought devoted to dreams of social stability and obedience. His writing is open to the reader's agreement or dissent; it is not in

[5] S. Sontag, 'Against Interpretation', in *Against Interpretation and Other Essays* (Farrer, Strauss & Giroux: New York, 1966), 4–5.

pursuit of disciples. His tone is democratic and secular; even now, this can make him seem a moving, and even exemplary, figure.

NOTE ON THE TEXT

I HAVE drawn on P. P. Howe's *Complete Works of William Hazlitt* for the text of Hazlitt's writings published in this selection. The time and place of first publication for each of the pieces printed here is given in the notes at the back of the volume.

The classification of Hazlitt's writing in this edition is my own invention and does not correspond to any distinctions made by Hazlitt about his own work. Hazlitt wrote before the current division of knowledge into separate specialisms and did not define himself exclusively as a literary critic or a philosopher or critic of art or political commentator. This has the positive effect of making him difficult to classify, but his work can also seem bewilderingly various. The headings which organize this edition are no more than signposts, designed to help readers negotiate the variety of Hazlitt's writing. It will be obvious that some of the pieces printed here could appear under more than one heading.

Hazlitt's writing can also be an editor's nightmare. His work is full of allusions, quotations, and echoes of the work of other writers. This edition is not intended to be exhaustive in its scholarship, but the notes do provide as many of the sources for quotations and allusions as I have been able to find. In most cases original spellings have been retained, except for printer's errors which have been silently corrected.

SELECT BIBLIOGRAPHY

Collected Editions. The standard edition is the *Complete Works of William Hazlitt*, ed. P. P. Howe (21 vols.; J. M. Dent & Sons Ltd.: London, 1930–4). Howe's work builds on the earlier edition of Hazlitt's writings edited by A. R. Waller and A. Glover between 1902 and 1906.

Individual Works. A small number of Hazlitt's individual works are available. They include: *The Round Table and Characters of Shakespeare's Plays*, with an introduction by C. M. Maclean (J. M. Dent & Sons, Everyman Library: London, last reprinted 1960); *Table Talk*, with an introduction by C. M. Maclean (J. M. Dent & Sons: London, last reprinted 1961); *Lectures on the English Poets and The Spirit of the Age*, with an introduction by C. M. Maclean (J. M. Dent & Sons: London, last reprinted 1960); *The Spirit of the Age* (The World's Classics; Oxford University Press: London, last reprinted 1970); *The Spirit of the Age*, ed. E. D. Mackerness (Collins Annotated Students Texts; Collins: London, 1969); *Liber Amoris: or, the New Pygmalion*, with an introduction by M. Neave (Hogarth Press: London, 1985); *Liber Amoris: or, the New Pygmalion*, edited with an introduction by G. Lahey (The Gotham Library; New York University Press: New York, 1980).

Selections. Selected Essays of William Hazlitt, ed. G. Keynes (Nonesuch Press: London, 1930); *William Hazlitt, Selected Writings*, edited with an introduction by R. Blythe (Penguin Books: Harmondsworth, 1970); *Selected Writings of William Hazlitt*, edited with an introduction by C. Salvesen (New American Library: New York, 1972).

Correspondence, Biography. Hazlitt's letters are collected in *The Letters of William Hazlitt*, ed. H. M. Sikes, W. H. Bonner, and G. Lahey (New York University Press: New York, 1978). Biographies include: H. Baker, *William Hazlitt* (Harvard University Press: Cambridge, Mass., 1962); *The Life of William Hazlitt*, by P. P. Howe (Martin Secker: London, 1922); *Born Under Saturn*, by C. M. Maclean (Collins: London, 1943); H. Pearson, *The Fool of Love* (Hamish Hamilton: London, 1934); R. M. Wardle, *Hazlitt* (University of Nebraska Press: Lincoln, 1971). A new standard biography by Stanley Jones, *Hazlitt, A Life, From Winterslow to Frith Street*, was published by Oxford University Press in 1989. For writing about Hazlitt by his contemporaries or near contemporaries, see B. R. Haydon, *Autobiography and Memoirs*, ed. T. Taylor (Peter Davies: London, 1926, first published 1853); W. C. Hazlitt, *Memoirs of William Hazlitt* (2 vols.; Bentley: London, 1867); Leigh Hunt,

SELECT BIBLIOGRAPHY xli

Autobiography, ed. R. Ingpen (Constable: London, 1903, first published 1850); P. G. Patmore, *My Friends and Acquaintances* (3 vols.; (Saunders and Otley: London, 1854); B. W. Procter [Barry Cornwall], *An Autobiographical Fragment and Biographical Notes* (George Bell & Sons: London, 1877); H. C. Robinson, *Diary, Reminiscences, Correspondence*, ed. T. Sadler (3 vols.; Macmillan: London, 1869). For De Quincey's account of Hazlitt, see *De Quincey as Critic*, ed. J. E. Jackson (Routledge and Kegan Paul: London, 1973).

Criticism: The best recent full-length critical study of Hazlitt is D. Bromwich, *Hazlitt: The Mind of a Critic* (Oxford University Press: New York and Oxford, 1983). Other valuable studies include: W. P. Albrecht, *Hazlitt and the Creative Imagination* (University of Kansas Press: Lawrence, 1965); J. W. Kinnaird, *Hazlitt, Critic of Power* (Columbia University Press: New York, 1978); R. Park, *Hazlitt and the Spirit of the Age* (Oxford University Press: Oxford, 1971); Tom Paulin, *Day-Star of Liberty: William Hazlitt's Radical Style* (Faber: London, 1998); J. B. Priestley, *William Hazlitt* (Longman: London, 1961); E. Schneider, *The Aesthetics of William Hazlitt* (University of Pennsylvania Press: Philadelphia, 1933).

A number of critical books contain substantial discussion of Hazlitt's writings. These include: M. Abrams, *The Mirror and the Lamp* (Oxford University Press: New York, 1954); D. Aers, J. Cook, D. Punter, *Romanticism and Ideology* (Routledge and Kegan Paul: London, 1981); J. Barrell, *The Political Theory of Painting from Reynolds to Hazlitt* (Yale University Press: New Haven and London, 1986); J. Bate, *Shakespeare and the English Romantic Imagination* (Oxford University Press: Oxford, 1986) and *Shakespearian Constitutions* (Oxford University Press: Oxford, 1989); M. Butler, *Romantics, Rebels and Reactionaries* (Oxford University Press: Oxford, 1981); M. Foot, *Debts of Honour* (Davis-Poynter: London, 1980); J. O. Hayden, *The Romantic Reviewers, 1802–24* (Routledge and Kegan Paul: London, 1969); I. Jack, *Keats and the Mirror of Art* (Oxford University Press: Oxford, 1967); T. McFarlane, *Romantic Cruxes, the English Essayists and the Spirit of the Age* (Oxford University Press: Oxford, 1987); P. Parrinder, *Authors and Authority* (Routledge and Kegan Paul: London, 1977); R. Wellek, *A History of Modern Criticism*, Vol. 2 (Jonathan Cape: London, 1955).

Other books that provide a useful context for reading Hazlitt include: R. Sales, *Literature in History 1780–1830, Pastoral and Politics* (Hutchinson: London, 1983); O. Smith, *The Politics of Language, 1791–1819* (Oxford University Press: Oxford, 1987); E. P. Thompson, *The Making of the English Working Class* (V. Gollancz: London, 1963).

Critical articles and essays include: M. Butler, 'Satire and the Images of Self in the Romantic Period: The Long Tradition of Hazlitt's *Liber*

Amoris', *The Yearbook of English Studies*, 14(1984), 209–25; C. D. Thorpe, 'Keats and Hazlitt', *Proceedings of the Modern Language Association*, 62(1947), 487–503; C. I. Patterson, 'Hazlitt as a Critic of Prose Fiction', *Proceedings of the Modern Language Association*, 68(1953), 1001–1016; L. M. Trawick, 'Hazlitt, Reynolds and the Ideal', *Studies in Romanticism*, 4(1964–5), 240–7; J. Whale, 'Hazlitt on Burke: The Ambivalent Position of a Radical Essayist', *Studies in Romanticism*, 25(1986), 446–83; V. Woolf, 'William Hazlitt', in *Collected Essays* (Hogarth Press: London, 1966), 155–65.

Bibliography: For further bibliographical information, see J. A. Houck, *William Hazlitt, A Reference Guide* (G. K. Hall & Co.: Boston, 1977); G. Keynes, *Bibliography of Hazlitt* (Nonesuch Press: London, 1931).

A CHRONOLOGY OF
WILLIAM HAZLITT

1778 Born in Maidstone, the youngest son of William and Grace Hazlitt. Of the four children, three survive: William, his brother, John, and sister, Margaret. Hazlitt's father is a prominent Unitarian minister. Rousseau dies.

1780 Hazlitt's father openly advocates the cause of the Americans in the War of Independence. This leads to a rift with his congregation in Maidstone and the family move to Bandon in Ireland where Hazlitt's father befriends American prisoners-of-war and protests about their treatment by the British Army.

1783 The family moves to America where Hazlitt's father establishes the first Unitarian church in Boston, and is active in theological and political controversy.

1787 The family returns to England where Hazlitt's father takes up a ministry in Wem, Shropshire. Hazlitt's brother, John, moves to London to study painting with Sir Joshua Reynolds and becomes acquainted with the Godwin circle.

1789 Fall of the Bastille.

1790 Burke's *Reflections on the Revolution in France* and Wollstonecraft's *A Vindication of the Rights of Men* both published.

1791 Paine's *Rights of Man* published.

1792 Wollstonecraft's *A Vindication of the Rights of Woman* published. September Massacres in Paris.

1793 Hazlitt attends the New Unitarian College at Hackney in London. The college, founded by Joseph Priestley, is regarded by Anti-Jacobins as a seditious and heretical institution. It is here that Hazlitt begins his writing on the nature of human motivation and reads Hume, Berkley, Hartley, and the French philosophers Condorcet, D'Holbach, and Helvetius. Godwin publishes *Political Justice*. Execution of Louis XVI. England declares war on France.

1794 Hazlitt continues at the New Unitarian College. Visits the theatre where he sees Sarah Siddons act. Hardy, Horne Tooke, and Thelwall tried for high treason and acquitted.

1795   Hazlitt refuses to follow his father's profession as a Unitarian minister. Withdraws from the New Unitarian College during the summer and lives with his brother in London. Meets Godwin.

1796   Living in London and at Wem. Meets Wollstonecraft; reads widely in the English poets and Burke and Rousseau; continues with his efforts at philosophical writing.

1797   Mutinies in the British Navy at Spithead and the Nore.

1798   Meets Coleridge in January when the latter comes to preach at Wem (see *My First Acquaintance with Poets*). Hazlitt visits Coleridge in Somerset, meets Wordsworth, and reads *Lyrical Ballads* in manuscript, shortly before their first publication. Decides to become a painter and begins a stay at Bury St Edmunds with his brother John who by this time has established himself as a successful miniaturist. In December Hazlitt attends an exhibition of Italian Renaissance painting at the Orleans Gallery in London.

1799   Hazlitt in London and travelling around the country in search of portrait commissions. In France the Directory is overthrown and Napoleon becomes First Consul. In England the Combination Act is passed, strengthening existing legislation against trade union activity.

1802   Hazlitt's portrait of his father is exhibited at the Royal Academy. After the Peace of Amiens Hazlitt visits Paris and engages in an intensive study of paintings in the Louvre. Meets Charles James Fox.

1803   Back in England, Hazlitt renews his acquaintance with Coleridge. Visits Coleridge and Wordsworth in the Lake District. Evidence of increasing political disagreement between them. Hazlitt has to end his visit because of a sexual scandal. Renewal of war between England and France.

1804   Meets Charles and Mary Lamb. Hazlitt paints Lamb's portrait, but is becoming increasingly uncertain about following painting as a career; resumes his philosophical writing.

1805   Living in London and Wem. Publication of his first book, *An Essay on the Principles of Human Action.*

1806   Publication of Hazlitt's *Free Thoughts on Human Affairs.*

1807   Publication of *An Abridgement of the Light of Nature Pursued by Abraham Tucker, A Reply to the Essay on Population,* and *The*

Eloquence of the British Senate. Wordsworth's *Poems in Two Volumes* published.

1808   Marries Sarah Stoddart. Moves to Winterslow, near Salisbury.

1810   *A New and Improved Grammar of the English Tongue* published.

1811   Birth of son, William. Hazlitt in London planning a series of lectures on English philosophy.

1812   Hazlitt's first series of public lectures, on English philosophy, delivered at the Russell Institution, London. Starts work as a reporter of parliamentary speeches for the *Morning Chronicle.* Moves to 19 York Street, Westminster, which he rents from Jeremy Bentham. Meets Leigh Hunt at Haydon's studio. Probably meets Shelley at some stage between 1812 and 1814. The first two cantos of Byron's *Childe Harold* published. Napoleon invades Russia.

1813   Writing short essays and drama reviews for the *Morning Chronicle.* Southey becomes Poet Laureate. John and Leigh Hunt, editors of the *Examiner,* sentenced to two years in prison for a libel on the Prince Regent.

1814   First sees Edmund Kean on the London stage. Hazlitt leaves the *Morning Chronicle* after disagreements with its editor, James Perry. He starts writing for the *Champion,* the *Examiner,* and the *Edinburgh Review.* Writes a lengthy review of Wordsworth's *Excursion* for the *Examiner.*

1815   Writing on drama and painting for the *Champion,* miscellaneous essays for the *Examiner,* and continues to contribute to the *Edinburgh Review.*

1816   Writing political and literary journalism. Completes *The Memoirs of Thomas Holcroft* for publication. Byron and Shelley leave England and travel in Europe. Hazlitt in poor health.

1817   At the beginning of the year Hazlitt meets Keats; discussing monarchy and republicanism with Shelley. *The Round Table* and *Characters of Shakespeare's Plays* published. Coleridge's *Biographia Literaria* published and reviewed unfavourably by Hazlitt.

1818   Gives two lecture series, on English Poetry and on English Comic Writers, at the Surrey Institution. *A View of the English Stage* and *Lectures on the English Poets* published. Hazlitt is attacked by the Tory *Blackwood's Magazine,* as part of their campaign against 'the Cockney School'. He sues the magazine for libel.

1819   *A Letter to William Gifford, Lectures on the English Comic Writers,* and *Political Essays* published. Hazlitt is described in the *Morning Chronicle* as 'one of the ablest and most eloquent critics of our nation'.

1820   Begins writing for the *London Magazine. Lectures on the Dramatic Literature of the Age of Elizabeth* published.

1821   Beginning of his infatuation with Sarah Walker. *Table Talk or Original Essays* published. In February Keats dies in Rome.

1822   Divorces his wife in Edinburgh in the hope of marrying Sarah Walker but she refuses him. In July Shelley is drowned.

1823   *Liber Amoris; or, the New Pygmalion* and *Characteristics* published. Hazlitt is briefly arrested for debt. Living in London and Winterslow.

1824   Marries Isabella Bridgewater. *Sketches of the Principal Picture Galleries in England* published; edits *Selected British Poets.* Relieved from financial worry by his wife's private income, Hazlitt travels with her in France and Italy. He meets Stendhal in Paris. Byron dies.

1825   *Table Talk or Original Essays* published in Paris; *The Spirit of the Age* published in London. Returns to England in October.

1826   *The Plain Speaker* and *Notes of a Journey through France and Italy* published. Hazlitt returns to Paris to work on his biography of Napoleon.

1827   Lives in Paris for the first part of the year. On his return to England, separates from Isabella, probably as the result of increasing tensions between Isabella and Hazlitt's son by his first marriage. Lives in Winterslow. Suffers increasing ill health.

1828   Publication of the first volume of *The Life of Napoleon.*

1830   Publication of *Conversations with James Northcote.* Hazlitt continues working, although mortally ill. He dies in his lodgings at Frith Street, Soho on 16 September and is buried in the churchyard of St Anne's, Soho, on 23 September. *The Life of Napoleon* is published in its entirety shortly after his death.

POLITICS

WHAT IS THE PEOPLE?

—AND who are you that ask the question? One of the people. And yet you would be something! Then you would not have the People nothing. For what is the People? Millions of men, like you, with hearts beating in their bosoms, with thoughts stirring in their minds, with the blood circulating in their veins, with wants and appetites, and passions and anxious cares, and busy purposes and affections for others and a respect for themselves, and a desire of happiness, and a right to freedom, and a will to be free. And yet you would tear out this mighty heart of a nation, and lay it bare and bleeding at the foot of despotism: you would slay the mind of a country to fill up the dreary aching void with the old, obscene, drivelling prejudices of superstition and tyranny: you would tread out the eye of Liberty (the light of nations) like 'a vile jelly',* that mankind may be led about darkling to its endless drudgery, like the Hebrew Sampson (shorn of his strength and blind), by his insulting taskmasters: you would make the throne every thing, and the people nothing, to be yourself less than nothing, a very slave, a reptile, a creeping, cringing sycophant, a court favourite, a pander to Legitimacy*—that detestable fiction, which would make you and me and all mankind its slaves or victims; which would, of right and with all the sanctions of religion and morality, sacrifice the lives of millions to the least of its caprices; which subjects the rights, the happiness, and liberty of nations, to the will of some of the lowest of the species; which rears its bloated hideous form to brave the will of a whole people; that claims mankind as its property, and allows human nature to exist only upon sufferance; that haunts the understanding like a frightful spectre, and oppresses the very air with a weight that is not to be borne; that like a witch's spell covers the earth with a dim and envious mist, and makes us turn our eyes from the light of heaven, which we have no right to look at without its leave: robs us of 'the unbought grace of life',* the pure delight and

conscious pride in works of art or nature; leaves us no thought
or feeling that we dare call our own; makes genius its lacquey,
and virtue its easy prey; sports with human happiness, and
mocks at human misery; suspends the breath of liberty, and
almost of life; exenterates us of our affections, blinds our
understandings, debases our imaginations, converts the very
hope of emancipation from its yoke into sacrilege, binds the
successive countless generations of men together in its chains
like a string of felons or galley-slaves, lest they should
'resemble the flies of a summer', considers any remission of
its absolute claims as a gracious boon, an act of royal clemency
and favour, and confounds all sense of justice, reason, truth,
liberty, humanity, in one low servile deathlike dread of power
without limit and without remorse!

Such is the old doctrine of Divine Right, new-vamped up
under the style and title of Legitimacy. 'Fine word, Legitimate!'* We wonder where our English politicians picked it up.
Is it an echo from the tomb of the martyred monarch, Charles
the First? Or was it the last word which his son, James the
Second, left behind him in his flight, and bequeathed with
his *abdication*, to his legitimate successors? It is not written in
our annals in the years 1688, in 1715, or 1745. It was not
sterling then, which was only fifteen years before his present
Majesty's accession to the throne. Has it become so since? Is
the Revolution of 1688 at length acknowledged to be a blot
in the family escutcheon of the Prince of Orange or the
Elector of Hanover? Is the choice of the people, which raised
them to the throne, found to be the only flaw in their title to
the succession; the weight of royal gratitude growing more
uneasy with the distance of the obligation? Is the alloy of
liberty, mixed up with it, thought to debase that *fine carat*,
which should compose the regal diadem? Are the fire-new
specimens of the principles of the Right-Liners, and of Sir
Robert Filmer's* patriarchal scheme, to be met with in *The
Courier, The Day, The Sun*, and some time back, in *The Times*,
handed about to be admired in the highest circle, like the
new gold coinage of sovereigns and half- sovereigns? We do
not know. It may seem to be *Latter Lammas** with the doctrine
at this time of day; but better late than never. By taking root

in the soil of France, from which it was expelled (not quite so long as from our own), it may in time stretch out its feelers and strong suckers to this country; and present an altogether curious and novel aspect, by ingrafting the principles of the House of Stuart on the illustrious stock of the House of Brunswick.

'Miraturque novas frondes, et non sua poma.'*

What then is the People? We will answer first, by saying what it is not; and this we cannot do better than in the words of a certain author,* whose testimony on the subject is too important not to avail ourselves of it again in this place. That infatuated drudge of despotism, who at one moment asks, 'Where is the madman that maintains the doctrine of divine right?' and the next affirms, that 'Louis XVIII has the same right to the throne of France, independently of his merits or conduct, that Mr Coke of Norfolk has to his estate at Holkham,' has given us a tolerable clue to what we have to expect from that mild paternal sway to which he would so kindly make us and the rest of the world over, in hopeless perpetuity. In a violent philippic against the author of the *Political Register*, he thus inadvertently expresses himself:—'Mr Cobbett had been sentenced to two years' imprisonment for a libel, and during the time that he was in Newgate, it was discovered that he had been in treaty with Government to avoid the sentence passed upon him; and that he had proposed to certain of the agents of Ministers, that if they would let him off, they might make what future use they pleased of him; *he would entirely betray the cause of the people*; he would either write or not write, or *write against them*, as he had once done before, just as Ministers thought proper. To this, however, it was replied, that 'Cobbett had written on too many sides already *to be worth a groat for the service of Government*'; and he accordingly suffered his confinement!'—We here then see plainly enough what it is that, in the opinion of this very competent judge, alone renders any writer 'worth a groat for the service of Government,' *viz.* that he shall be able and willing entirely to betray the cause of the people. It follows from this principle (by which he seems to estimate the value of his lucubrations in

the service of Government—we do not know whether the
Government judge of them in the same way), that the cause
of the people and the cause of the Government, who are
represented as thus anxious to suborn their creatures to write
against the people, are not the same but the reverse of one
another. This slip of the pen in our professional retainer of
legitimacy, though a libel on our own Government,* is, notwithstanding, a general philosophic truth (the only one he
ever hit upon), and an axiom in political mechanics, which
we shall make the text of the following commentary.

What are the interests of the people? Not the interests of
those who would betray them. Who is to judge of those interests? Not those who would suborn others to betray them. That
Government is instituted for the benefit of the governed,
there can be little doubt; but the interests of the Government
(when once it becomes absolute and independent of the
people) must be directly at variance with those of the governed. The interests of the one are common and equal rights:
of the other, exclusive and invidious privileges. The essence
of the first is to be shared alike by all, and to benefit the
community in proportion as they are spread: the essence of
the last is to be destroyed by communication, and to subsist
only—in wrong of the people. Rights and privileges are a
contradiction in terms: for if one has more than his right,
others must have less. The latter are the deadly nightshade of
the commonwealth, near which no wholesome plant can
thrive,—the ivy clinging round the trunk of the British oak,
blighting its verdure, drying up its sap, and oppressing its
stately growth. The insufficient checks and balances opposed
to the overbearing influence of hereditary rank and power in
our own Constitution, and in every Government which retains
the least trace of freedom, are so many illustrations of this
principle, if it needed any. The tendency in arbitrary power
to encroach upon the liberties and comforts of the people,
and to convert the public good into a stalking-horse to its own
pride and avarice, has never (that we know) been denied by
any one but 'the professional gentleman', who writes in *The
Day and New Times*. The great and powerful, in order to be
what they aspire to be, and what this gentleman would have

them, perfectly independent of the will of the people, ought also to be perfectly independent of the assistance of the people. To be formally invested with the attributes of Gods upon earth, they ought first to be raised above its petty wants and appetites: they ought to give proofs of the beneficence and wisdom of Gods, before they can be trusted with the power. When we find them seated above the world, sympathizing with the welfare, but not feeling the passions of men, receiving neither good nor hurt, neither tilth nor tythe from them, but bestowing their benefits as free gifts on all, they may then be expected, but not till then, to rule over us like another Providence. We may make them a present of all the taxes they do not apply to their own use: they are perfectly welcome to all the power, to the possession of which they are perfectly indifferent, and to the abuse of which they can have no possible temptation. But Legitimate Governments (flatter them as we will) are not another Heathen mythology. They are neither so cheap nor so splendid as the Delphin edition of Ovid's Metamorphoses.* They are indeed 'Gods to punish', but in other respects 'men of our infirmity'.* They do not feed on ambrosia or drink nectar; but live on the common fruits of the earth, of which they get the largest share, and the best. The wine they drink is made of grapes: the blood they shed is that of their subjects: the laws they make are not against themselves: the taxes they vote, they afterwards devour. They have the same wants that we have: and having the option, very naturally help themselves first, out of the common stock, without thinking that others are to come after them. With the same natural necessities, they have a thousand artificial ones besides; and with a thousand times the means to gratify them, they are still voracious, importunate, unsatisfied. Our State-paupers have their hands in every man's dish, and fare sumptuously every day. They live in palaces, and loll in coaches. In spite of Mr Malthus,* their studs of horses consume the produce of our fields, their dog-kennels are glutted with the food which would maintain the children of the poor. They cost us so much a year in dress and furniture, so much in stars and garters, blue ribbons, and grand crosses,—so much in dinners, breakfasts, and suppers, and so much in suppers, breakfasts, and dinners. These heroes of the Income-tax, Worthies of the Civil List, Saints of the Court calendar (*compagnons du lys*),* have their naturals and non-naturals, like the rest of the world, but at a dearer rate. They are real *bona fide* personages, and do not live upon air. You will find it easier to keep them a week than a month; and at the end of that time, waking from the sweet dream of Legitimacy, you may say with Caliban, 'Why, what a fool was I to take this drunken monster for a God!'* In fact, the case on the part of the people is so far self-evident. There is but a limited earth and a limited fertility to supply the demands both of Government and people; and what the one gains in the division of the spoil, beyond its average proportion, the other must needs go without. Do you suppose that our gentlemen-placemen and pensioners would suffer so many wretches to be perishing in our streets and highways, if they could relieve their extreme misery without parting with any of their own superfluities? If the Government take a fourth of the produce of the poor man's labour, they will be rich, and he will be in want. If they can contrive to take one half of it by legal means, or by a stretch of arbitrary power, they will be just twice as rich, twice as insolent and tyrannical, and he will be twice as poor, twice as miserable and oppressed, in a mathematical ratio to the end of the chapter, that is, till the one can extort and the other endure no more. It is the same with respect to power. The will and passions of the great are not exerted in regulating the seasons, or rolling the planets round their orbits for our good, without fee or reward, but in controlling the will and passions of others, in making the follies and vices of mankind subservient to their own, and marring,

'Because men suffer it, their toy, the world.'*

This is self-evident, like the former. Their will cannot be paramount, while any one in the community, or the whole community together, has the power to thwart it. A King cannot attain absolute power, while the people remain perfectly free; yet what King would not attain absolute power? While any trace of liberty is left among a people, ambitious Princes will never be easy, never at peace, never of sound mind; nor will they ever rest or leave one stone unturned, till they have succeeded in destroying the very name of liberty, or making it into a by-word,* and in rooting out the germs of every popular right and liberal principle from a soil once sacred to liberty. It is not enough that they have secured the whole power of the state in their hands,—that they carry every measure they please without the chance of an effectual opposition to it: but a word uttered against it is torture to their ears,—a thought that questions their wanton exercise of the royal prerogative rankles in their breasts like poison. Till all distinctions of right and wrong, liberty and slavery, happiness and misery, are looked upon as matters of indifference, or as saucy, insolent pretensions,—are sunk and merged in their idle caprice and pampered self-will, they will still feel themselves 'cribbed, confined, and cabin'd in':* but if they can once more set up the doctrine of Legitimacy, 'the right divine of Kings to govern wrong',* and set mankind at defiance with impunity, they will then be 'broad and casing as the general air, whole as the rock'.* This is the point from which they set out, and to which by the grace of God and the help of man they may return again. Liberty is short and fleeting, a transient grace that lights upon the earth by stealth and at long intervals—

> 'Like the rainbow's lovely form,
> Evanishing amid the storm;
> Or like the Borealis race,
> That shift ere you can point their place;
> Or like the snow falls in the river,
> A moment white, then melts for ever.'*

But power is eternal; it is 'enthroned in the hearts of Kings'.* If you want the proofs, look at history, look at geography, look abroad; but do not look at home!

The power of an arbitrary King or an aspiring Minister does not increase with the liberty of the subject, but must be circumscribed by it. It is aggrandized by perpetual, systematic, insidious, or violent encroachments on popular freedom and natural right, as the sea gains upon the land by swallowing it up.—What then can we expect from the mild paternal sway of absolute power, and its sleek minions? What the world has always received at its hands, an abuse of power as vexatious, cowardly, and unrelenting, as the power itself was unprincipled, preposterous, and unjust. They who get wealth and power from the people, who drive them like cattle to slaughter or to market, 'and levy cruel wars, wasting the earth';* they who wallow in luxury, while the people are 'steeped in poverty to the very lips',* and bowed to the earth with unremitting labour, can have but little sympathy with those whose loss of liberty and property is their gain. What is it that the wealth of thousands is composed of? The tears, the sweat, and blood of millions. What is it that constitutes the glory of the Sovereigns of the earth? To have millions of men their slaves. Wherever the Government does not emanate (as in our own excellent Constitution) from the people, the principle of the Government, the *esprit de corps*, the point of honour, in all those connected with it, and raised by it to privileges above the law and above humanity, will be hatred to the people. Kings who would be thought to reign in contempt of the people, will shew their contempt of them in every act of their lives. Parliaments, not chosen by the people, will only be the instruments of Kings, who do not reign in the hearts of the people, 'to betray the cause of the people'. Ministers, not responsible to the people, will squeeze the last shilling out of them. *Charity begins at home*, is a maxim as true of Governments as of individuals. When the English Parliament insisted on its right of taxing the Americans without their consent, it was not from an apprehension that the Americans would, by being left to themselves, lay such heavy duties on their own produce and manufactures, as would afflict the generosity of the mother-country, and put the mild paternal sentiments of Lord North to the blush. If any future King of England should keep a wistful eye on the map of that country, it would rather be to hang it up as a trophy of legitimacy, and to 'punish the last successful example of a democratic rebellion',* than from any yearnings of fatherly goodwill to the American people, or from finding his 'large heart' and capacity for good government, 'confined in too narrow room'* in the united kingdoms of Great Britain, Ireland, and Hanover. If Ferdinand VII*

refuses the South American patriots leave to plant the olive
or the vine, throughout that vast continent, it is his pride, not
his humanity, that steels his royal resolution.

In 1781, the Controller-general of France, under Louis XVI
Monsieur Joli de Fleuri, defined the people of France to be
*un peuple serf, corveable et baillable, à merci et misericorde.** When
Louis XVIII as the Count de Lille, protested against his
brother's accepting the Constitution of 1792 (he has since
become an accepter of Constitutions himself, if not an observer of them,) as compromising the rights and privileges of
the noblesse and clergy as well as of the crown, he was right
in considering the Bastile, or 'King's castle', with the picturesque episode of the Man in the Iron Mask, the fifteen
thousand *lettres de cachet,** issued in the mild reign of Louis
XV, *corvées,** tythes, game-laws, holy water, the right of pilla-
ging, imprisoning, massacring, persecuting, harassing, insulting, and ingeniously tormenting the minds and bodies of the
whole French people at every moment of their lives, on every
possible pretence, and without any check or control but their
own mild paternal sentiments towards them, as among the
*menus plaisirs,** the chief points of etiquette, the immemorial
privileges, and favourite amusements of Kings, Priests, and
Nobles, from the beginning to the end of time, without which
the bare title of King, Priest, or Noble, would not have been
worth a groat.

The breasts of Kings and Courtiers then are not the safest
depository of the interests of the people. But they know best
what is for their good! Yes—to prevent it! The people may
indeed feel their grievance, but their betters, it is said, must
apply the remedy—which they take good care never to do! If
the people want judgment in their own affairs (which is not
certain, for they only meddle with their own affairs when they
are forcibly brought home to them in a way which they can
hardly misunderstand), this is at any rate better than the want
of sincerity, which would constantly and systematically lead
their superiors to betray those interests, from their having
other ends of their own to serve. It is better to trust to ignorance than to malice—to run the risk of sometimes miscalculat-
ing the odds than to play against loaded dice. The people

would in this way stand as little chance in defending their
purses or their persons against Mr C——or Lord C——,* as
an honest country gentleman would have had in playing at
put or hazard with Count Fathom or Jonathan Wild.* A certain degree of folly, or rashness, or indecision, or even violence in attaining an object, is surely less to be dreaded than
a malignant, deliberate, mercenary intention in others to
deprive us of it. If the people must have attorneys, and the
advice of counsel, let them have attorneys and counsel of their
own chusing, not those who are employed by special retainer
against them, or who regularly hire others *to betray their cause.*

—— —— ——'O silly sheep,
Come ye to seek the lamb here of the wolf?'*

This then is the cause of the people, the good of the people,
judged of by common feeling and public opinion. Mr Burke
contemptuously defines the people to be 'any faction that at
the time can get the power of the sword into its hands'.* No:
that may be a description of the Government, but it is not of
the people. The people is the hand, heart, and head of the
whole community acting to one purpose, and with a mutual
and thorough consent. The hand of the people so employed
to execute what the heart feels, and the head thinks, must be
employed more beneficially for the cause of the people, than
in executing any measures which the cold hearts, and contriv-
ing heads of any faction, with distinct privileges and interests,
may dictate to betray their cause. The will of the people
necessarily tends to the general good as its end; and it must
attain that end, and can only attain it, in proportion as it is
guided—First, by popular feeling, as arising out of the immediate wants and wishes of the great mass of the people,—
secondly, by public opinion, as arising out of the impartial
reason and enlightened intellect of the community. What is
it that determines the opinion of any number of persons in
things they actually feel in their practical and home results?
Their common interest. What is it that determines their opinion in things of general inquiry, beyond their immediate
experience or interest? Abstract reason. In matters of feeling
and common sense, of which each individual is the best judge,

the majority are in the right; in things requiring a greater strength of mind to comprehend them, the greatest power of understanding will prevail, if it has but fair play. These two, taken together, as the test of the practical measures or general principles of Government, must be right, cannot be wrong. It is an absurdity to suppose that there can be any better criterion of national grievances, or the proper remedies for them, than the aggregate amount of the actual, dear-bought experience, the honest feelings, and heart-felt wishes of a whole people, informed and directed by the greatest power of understanding in the community, unbiassed by any sinister motive. Any other standard of public good or ill must, in proportion as it deviates from this, be vitiated in principle, and fatal in its effects. *Vox populi vox Dei,** is the rule of all good Government: for in that voice, truly collected and freely expressed (not when it is made the servile echo of a corrupt Court, or a designing Minister), we have all the sincerity and all the wisdom of the community. If we could suppose society to be transformed into one great animal (like Hobbes's Leviathan), each member of which had an intimate con-nexion with the head or Government, so that every individual in it could be made known and have its due weight, the State would have the same consciousness of its own wants and feelings, and the same interest in providing for them, as an individual has with respect to his own welfare. Can any one doubt that such a state of society in which the greatest know-ledge of its interests was thus combined with the greatest sympathy with its wants, would realize the idea of a perfect Commonwealth? But such a Government would be the precise idea of a truly popular or *representative* Government. The opposite extreme is the purely hereditary and despotic form of Government, where the people are an inert, torpid mass, without the power, scarcely with the will, to make its wants or wishes known: and where the feelings of those who are at the head of the State, centre in their own exclusive interests, pride, passions, prejudices; and all their thoughts are employed in defeating the happiness and undermining the liberties of a country.*

· · · · ·

It is not denied that the people are best acquainted with their own wants, and most attached to their own interests. But then a question is started, as if the persons asking it were at a great loss for the answer,—Where are we to find the intellect of the people? Why, all the intellect that ever was is theirs. The public opinion expresses not only the collective sense of the whole people, but of all ages and nations, of all those minds that have devoted themselves to the love of truth and the good of mankind,—who have bequeathed their instructions, their hopes, and their example to posterity,—who have thought, spoke, written, acted, and suffered in the name and on the behalf of our common nature. All the greatest poets, sages, heroes, are ours originally, and by right. But surely Lord Bacon* was a great man? Yes; but not because he was a lord. There is nothing of hereditary growth but pride and prejudice. That 'fine word Legitimate' never produced any thing but bastard philosophy and patriotism! Even Burke was one of the people, and would have remained with the people to the last, if there had been no court-side for him to go over to. The King gave him his pension, not his understanding or his eloquence. It would have been better for him and for mankind if he had kept to his principles, and gone without his pension. It is thus that the tide of power constantly setting in against the people, swallows up natural genius and acquired knowledge in the vortex of corruption, and then they reproach us with our want of leaders of weight and influence, to stem the torrent. All that has ever been done for society, has, however, been done for it by this intellect, before it was cheapened to be a cat's-paw of divine right. All discoveries and all improvements in arts, in science, in legislation, in civilization, in every thing dear and valuable to the heart of man, have been made by this intellect—all the triumphs of human genius over the rudest barbarism, the darkest ignorance, the grossest and most inhuman superstition, the most unmitigated and remorseless tyranny, have been gained for themselves by the people. Great Kings, great law-givers, great founders, and great reformers of religion, have almost all arisen from among the people. What have hereditary Monarchs, or regular Governments, or established priesthoods, ever done for the people? Did the Pope and Cardinals first set on foot the Reformation? Did the Jesuits attempt to abolish the Inquisition? For what one measure of civil or religious liberty did our own Bench of Bishops ever put themselves forward? What judge ever proposed a reform in the laws! Have not the House of Commons, with all their 'tried wisdom', voted for every measure of Ministers for the last twenty-five years, except the Income-tax? It is the press that has done every thing for the people, and even for Governments.—'If they had not ploughed with our heifer, they would not have found out our riddle.'* And it has done this by slow degrees, by repeated, incessant, and incredible struggles with the oldest, most inveterate, powerful, and active enemies of the freedom of the press and of the people, who wish, in spite of the nature of things and of society, to retain the idle and mischievous privileges they possess as the relics of barbarous and feudal times, who have an exclusive interest as a separate cast in the continuance of all existing abuses, and who plead a permanent *vested right* in the prevention of the progress of reason, liberty, and civilization. Yet they tax us with our want of intellect; and *we* ask them in return for their court-list of great names in arts or philosophy, for the coats of arms of their heroic vanquishers of error and intolerance, for their devout benefactors and royal martyrs of humanity. What are the claims of the people—the obvious, undoubted rights of common justice and humanity, forcibly withheld from them by pride, bigotry, and selfishness,—demanded for them, age after age, year after year, by the wisdom and virtue of the enlightened and disinterested part of mankind, and only grudgingly yielded up, with indecent, disgusting excuses, and sickening delays, when the burning shame of their refusal can be no longer concealed by fear or favour from the whole world. What did it not cost to abolish the Slave Trade? How long will the Catholic Claims* be withheld by our State-jugglers? How long, and for what purpose? We may appeal, in behalf of the people, from the interested verdict of the worst and weakest men now living, to the disinterested reason of the best and wisest men among the living and the dead. We appeal from the corruption of Courts, the hypocrisy of zealots, and the dotage of hereditary imbecility, to the innate love of liberty in the human breast, and to the growing intellect of the world. We appeal to the pen, and they answer us with the point of the bayonet; and, at one time, when that had failed, they were for recommending the dagger.* They quote Burke, but rely on the Attorney-General. They hold Universal Suffrage to be the most dreadful of all things, and a Standing Army the best representatives of the people abroad and at home. They think Church-and-King mobs good things, for the same reason that they are alarmed at a meeting to petition for a Reform of Parliament. They consider the cry of 'No Popery' a sound, excellent, and constitutional cry,—but the cry of a starving population for food, strange and unnatural. They exalt the war-whoop of the Stock-Exchange into the voice of undissembled patriotism, while they set down the cry for peace as the work of the Jacobins, the ventriloquism of the secret enemies of their country. The writers on the popular side of the question are factious, designing demagogues, who delude the people to make tools of them: but the government-writers, who echo every calumny, and justify every encroachment on the people, are profound philosophers and very honest men. Thus when Mr John Gifford, the Editor of the 'Anti-Jacobin' (not Mr William Gifford,* who at present holds the same office under Government, as the Editor of the *Quarterly Review*), denounced Mr Coleridge as a person, who had 'left his wife destitute and his children fatherless', and proceeded to add—'*Ex hoc disce* his friends Lamb and Southey'—we are to suppose that he was influenced in this gratuitous statement purely by his love for his King and country. Loyalty, patriotism, and religion, are regarded as the natural virtues and plain unerring instincts of the common people: the mixture of ignorance or prejudice is never objected to in these: it is only their love of liberty or hatred of oppression that are discovered, by the same liberal-minded junto, to be proofs of a base and vulgar disposition. The Bourbons are set over the immense majority of the French people against their will, because a talent for governing does not go with numbers. This argument was not thought of when Bonaparte tried to shew his talent for governing the people of the Continent against their will, though he had quite as much talent as the Bourbons. Mr Canning rejoiced that the first successful resistance to Bonaparte was made in Russia, a country of barbarians and slaves. The heroic struggles of 'the universal Spanish nation'* in the cause of freedom and independence, have ended in the destruction of the Cortes and the restoration of the Inquisition, but without making the Duke of Wellington look thoughtful:—not a single renegado poet has vented his indignation in a single ode, elegy, or sonnet; nor does Mr Southey 'make him a willow cabin at its gate, write loyal cantos of contemned love, and sing them loud even in the dead of the night!'* He indeed assures us in the *Quarterly Review*, that the Inquisition was restored by the voice of the Spanish people. He also asks, in the same place, 'whether the voice of God was heard in the voice of the people at Jerusalem, when they cried, "Crucify him, crucify him"?' We do not know; but we suppose, he would hardly go to the Chief Priests and Pharisees to find it. This great historian, politician, and logician, breaks out into a rhapsody against the old maxim, *vox populi vox Dei*, in the midst of an article of 55 pages,* written expressly to prove that the last war was 'the most popular, *because* the most just and necessary war that ever was carried on'. He shrewdly asks, 'Has the *vox populi* been the *vox Dei* in France for the last twenty-five years?' But, at least, according to his own shewing, it has been so in this country for all that period. We, however, do not think so. The voice of the country has been for war, because the voice of the King was for it, which was echoed by Parliament, both Lords and Commons, by Clergy and Gentry, and by the populace, till, as Mr Southey himself states in the same connected chain of reasoning, the cry for war became *so* popular, that all those who did not join in it (of which number the Poet-laureate himself was one) were 'persecuted, insulted, and injured in their persons, fame, and fortune'. This is the true way of accounting for the fact, but it unfortunately knocks the Poet's inference on the head. Mr Locke has observed,* that there are not so many wrong opinions in the world as we are apt to believe, because most people take their opinions on trust from others. Neither are the opinions of the people their own, when they have been bribed or bullied into them by a mob of Lords and Gentlemen, following in full cry at the heels of the Court. The *vox populi* is the *vox Dei* only when it springs from the individual, unbiassed feelings, and unfettered, independent opinion of the people. Mr Southey does not understand the terms of this good old adage, now that he is so furious against it: we fear, he understood them no better when he was as loudly in favour of it.

All the objections, indeed, to the voice of the people being the best rule for Government to attend to, arise from the stops and impediments to the expression of that voice, from the attempts to stifle or to give it a false bias, and to cut off its free and open communication with the head and heart of the people—by the Government itself. The sincere expression of the feelings of the people must be true, the full and free development of the public opinion must lead to truth, to the gradual discovery and diffusion of knowledge in this, as in all other departments of human inquiry. It is the interest of Governments in general to keep the people in a state of vassalage as long as they can—to prevent the expression of their sentiments, and the exercise and improvement of their understandings, by all the means in their power. They have a patent, and a monopoly, which they do not like to have looked into or to share with others. The argument for keeping the people in a state of lasting wardship, or for treating them as lunatics, incapable of self-government, wears a very suspicious aspect, as it comes from those who are trustees to the estate, or keepers of insane asylums. The long minority of the people would, at this rate, never expire, while those who had an interest had also the power to prevent them from arriving at years of discretion: their government-keepers have nothing to do but to drive the people mad by ill-treatment, and to keep them so by worse, in order to retain the pretence for applying the gag, the strait waistcoat, and the whip as long as they please. It is like the dispute between Mr Epps, the angry shopkeeper in the Strand, and his journeyman, whom he would restrict from setting up for himself. Shall we never serve out our apprenticeship to liberty? Must our indentures to slavery bind us for life? It is well, it is perfectly well. You teach us nothing, and you will not let us learn. You deny us education, like Orlando's eldest brother,* and then 'stying us' in the den of legitimacy, you refuse to let us take the management of our own affairs into our own hands, or to seek our fortunes in the world ourselves. You found a right to treat us with indignity on the plea of your own neglect and injustice. You abuse a trust in order to make it perpetual. You profit of our ignorance and of your own wrong. You degrade, and then enslave us; and by enslaving, you degrade us more, to make us more and more incapable of ever escaping from your selfish, sordid yoke. There is no end of this. It is the fear of the progress of knowledge and a *Reading Public*, that has produced all the fuss and bustle and cant about Bell and Lancaster's plans, Bible and Missionary, and Auxiliary and Cheap Tract Societies,* and that when it was impossible to prevent our reading something, made the Church and State so anxious to provide us with that sort of food for our stomachs, which they thought best. The Bible is an excellent book; and when it becomes the Statesman's Manual, in its precepts of charity—not of beggarly almsgiving, but of peace on earth and good will to man, the people may read nothing else. It reveals the glories of the world to come, and records the preternatural dispensations of Providence to mankind two thousand years ago. But it does not describe the present state of Europe, or give an account of the measures of the last or of the next reign, which yet it is important the people of England should look to. We cannot learn from Moses and the Prophets what Mr Vansittart and the Jews are about in 'Change-alley.* Those who prescribe us the study of the miracles and prophecies, themselves laugh to scorn the promised deliverance of Joanna Southcott* and the Millennium. Yet they would have us learn patience and resignation from the miraculous interpositions of Providence recorded in the Scriptures. '*When the sky falls*'*—the proverb is somewhat musty. The worst compliment ever paid to the Bible was the recommendation of it as a political palliative by the Lay Preachers of the day.

To put this question in a different light, we might ask, What is the public? and examine what would be the result of

depriving the people of the use of their understandings in
other matters as well as government—to subject them to the
trammels of prescriptive prejudice and hereditary pretension.
Take the stage as an example. Suppose Mr Kean* should have
a son, a little crook-kneed, raven-voiced, disagreeable, mischievous, stupid urchin, with the faults of his father's acting
exaggerated tenfold, and none of his fine qualities,—what if
Mr Kean should take it into his head to get out letters-patents
to empower him and his heirs for ever, with this hopeful
commencement, to play all the chief parts in tragedy, by the
grace of God and the favour of the Prince Regent! What a
precious race of tragedy kings and heroes we should have!
They would not even play the villain with a good grace. The
theatres would soon be deserted, and the race of the Keans
would 'hold a barren sceptre'* over empty houses, to be
'wrenched from them by an unlineal hand!'—But no! For it
would be necessary to uphold theatrical order, the cause of
the legitimate drama, and so to levy a tax on all those who
staid away from the theatre, or to drag them into it by force.
Every one seeing the bayonet at the door, would be compelled
to applaud the hoarse tones and lengthened pauses of the
illustrious house of Kean; the newspaper critics would grow
wanton in their praise, and all those would be held as rancor-
ous enemies of their country, and of the prosperity of the
stage, who did not join in the praises of the best of actors.
What a falling off there would be from the present system of
universal suffrage and open competition among the candidates, the frequency of rows in the pit, the noise in the gallery,
the whispers in the boxes, and the lashing in the newspapers
the next day!

  In fact, the argument drawn from the supposed incapacity
of the people against a representative Government, comes
with the worst grace in the world from the patrons and admirers of hereditary government. Surely, if government were
a thing requiring the utmost stretch of genius, wisdom, and
virtue, to carry it on, the office of King would never even have
been dreamt of as hereditary, any more than that of poet,
painter, or philosopher. It is easy here 'for the Son to tread
in the Sire's steady steps'.* It requires nothing but the will to

do it. Extraordinary talents are not once looked for. Nay, a
person, who would never have risen by natural abilities to the
situation of churchwarden or parish beadle, succeeds by un-
questionable right to the possession of a throne and wields
the energies of an empire, or decides the fate of the world,
with the smallest possible share of human understanding. The
line of distinction which separates the regal purple from the
slabbering-bib, is sometimes fine indeed; as we see in the case
of the two Ferdinands.* Any one above the rank of an ideot
is supposed capable of exercising the highest functions of
royal state. Yet these are the persons who talk of the people
as a swinish multitude,* and taunt them with their want of
refinement and philosophy.

The great problem of political science is not of so profoundly
metaphysical or highly poetical a cast as Mr Burke represents
it. It is simply a question on the one part, with how little
expense of liberty and property the Government, 'that complex constable',* as it has been quaintly called, can keep the
peace; and on the other part, for how great a sacrifice of both,
the splendour of the throne and the safety of the state can be
made a pretext. Kings and their Ministers generally strive to
get their hands in our pockets, and their feet on our necks;
the people and their representatives will be wise enough, if
they can only contrive to prevent them; but this, it must be
confessed, they do not always succeed in. For a people to be
free, it is sufficient that they will to be free. But the love of
liberty is less strong than the love of power; and is guided by
a less sure instinct in attaining its object. Milton only spoke
the sentiments of the English people of his day (sentiments
too which they had acted upon), in strong language, when he
said, in answer to a foreign pedant:—'*Liceat, quæso, populo qui
servitutis jugum in cervicibus grave sentit, tam sapienti esse, tam
docto, tamque nobili, ut sciat quid tyranno suo faciendum sit, etiamsi
neque exteros neque grammaticos sciscitatum mittat.*'—(*Defensio pro
populo Anglicano.*)* Happily the whole of the passage is not
applicable to their descendants in the present day; but at all
times a people may be allowed to know when they are oppressed, enslaved, and miserable, to feel their wrongs and to

demand a remedy—from the superior knowledge and humanity of Ministers, who, if they cannot cure the State-malady,
ought in decency, like other doctors, to resign their authority
over the patient. The people are not subject to fanciful wants,
speculative longings, or hypochondriacal complaints. Their
disorders are real, their complaints substantial and well-
founded. Their grumblings are in general seditions of the
belly. They do not cry out till they are hurt. They do not stand
upon nice questions, or trouble themselves with Mr Burke's
Sublime and Beautiful;* but when they find the money con-
jured clean out of their pockets, and the Constitution suspended over their heads, they think it time to look about
them. For example, poor Evans,* that amateur of music and
politics (strange combination of tastes), thought it hard, no
doubt to be sent to prison and deprived of his flute by a State-
warrant, because there was no ground for doing it by law; and
Mr Hiley Addington, being himself a flute-player, thought so
too: though, in spite of this romantic sympathy, the Minister
prevailed over the musician, and Mr Evans has, we believe,
never got back his flute. For an act of injustice, by the new
system, if complained of 'forsooth', becomes justifiable by the
very resistance to it: if not complained of, nobody knows any
thing about it, and so it goes equally unredressed in either
way. Or to take another obvious instance and sign of the times:
a tenant or small farmer who has been distrained upon and
sent to gaol or to the workhouse, probably thinks, and with
some appearance of reason, that he was better off before this
change of circumstances; and Mr Cobbett, in his two-penny
Registers, proves to him so clearly, that this change for the
worse is owing to the war and taxes, which have driven him
out of his house and home, that Mr Cobbett himself has been
forced to quit the country to argue the question, whether two
and two make four, with Mr Vansittart, upon safer ground to
himself, and more equal ground to the Chancellor of the
Exchequer. Such questions as these are, one would think,
within the verge of common sense and reason. For any thing
we could ever find, the people have as much common sense
and sound judgment as any other class of the community.
Their folly is second-hand, derived from their being the dupe

of the passions, interests, and prejudices of their superiors. When they judge for themselves, they in general judge right. At any rate, the way to improve their judgment in their own concerns (and if they do not judge for themselves, they will infallibly be cheated both of liberty and property, by those who kindly insist on relieving them of that trouble) is not to deny them the use and exercise of their judgment altogether. Nothing can be pleasanter than one of the impositions of late attempted to be put upon the people, by persuading them that economy is no part of a wise Government. The people must be pretty competent judges of the cheapness of a Government. But it is pretended by our high-flying sinecurists and pensioners, that this is a low and vulgar view of the subject, taken up by interested knaves, like Paine and Cobbett, to delude, and, in the end, make their market of the people. With all the writers and orators who compose the band of gentlemen pensioners and their patrons, politics is entirely a thing of sentiment and imagination. To speak of the expenses of Government, as if it were a little paltry huckstering calculation of profit and loss, quite shocks their lofty, liberal, and disinterested notions. They have no patience with the people if they are not ready to sacrifice their all for the public good! This is something like a little recruiting cavalry-lieutenant we once met with, who, sorely annoyed at being so often dunned for the arrears of board and lodging by the people where he took up his quarters, exclaimed with the true broad Irish accent and emphasis— '*Vulgar ideas! These wretches always expect one to pay for what one has of them!*' Our modest lieutenant thought, that while he was employed on his Majesty's service, he had a right to pick the pockets of his subjects, and that if they complained of being robbed of what was their own, they were blackguards and *no gentlemen!* Mr Canning hit upon nothing so good as this, in his luminous defence of his Lisbon Job!*

But allow the people to be as gross and ignorant as you please, as base and stupid as you can make them or keep them, 'duller than the fat weed that roots itself at ease on Lethe's wharf',* —is nothing ever to rouse them? Grant that they are slow of apprehension—that they do not see till they feel. Is

that a reason that they are not to feel then, neither? Would
you blindfold them with the double bandages of bigotry, or
quench their understandings with 'the dim suffusion', 'the
drop serene', of Legitimacy, that 'they may roll in vain and
find no dawn'* of liberty, no ray of hope? Because they do
not see tyranny till it is mountain high, 'making Ossa like a
wart',* are they not to feel its weight when it is heaped upon
them, or to throw it off with giant strength and a convulsive
effort? If they do not see the evil till it has grown enormous,
palpable, and undeniable, is that a reason why others should
then deny that it exists, or why it should not be removed?
They do not snuff arbitrary power a century off: they are not
shocked at it on the other side of the globe, or of the Channel:
are they not therefore to see it, could it in time be supposed
to stalk over their heads, to trample and grind them to the
earth? If in their uncertainty how to deal with it, they sometimes strike random blows, if their despair makes them
dangerous, why do not they, who, from their elevated situation, see so much farther and deeper into the principles and
consequences of things—in their boasted wisdom prevent the
causes of complaint in the people before they accumulate to
a terrific height, and burst upon the heads of their oppres-
sors? The higher classes, who would disqualify the people
from taking the cure of their disorders into their own hands,
might do this very effectually, by preventing the first symptoms
of their disorders. They would do well, instead of abusing the
blunders and brutishness of the multitude, to shew their superior penetration and zeal in detecting the first approaches
of mischief, in withstanding every encroachment on the comforts and rights of the people, in guarding every bulwark
against the influence and machinations of arbitrary power, as
a precious, inviolable, sacred trust. Instead of this, they are
the first to be lulled into security, a security 'as gross as ignorance made drunk'* —the last to believe the consequences,
because they are the last to feel them. Instead of this, the
patience of the lower classes, in submitting to privations and
insults, is only surpassed by the callousness of their betters in
witnessing them. The one never set about the redress of
grievances or the reform of abuses, till they are no longer to

be borne; the others will not hear of it even then. It is for this reason, among others, that the *vox populi* is the *vox Dei*, that it is the agonizing cry of human nature raised, and only raised, against intolerable oppression and the utmost extremity of human suffering. The people do not rise up till they are trod down. They do not turn upon their tormentors till they are goaded to madness. They do not complain till the thumbscrews have been applied, and have been strained to the last turn. Nothing can ever wean the affections or confidence of a people from a Government (to which habit, prejudice, natural pride, perhaps old benefits and joint struggles for liberty have attached them) but an excessive degree of irritation and disgust, occasioned either by a sudden and violent stretch of power, contrary to the spirit and forms of the established Government, or by a blind and wilful adherence to old abuses and established forms, when the changes in the state of manners and opinion have rendered them as odious as they are ridiculous. The Revolutions of Switzerland, the Low Countries, and of America, are examples of the former—the French Revolution of the latter: our own Revolution of 1688 was a mixture of the two. As a general rule, it might be laid down, that for every instance of national resistance to tyranny, there ought to have been hundreds, and that all those which have been attempted ought to have succeeded. In the case of Wat Tyler,* for instance, which has been so naturally dramatised by the poet-laureate, the rebellion was crushed, and the ringleaders hanged by the treachery of the Government; but the grievances of which they had complained were removed a few years after, and the rights they had claimed granted to the people, from the necessary progress of civilization and knowledge. Did not Mr Southey know, when he applied for an injunction against Wat Tyler, that the feudal system had been abolished long ago?—Again, as nothing rouses the people to resistance but extreme and aggravated injustice, so nothing can make them persevere in it, or push their efforts to a successful and triumphant issue, but the most open and unequivocal determination to brave their cries and insult their misery. They have no principle of union in themselves, and nothing brings or holds them together, but the strong pressure of want, the stern hand of necessity—'a necessity that is not chosen, but chuses,—a necessity paramount to deliberation, that admits of no discussion and demands no evidence, that can alone, (according to Mr Burke's theory) justify a resort to anarchy',* and that alone ever did or can produce it. In fine, there are but two things in the world, might and right. Whenever one of these is overcome, it is by the other. The triumphs of the people, or the stand which they at any time make against arbitrary sway, are the triumphs of reason and justice over the insolence of individual power and authority, which, unless as it is restrained, curbed, and corrected by popular feeling or public opinion, can be guided only by its own drunken, besotted, mad pride, selfishness and caprice, and must be productive of all the mischief, which it can wantonly or deliberately commit with impunity.

The people are not apt, like a fine lady, to affect the vapours of discontent; nor to volunteer a rebellion for the theatrical eclat of the thing. But the least plausible excuse, one kind word, one squeeze of the hand, one hollow profession of good will, subdues the soft heart of rebellion, (which is 'too foolish fond and pitiful'* to be a match for the callous hypocrisy opposed to it) dissolves and melts the whole fabric of popular innovation like butter in the sun. Wat Tyler is a case in point again. The instant the effeminate king and his unprincipled courtiers gave them fair words, they dispersed, relying in their infatuation on the word of the King as binding, on the oath of his officers as sincere; and no sooner were they dispersed than they cut off their leaders' heads, and poor John Ball's* along with them, in spite of all his texts of Scripture. The story is to be seen in all the shop-windows, *written in very choice blank verse!*—That the people are rash in trusting to the promises of their friends, is true; they are more rash in believing their enemies. If they are led to expect too much in theory, they are satisfied with too little in reality. Their anger is sometimes fatal while it lasts, but it is not roused very soon, nor does it last very long. Of all dynasties, anarchy is the shortest lived. They are violent in their revenge, no doubt; but it is because justice has been long denied them, and they have to pay off a very long score at a very short notice. What Caesar says of himself, might be applied well enough to the people, that they 'did never wrong but with just cause'.* The errors of the people are the crimes of Governments. They apply sharp remedies to lingering diseases, and when they get sudden power in their hands, frighten their enemies, and wound themselves with it. They rely on brute force and the fury of despair, in proportion to the treachery which surrounds them, and to the degradation, the want of general information and mutual co-operation, in which they have been kept, on purpose to prevent them from ever acting in concert, with wisdom, energy, confidence, and calmness, for the public good. The American Revolution produced no horrors, because its enemies could not succeed in sowing the seeds of terror, hatred, mutual treachery, and universal dismay in the hearts of the people. The French Revolution, under the auspices of Mr Burke, and other friends of social order, was tolerably prolific of these horrors. But that should not be charged as the fault of the Revolution or of the people. Timely Reforms are the best preventives of violent Revolutions. If Governments are determined that the people shall have no redress, no remedies for their acknowledged grievances, but violent and desperate ones, they may thank themselves for the obvious consequences. Despotism must always have the most to fear from the re-action of popular fury, where it has been guilty of the greatest abuses of power, and where it has shewn the greatest tenaciousness of those abuses, putting an end to all prospect of amicable arrangement, and provoking the utmost vengeance of its oppressed and insulted victims. This tenaciousness of power is the chief obstacle to improvement, and the cause of the revulsions which follow the attempts at it. In America, a free Government was easy of accomplishment, because it was not necessary, in building up, to pull down: there were no nuisances to abate. The thing is plain. Reform in old Governments is just like the new improvements in the front of Carlton House,* that would go on fast enough but for the vile, old, dark, dirty, crooked streets, which cannot be removed without giving the inhabitants notice to quit. Mr Burke, in regretting these old institutions as the result of the wisdom of ages, and not the remains of Gothic ignorance and barbarism, played the part of *Crockery*, in the farce of *Exit by Mistake*,* who sheds tears of affection over the loss of the old windows and buttresses of the houses that no longer jut out to meet one another, and stop up the way.

There is one other consideration which may induce hereditary Sovereigns to allow some weight to the arguments in favour of popular feeling and public opinion. They are the only security which they themselves possess individually for the continuance of their splendour and power. Absolute monarchs have nothing to fear from the people, but they have every thing to fear from their slaves and one another. Where power is lifted beyond the reach of the law or of public opinion, there is no principle to oppose it, and he who can obtain possession of the throne (by whatever means) is always the rightful possessor of it, till he is supplanted by a more fortunate or artful successor, and so on in a perpetual round of treasons, conspiracies, murders, usurpations, regicides, and rebellions, with which the people have nothing to do, but as passive, unconcerned spectators. —Where the son succeeds to the father's throne by assassination, without being amenable to public justice, he is liable to be cut off himself by the same means, and with the same impunity. The only thing that can give stability or confidence to power, is that very will of the people, and public censure exercised upon public acts, of which legitimate Sovereigns are so disproportionately apprehensive. For one regicide committed by the people, there have been thousands committed by Kings themselves. A Constitutional King of England reigns in greater security than the Persian Sophi, or the Great Mogul; and the Emperor of Turkey, or the Autocrat of all the Russias, has much more to fear from a cup of coffee or the bow-string, than the Prince Regent from the speeches and writings of all the Revolutionists in Europe. By removing the barrier of public opinion, which interferes with their own lawless acts, despotic Kings lay themselves open to the hand of the assassin,—and while they reign in contempt of the will, the voice, the heart and mind of a whole people, hold their crowns, and every moment of their lives at the mercy of the meanest of their slaves.

ON CONSISTENCY OF OPINION

'——Servetur ad imum
Qualis ab inceptu processerit, et sibi constet.'*

MANY people boast of being masters in their own house. I pretend to be master of my own mind. I should be sorry to have an ejectment served upon me for any notions I may chuse to entertain there. Within that little circle I would fain be an absolute monarch. I do not profess the spirit of martyrdom; I have no ambition to march to the stake or up to a masked battery, in defence of an hypothesis: I do not court the rack: I do not wish to be flayed alive for affirming that two and two make four, or any other intricate proposition: I am shy of bodily pains and penalties, which some are fond of, imprisonment, fine, banishment, confiscation of goods: but if I do not prefer the independence of my mind to that of my body, I at least prefer it to every thing else. I would avoid the arm of power, as I would escape from the fangs of a wild beast: but as to the opinion of the world, I see nothing formidable in it. 'It is the eye of childhood that fears a painted devil.'* I am not to be brow-beat or wheedled out of any of my settled convictions. Opinion to opinion, I will face any man. Prejudice, fashion, the cant of the moment, go for nothing; and as for the reason of the thing, it can only be supposed to rest with me or another, in proportion to the pains we have taken to ascertain it. Where the pursuit of truth has been the habitual study of any man's life, the love of truth will be his ruling passion. 'Where the treasure is, there the heart is also.'* Every one is most tenacious of that to which he owes his distinction from others. Kings love power, misers gold, women flattery, poets reputation—and philosophers truth, when they can find it. They are right in cherishing the only privilege they inherit. If 'to be wise were to be obstinate',* I might set up for as great a philosopher as the best of them; for some of my conclusions are as fixed and as incorrigible to proof as need be. I am attached to them in consequence of the pains, the anxiety, and the waste of time they have cost me. In fact, I should not well know what to do without them at this time of day; nor how to get others to supply their place. I would quarrel with the best friend I have sooner than acknowledge the absolute right of the Bourbons. I see Mr —— seldomer than I did, because I cannot agree with him about the *Catalogue Raisonnée.** I remember once saying to this gentleman, a great while ago, that I did not seem to have altered any of my ideas since I was sixteen years old. 'Why then,' said he, 'you are no wiser now than you were then!' I might make the same confession, and the same retort would apply still. Coleridge used to tell me, that this pertinacity was owing to a want of sympathy with others. What he calls *sympathising with others* is their admiring him, and it must be admitted that he varies his battery pretty often, in order to accommodate himself to this sort of mutual understanding. But I do not agree in what he says of me. On the other hand, I think that it is my sympathising *beforehand* with the different views and feelings that may be entertained on a subject, that prevents my retracting my judgment, and flinging myself into the contrary extreme *afterwards.** If you proscribe all opinion opposite to your own, and impertinently exclude all the evidence that does not make for you, it stares you in the face with double force when it breaks in unexpectedly upon you, or if at any subsequent period it happens to suit your interest or convenience to listen to objections which vanity or prudence had hitherto overlooked. But if you are aware from the first suggestion of a subject, either by subtlety of tact, or close attention, of the full force of what others possibly feel and think of it, you are not exposed to the same vacillation of opinion. The number of grains and scruples, of doubts and difficulties, thrown into the scale while the balance is yet undecided, add to the weight and steadiness of the determination. He who anticipates his opponent's arguments, confirms while he corrects his own reasonings. When a question has been carefully examined in all its bearings, and a principle is once established, it is not liable to be overthrown by any new facts which have been arbitrarily and petulantly set aside, nor by every wind of idle doctrine rushing into the interstices of a hollow speculation, shattering it in pieces, and leaving it a mockery and a bye-word;* like those tall, gawky, staring, pyramidal erections which are seen scattered over different parts of the country, and are called the *Follies* of different gentlemen! A man may be confident in maintaining a side, as he has been cautious in chusing it. If after making up his mind strongly in one way, to the best of his capacity and judgment, he feels himself inclined to a very violent revulsion of sentiment, he may generally rest assured that the change is in himself and his motives, not in the reason of things.

I cannot say that, from my own experience, I have found that the persons most remarkable for sudden and violent changes of principle have been cast in the softest or most susceptible mould. All their notions have been exclusive, bigoted, and intolerant. Their want of consistency and moderation has been in exact proportion to their want of candour and comprehensiveness of mind. Instead of being the creatures of sympathy, open to conviction, unwilling to give offence by the smallest difference of sentiment, they have (for the most part) been made up of mere antipathies—a very repulsive sort of personages—at odds with themselves, and with every body else. The slenderness of their pretensions to philosophical inquiry has been accompanied with the most presumptuous dogmatism. They have been persons of that narrowness of view and headstrong self-sufficiency of purpose, that they could see only one side of a question at a time, and whichever they pleased. There is a story somewhere in *Don Quixote*, of two champions coming to a shield hung up against a tree with an inscription written on each side of it. Each of them maintained, that the words were what was written on the side next him, and never dreamt, till the fray was over, that they might be different on the opposite side of the shield. It would have been a little more extraordinary if the combatants had changed sides in the heat of the scuffle, and stoutly denied that there were any such words on the opposite side as they had before been bent on sacrificing their lives to prove were the only ones it contained. Yet such is the very situation of some of our modern polemics. They have been of all sides of the question, and yet they cannot conceive how an honest man can be of any but one—that which they hold at present. It seems that they are afraid to look their old opinions in the face, lest they should be fascinated by them once more. They banish all doubts of their own sincerity by inveighing against the motives of their antagonists. There is no salvation out of the pale of their strange inconsistency. They reduce common sense and probity to the straitest possible limits—the breasts of themselves and their patrons. They are like people out at sea on a very narrow plank, who try to push every body else off. Is it that they have so little faith in the cause to which they have become such staunch converts, as to suppose that, should they allow a grain of sense to their old allies and new antagonists, they will have more than they? Is it that they have so little consciousness of their own disinterestedness, that they feel if they allow a particle of honesty to those who now differ with them, they will have more than they? These opinions must needs be of a very fragile texture which will not stand the shock of the least acknowledged opposition, and which lay claim to respectability by stigmatising all who do not hold them as 'sots, and knaves, and cowards'.* There is a want of well-balanced feeling in every such instance of extravagant versatility; a something crude, unripe, and harsh, that does not hit a judicious palate, but sets the teeth on edge to think of. 'I had rather hear my mother's cat mew, or a wheel grate on the axle-tree, than one of these same metre-ballad-mongers'* chaunt his incondite retrograde lays without rhyme and without reason.

The principles and professions change: the man remains the same. There is the same spirit at the bottom of all this pragmatical fickleness and virulence, whether it runs into one extreme or another:—to wit, a confinement of view, a jealousy of others, an impatience of contradiction, a want of liberality in construing the motives of others either from monkish pedantry, or a conceited overweening reference of every thing to our own fancies and feelings. There is something to be said, indeed, for the nature of the political machinery, for the whirling motion of the revolutionary wheel which has of late wrenched men's understandings almost asunder, and 'amazed the very faculties of eyes and ears';* but still this is hardly a sufficient reason, why the adept in the old as well as the new school should take such a prodigious latitude himself, while at the same time he makes so little allowance for others. His whole creed need not be turned topsy-turvy, from the top to the bottom, even in times like these. He need not, in the rage of party-spirit, discard the proper attributes of humanity, the common dictates of reason. He need not outrage every former feeling, nor trample on every customary decency, in his zeal for reform, or in his greater zeal against it. If his mind, like his body, has undergone a total change of essence, and purged off the taint of all its early opinions, he need not carry about with him, or be haunted in the persons of others with, the phantoms of his altered principles to loathe and execrate them. He need not (as it were) pass an act of attainder on all his thoughts, hopes, wishes, from youth upwards, to offer them at the shrine of matured servility: he need not become one vile antithesis, a living and ignominious satire on himself. Mr Wordsworth has hardly, I should think, so much as a single particle of feeling left in his whole composition, the same that he had twenty years ago; not 'so small a drop of pity',* for what he then was, 'as a wren's eye,'—except that I do not hear that he has given up his theory that poetry should be written in the language of prose, or applied for an injunction against the *Lyrical Ballads.* I will wager a trifle, that our ingenious poet will not concede to any patron, (how noble and munificent soever), that the Leech Gatherer is not a fit subject of the Muse, and would sooner resign the stamp-distributorship of two counties, than burn that portion of the *Recluse*, a Poem, which has been given to the world under the title of the *Excursion.* The tone, however, of Mr Wordsworth's poetical effusions requires a little revision to adapt it to the progressive improvement in his political sentiments: for, as far as I under-stand the Poems themselves or the Preface, his whole system turns upon this, that the thoughts, the feelings, the expres-sions of the common people in country places are the most refined of all others; at once the most pure, the most simple, and the most sublime:—yet, with one stroke of his prose-pen, he disfranchises the whole rustic population* of Westmoreland and Cumberland from voting at elections, and says there is not a man among them that is not a knave in grain. In return, he lets them still retain the privilege of expressing their sentiments in select and natural language in the *Lyrical Ballads*. So much for poetical justice and political severity! An author's political theories sit loose upon him, and may be changed like his clothes. His literary vanity, alas! sticks to him like his skin, and survives in its first gloss and sleekness, amidst

'The wreck of matter, and the crush of worlds.'

Mr Southey still makes experiments on metre, not on governments, and seems to think the last resort of English liberty is in court-iambics. Still the same upstart self-sufficiency, still the same itch of new-fangled innovation directed into a new channel, still the same principle of favouritism, still the same overcharged and splenetic hostility—all is right that he approves, all is wrong that opposes his views in the smallest particular. There is no inconsistency in all these anomalies. Absurdity is uniform; egotism is the same thing; a limited range of comprehension is a habit of mind that a man seldom gets the better of, and may distinguish equally the Pantisocratist or Constitutional Association-monger.*

To quit this, which is rather a stale topic, as well as a hopeless one, and give some instances of a change of sentiment in individuals, which may serve for materials of a history of opinion in the beginning of the 19th century:—A gentleman went to live, some years ago, in a remote part of the country, and as he did not wish to affect singularity he used to have two candles on his table of an evening. A romantic acquaintance* of his in the neighbourhood, smit with the love of simplicity and equality, used to come in, and without ceremony snuff one of them out, saying, it was a shame to indulge in such extravagance, while many a poor cottager had not even a rush-light to see to do their evening's work by. This might be about the year 1802, and was passed over as among the ordinary occurrences of the day. In 1816 (oh! fearful lapse of time, pregnant with strange mutability), the same enthusiastic lover of economy, and hater of luxury, asked his

thoughtless friend to dine with him in company with a certain
lord, and to lend him his man servant to wait at table; and
just before they were sitting down to dinner, he heard him say
to the servant in a sonorous whisper—'and be sure you don't
forget to have six candles on the table!' Extremes meet. The
event here was as true to itself as the oscillation of the pen-
dulum. My informant, who understands moral equations, had
looked for this reaction, and noted it down as characteristic.
The impertinence in the first instance was the cue to the
ostentatious servility in the second. The one was the fulfilment
of the other, like the type and anti-type of a prophecy. No—
the keeping of the character at the end of fourteen years was
as unique as the keeping of the thought to the end of the
fourteen lines of a Sonnet! Would it sound strange if I were
to whisper it in the reader's ear, that it was the same person
who was thus anxious to see six candles on the table to receive
a lord, who once (in ages past) said to me, that 'he saw
nothing to admire in the eloquence of such men as Mansfield
and Chatham; and what did it all end in, but their being made
Lords?' It is better to be a lord than a lacquey to a lord. So
we see that the swelling pride and proposterous self-opinion
which exalts itself above the mightiest, looking down upon,
and braving the boasted pretensions of the highest rank and
the most brilliant talents as nothing, compared with its own
conscious powers and silent unmoved self-respect, grovels and
licks the dust before titled wealth, like a lacquered slave, the
moment it can get wages and a livery! Would Milton or Marvel
have done thus?

Mr Coleridge, indeed, sets down this outrageous want of
keeping to an excess of sympathy,* and there is, after all, some
truth in his suggestion. There is a craving after the approbation and concurrence of others natural to the mind of man.
It is difficult to sustain the weight of an opinion singly for any
length of way. The intellect languishes without cordial encouragement and support. It exhausts both strength and patience
to be always striving against the stream. *Contra audentior ito**
—is the motto but of few. Public opinion is always pressing
upon the mind, and, like the air we breathe, acts unseen,
unfelt. It supplies the living current of our thoughts, and

infects without our knowledge. It taints the blood, and is taken into the smallest pores. The most sanguine constitutions are, perhaps, the most exposed to its influence. But public opinion* has its source in power, in popular prejudice, and is not always in accord with right reason, or a high and abstracted imagination. Which path to follow where the two roads part? The heroic and romantic resolution prevails at first in high and heroic tempers. They think to scale the heights of truth and virtue at once with him 'whose genius had angelic wings, and fed on manna',* —but after a time find themselves baffled, toiling on in an uphill road, without friends, in a cold neighbourhood, without aid or prospect of success. The poet

'Like a worm goes by the way'.*

He hears murmurs loud or suppressed, meets blank looks or scowling faces, is exposed to the pelting of the pitiless press, and is stunned by the shout of the mob, that gather round him to see what sort of a creature a poet and a philosopher is. What is there to make him proof against all this? A strength of understanding steeled against temptation, and a dear love of truth that smiles opinion to scorn? These he perhaps has not. A lord passes in his coach. Might he not get up, and ride out of the reach of the rabble-rout? He is invited to stop dinner. If he stays he may insinuate some wholesome truths. He drinks in rank poison—flattery! He recites some verses to the ladies, who smile delicious praise, and thank him through their tears. The master of the house suggests a happy allusion in the turn of an expression. 'There's sympathy.'* This is better than the company he lately left. Pictures, statues meet his raptured eye. Our Ulysses finds himself in the gardens of Alcinous:* our truant is fairly caught. He wanders through enchanted ground. Groves, classic groves, nod unto him, and he hears 'ancestral voices'* hailing him as brother-bard! He sleeps, dreams, and wakes cured of his thriftless prejudices and morose philanthropy. He likes this courtly and popular sympathy better. 'He looks up with awe to kings; with honour to nobility; with reverence to magistrates,' &c. He no longer breathes the air of heaven and his own thoughts, but is steeped in that of palaces and courts, and finds it agree better

with his constitutional temperament. Oh! how sympathy alters
a man from what he was!

> 'I've heard of hearts unkind,
> Kind deeds with coldness still returning;
> Alas! the gratitude of man
> Has oftener set me mourning.'*

... An overstrained enthusiasm produces a capriciousness in
taste, as well as too much indifference. A person who sets no
bounds to his admiration takes a surfeit of his favourites. He
over-does the thing. He gets sick of his own everlasting praises,
and affected raptures. His preferences are a great deal too
violent to last. He wears out an author in a week, that might
last him a year, or his life, by the eagerness with which he
devours him. Every such favourite is in his turn the greatest
writer in the world. Compared with the lord of the ascendant
for the time being, Shakespeare is commonplace, and Milton
a pedant, a little insipid or so. Some of these prodigies require
to be dragged out of their lurking-places, and cried up to the
top of the compass;* —their traits are subtle, and must be
violently obtruded on the sight. But the effort of exaggerated
praise, though it may stagger others, tires the maker, and we
hear of them no more after a while. Others take their turns,
are swallowed whole, undigested, ravenously, and disappear
in the same manner. Good authors share the fate of bad, and
a library in a few years is nearly dismantled. It is a pity thus
to outlive our admiration, and exhaust our relish of what is
excellent. Actors and actresses are disposed of in the same
conclusive peremptory way: some of them are talked of for
months, nay, years; then it is almost an offence to mention
them. Friends, acquaintance, go the same road;—are now
asked to come six days in the week, then warned against
coming the seventh. The smallest faults are soon magnified
in those we think too highly of: but where shall we find
perfection? If we will put up with nothing short of that, we
shall have neither pictures, books, nor friends left—we shall
have nothing but our own absurdities to keep company with!
'In all things a regular and moderate indulgence is the best
security for a lasting enjoyment.'—BURKE.*

There are numbers who judge by the event, and change with fortune. They extol the hero of the day, and join the prevailing clamour whatever it is; so that the fluctuating state of public opinion regulates their feverish, restless enthusiasm, like a thermometer. They blow hot or cold, according as the wind sets favourably or otherwise. With such people the only infallible test of merit is success; and no arguments are true that have not a large or powerful majority on their side. They go by appearances. Their vanity, not the truth, is their ruling object. They are not the last to quit a falling cause, and they are the first to hail the rising sun Their minds want sincerity, modesty, and keeping. With them

> ——'To have done is to hang
> Quite out of fashion, like a rusty mail
> In monumental mockery.'

They still, 'with one consent, praise new-born gauds', and Fame, as they construe it, is—

> ——'Like a fashionable host,
> That slightly shakes his parting guest by the hand:
> And with his arms outstretch'd, as he would fly,
> Grasps-in the comer. Welcome ever smiles,
> And Farewell goes out sighing.'*

Such servile flatterers made an idol of Buonaparte while fortune smiled upon him, but when it left him, they removed him from his pedestal in the cabinet of their vanity, as we take down the picture of a relation that has died without naming us in his will. The opinion of such triflers is worth nothing: it is merely an echo. We do not want to be told the event of a question, but the rights of it. Truth is in their theory nothing but 'noise and inexplicable dumb show.'* They are the heralds, outriders, and trumpeters in the procession of fame; are more loud and boisterous than the rest, and give themselves great airs, as the avowed patrons and admirers of genius and merit.

As there are many who change their sentiments with circumstances, (as they decided lawsuits in Rabelais with the dice), so there are others who change them with their acquaintance. 'Tell me your company, and I'll tell you your opinions,'* might be said to many a man who piques himself on a select and superior view of things, distinct from the vulgar. Individuals of this class are quick and versatile, but they are not beforehand with opinion. They catch it, when it is pointed out to them, and take it at the rebound, instead of giving the first impulse. Their minds are a light, luxuriant soil, into which thoughts are easily transplanted, and shoot up with uncommon sprightliness and vigour. They wear the dress of other people's minds very gracefully and unconsciously. They tell you your own opinion, or very gravely repeat an observation you have made to them about half a year afterwards. They let you into the delicacies and luxuries of Spenser with great disinterestedness, in return for your having introduced that author to their notice. They prefer West to Raphael, Stothard* to Rubens, till they are told better. Still they are acute in the main, and good judges in their way. By trying to improve their taste, and reform their notions according to an ideal standard, they perhaps spoil and muddle their native faculties, rather than do them any good. Their first manner is their best, because it is the most natural. It is well not to go out of ourselves, and to be contented to take up with what we are, for better for worse. We can neither beg, borrow, nor steal characteristic excellences. Some views and modes of thinking suit certain minds, as certain colours suit certain complexions. We may part with very shining and very useful qualities without getting better ones to supply them. Mocking is catching, only in regard to defects. Mimicry is always dangerous.

It is not necessary to change our road in order to advance on our journey. We should cultivate the spot of ground we possess to the utmost of our power, though it may be circumscribed and comparatively barren. *A rolling stone gathers no moss.* People may collect all the wisdom they will ever attain, quite as well by staying at home as by travelling abroad. There is no use in shifting from place to place, from side to side, or from subject to subject. You have always to begin again, and never finish any course of study or observation. By adhering to the same principles you do not become stationary. You enlarge, correct, and consolidate your reasonings, without contradicting and shuffling about in your conclusions. If truth consisted in hasty assumptions and petulant contradictions, there might be some ground for this whiffling and violent inconsistency. But the face of truth, like that of nature, is different and the same. The first outline of an opinion, and the general tone of thinking, may be sound and correct, though we may spend any quantity of time and pains in working up and uniting the parts at subsequent sittings. If we have mistaken the character of the countenance altogether at first, no alterations will bring it right afterwards. Those who mistake white for black in the first instance, may as well mistake black for white when they reverse their canvass. I do not see what security they can have in their present opinions, who build their pretension to wisdom on the total folly, rashness, and extravagance (to say no worse) of their former ones. The perspective may change with years and experience: we may see certain things nearer, and others more remote; but the great masses and landmarks will remain, though thrown into shadow and tinged by the intervening atmosphere: so the laws of the understanding, the truth of nature, will remain, and cannot be thrown into utter confusion and perplexity by our blunders or caprice, like the objects in Hogarth's Rules of Perspective,* where every thing is turned upside down, or thrust out of its well-known place. I cannot understand how our political Harlequins feel after all their summersaults and metamorphoses. They can hardly, I should think, look at themselves in the glass, or walk across the room without stumbling. This at least would be the case if they had the least reflection or self-knowledge. But they judge from pique and vanity solely. There should be a certain decorum in life as in a picture, without which it is neither useful nor agreeable. If my opinions are not right, at any rate they are the best I have been able to form, and better than any others I could take up at random, or out of perversity, now. Certainly opinions vitiate one another, and destroy the simplicity and clearness of the mind: nothing is good that has not a beginning, a middle, and an end; and I would wish my thoughts to be

'Linked each to each by natural piety!'*

ILLUSTRATIONS OF
'THE TIMES' NEWSPAPER

ON MODERN LAWYERS AND POETS

—— —— ——'Facilis descensus Averni;
Noctes atque dies patet atri janua Ditis;
Sed revocare gradum superasque evadere ad auras,
Hoc opus, hic labor est.'*

THE meaning of which passage is, that it is easier to sail with
the stream, than to strive against it. Our classical reformers
should have known this passage in Virgil. They should have
known themselves too; but they did not. 'Let no man go about
to cozen honesty,'* or to be a knave by halves. The man, as
well as the woman, who deliberates between his principle and
the price of its sacrifice, is lost. The same rule holds with
respect to literary as to any other kind of prostitution. It is the
first false step that always costs the most; and which is, for that
reason, always fatal. It requires an effort of resolution, or at
least obstinate prejudice, for a man to maintain his opinions
at the expense of his interest. But it requires a much greater
effort of resolution for a man to give up his interest to recover
his independence; because, with the consistency of his character, he has lost the habitual energy of his mind, and the
indirect aid of prejudice and obstinacy, which are sometimes
as useful to virtue as they are to vice. A man, in adhering to
his principles in contradiction to the decisions of the world,
has many disadvantages. He has nothing to support him* but
the supposed sense of right; and any defect in the justice of
his cause, or the force of his conviction, must prey on his
mind, in proportion to the delicacy and sensitiveness of its
texture: he is left alone in his opinions; and, like *Sam Sharpset,**
in Mr Morton's new comedy (when he gets into solitary confinement in the spunging-house,) grows nervous, melancholy,
fantastical, and would be glad of *somebody* or *anybody* to sympathize with him; but when he has once gone over to the
strong side of the question (perhaps from these very scruples
of conscience, suggested by weakness and melancholy, as 'the
Devil is very potent with such spirits, and abuses them to damn

them')* our wavering sceptic no longer finds the same
scruples troublesome; the air of a court promotes their diges-
tion wonderfully; the load on his conscience falls off at the
foot of the throne. The poet-laureate,* standing with his
laurel-wreath amidst 'Britain's warriors, her statesmen, and
her fair', thinks no more or says no more about the patriots
of Spain pining in dungeons or consigned to the torture,
though it was his zeal, his virtuous, patriotic, romantic, disinterested zeal for them, which brought *them* there, and him
to court. His Prince's smile soothes the involuntary pang of
sympathy rising in his breast; and Mr Croker's* whispers
drown their agonizing shrieks. When we are at Rome, we must
do as the people at Rome do. A man in a crowd must go along
with the crowd, and cannot stop to pick his way; nor need he
be so particular about it. He has friends to back him: appearances are for him; the world is on his side; his interest becomes surety for his honour, his vanity makes him blind to
objections, or overrules them, and he is not so much ashamed
of being in the wrong in such good company. It requires some
fortitude to oppose one's opinion, however right, to that of
all the world besides; none at all to agree with it, however
wrong. Nothing but the strongest and clearest conviction can
support a man in a losing minority: any excuse or quibble is
sufficient to salve his conscience, when he has made sure of
the main chance, and his understanding has become the
stalking-horse of his ambition. It is this single circumstance of
not being answerable for one's opinions one's-self, but being
able to put them off to other men's shoulders in all crowds
and collections of men, that is the reason of the violence of
mobs, the venality of courts, and the corruption of all corpor-
ate bodies. It is also the reason of the degeneracy of modern
apostates and reformed Jacobins, who find the applause of
their king and country doubly cheering after being so long
without it, and who go all lengths in adulation and servility,
to make up for their former awkward singularity.

Many of the persons we have known, who have deserted the
cause of the people to take a high tone against those who did
not chuse to desert it, have been lawyers or poets. The last

took their leave of it by a poetic license; the first slunk out of it by some loop-hole of the law. We shall say a word of each.

'Our's is an honest employment,'* says *Peachum*; 'and so is a lawyer's.' It is a lawyer's business to confound truth and falsehood in the minds of his hearers; and the natural consequence is, that he confounds them in his own. He takes his opinion of right and wrong from his brief: his soul is in his fee. His understanding is *upon the town*, and at the service of any cause that is paid for beforehand. He is not a hired suborner of *facts*, but of *reasons*; and though he would not violate the sacred obligation of an oath, as Lord Ellenborough* calls it, by swearing that black is white, he holds himself at all times in readiness and bound in duty, to prove it so. He will not swear to an untruth to get himself hanged, but he will assert it roundly by the hour together to hang other persons, however innocent,—if he finds it in his retainer. We do not wish to say any thing illiberal of any profession or set of men in the abstract. But we think it possible, that they who are employed to argue away men's lives at a venture in a court of justice, may be tempted to write them away deliberately in a newspaper. They who find it consistent with their honour to do this under the sanction of the court, may find it to their interest to do the same thing at the suggestion of a court. A lawyer is a sophist by profession; that is, a person who barters his opinion, and speaks what he knows to be false in defence of wrong, and to the prejudice of right. Not only the confirmed habit of looking at any side of a question with a view to make the worse appear the better reason, from a motive always foreign to the question itself, must make truth and falsehood sit loose upon him, and lead him to 'look on both indifferently',* as his convenience prompts; but the quibbles and quillets of the law give a handle to all that is petty and perverse in his understanding, and enable him to tamper with his principles with impunity. Thus the intricacy and verbal distinctions of the profession promote the practical duplicity of its professors; and folly and knavery become joint securities for one another. The bent of a lawyer's mind is to pervert his talents, if he has any, and to keep down his feelings, if they are at all in his way. He lives by forging and uttering counterfeit pretexts; he says not what he believes to be true, but any thing that by any trick or sleight he can make others believe; and the more petty, artificial, and far-fetched the contrivance, the more low, contemptible, and desperate the shift, the more is he admired and cried up in his profession. A perfect lawyer is one whose understanding always keeps pace with the inability of words to keep pace with ideas: who by natural conformation of mind cannot get beyond the letter to the spirit of any thing; who, by a happy infirmity of soul, is sure never to lose the form in grasping at the substance. Such a one is sure to arrive at the head of his profession! Look at the lawyers in the House of Commons (of course at the head of their profession)—look at Garrow.* We have heard him stringing contradictions there with the fluency of water, every third sentence giving the lie to the two former; gabbling folly as if it were the last opportunity he might ever have, and as regularly put down as he rose up—not for false statements, not for false reasoning, not for common-place absurdities or vulgar prejudices, (there is enough of these to be found there without going to the bar), but for such things as nobody but a lawyer could utter, and as nobody (not even a lawyer) could believe. The only thing that ever gave us a good opinion of the House of Commons was to see the contempt with which they treat lawyers there. The reason is, that no one there but a lawyer fancies himself holding a brief in his hand as a *carte blanche* for vanity and impertinence—no one else thinks he has got an *ad libitum* right to express any absurd or nonsensical opinions he pleases, because he is not supposed to hold the opinions he expresses—no one else thinks it necessary to confound the distinctions of common-sense to subject them to those of the law (even Lord Castlereagh* would never think of maintaining it to be lawful to detain a person kidnapped from France, on the special plea, that the law in that case *not provided* had *not declared* it lawful to detain persons so kidnapped, if not reclaimed by their own country)—no one else thinks of huddling contradictions into self-evident truths by legal volubility, or of sharpening nonsense into sense by legal acuteness, or of covering shallow assumptions under the solemn disguises of the long robe. The opinions of the gentlemen of the bar go for nothing in the House of Commons: but their votes tell; and are always sure—in the end! The want of principle makes up for the want of talent. What a tool in the hands of a minister is a whole profession, habitually callous to the distinctions of right and wrong, but perfectly alive to their own interest, with just ingenuity enough to be able to trump up some fib or sophistry for or against any measure, and with just understanding enough to see no more of the real nature or consequences of any measure than suits their own or their employer's convenience! What an acquisition to 'the tried wisdom of parliament'* in the approaching hard season!

But all this, though true, seems to fall short of the subject before us. The weak side of the professional character is rather an indifference to truth and justice, than an outrageous and inveterate hatred to them. They are chargeable, as a general class of men, with levity, servility, and selfishness; but it seems to be quite out of their character to commence furious and illiberal fanatics against those who have more principle than themselves. But not when this character is ingrafted on that of a true Jacobin renegado. Such a person* (and no one else) would be fit to write the leading article in *The Times*. It is this union of rare accomplishments (there seems, after all, to be nothing contradictory in the coalition of the vices) that enables that nondescript person to blend the violence of the bravo with the subtlety of a pettifogging attorney—to interlard his furious appeals to the lowest passions of the middle and upper classes, with nice points of law, reserved for the opinion of the adepts in the profession—to appeal to the passions of his city readers when any thing wrong is to be done, and to their cooler and dispassionate judgments when any thing right is to be done—that makes him stick (spell-bound) to the letter of the law when it is in his favour, and set every principle of justice and humanity at defiance when it interferes with his pragmatical opinion— that makes him disregard all decency as well as reason out of 'the lodged hatred'* he bears to the cause he has deserted, and to all who have not, like himself, deserted it—that made him urge the foul death of the brave Marshal Ney,* by putting a legal interpretation on a military convention—that tempted him to make out his sanguinary list of proscribed rebels and regicides (he was not for making out any such list in the year 1793, nor long after the event he now deplores with such well-timed indignation)—that makes him desperately bent on hanging wretches at home in cobweb chains spun from his own brains—that makes him stake the liberty of nations or the independence of states on a nickname or a law-quillet, as his irritable humour or professional habits prevail—that sets him free from all restraints or deference to others in forming his own opinions, and which would induce him to subject all the rest of the world to his unprincipled and frantic dogmas, by entangling them in the quirks and technicalities of the law! No one else would heroically consign a whole continent to the most odious and despicable slavery in the world, on the strength of a flaw in a proclamation: or call that piece of diplomatic atrocity, the declaration of the 25th of March,* a *delicious* declaration. Such a man might sell his country, or enslave his species, and justify it to his conscience and the world by some law-term! Such men are very dangerous, unless when they are tied up in the forms of a profession, where form is opposed to form, where no-meaning baffles want of sense, and where no great harm is done, because there is not much to do: but when chicane and want of principle are let loose upon the world, 'with famine, sword, and fire at their heels, leashed in like hounds',* when they have their prey marked out for them by the passions, when they are backed by force—when the pen of the Editor of *The Times* is seconded by eleven hundred thousand bayonets—then such men are very mischievous.

'My soul, turn from them: turn we to survey'* where poetry, joined hand in hand with liberty, renews the golden age in 1793, during the reign of Robespierre, which was hardly thought a blot in their escutcheon, by those who said and said truly, for what we know, that he destroyed the lives of hundreds, to save the lives of thousands: (Mark; then, as now, 'Carnage was the daughter of Humanity.'* It is true, these men have changed sides, but not parted with their principles, that is, with their presumption and egotism)—let us turn where Pantisocracy's* equal hills and vales arise in visionary pomp, where Peace and Truth have kissed each other 'in Philarmonia's undivided dale'; and let us see whether the fictions and the forms of poetry give any better assurance of political consistency than the fictions and forms of law.

The spirit of poetry is in itself favourable to humanity and liberty: but, we suspect, not in times like these—not in the present reign. The spirit of poetry is not the spirit of mortification or of martyrdom. Poetry dwells in a perpetual Utopia of its own, and is, for that reason, very ill calculated to make a Paradise upon earth, by encountering the shocks and disappointments of the world. Poetry, like the law, is a fiction; only a more agreeable one. It does not create difficulties where they do not exist; but contrives to get rid of them, whether they exist or not. It is not entangled in cobwebs of its own making, but soars above all obstacles. It cannot be 'constrained by mastery'. It has the range of the universe; it traverses the empyreum, and looks down on nature from a higher sphere. When it lights upon the earth, it loses some of its dignity and its use. Its strength is in its wings; its element the air. Standing on its feet, jostling with the crowd, it is liable to be overthrown, trampled on, and defaced; for its wings are of a dazzling brightness, 'heaven's own tinct', and the least soil upon them shews to disadvantage. Sunk, degraded as we have seen it, we shall not insult over it, but leave it to time to take out the stains, seeing it is a thing immortal as itself. 'Being so majestical, we should do it wrong to offer it but the shew of violence.' But the best things, in their abuse, often become the worst; and so it is with poetry when it is diverted from its proper end. Poets live in an ideal world, where they make every thing out according to their wishes and fancies. They either find things delightful, or make them so. They feign the beautiful and grand out of their own minds, and imagine all things to be, not what they are, but what they ought to be. They are naturally inventors, creators not of truth but beauty: and while they speak to us from the sacred shrine of their own hearts, while they pour out the pure treasures of thought to the world, they cannot be too much admired and applauded: but when, forgetting their high calling, and becoming tools and puppets in the hands of others, they would pass off the gewgaws of corruption and love-tokens of self-interest, as the gifts of the Muse, they cannot be too much despised and shunned. We do not like novels founded on facts, nor do we like poets turned courtiers. Poets, it has been said, succeed best in fiction: and they should for the most part stick to it. Invention, not upon an imaginary subject, is a lie: the varnishing over the vices or deformity of actual objects, is hypocrisy. Players leave their finery at the stage-door, or they would be hooted: poets come out into the world with all their bravery on, and yet they would pass for *bonâ fide* persons. They lend the colours of fancy to whatever they see: whatever they touch becomes gold, though it were lead. With them every Joan is a lady: and kings and queens are human. Matters of fact they embellish at their will, and reason is the plaything of their passions, their caprice, or interest. . .

Man is a toad-eating animal. The admiration of power in others is as common to man as the love of it in himself: the one makes him a tyrant, the other a slave. It is not he alone, who wears the golden crown, that is proud of it: the wretch who pines in a dungeon, and in chains, is dazzled with it; and if he could but shake off his own fetters, would care little about the wretches whom he left behind him, so that he might have an opportunity, on being set free himself, of gazing at this glittering gew-gaw 'on some high holiday of once a year'. The slave, who has no other hope or consolation, clings to the apparition of royal magnificence, which insults his misery and his despair; stares through the hollow eyes of famine at the insolence of pride and luxury which has occasioned it, and hugs his chains the closer, because he has nothing else left. The French, under the old regime, made the glory of their *Grand Monarque* a set-off against rags and hunger, equally satisfied with *shows or bread*; and the poor Spaniard, delivered from temporary to permanent oppression, looks up once more with pious awe, to the time-hallowed towers of the Holy Inquisition. As the herd of mankind are stripped of every thing, in body and mind, so are they thankful for what is left; as is the desolation of their hearts and the wreck of their little all, so is the pomp and pride which is built upon their ruin, and their fawning admiration of it.

> 'I've heard of hearts unkind, kind deeds
> With coldness still returning:
> Alas! the gratitude of men
> Has oftener set me mourning.'*

There is something in the human mind, which requires an object for it to repose on; and, driven from all other sources of pride or pleasure, it falls in love with misery, and grows enamoured of oppression. It gazes after the liberty, the happiness, the comfort, the knowledge, which have been torn from it by the unfeeling gripe of wealth and power, as the poor debtor gazes with envy and wonder at the Lord Mayor's show. Thus is the world by degrees reduced to a spital or lazar-house, where the people waste away with want and disease, and are thankful if they are only suffered to crawl forgotten to their graves. Just in proportion to the systematic tyranny exercised over a nation, to its loss of a sense of freedom and the spirit of resistance, will be its loyalty; the most abject submission will always be rendered to the most confirmed despotism. The most wretched slaves are the veriest sycophants. The lacquey, mounted behind his master's coach, looks down with contempt upon the mob, forgetting his own origin and his actual situation, and comparing them only with that standard of gentility which he has perpetually in his eye. The hireling of the press (a still meaner slave) wears his livery, and is proud of it. He measures the greatness of others by his own meanness; their lofty pretensions indemnify him for his servility; he magnifies the sacredness of their persons to cover the laxity of his own principles. He offers up his own humanity, and that of all men, at the shrine of royalty. He sneaks to court; and the bland accents of power close his ears to the voice of freedom ever after; its velvet touch makes his heart marble to a people's sufferings. He is the intellectual pimp of power, as others are the practical ones of the pleasures of the great, and often on the same disinterested principle. For one tyrant, there are a thousand ready slaves. Man is naturally a worshipper of idols and a lover of kings. It is the excess of

individual power, that strikes and gains over his imagination:
the general misery and degradation which are the necessary
consequences of it, are spread too wide, they lie too deep,
their weight and import are too great, to appeal to any but
the slow, inert, speculative, imperfect faculty of reason. The
cause of liberty is lost in its own truth and magnitude; while
the cause of despotism flourishes, triumphs, and is irresistible
in the gross mixture, the *Belle Alliance*, of pride and ignorance.

Power is the grim idol that the world adore; that arms itself
with destruction, and reigns by terror in the coward heart of
man; that dazzles the senses, haunts the imagination, confounds the understanding, and tames the will, by the vastness
of its pretensions, and the very hopelessness of resistance to
them. Nay more, the more mischievous and extensive the
tyranny—the longer it has lasted, and the longer it is likely to
last—the stronger is the hold it takes of the minds of its
victims, the devotion to it increasing with the dread. It does
not satisfy the enormity of the appetite for servility, till it has
slain the mind of a nation, and becomes like the evil principle
of the universe, from which there is no escape. So in some
countries, the most destructive animals are held sacred,
despair and terror completely overpowering reason. The
prejudices of superstition (religion is another name for fear)
are always the strongest in favour of those forms of worship
which require the most bloody sacrifices; the foulest idols are
those which are approached with the greatest awe; for it
should seem that those objects are the most sacred to passion
and imagination, which are the most revolting to reason and
common sense. No wonder that the Editor of *The Times* bows
his head before the idol of Divine Right, or of Legitimacy, (as
he calls it) which has had more lives sacrificed to its ridiculous
and unintelligible pretensions, in the last twenty-five years,
than were ever sacrificed to any other idol in all preceding
ages. Never was there any thing so well contrived as this fiction
of Legitimacy, to suit the fastidious delicacy of modern sycophants. It hits their grovelling servility and petulant egotism
exactly between wind and water. The contrivers or re-model-
lers of this idol, beat all other idol-mongers, whether Jews,
Gentiles or Christians, hollow. The principle of an idolatry is

the same: it is the want of something to admire, without knowing what or why: it is the love of an effect without a cause; it is a voluntary tribute of admiration which does not compromise our vanity: it is setting something up over all the rest of the world, to which we feel ourselves to be superior, for it is our own handy-work; so that the more perverse the homage we pay to it, the more it pampers our self-will: the meaner the object, the more magnificent and pompous the attributes we bestow upon it; the greater the lie, the more enthusiastically it is believed and greedily swallowed:

> 'Of whatsoever race his godhead be,
> Stock, stone, or other homely pedigree,
> In his defence his servants are as bold
> As if he had been made of beaten gold.'*

In this inverted ratio, the bungling impostors of former times, and less refined countries, got no further than stocks and stones: their utmost stretch of refinement in absurdity went no further than to select the most mischievous animals or the most worthless objects for the adoration of their besotted votaries: but the framers of the new law-fiction of legitimacy have started a nonentity. The ancients sometimes worshipped the sun or stars, or deified heroes and great men: the moderns have found out the image of the divinity in Louis XVIII!* They have set up an object for their idolatry, which they themselves must laugh at, if hypocrisy were not with them the most serious thing in the world. They offer up thirty millions of men to it as its victims, and yet they know that it is nothing but a scare-crow to keep the world in subjection to their renegado whimsies and preposterous hatred of the liberty and happiness of mankind. They do not think kings gods, but they make believe that they do so, to degrade their fellows to the rank of brutes. Legitimacy answers every object of their meanness and malice—*omne tulit punctum.**—This mock-doctrine, this little Hunchback, which our resurrection-men, the Humane Society of Divine Right, have foisted on the altar of Liberty, is not only a phantom of the imagination, but a contradiction in terms; it is a prejudice, but an exploded prejudice; it is an imposture, that imposes on nobody; it is powerful only in impotence, safe in absurdity, courted from fear and hatred, a dead prejudice linked to the living mind; the sink of honour, the grave of liberty, a palsy in the heart of a nation; it claims the species as its property, and derives its right neither from God nor man; not from the authority of the Church, which it treats cavalierly, and yet in contempt of the will of the people, which it scouts as opposed to its own: its two chief supporters are, the sword of the Duke of Wellington and the pen of the Editor of *The Times*! The last of these props has, we understand, just failed it.*

We formerly gave the Editor of *The Times* a definition of a true Jacobin, as one 'who had seen the evening star set over a poor man's cottage, and connected it with the hope of human happiness'. The city-politician laughed this pastoral definition to scorn, and nicknamed the person who had very innocently laid it down, 'the true Jacobin who writes in the Chronicle',—a nickname by which we profited as little as he has by our Illustrations. Since that time our imagination has grown a little less romantic: so we will give him another, which he may chew the cud upon at his leisure. A true Jacobin, then, is one who does not believe in the divine right of kings, or in any other *alias* for it, which implies that they reign 'in contempt of the will of the people';* and he holds all such kings to be tyrants, and their subjects slaves. To be a true Jacobin,* a man must be a good hater; but this is the most difficult and the least amiable of all the virtues: the most trying and the most thankless of all tasks. The love of liberty consists in the hatred of tyrants. The true Jacobin hates the enemies of liberty as they hate liberty, with all his strength and with all his might, and with all his heart and with all his soul. His memory is as long, and his will as strong as theirs, though his hands are shorter. He never forgets or forgives an injury done to the people, for tyrants never forget or forgive one done to themselves. There is no love lost between them. He does not leave them the sole benefit of their old motto, *Odia in longum jaciens quæ conderet auctaque promeret.** He makes neither peace nor truce with them. His hatred of wrong only ceases with the wrong. The sense of it, and of the barefaced assumption of the right to inflict it, deprives him of his rest. It stagnates in his blood. It loads his heart with aspics' tongues, deadly to venal pens. It settles in his brain—it puts him beside himself. Who will not feel all this for a girl, a toy, a turn of the dice, a word, a blow, for any thing relating to himself; and will not the friend of liberty feel as much for mankind? The love of truth is a passion in his mind, as the love of power is a passion in the minds of others. Abstract reason, unassisted by passion, is no match for power and prejudice, armed with force and cunning. The love of liberty is the love of others; the love of power is the love of ourselves. The one is real; the other often but an empty dream. Hence the defection of modern apostates. While they are looking about, wavering and distracted, in pursuit of universal good or universal fame, the eye of power is upon them, like the eye of Providence, that neither slumbers nor sleeps, and that watches but for one object, its own good. They take no notice of it at first, but it is still upon them, and never off them. It at length catches theirs, and they bow to its sacred light; and like the poor fluttering bird, quail beneath it, are seized with a vertigo, and drop senseless into its jaws, that close upon them for ever, and so we see no more of them, which is well.

'And we saw three poets in a dream,* walking up and down on the face of the earth, and holding in their hands a human heart, which, as they raised their eyes to heaven, they kissed and worshipped; and a mighty shout arose and shook the air, for the towers of the Bastile had fallen, and a nation had become, of slaves, freemen; and the three poets, as they heard the sound, leaped and shouted, and made merry, and their voice was choked with tears of joy, which they shed over the human heart, which they kissed and worshipped. And not long after, we saw the same three poets, the one with a receipt-stamp in his hand, the other with a laurel on his head, and the third with a symbol which we could make nothing of, for it was neither literal nor allegorical, following in the train of the Pope and the Inquisition and the Bourbons, and worshipping the mark of the Beast, with the emblem of the human heart thrown beneath their feet, which they trampled and spit upon!'—This apologue is not worth finishing, nor are the people to whom it relates worth talking of. We have done with them.

CHARACTER OF MR BURKE

I

. . . IT has always been with me a test of the sense and candour of any one belonging to the opposite party, whether he allowed Burke to be a great man. Of all the persons of this description that I have ever known, I never met with above one or two who would make this concession; whether it was that party feelings ran too high to admit of any real candour, or whether it was owing to an essential vulgarity in their habits of thinking, they all seemed to be of opinion that he was a wild enthusiast, or a hollow sophist, who was to be answered by bits of facts, by smart logic, by shrewd questions, and idle songs. They looked upon him as a man of disordered intellects, because he reasoned in a style to which they had not been used and which confounded their dim perceptions. If you said that though you differed with him in sentiment, yet you thought him an admirable reasoner, and a close observer of human nature, you were answered with a loud laugh, and some hackneyed quotation. 'Alas! Leviathan was not so tamed!'* They did not know whom they had to contend with. The corner stone, which the builders rejected, became the head-corner, though to the Jews* a stumbling block, and to the Greeks foolishness; for indeed I cannot discover that he was much better understood by those of his own party, if we may judge from the little affinity there is between his mode of reasoning and theirs.—The simple clue to all his reasonings on politics is, I think, as follows. He did not agree with some writers, that that mode of government is necessarily the best which is the cheapest. He saw in the construction of society other principles at work, and other capacities of fulfilling the desires, and perfecting the nature of man, besides those of securing the equal enjoyment of the means of animal life, and doing this at as little expense as possible. He thought that the wants and happiness of men were not to be provided for, as we provide for those of a herd of cattle, merely by attending to their physical necessities. He thought more nobly of his fellows. He knew that man had affections and passions and powers of imagination, as well as hunger and thirst and the sense of heat and cold. He took his idea of political society from the pattern of private life, wishing, as he himself expresses it, to incorporate the domestic charities with the orders of the state, and to blend them together. He strove to establish an analogy between the compact that binds together the community at large, and that which binds together the several families that compose it. He knew that the rules that form the basis of private morality are not founded in reason, that is, in the abstract properties of those things which are the subjects of them, but in the nature of man, and his capacity of being affected by certain things from habit, from imagination, and sentiment, as well as from reason.

Thus, the reason why a man ought to be attached to his wife and children is not, surely, that they are better than others, (for in this case every one else ought to be of the same opinion) but because he must be chiefly interested in those things which are nearest to him, and with which he is best acquainted, since his understanding cannot reach equally to every thing; because he must be most attached to those objects which he has known the longest, and which by their situation have actually affected him the most, not those which in themselves are the most affecting, whether they have ever made any impression on him or no; that is, because he is by his nature the creature of habit and feeling, and because it is reasonable that he should act in conformity to his nature. Burke was so far right in saying that it is no objection to an institution, that it is founded in *prejudice*, but the contrary, if that prejudice is natural and right; that is, if it arises from those circumstances which are properly subjects of feeling and association, not from any defect or perversion of the understanding in those things which fall strictly under its jurisdiction. On this profound maxim he took his stand. Thus he contended, that the prejudice in favour of nobility was natural and proper, and fit to be encouraged by the positive institutions of society; not on account of the real or personal merit of the individuals, but because such an institution has a tendency to enlarge and raise the mind, to keep alive the memory of past greatness, to connect the different ages of the world together, to carry back the imagination over a long tract of time, and feed it with the contemplation of remote events: because it is natural to think highly of that which inspires us with high thoughts, which has been connected for many generations with splendour, and affluence, and dignity, and power, and privilege. He also conceived, that by transferring the respect from the person to the thing, and thus rendering it steady and permanent, the mind would be habitually formed to sentiments of deference, attachment, and fealty, to whatever else demanded its respect: that it would be led to fix its view on what was elevated and lofty, and be weaned from that low and narrow jealousy which never willingly or heartily admits of any superiority in others, and is glad of every opportunity to bring down all excellence to a level with its own miserable standard. Nobility did not therefore exist to the prejudice of the other orders of the state, but by, and for them. The inequality of the different orders of society did not destroy the unity and harmony of the whole. The health and well-being of the moral world was to be promoted by the same means as the beauty of the natural world; by contrast, by change, by light and shade, by variety of parts, by order and proportion. To think of reducing all mankind to the same insipid level, seemed to him the same absurdity as to destroy the inequalities of surface in a country, for the benefit of agriculture and commerce. In short, he believed that the interests of men in society should be consulted, and their several stations and employments assigned, with a view to their nature, not as physical, but as moral beings, so as to nourish their hopes, to lift their imagination, to enliven their fancy, to rouse their activity, to strengthen their virtue, and to furnish the greatest number of objects of pursuit and means of enjoyment to beings constituted as man is, consistently with the order and stability of the whole.

The same reasoning might be extended farther. I do not say that his arguments are conclusive; but they are profound and *true*, as far as they go. There may be disadvantages and abuses necessarily interwoven with his scheme, or opposite advantages of infinitely greater value, to be derived from another order of things and state of society. This however does not invalidate either the truth or importance of Burke's reasoning; since the advantages he points out as connected with the mixed form of government are really and necessarily inherent in it: since they are compatible in the same degree with no other; since the principle itself on which he rests his argument (whatever we may think of the application) is of the utmost weight and moment; and since on whichever side the truth lies, it is impossible to make a fair decision without having the opposite side of the question clearly and fully stated to us. This Burke has done in a masterly manner. He presents to you one view or face of society. Let him, who thinks he can, give the reverse side with equal force, beauty, and clearness. It is said, I know, that truth is *one*; but to this I cannot subscribe, for it appears to me that truth is *many*. There are as many truths as there are things and causes of action and contradictory principles at work in society. In making up the account of good and evil, indeed, the final result must be one way or the other; but the particulars on which that result depends are infinite and various.

It will be seen from what I have said, that I am very far from agreeing with those who think that Burke was a man without understanding, and a merely florid writer. There are two causes which have given rise to this calumny; namely, that narrowness of mind which leads men to suppose that the truth lies entirely on the side of their own opinions, and that whatever does not make for them is absurd and irrational; secondly, a trick we have of confounding reason with judgment, and supposing that it is merely the province of the understanding to pronounce sentence, and not to give in evidence, or argue the case, in short, that it is a passive, not an active faculty. Thus there are persons who never run into any extravagance, because they are so buttressed up with the opinions of others on all sides, that they cannot lean much to one side or the other; they are so little moved with any kind of reasoning, that they remain at an equal distance from every extreme, and are never very far from the truth, because the slowness of their faculties will not suffer them to make much progress in error. These are persons of great judgment. The scales of the mind are pretty sure to remain even, when there is nothing in them. In this sense of the word, Burke must be allowed to have wanted judgment, by all those who think that he was wrong in his conclusions. The accusation of want of judgment, in fact, only means that you yourself are of a different opinion. But if in arriving at one error he discovered a hundred truths, I should consider myself a hundred times more indebted to him than if, stumbling on that which I consider as the right side of the question, he had committed a hundred absurdities in striving to establish his point. I speak of him now merely as an author, or as far as I and other readers are concerned with him; at the same time, I should not differ from any one who may be disposed to contend that the consequences of his writings as instruments of political power have been tremendous, fatal, such as no exertion of wit or knowledge or genius can ever counteract or atone for.

Burke also gave a hold to his antagonists by mixing up sentiment and imagery with his reasoning; so that being unused to such a sight in the region of politics, they were deceived, and could not discern the fruit from the flowers. Gravity is the cloke of wisdom; and those who have nothing else think it an insult to affect the one without the other, because it destroys the only foundation on which their pretensions are built. The easiest part of reason is dulness; the generality of the world are therefore concerned in discouraging any example of unnecessary brilliancy that might tend to shew that the two things do not always go together. Burke in some measure dissolved the spell. It was discovered, that his gold was not the less valuable for being wrought into elegant shapes, and richly embossed with curious figures; that the solidity of a building is not destroyed by adding to it beauty and ornament; and that the strength of a man's understanding is not always to be estimated in exact proportion to his want of imagination. His understanding was not the less real, because it was not the only faculty he possessed. He justified the description of the poet,—

'How charming is divine philosophy!
Not harsh and crabbed as dull fools suppose,
But musical as is Apollo's lute!'*

Those who object to this union of grace and beauty with
reason, are in fact weak-sighted people, who cannot distinguish the noble and majestic form of Truth from that of
her sister Folly, if they are dressed both alike! But there is
always a difference even in the adventitious ornaments they.
wear, which is sufficient to distinguish them.

Burke was so far from being a gaudy or flowery writer, that
he was one of the severest writers we have. His words are the
most like things; his style is the most strictly suited to the
subject. He unites every extreme and every variety of composition; the lowest and the meanest words and descriptions with
the highest. He exults in the display of power, in shewing the
extent, the force, and intensity of his ideas; he is led on by
the mere impulse and vehemence of his fancy, not by the
affectation of dazzling his readers by gaudy conceits or pompous images. He was completely carried away by his subject.
He had no other object but to produce the strongest impression on his reader, by giving the truest, the most characteristic,
the fullest, and most forcible descriptions of things, trusting
to the power of his own mind to mould them into grace and
beauty. He did not produce a splendid effect by setting fire
to the light vapours that float in the regions of fancy, as the
chemists make fine colours with phosphorus, but by the eagerness of his blows struck fire from the flint, and melted the
hardest substances in the furnace of his imagination. The
wheels of his imagination did not catch fire from the rotten-
ness of the materials, but from the rapidity of their motion.
One would suppose, to hear people talk of Burke, that his
style was such as would have suited the 'Lady's Magazine';*
soft, smooth, showy, tender, insipid, full of fine words, without
any meaning. The essence of the gaudy or glittering style
consists in producing a momentary effect by fine words and
images brought together, without order or connexion. Burke
most frequently produced an effect by the remoteness and
novelty of his combinations, by the force of contrast, by the

striking manner in which the most opposite and unpromising materials were harmoniously blended together; not by laying his hands on all the fine things he could think of, but by bringing together those things which he knew would blaze out into glorious light by their collision. The florid style is a mixture of affectation and common-place. Burke's was an union of untameable vigour and originality.

Burke was not a verbose writer. If he sometimes multiplies words, it is not for want of ideas, but because there are no words that fully express his ideas, and he tries to do it as well as he can by different ones. He had nothing of the *set* or formal style, the measured cadence, and stately phraseology of Johnson, and most of our modern writers. This style, which is what we understand by the *artificial*, is all in one key. It selects a certain set of words to represent all ideas whatever, as the most dignified and elegant, and excludes all others as low and vulgar. The words are not fitted to the things, but the things to the words. Every thing is seen through a false medium. It is putting a mask on the face of nature, which may indeed hide some specks and blemishes, but takes away all beauty, delicacy, and variety. It destroys all dignity or elevation, because nothing can be raised where all is on a level, and completely destroys all force, expression, truth, and character, by arbitrarily confounding the differences of things, and reducing every thing to the same insipid standard. To suppose that this stiff uniformity can add any thing to real grace or dignity, is like supposing that the human body in order to be perfectly graceful, should never deviate from its upright posture. Another mischief of this method is, that it confounds all ranks in literature. Where there is no room for variety, no discrimination, no nicety to be shewn in matching the idea with its proper word, there can be no room for taste or elegance. A man must easily learn the art of writing, when every sentence is to be cast in the same mould: where he is only allowed the use of one word, he cannot choose wrong, nor will he be in much danger of making himself ridiculous by affectation or false glitter, when, whatever subject he treats of, he must treat of it in the same way. This indeed is to wear golden chains for the sake of ornament.

Burke was altogether free from the pedantry which I have here endeavoured to expose. His style was as original, as expressive, as rich and varied, as it was possible; his combinations were as exquisite, as playful, as happy, as unexpected, as bold and daring, as his fancy. If any thing, he ran into the opposite extreme of too great an inequality, if truth and nature could ever be carried to an extreme.

Those who are best acquainted with the writings and speeches of Burke will not think the praise I have here bestowed on them exaggerated. Some proof will be found of this in the following extracts.* But the full proof must be sought in his works at large, and particularly in the *Thoughts on the Discontents*; in his *Reflections on the French Revolution*; in his *Letter to the Duke of Bedford*; and in the *Regicide Peace*. The two last of these are perhaps the most remarkable of all his writings, from the contrast they afford to each other. The one is the most delightful exhibition of wild and brilliant fancy, that is to be found in English prose, but it is too much like a beautiful picture painted upon gauze; it wants something to support it: the other is without ornament, but it has all the solidity, the weight, the gravity of a judicial record. It seems to have been written with a certain constraint upon himself, and to shew those who said he could not *reason*, that his arguments might be stripped of their ornaments without losing any thing of their force. It is certainly, of all his works, that in which he has shewn most power of logical deduction, and the only one in which he has made any important use of facts. In general he certainly paid little attention to them: they were the playthings of his mind. He saw them as he pleased, not as they were; with the eye of the philosopher or the poet, regarding them only in their general principle, or as they might serve to decorate his subject. This is the natural consequence of much imagination: things that are probable are elevated into the rank of realities. To those who can reason on the essences of things, or who can invent according to nature, the experimental proof is of little value. This was the case with Burke. In the present instance, however, he seems to have forced his mind into the service of facts: and he succeeded completely. His comparison between our connexion with France or Algiers, and his account of the conduct of the war, are as clear, as convincing, as forcible examples of this kind of reasoning, as are any where to be met with. . .

II

It is not without reluctance that we speak of the vices and infirmities of such a mind as Burke's: but the poison of high example has by far the widest range of destruction: and, for the sake of public honour and individual integrity, we think it right to say, that however it may be defended upon other grounds, the political career of that eminent individual has no title to the praise of consistency. Mr Burke, the opponent of the American war,* and Mr Burke, the opponent of the French Revolution, are not the same person, but opposite persons—not opposite persons only, but deadly enemies. In the latter period, he abandoned not only all his practical conclusions, but all the principles on which they were founded. He proscribed all his former sentiments, denounced all his former friends, rejected and reviled all the maxims to which he had formerly appealed as incontestable. In the American war, he constantly spoke of the rights of the people as inherent, and inalienable: after the French Revolution, he began by treating them with the chicanery of a sophist, and ended by raving at them with the fury of a maniac. In the former case, he held out the duty of resistance to oppression, as the palladium and only ultimate resource of natural liberty; in the latter, he scouted, prejudged, vilified, and nicknamed, all resistance in the abstract, as a foul and unnatural union of rebellion and sacrilege. In the one case, to answer the purposes of faction, he made it out, that the people are always in the right; in the other, to answer different ends, he made it out that they are always in the wrong—lunatics in the hands of their royal keepers, patients in the sick-wards of an hospital, or felons in the condemned cells of a prison. In the one, he considered that there was a constant tendency on the part of the prerogative to encroach on the rights of the people, which ought always to be the object of the most watchful jealousy, and of resistance, when necessary: in the other, he pretended to regard it as the sole occupation and ruling passion of those in power, to watch over the liberties and happiness of their subjects. The burthen of all his speeches on the American war, was conciliation, concession, timely reform, as the only practicable or desirable alternative of rebellion: the object of all his writings on the French Revolution was, to deprecate and explode all concession and all reform, as encouraging rebellion, and as an irretrievable step to revolution and anarchy. In the one, he insulted kings personally, as among the lowest and worst of mankind; in the other, he held them up to the imagination of his readers, as sacred abstractions. In the one case, he was a partisan of the people, to court popularity; in the other, to gain the favour of the Court, he became the apologist of all courtly abuses. In the one case, he took part with those who were actually rebels against his Sovereign: in the other, he denounced as rebels and traitors, all those of his own countrymen who did not yield sympathetic allegiance to a foreign Sovereign, whom we had always been in the habit of treating as an arbitrary tyrant.

Nobody will accuse the principles of his present Majesty, or the general measures of his reign, of inconsistency. If they had no other merit, they have, at least, that of having been all along actuated by one uniform and constant spirit: yet Mr Burke at one time vehemently opposed, and afterwards most intemperately extolled them: and it was for his recanting his opposition, not for his persevering in it, that he received his pension. He does not himself mention his flaming speeches in the American war, as among the public services which had entitled him to this remuneration.

The truth is, that Burke was a man of fine fancy and subtle reflection; but not of sound and practical judgment, nor of high or rigid principles.—As to his understanding, he certainly was not a great philosopher; for his works of mere abstract reasoning are shallow and inefficient:—nor was he a man of sense and business; for, both in counsel, and in conduct, he alarmed his friends as much at least as his opponents:—but he was an acute and accomplished man of letters—an ingenious political essayist. He applied the habit of reflection, which he had borrowed from his metaphysical studies, but which was not competent to the discovery of any elementary

truth in that department, with great facility and success, to
the mixed mass of human affairs. He knew more of the political machine than a recluse philosopher; and he speculated
more profoundly on its principles and general results than a
mere politician. He saw a number of fine distinctions and
changeable aspects of things, the good mixed with the ill, and
the ill mixed with the good; and with a sceptical indifference,
in which the exercise of his own ingenuity was obviously the
governing principle, suggested various topics to qualify or
assist the judgment of others. But for this very reason, he was
little calculated to become a leader or a partizan in any important practical measure. For the habit of his mind would
lead him to find out a reason for or against any thing: and it
is not on speculative refinements, (which belong to *every* side
of a question), but on a just estimate of the aggregate mass
and extended combinations of objections and advantages,
that we ought to decide or act. Burke had the power of
throwing true or false weights into the scales of political casu-
istry, but not firmness of mind (or, shall we say, honesty
enough) to hold the balance. When he took a side, his vanity
or his spleen more frequently gave the casting vote than his
judgment; and the fieriness of his zeal was in exact proportion
to the levity of his understanding, and the want of conscious
sincerity.

He was fitted by nature and habit for the studies and labours
of the closet; and was generally mischievous when he came
out; because the very subtlety of his reasoning, which, left to
itself, would have counteracted its own activity, or found its
level in the common sense of mankind, became a dangerous
engine in the hands of power, which is always eager to make
use of the most plausible pretexts to cover the most fatal
designs. That which, if applied as a general observation to
human affairs, is a valuable truth suggested to the mind, may,
when forced into the interested defence of a particular measure or system, become the grossest and basest sophistry. Facts
or consequences never stood in the way of this speculative
politician. He fitted them to his preconceived theories, instead of conforming his theories to them. They were the
playthings of his style, the sport of his fancy. They were the

straws of which his imagination made a blaze, and were consumed, like straws, in the blaze they had served to kindle. The fine things he said about Liberty and Humanity, in his speech on the Begum's affairs, told equally well, whether Warren Hastings* was a tyrant or not: nor did he care one jot who caused the famine he described, so that he described it in a way that no one else could. On the same principle, he represented the French priests and nobles under the old regime as excellent moral people, very charitable and very religious, in the teeth of notorious facts—to answer to the handsome things he had to say in favour of priesthood and nobility in general; and, with similar views, he falsifies the records of our English Revolution, and puts an interpretation on the word *abdication*,* of which a schoolboy would be ashamed. He constructed his whole theory of government, in short, not on rational, but on picturesque and fanciful principles; as if the king's crown were a painted gewgaw, to be looked at on gala-days; titles an empty sound to please the ear; and the whole order of society a theatrical procession. His lamentations over the age of chivalry, and his projected crusade to restore it, are about as wise as if any one, from reading the *Beggar's Opera*,* should take to picking of pockets: or, from admiring the landscapes of Salvator Rosa,* should wish to convert the abodes of civilized life into the haunts of wild beasts and banditti. On this principle of false refinement, there is no abuse, nor system of abuses, that does not admit of an easy and triumphant defence; for there is something which a merely speculative enquirer may always find out, good as well as bad, in every possible system, the best or the worst; and if we can once get rid of the restraints of common sense and honesty, we may easily prove, by plausible words, that liberty and slavery, peace and war, plenty and famine, are matters of perfect indifference. This is the school of politics, of which Mr Burke was at the head; and it is perhaps to his example, in this respect, that we owe the prevailing tone of many of those newspaper paragraphs, which Mr Coleridge thinks so invaluable an accession to our political philosophy.*

Burke's literary talents were, after all, his chief excellence. His style has all the familiarity of conversation, and all the research of the most elaborate composition. He says what he wants to say, by any means, nearer or more remote, within his reach. He makes use of the most common or scientific terms, of the longest or shortest sentences, of the plainest and most downright, or of the most figurative modes of speech. He gives for the most part loose reins to his imagination, and follows it as far as the language will carry him. As long as the one or the other has any resources in store to make the reader feel and see the thing as he has conceived it, in its nicest shades of difference, in its utmost degree of force and splendour, he never disdains, and never fails to employ them. Yet, in the extremes of his mixed style, there is not much affectation, and but little either of pedantry or of coarseness. He everywhere gives the image he wishes to give, in its true and appropriate colouring: and it is the very crowd and variety of these images that has given to his language its peculiar tone of animation, and even of passion. It is his impatience to transfer his conceptions entire, living, in all their rapidity, strength, and glancing variety, to the minds of others, that constantly pushes him to the verge of extravagance, and yet supports him there in dignified security—

> 'Never so sure our rapture to create,
> As when he treads the brink of all we hate.'*

He is the most poetical of our prose writers, and at the same time his prose never degenerates into the mere effeminacy of poetry; for he always aims at overpowering rather than at pleasing; and consequently sacrifices beauty and delicacy to force and vividness. He has invariably a task to perform, a positive purpose to execute, an effect to produce. His only object is therefore to strike hard, and in the right place; if he misses his mark, he repeats his blow; and does not care how ungraceful the action, or how clumsy the instrument, provided it brings down his antagonist.

MALTHUS

'A swaggering paradox, when once explained, soon sinks into an unmeaning common-place.'*

I

THIS excellent saying of a great man was never more strictly applicable to any system than it is to Mr Malthus's paradox, and his explanation of it. It seemed, on the first publication of the Essay on Population,* as if the whole world was going to be turned topsy-turvy, all our ideas of moral good and evil, were in a manner confounded, we scarcely knew whether we stood on our head or our heels: but after exciting considerable expectation, giving us a good shake, and making us a little dizzy, Mr Malthus does as we do when we shew the children *London*,—sets us on our feet again, and every thing goes on as before. The common notions that prevailed on this subject, till our author's first population-scheme tended to weaken them, were that life is a blessing, and that the more people could be maintained in any state in a tolerable degree of health, comfort and decency, the better: that want and misery are not desirable in themselves, that famine is not to be courted for its own sake, that wars, disease and pestilence are not what every friend of his country or his species should pray for in the first place: that vice in its different shapes is a thing that the world could do very well without, and that if it could be got rid of altogether, it would be a great gain. In short, that the object both of the moralist and politician was to diminish as much as possible the quantity of vice and misery existing in the world: without apprehending that by thus effectually introducing more virtue and happiness, more reason and good sense, that by improving the manners of a people, removing pernicious habits and principles of acting, or securing greater plenty, and a greater number of mouths to partake of it, they were doing a disservice to humanity. Then comes Mr Malthus with his octavo book, and tells us there is another great evil, which had never been found out, or at least not sufficiently attended to till his time, namely, excessive population: that this evil was infinitely greater and more to be dreaded than all others put together; and that its approach could only be checked by vice and misery: that any increase of virtue or happiness was the direct way to hasten it on; and that in proportion as we attempted to improve the condition of mankind, and lessened the restraints of vice and misery, we threw down the only barriers that could protect us from this most formidable scourge of the species, population. Vice and misery were indeed evils, but they were absolutely necessary evils; necessary to prevent the introduction of others of an incalculably and inconceivably greater magnitude; and that every proposal to lessen their actual quantity, on which the measure of our safety depended, might be attended with the most ruinous consequences, and ought to be looked upon with horror. I think that this description of the tendency and complexion of Mr Malthus's first essay is not in the least exaggerated, but an exact and faithful picture of the impression, which is made on every one's mind.

After taking some time to recover from the surprise and hurry into which so great a discovery would naturally throw him, he comes forward again with a large quarto,* in which he is at great pains both to say and unsay all that he has said in his former volume; and upon the whole concludes, that population is in itself a good thing, that it is never likely to do much harm, that virtue and happiness ought to be promoted by every practicable means, and that the most effectual as well as desirable check to excessive population is *moral restraint.* The mighty discovery thus reduced to, and pieced out by common sense, the wonder vanishes, and we breathe a little freely again. Mr Malthus is, however, by no means willing to give up his old doctrine, or *eat his own words*: he stickles stoutly for it at times. He has his fits of reason and his fits of extravagance, his yielding and his obstinate moments, fluctuating between the two, and vibrating backwards and forwards with a dexterity of self-contradiction which it is wonderful to behold. The following passage is so curious in this respect that I cannot help quoting it in this place. Speaking

of the Reply of the author of the *Political Justice** to his former
work, he observes, 'But Mr. Godwin says, that if he looks into
the past history of the world, he does not see that increasing
population has been controlled and confined by vice and
misery *alone. In this observation I cannot agree with him.* I will
thank Mr. Godwin to name to me any check, that in past ages
has contributed to keep down the population to the level of
the means of subsistence, that does not fairly come under
some form of vice or misery; except indeed the check of *moral
restraint, which I have mentioned in the course of this work*; and
which to say the truth, whatever hopes we may entertain of its
prevalence in future, has undoubtedly in past ages operated
with very inconsiderable force.' When I assure the reader that
I give him this passage fairly and fully, I think he will be of
opinion with me, that it would be difficult to produce an
instance of a more miserable attempt to reconcile a contradiction by childish evasion, to insist upon an argument, and give
it up in the same breath. Does Mr Malthus really think that
he has such an absolute right and authority over this subject
of population, that provided he mentions a principle, or shews
that he is not ignorant of it, and cannot be caught *napping* by
the critics, he is at liberty to say that it has or has not had any
operation, just as he pleases, and that the state of the fact is
a matter of perfect indifference? He contradicts the opinion
of Mr Godwin that vice and misery are not the only checks to
population, and gives as a proof of his assertion, that he
himself truly has mentioned another check. Thus after flatly
denying that moral restraint has any effect at all, he modestly
concludes by saying that it has had some, no doubt, but
promises that it will never have a great deal. Yet in the very
next page, he says, 'On this sentiment, whether virtue, prudence or pride, which I have already noticed under the name
of moral restraint, or of the more comprehensive title, the
preventive check, it will appear, that in the sequel of this work,
I shall lay considerable stress.' This kind of reasoning is
enough to give one the headache.

The most singular thing in this singular performance of our
author is, that it should have been originally ushered into the
world as the most complete and only satisfactory answer to

the speculations of Godwin, Condorcet* and others, or to
what has been called the modern philosophy. A more complete piece of wrong-headedness, a more strange perversion
of reason could hardly be devised by the wit of man. Whatever
we may think of the doctrine of the progressive improvement
of the human mind, or of a state of society in which every
thing will be subject to the absolute control of reason, however
absurd, unnatural, or impracticable we may conceive such a
system to be, certainly it cannot without the grossest inconsistency be objected to it, that such a system would necessarily
be rendered abortive, because if reason should ever get the
mastery over all our actions, we shall then be governed entirely by our physical appetites and passions, without the least
regard to consequences. This appears to me a refinement on
absurdity. Several philosophers and speculatists had supposed
that a certain state of society very different from any that has
hitherto existed was in itself practicable; and that if it were
realised, it would be productive of a far greater degree of
human happiness than is compatible with the present institutions of society. I have nothing to do with either of these
points. I will allow to any one who pleases that all such
schemes are 'false, sophistical, unfounded in the extreme'.
But I cannot agree with Mr Malthus that they would be *bad*,
in proportion as they were *good*; that their excellence would
be their ruin; or that the true and only unanswerable objection against all such schemes is that very degree of happiness,
virtue, and improvement, to which they are supposed to give
rise. And I cannot agree with him in this, because it is contrary
to common sense, and leads to the subversion of every principle of moral reasoning. Without perplexing himself with the
subtle arguments of his opponents, Mr Malthus comes boldly
forward, and says, 'Gentlemen, I am willing to make you large
concessions, I am ready to allow the practicability and the
desirableness of your schemes; the more happiness, the more
virtue, the more refinement they are productive of, the better;
all these will only add to the "exuberant strength of my argument";* I have a short answer to all objections, to be sure I
found it in an old political receipt-book, called Prospects, &c.
by one Wallace,* a man not much known, but no matter for

that, *finding is keeping*, you know:' and with one smart stroke of his wand, on which are inscribed certain mystical characters, and algebraic proportions, he levels the fairy enchantment with the ground. For, says Mr Malthus, though this improved state of society were actually realised, it could not possibly continue, but must soon terminate in a state of things pregnant with evils far more insupportable than any we at present endure, in consequence of the excessive population which would follow, and the impossibility of providing for its support.

This is what I do not understand. It is, in other words, to assert that the doubling the population of a country, for example, after a certain period, will be attended with the most pernicious effects, by want, famine, bloodshed, and a state of general violence and confusion; this will afterwards lead to vices and practices still worse than the physical evils they are designed to prevent, &c. and yet that at this period those who will be the most interested in preventing these consequences, and the best acquainted with the circumstances that lead to them, will neither have the understanding to foresee, nor the heart to feel, nor the will to prevent the sure evils to which they expose themselves and others, though this advanced state of population, which does not admit of any addition without danger is supposed to be the immediate result of a more general diffusion of the comforts and conveniences of life, of more enlarged and liberal views, of a more refined and comprehensive regard to our own permanent interests, as well as those of others, of correspondent habits and manners, and of a state of things, in which our gross animal appetites will be subjected to the practical control of reason. The influence of rational motives, of refined and long-sighted views of things is supposed to have taken the place of narrow, selfish, and merely sensual motives: this is implied in the very statement of the question. 'What conjuration and what mighty magic'* should thus blind our philosophical descendants on this single subject in which they are more interested than in all the rest, so that they should stand with their eyes open on the edge of a precipice, and instead of retreating from it, should throw themselves down headlong, I cannot comprehend;

unless indeed we suppose that the impulse to propagate the species is so strong and uncontrolable, that reason has no power over it. This is what Mr Malthus was at one time strongly disposed to assert, and what he is at present half inclined to retract. Without this foundation to rest on, the whole of his reasoning is unintelligible. It seems to me a most childish way of answering any one, who chooses to assert that mankind are capable of being governed entirely by their reason, and that it would be better for them if they were, to say, No, for if they were governed entirely by it, they would be much less able to attend to its dictates than they are at present: and the evils, which would thus follow from the unrestrained increase of population, would be excessive.—Almost every little Miss, who has had the advantage of a boarding-school education, or been properly tutored by her mamma, whose hair is not of an absolute flame-colour, and who has hopes in time, if she behaves prettily, of getting a good husband, waits patiently year after year, looks about her, rejects or trifles with half a dozen lovers, favouring one, laughing at another, chusing among them 'as one picks pears, saying, this I like, that I loathe',* with the greatest indifference, as if it were no such very pressing affair, and *all the while behaves very prettily*:—why, what an idea does Mr Malthus give us of the grave, masculine genius of our Utopian philosophers, their sublime attainments and gigantic energy, that they will not be able to manage these matters as decently and cleverly as the silliest woman can do at present! Mr Malthus indeed endeavours to soften the absurdity by saying that moral restraint at present owes its strength to selfish motives: what is that to the purpose? If Mr Malthus chooses to say, that men will always be governed by the same gross mechanical motives that they are at present, I have no objection to make to it; but it is shifting the question: it is not arguing against the state of society we are considering from the consequences to which it would give rise, but against the possibility of its ever existing. It is absurd to object to a system on account of the consequences which would follow if we once suppose men to be actuated by entirely different motives and principles from what they are at present, and then to say, that those consequences would necessarily follow, because men would never be what we suppose them. It is very idle to alarm the imagination by deprecating the evils that must follow from the practical adoption of a particular scheme, yet to allow that we have no reason to dread those consequences, but because the scheme itself is impracticable.—But I am ashamed of wasting the reader's time and my own in thus beating the air. It is not however my fault that Mr Malthus has written nonsense, or that others have admired it. It is not Mr Malthus's nonsense, but the opinion of the world respecting it, that I would be thought to compliment by this serious refutation of what in itself neither deserves nor admits of any reasoning upon it. If, however, we recollect the source from whence Mr Malthus borrowed his principle and the application of it to improvements in political philosophy, we must allow that he is merely passive in error. The principle itself would not have been worth a farthing to him without the application, and accordingly he took them as he found them lying snug together; and as Trim having converted the old jack-boots into a pair of new mortars immediately planted them against whichever of my uncle Toby's* garrisons the allies were then busy in besieging, so the public-spirited gallantry of our modern engineer directed him to bend the whole force of his clumsy discovery against that system of philosophy which was the most talked of at the time, but to which it was the least applicable of all others. Wallace, I have no doubt, took up his idea either as a paradox, or a *jeu d'esprit*, or because any thing, he thought, was of weight enough to overturn what had never existed any where but in the imagination; or he was led into a piece of false logic by an error we are very apt to fall into, of supposing because he had never been struck himself by the difficulty of population in such a state of society, that therefore the people themselves would not find it out, nor make any provision against it. But though I can in some measure excuse a lively paradox, I do not think the same favour is to be shewn to the dull, dogged, voluminous repetition of an absurdity.

I cannot help thinking that our author has been too much influenced in his different feelings on this subject, by the particular purpose he had in view at the time. Mr Malthus might not improperly have taken for the motto of his first edition,—'These three bear record on earth, vice, misery, and population.'* In his answer to Mr Godwin, this principle was represented as an evil, for which no remedy could be found but in evil;—that its operation was mechanical, unceasing, necessary; that it went straight forward to its end, unchecked by fear, or reason, or remorse; that the evils, which it drew after it, could only be avoided by other evils, by actual vice and misery. Population was, in fact, the great Devil, the un-tamed Beelzebub that was only kept chained down by vice and misery, and which, if it were once let loose from these res-traints, would go forth, and ravage the earth. That they were, of course, the two main props and pillars of society, and that the lower and weaker they kept this principle, the better able they were to contend with it: that therefore any diminution of that degree of them, which at present prevails, and is found sufficient to keep the world in order, was of all things chiefly to be dreaded.—Mr Malthus seems fully aware of the impor-tance of the stage-maxim,* To elevate and surprise. Having once heated the imaginations of his readers, he knows that he can afterwards mould them into whatever shape he pleases. All this bustle and terror, and stage-effect, and theat-rical mummery was only to serve a temporary purpose, for all of a sudden the scene is shifted, and the storm subsides. Having frighted away the boldest champions of modern philo-sophy, this monstrous appearance, full of strange and inex-plicable horrors, is suffered quietly to shrink back to its natural dimensions, and we find it to be nothing more than a common-sized tame looking animal, which however re-quires a chain and the whip of its keeper to prevent it from becoming mischievous. Mr Malthus then steps forward and says, 'The evil we were all in danger of was not population,—but philosophy. Nothing is to be done with the latter by mere reasoning. I, therefore, thought it right to make use of a little terror to accomplish the end. As to the principle of popula-tion you need be under no alarm; only leave it to me, and I shall be able to manage it very well. All its dreadful conse-quences may be easily prevented by a proper application of the motives of common prudence and common decency.' If,

however, any one should be at a loss to know how it is possible
to reconcile such contradictions, I would suggest to Mr
Malthus the answer which Hamlet makes to his friend Guilder-
stern, ' 'Tis as easy as lying: govern these ventiges (the poor-
rates and private charity) with your fingers and thumb, and
this same instrument will discourse most excellent music; look
you, here are the stops,'* (namely, Mr Malthus's Essay and Mr
Whitbread's Poor Bill).*

II

In speaking of the abolition of the Poor Laws, Mr Malthus
says:—

'To this end, I should propose a regulation to be made,
declaring, that no child born from any marriage, taking place
after the expiration of a year from the date of the law, and no
illegitimate child born two years from the same date, should
ever be entitled to parish assistance. And to give a more
general knowledge of this law, and to enforce it more strongly
on the minds of the lower classes of people, the clergyman of
each parish should, after the publication of banns, read a
short address, stating the strong obligation on every man to
support his own children; the impropriety, and even immoral-
ity, of marrying without a prospect of being able to do this;
the evils which had resulted to the poor themselves from the
attempt which had been made to assist by public institutions
in a duty which ought to be exclusively appropriated to
parents; and the absolute necessity which had at length appeared of abandoning all such institutions, on account of
their producing effects totally opposite to those which were
intended.

'This would operate as a fair, distinct, and precise notice,
which no man could well mistake, and, without pressing hard
on any particular individuals, would at once throw off the
rising generation from that miserable and helpless dependence upon the government and the rich, the moral as well as
physical consequences of which are almost incalculable.

'After the public notice which I have proposed had been
given, and the system of poor-laws had ceased with regard to
the rising generation, if any man chose to marry, without a

prospect of being able to support a family, he should have the most perfect liberty so to do. Though to marry, in this case, is, in my opinion, clearly an immoral act, yet it is not one which society can justly take upon itself to prevent or punish; because the punishment provided for it by the laws of nature falls directly and most severely upon the individual who commits the act, and through him, only more remotely and feebly, on the society. When Nature will govern and punish for us, it is a very miserable ambition to wish to snatch the rod from her hands, and draw upon ourselves the odium of executioner. To the punishment therefore of Nature he should be left, the punishment of want. He has erred in the face of a most clear and precise warning, and can have no just reason to complain of any persons but himself when he feels the consequences of his error. All parish assistance should be most rigidly denied him; and he should be left to the uncertain support of private charity. He should be taught to know, that the laws of Nature, which are the laws of God, had doomed him and his family to starve, for disobeying their repeated admonitions; that he had no claim of *right* on society for the smallest portion of food, beyond that which his labour would fairly purchase; and that if he and his family were saved from feeling the natural consequences of his imprudence, he would owe it to the pity of some kind benefactor, to whom, therefore, he ought to be bound by the strongest ties of gratitude.'*

This passage has been well answered by Mr Cobbett* in one word, 'Parson';—the most expressive apostrophe that ever was made; and it might be answered as effectually by another word, which I shall omit. When Mr Malthus asserts, that the poor man and his family have been doomed to starve by the laws of nature, which are the laws of God, he means by the laws of God and nature, the physical and necessary inability of the earth to supply food for more than a certain number of human beings; but if he means that the wants of the poor arise from the impossibility of procuring food for them, while the rich roll in abundance, or, we will say, maintain their dogs and horses, &c. out of their ostentatious superfluities, he asserts what he knows not to be true. Mr Malthus wishes to confound the necessary limits of the produce of the earth with the arbitrary and artificial distribution of that produce according to the institutions of society, or the caprice of individuals, the laws of God and nature with the laws of man. And what proves the fallacy is, that the laws of man in the present case actually afford the relief, which he would wilfully deny; he proposes to repeal those laws, and then to tell the poor man impudently, that 'the laws of God and nature have doomed him and his family to starve, for disobeying their repeated admonitions,' stuck on the church-door for the last twelve months! 'Tis much.

I have in a separate work* made the following remarks on the above proposal, which are a little cavalier, not too cavalier;—a little contemptuous, not too contemptuous; a little gross, but not too gross for the subject.—

'I am not sorry that I am at length come to this passage. It will I hope decide the reader's opinion of the benevolence, wisdom, piety, candour, and disinterested simplicity of Mr Malthus's mind. Any comments that I might make upon it to strengthen this impression must be faint and feeble. I give up the task of doing justice to the moral beauties that pervade every line of it, in despair. There are some instances of an heroical contempt for the narrow prejudices of the world, of a perfect refinement from the vulgar feelings of human nature, that must only suffer by a comparison with any thing else.

I shall not myself be so uncandid as not to confess, that I think the poor laws bad things; and that it would be well, if they could be got rid of, consistently with humanity and justice. This I do not think they could in the present state of things, and other circumstances remaining as they are. The reason why I object to Mr Malthus's plan is, that it does not go to the root of the evil, or attack it in its principle, but its effects. He confounds the cause with the effect. The wide spreading tyranny, dependence, indolence, and unhappiness, of which Mr Malthus is so sensible, are not occasioned by the increase of the poor-rates, but these are the natural consequence of that increasing tyranny, dependence, indolence, and unhappiness occasioned by other causes.

Mr Malthus desires his readers to look at the enormous proportion in which the poor-rates have increased within the last ten years. But have they increased in any greater proportion than the other taxes, which rendered them necessary, and, which I think, were employed for much more mischievous purposes? I would ask, what have the poor got by their encroachments for the last ten years? Do they work less hard? Are they better fed? Do they marry oftener, and with better prospects? Are they grown pampered and insolent? Have they changed places with the rich? Have they been cunning enough, by means of the poor-laws, to draw off all their wealth and superfluities from the men of property? Have they got so much as a quarter of an hour's leisure, a farthing candle, or a cheese-paring more than they had? Has not the price of provisions risen enormously? Has not the price of labour almost stood still? Have not the government and the rich had their way in every thing? Have they not gratified their ambition, their pride, their obstinacy, their ruinous extravagance? Have they not squandered the resources of the country as they pleased? Have they not heaped up wealth on themselves, and their dependents? Have they not multiplied sinecures, places, and pensions? Have they not doubled the salaries of those that existed before? Has there been any want of new creations of peers, who would thus be impelled to beget heirs to their titles and estates, and saddle the younger branches of their rising families, by means of their new influence, on the country at large? Has there been any want of contracts, of loans, of monopolies of corn, of a good understanding between the rich and the powerful to assist one another, and to fleece the poor? Have the poor prospered? Have the rich declined? What then have they to complain of? What ground is there for the apprehension, that wealth is secretly changing hands, and that the whole property of the country will shortly be absorbed in the poor's fund? Do not the poor create their own fund? Is not the necessity for such a fund first occasioned by the unequal weight with which the rich press upon the poor; and has not the increase of that fund in the last ten years been occasioned by the additional exorbitant demands, which have been made upon the poor and industrious, which, without some assistance from the public, they could not possibly have answered? Whatever is the increase in the nominal amount of the poor's fund, will not the rich always be able ultimately to throw the burthen of it on the poor themselves? But Mr Malthus is a man of general principles. He cares little about these circumstantial details, and petty objections. He takes higher ground. He deduces all his conclusions, by an infallible logic, from the laws of God and nature. When our Essayist shall prove to me, that by these paper bullets of the brain,* by his ratios of the increase of food, and the increase of mankind, he has prevented one additional tax, or taken off one oppressive duty, that he has made a single rich man retrench one article at his table: that he has made him keep a dog or a horse the less, or part with a single vice, arguing from a mathematical admeasurement of the size of the earth, and the number of inhabitants it can contain, he shall have my perfect leave to disclaim the right of the poor to subsistence, and to tie them down by severe penalties to their good behaviour, on the same profound principles. But why does Mr Malthus practise his demonstrations on the poor only? Why are they to have a perfect system of rights and duties prescribed to them? I do not see why they alone should be put to live on these metaphysical board-wages, why they should be forced to submit to a course of *abstraction*; or why it should be meat and drink to them, more than to others, to do the will of God. Mr Malthus's gospel is preached only to the poor!— Even if I approved of our author's plan, I should object to the principle on which it is founded. The parson of the parish, when a poor man comes to be married—No, not so fast. The author does not say, whether the lecture he proposes is to be read to the poor only, or to all ranks of people. Would it not sound oddly, if when the squire, who is himself worth a hundred thousand pounds, is going to be married to the rector's daughter, who is to have fifty, the curate should read them a formal lecture on their obligation to maintain their own children and not turn them on the parish? Would it be necessary to go through the form of the address, when an

amorous couple of eighty presented themselves at the altar?
If the admonition were left to the parson's own discretion,
what affronts would he not subject himself to, from his neglect
of old maids, and superannuated widows, and from his applying himself familiarly to the little shopkeeper, or thriving
mechanic? Well, then, let us suppose that a very poor hard-
working man comes to be married, and that the clergyman
can take the liberty with him: he is to warn him first against
fornication, and in the next place against matrimony. These
are the two greatest sins which a poor man can commit, who
can neither be supposed to keep his wife, nor his girl. Mr
Malthus, however, does not think them equal: for he objects
strongly to a country fellow's marrying a girl whom he has
debauched, or, as the phrase is, making an honest woman of
her, as aggravating the crime; because, by this means, the
parish will probably have three or four children to maintain
instead of one. However, as it seems rather too late to give
advice to a man who is actually come to be married, it is most
natural to suppose that he would marry the young woman in
spite of the lecture. Here then he errs in the face of a precise
warning, and should be left to the punishment of *nature*, the
punishment of severe want. When he begins to feel the consequences of his error, all parish assistance is to be rigidly
denied him, and the interests of humanity imperiously require that all other assistance should be withheld from him,
or most sparingly administered. In the meantime, to reconcile
him to this treatment, and let him see that he has nobody to
complain of but himself, the parson of the parish comes to
him with the certificate of his marriage, and a copy of the
warning he had given him at the time, by which he is taught
to know that the laws of nature, which are the laws of God,
had doomed him and his family to starve for disobeying their
repeated admonitions; that he had no claim of right to the
smallest portion of food beyond what his labour would actually purchase; and that he ought to kiss the feet and lick the
dust off the shoes of him, who gave him a reprieve from the
just sentence which the laws of God and nature had passed
upon him. To make this clear to him, it would be necessary
to put the Essay on Population into his hands, to instruct him

in the nature of a geometrical and arithmetical series, in the necessary limits to population from the size of the earth; and here would come in Mr Malthus's plan of education for the poor, writing, arithmetic, the use of the globes, &c. for the purpose of proving to them the necessity of their being starved. It cannot be supposed that the poor man (what with his poverty and what with being priest-ridden) should be able to resist this body of evidence, he would open his eyes to his error, and "would submit to the sufferings that were absolutely irremediable, with the fortitude of a man, and the resignation of a Christian".* He and his family might then be sent round the parish in a starving condition, accompanied by the constables and *quondam* overseers of the poor, to see that no person, blind to "the interests of humanity",* practised upon them the abominable deception of attempting to relieve their remediless sufferings; and by the parson of the parish, to point out to the spectators the inevitable consequences of sinning against the laws of God and man. By celebrating a number of these *Autos-da-fé* * yearly in every parish, the greatest publicity would be given to the principle of population, "the strict line of duty would be pointed out to every man",* enforced by the most powerful sanctions; justice and humanity would flourish, they would be understood to signify that the poor have no right to live by their labour, and that the feelings of compassion and benevolence are best shewn by denying them charity; the poor would no longer be dependent on the rich, the rich could no longer wish to reduce the poor into a more complete subjection to their will, all causes of contention, of jealousy, and of irritation would have ceased between them, the struggle would be over, each class would fulfil the task assigned by heaven; the rich would oppress the poor without remorse, the poor would submit to oppression with a pious gratitude and resignation; the greatest harmony would prevail between the government and the people; there would be no longer any seditions, tumults, complaints, petitions, partisans of liberty, or tools of power; no grumbling, no repining, no discontented men of talents proposing reforms, and frivolous remedies, but we should all have the same gaiety and lightness of heart, and the same happy spirit of resignation that a man feels when he is seized with the plague, who thinks no more of the physician, but knows that his disorder is without cure. The best-laid schemes are subject, however, to unlucky reverses. Some such seem to lie in the way of that pleasing Euthanasia, and contented submission to the grinding law of necessity, projected by Mr Malthus. We might never reach the philosophic temper of the inhabitants of modern Greece and Turkey in this respect. Many little things might happen to interrupt our progress, if we were put into ever so fair a train. For instance, the men might perhaps be talked over by the parson, and their understandings being convinced by the geometrical and arithmetical ratios, or at least so far puzzled, that they would have nothing to say for themselves, they might prepare to submit to their fate with a tolerable grace. But I am afraid that the women might prove refractory. They never will hearken to reason, and are much more governed by their feelings than by calculations. While the husband was instructing his wife in the principles of population, she might probably answer that "she did not see why her children should starve, when the squire's lady or the parson's lady kept half a dozen lap-dogs, and that it was but the other day, that being at the hall, or the parsonage-house, she heard Miss declare that not one of the brood that were just littered should be drowned—It was *so inhuman* to kill the poor little things— Surely the children of the poor are as good as puppy-dogs! Was it not a week ago that the rector had a new pack of terriers sent down, and did I not hear the squire swear a tremendous oath, that he would have Mr Such-a-one's fine hunter, if it cost him a hundred guineas? Half that sum would save us from ruin."—After this curtain- lecture,* I conceive that the husband might begin to doubt the force of the demonstrations he had read and heard, and the next time his clerical monitor came, might pluck up courage to question the matter with him; and as we of the male sex, though dull of apprehension, are not slow at taking a hint, and can draw tough inferences from it, it is not impossible but the parson might be *gravelled.** In consequence of these accidents happening more than once, it would be buzzed about that the laws of God and nature, on which so many families had been doomed to starve, were not so clear as had been pretended. This would soon get wind amongst the mob: and at the next grand procession of the Penitents of famine, headed by Mr Malthus in person, some discontented man of talents, who could not bear the distresses of others with the fortitude of a man and the resignation of a Christian, might undertake to question Mr Malthus, whether the laws of nature or of God, to which he had piously sacrificed so many victims, signified any thing more than the limited extent of the earth, and the natural impossibility of providing for more than a limited number of human beings; and whether those laws could be justly put in force, to the very letter, while the actual produce of the earth, by being better husbanded, or more equally distributed, or given to men and not to beasts, might maintain in comfort double the number that actually existed, and who, not daring to demand a *fair* proportion of the produce of their labour, humbly crave charity, and are refused out of regard to the interests of justice and humanity. Our philosopher, at this critical juncture not being able to bring into the compass of a few words all the history, metaphysics, morality, and divinity, or all the intricacies, subtleties, and callous equivocations contained in his quarto volume, might hesitate and be confounded—his own feelings and prejudices might add to his perplexity—his interrogator might persist in his question— the mob might become impatient for an answer, and not finding one to their minds, might proceed to extremities. Our unfortunate Essayist (who by that time would have become a bishop) might be ordered to the lamp-post, and his book committed to the flames,—I tremble to think of what would follow:—the poor-laws would be again renewed, and the poor no longer doomed to starve by the laws of God and nature! Some such, I apprehend, might be the consequences of attempting to enforce the abolition of the poor-laws, the extinction of private charity, and of instructing the poor in their metaphysical rights.'

THE FRENCH REVOLUTION

I

THE French Revolution might be described as a remote but inevitable result of the invention of the art of printing. The gift of speech, or the communication of thought by words, is that which distinguishes man from other animals. But this faculty is limited and imperfect without the intervention of books, which render the knowledge possessed by every one in the community accessible to all. There is no doubt, then, that the press (as it has existed in modern times) is the great organ of intellectual improvement and civilisation.* It was impossible in this point of view, that those institutions, which were founded in a state of society and manners long anterior to this second breathing of understanding into the life of man, should remain on the same proud footing after it, with all their disproportions and defects. Many of these, indeed, must be softened by the lapse of time and influence of opinion, and give way of their own accord: but others are too deeply rooted in the passions and interests of men to be wrenched asunder without violence, or by the mutual consent of the parties concerned; and it is this which makes revolutions necessary, with their train of lasting good and present evil. When a government, like an old-fashioned building, has become crazy and rotten, stops the way of improvement, and only serves to collect diseases and corruption, and the proprietors refuse to come to any compromise, the community proceed in this as in some other cases; they set summarily to work—'they pull down the house, they abate the nuisance.'* All other things had changed: why then should governments remain the same, an excrescence and an incumbrance on the state? It is only because they have most power and most interest to continue their abuses. This circumstance is a reason why it is doubly incumbent on those who are aggrieved by them to get rid of them; and makes the shock the greater, when opinion at last becomes a match for arbitrary power.

The feudal system was in full vigour almost up to the period of the discovery of printing. Much had been done since that time: but it was the object of the French Revolution to get rid at one blow of the frame-work and of the last relics of that system. Before the diffusion of knowledge and inquiry, governments were for the most part the growth of brute force or of barbarous superstition. Power was in the hands of a few, who used it only to gratify their own pride, cruelty, or avarice, and who took every means to extend and cement it by fear and favour. The lords of the earth, disdaining to rule by the choice or for the benefit of the mass of the community, whom they regarded and treated as no better than a herd of cattle, derived their title from the skies, pretending to be accountable for the exercise or abuse of their authority to God only— the throne rested on the altar, and every species of atrocity or wanton insult having power on its side, received the sanction of religion, which it was thenceforth impiety and rebellion against the will of Heaven to impugn. This state of things continued and grew worse and worse, while knowledge and power were confined within mere local and personal limits. Each petty sovereign shut himself up in his castle or fortress, and scattered havoc and dismay over the unresisting country around him. In an age of ignorance and barbarism, when force and interest decided every thing, and reason had no means of making itself heard, what was to prevent this, or act as a check upon it? The lord himself had no other measure of right than his own will: his pride and passions would blind him to every consideration of conscience or humanity; he would regard every act of disobedience as a crime of the deepest die, and to give unbridled sway to his lawless humours, would become the ruling passion and sole study of his life. How would it stand with those within the immediate circle of his influence or his vengeance? Fear would make them cringe, and lick the feet of their haughty and capricious oppressor: the hope of reward or the dread of punishment would stifle the sense of justice or pity; despair of success would make them cowards, habit would confirm them into slaves, and they would look up with bigotted devotion (the boasted *loyalty* of the good old times) to the right of the strongest as the only law. A king would only be the head of a confederation of such petty despots, and the happiness or rights of the people would be equally disregarded by them both. Religion, instead of curbing this state of rapine and licentiousness, became an accomplice and a party in the crime; gave absolution and plenary indulgence for all sorts of enormities; granting the forgiveness of Heaven in return for a rich jewel or fat abbey-lands, and setting up a regular (and what in the end proved an intolerable) traffic in violence, cruelty, and lust. As to the restraints of law, there was none but what resided in the breast of the *Grand Seigneur*, who hung up in his courtyard, without judge or jury, any one who dared to utter the slightest murmur against the most flagrant wrong. Such must be the consequence, as long as there was no common standard or impartial judge to appeal to; and this could only be found in public opinion, the offspring of books. As long as any unjust claim or transaction was confined to the knowledge of the parties concerned, the tyrant and the slave, which is the case in all unlettered states of society, *might* must prevail over *right*; for the strongest would bully, and the weakest must submit, even in his own defence, and persuade himself that he was in the wrong, even in his own despite: but the instant the world (that dread jury) are impannelled, and called to look on and be umpires in the scene, so that nothing is done by connivance or in a corner, then reason mounts the judgment-seat in lieu of passion or interest, and opinion becomes law, instead of arbitrary will; and farewell feudal lord and sovereign king!

From the moment that the press opens the eyes of the community beyond the actual sphere in which each moves, there is from that time inevitably formed the germ of a body of opinion directly at variance with the selfish and servile code that before reigned paramount, and approximating more and more to the manly and disinterested standard of truth and justice. Hitherto force, fraud, and fear decided every question of individual right or general reasoning; the possessor of rank and influence, in answer to any censure or objection to his conduct, appealed to God and to his sword:—now a new principle is brought into play which had never been so much as dreamt of, and before which he must make good his pretensions, or it will shatter his strongholds of pride and prejudice to atoms, as the pent-up air shatters whatever resists its expansive force. This power is public opinion, exercised upon men, things, and general principles, and to which mere physical power must conform, or it will crumble it to powder. Books alone teach us to judge of truth and good in the abstract: without a knowledge of things at a distance from us, we judge like savages or animals from our senses and appetites only; but by the aid of books and of an intercourse with the world of ideas, we are purified, raised, ennobled from savages into intellectual and rational beings. Our impressions of what is near to us are false, of what is distant feeble; but the last gaining strength from being united in public opinion, and expressed by the public voice, are like the congregated roar of many waters, and quail the hearts of princes. Who but the tyrant does not hate the tyrant? Who but the slave does not despise the slave? The first of these looks upon himself as a God, upon his vassal as a clod of the earth, and forces him to be of the same opinion: the philosopher looks upon them both as men, and instructs the world to do so. While they had to settle their pretensions by themselves, and in the night of ignorance, it is no wonder no good was done; while pride intoxicated the one, and fear stupefied the other. But let them be brought out of that dark cave of despotism and superstition, and let a thousand other persons, who have no interest but that of truth and justice, be called on to determine between them, and the plea of the lordly oppressor to make a beast of burden of his fellow-man becomes as ridiculous as it is odious. All that the light of philosophy, the glow of patriotism, all that the brain wasted in midnight study, the blood poured out upon the scaffold or in the field of battle can do or have done, is to take this question in all cases from before the first gross, blind and iniquitous tribunal, where power insults over weakness, and place it before the last more just, disinterested, and in the end more formidable one, where each individual is tried by his peers, and according to rules and principles which have received the common examination and the common consent. A public sense is thus formed, free from slavish awe or the traditional assumption of insolent superiority, which the more it is exercised becomes the more enlightened and enlarged, and more and more requires equal rights and equal laws. This new sense acquired by the people, this new organ of opinion and feeling, is like bringing a battering-train to bear upon some old Gothic castle, long the den of rapine and crime, and must finally prevail against all absurd and antiquated institutions, unless it is violently suppressed, and this engine of political reform turned by bribery and terror against itself. Who in reading history, where the characters are laid open and the circumstances fairly stated, and where he himself has no false bias to mislead him, does not take part with the oppressed against the oppressor? Who is there that admires Nero at the distance of two thousand years? Did not the *Tartuffe** in a manner hoot religious hypocrisy out of France; and was it not on this account constantly denounced by the clergy? What do those, who read the annals of the Inquisition, think of that dread tribunal? And what has softened its horrors but those annals being read? What figure does the massacre of St Bartholomew make in the eyes of posterity? But books anticipate and conform the decision of the public, of individuals, and even of the actors in such scenes, to that lofty and irrevocable standard, mould and fashion the heart and inmost thoughts upon it, so that something manly, liberal, and generous grows out of the fever of passion and the palsy of base fear; and this is what is meant by the progress of modern civilisation and modern philosophy.* An individual in a barbarous age and country throws another who has displeased him (without other warrant than his will) into a dungeon, where he pines for years, and then dies; and perhaps only the mouldering bones of the victim, discovered long after, disclose his fate: or if known at the time, the confessor gives absolution, and the few who are let into the secret are intimidated from giving vent to their feelings, and hardly dare disapprove in silence. Let this act of violence be repeated afterwards in story, and there is not an individual in the whole nation whose bosom does not swell with pity, or whose blood does not curdle within him at the recital of so foul a wrong. Why then should there be an individual in a nation privileged to do what no other individual in the nation can be found to approve? But he has the power, and will not part with it in spite of public opinion. Then that public opinion must become active, and break the moulds of prescription in which his right derived from his ancestors is cast, and this will be a Revolution. Is that a state of things to regret or bring back, the bare mention of which makes one shudder? But the form, the shadow of it only was left: then why keep up that form, or cling to a shadow of injustice, which is no less odious than contemptible, except to make an improper use of it? Let all the wrongs public and private produced in France by arbitrary power and exclusive privileges for a thousand years be collected in a volume, and let this volume be read by all who have hearts to feel or capacity to understand, and the strong, stifling sense of oppression and kindling burst of indignation that would follow will be that impulse of public opinion that led to the French Revolution. Let all the victims that have perished under the mild, paternal sway* of the ancient *régime*, in dungeons, and in agony, without a trial, without an accusation, without witnesses, be assembled together, and their chains struck off, and the shout of jubilee and exultation they would make, or that nature would make at the sight, will be the shout that was heard when the Bastille fell! The dead pause that ensued among the Gods of the earth, the rankling malice, the panic-fear, when they saw law and justice raised to an equality with their sovereign will, and mankind no longer doomed to be their sport, was that of fiends robbed of their prey: their struggles, their arts, their unyielding perseverance, and their final triumph was that of fiends when it is restored to them!

It has been sometimes pretended as if the French Revolution burst out like a volcano, without any previous warning, only to alarm and destroy—or was one of those comet-like appearances, the approach of which no one can tell till the shock and conflagration are felt. What is the real state of the case? There was not one of those abuses and grievances which the rough grasp of the Revolution shook to air, that had not been the butt of ridicule, the theme of indignant invective, the subject of serious reprobation for near a century. They had been held up without ceasing and without answer to the derision of the gay, the scorn of the wise, the sorrow of the good. The most witty, the most eloquent, the most profound writers were unanimous in their wish to remove or reform these abuses, and the most dispassionate and well-informed part of the community joined in the sentiment: it was only the self-interested or the grossly ignorant who obstinately clung to them. Every public and private complaint had been subjected to the touchstone of inquiry and argument; the page of history, of fiction, of the drama, of philosophy had been laid open, and their contents poured into the public ear, which turned away disgusted from the arts of sophistry or the menace of authority. It was this operation of opinion, enlarging its circle, and uniting nearly all the talents, the patriotism, and the independence of the country in its service, that brought about the events which followed. Nothing else did or could. It was not a dearth of provisions, the loss of the queen's jewels, that could overturn all the institutions and usages of a great kingdom—it was not the Revolution that produced the change in the face of society, but the change in the texture of society that produced the Revolution, and brought its outward appearance into a nearer correspondence with its inward sentiments. There is no other way of accounting for so great and sudden a transition. Power, prejudice, interest, custom, ignorance, sloth, and cowardice were against it: what then remained to counterbalance this weight, and to overturn all obstacles, but reason and conviction which were for it? *Magna est veritas, et prevalebit.** A king was no longer thought to be an image of the Divinity; a lord to be of a different species from other men; a priest to carry an immediate passport to heaven in his pocket. On what possible plea or excuse then, when the ground of opinion on which they rested was gone, attempt to keep up the same exclusive and exorbitant pretensions, without any equivalent to the community in the awe and veneration they felt for them? Why should a nobleman be permitted to spit in your face, to rob you of an estate, or to debauch your wife or daughter with impunity, when it was no longer deemed an honour for him to do so? If manners had undergone a considerable change in this respect, so that the right was rarely exercised, why not abrogate the insult implied in the very forbearance from the injury, alike intolerable to the free-born spirit of man? Why suspend the blow over your head, if it was not meant to descend upon it? Or why hold up claims in idle mockery, which good sense and reason alike disowned, as if there were really a distinction in the two classes of society, and the one were rightful lords over the other, instead of being by nature all equal? But the evil did not stop here; for it was never yet known that men wished to retain the semblance of a wrong, unless they aimed at profiting as far as in them lay by the practice of it. While the king wore the anointed crown that was supposed to be let down in a golden chain from heaven on his head, while the lord dyed his sword in blood, while the priest worked fancied miracles with a crucifix and beads, they did well to claim to be masters of the world, and to trample in triple phalanx on mankind: but why they should expect us to allow this claim in mere courtesy and goodwill, when it is no longer *backed* by fraud or force, is difficult to comprehend. What is a legitimate government? It is a government that professedly derives its title from the grace of God and its ancestors, that sets the choice or the good of the governed equally at defiance, and that is amenable for the use it makes of its power only to its own caprice, pride, or malice. It is an outrage and a burlesque on every principle of common sense or liberty. It puts the means for the end: mistakes a trust for a property, considers the honours and offices of the state as its natural inheritance, and the law as an unjust encroachment on its arbitrary will. What motive can there be for tolerating such a government a single instant, except from sheer necessity or blindfold ignorance? Or what chance of modifying it so as to answer any good purpose, without a total subversion of all its institutions, principles, or prejudices? The kings of France, tamed by opinion, conforming to the manners of the time, no longer stabbed a faithful counsellor in the presence-chamber, or strangled a competitor for the throne in a dungeon, or laid waste a country or fired a city for a whim: but they still made peace or war as they pleased, or hung the wealth of a province in a mistress's ear, or lost a battle by the promotion of a favourite, or ruined a treasury by the incapacity of a minister of high birth and connexions. The noble no longer, as in days of yore, hung up his vassal at his door for a disrespectful word or look (which was called the *haute justice*), or issued with a numerous retinue from his lofty portcullis to carry fire and sword into the neighbouring country; but he too laboured in his vocation, and in the proud voluptuous city drained the last pittance from the toil-worn peasant by taxes, grants, and exactions, to waste it on his own vanity, luxury, and vices. If he had a quarrel with an inferior or with a rival less favoured than himself, the king would issue his *lettre-de-cachet*,* and give the refractory and unsuspecting offender a lodging for life in what Mr Burke is pleased to call the *'king's castle!'** Had opinion put a stop to this crying abuse, had it rendered this odious privilege of royalty merely nominal? 'In the mild reign of Louis XV alone,' according to Blackstone, 'there were no less than 15,000 *lettres-de-cachet* issued.' Some persons will think this fact alone sufficient to account for and to justify the overturning of the government in the reign of his successor. The priests no longer tied their victim to the stake or devoted him to the assassin's poniard as of old; they thought it enough if they could wallow in the fat of the land, pander to the vices of the rich and the abuses of power, to which they looked for the continuance of wealth and influence, and fly-blow every liberal argument and persecute every liberal writer, from whom they dreaded their loss. From the moment that the ancient *régime* ceased to be supported by that system of faith and manners in which it had originated, the whole order of the state became warped and disunited, a wretched jumble of claims that were neither enforced nor relinquished. There was ill-blood sown between the government and the people; heart-burning, jealousy, and want of confidence between the different members of the community. Every advance in civilisation was regarded by one party with dislike and distrust, while by the other every privilege held by ancient tenure was censured as the offspring of pride and prejudice. The court was like a decayed beauty, that viewed her youthful rival's charms with scorn and apprehension. The nation, in the language of the day, *had hitherto been*

nothing, was every thing, and wanted to be something. The great
mass of society felt itself as a degraded *caste*, and was determined to wipe out the stigma with which every one of its
opinions, sentiments and pretensions was branded. This was
a thing no longer to be endured and must be got rid of at any
rate.

II

The excesses of the French Revolution have indeed been
considered as an anomaly in history, as a case taken out of
every rule or principle of morality by comparison with any
thing else. But there are three tests by which we may form a
tolerably fair estimate of the characters and motives of those
concerned in it. First, do we not see the hold which the love
of power and all strong excitement takes of the mind; how it
engrosses the faculties, stifles compunction, and deadens the
sense of shame, even when it is purely selfish or mischievous,
when it does not even pretend to have any good in view, and
when we have all the world against us? What then must be the
force and confidence in itself which any such passion, ambition, cruelty, revenge, must acquire when it is founded on
some lofty and high-sounding principle, patriotism, liberty,
resistance to tyrants; when it aims at the public good as its
consequence, and is strengthened by the applause of the
multitude? Evil is strong enough in itself; when it has good
for its end, it is conscience-proof. If the common bravo or
cut-throat who stabs another merely to fill his purse or revenge
a private grudge, can hardly be persuaded that he does wrong,
and postpones his remorse till long after—he who sheds
blood like water, but can contrive to do it with some fine-
sounding name on his lips, will be in his own eyes little less
than a saint or martyr. Robespierre was a professed admirer
of Rousseau's *Social Contract* and the *Profession of Faith of a
Savoyard Vicar*; and I do not conceive it impossible that he
thought of these when the mob were dancing round him at
his own door. He would certainly have sent any one to the
guillotine who should have confuted him in a dispute on the
one or have ridiculed the other; but this would not prove that
he had altered his opinion of either. He was a political pedant,

a violent dogmatist, weak in argument, and who wished to be
strong in fact. Every head he cut off, he felt his power the
greater; with the increase of power, he felt his opinions confirmed, and with the certainty of his opinions, the security for
the welfare and liberty of mankind. These were the rollers on
which his actions moved, spreading ruin and dismay in large
and sweeping circles; these were the theoretical moulds in
which cruelty, suspicion, and proscription were cast, which
according to the abstractedness, or what in the cant of the day
was called the *purity* of his principles, embraced a wider
sphere, and called for unlimited sacrifices. The habitual and
increasing lust of power and gratification in counting his
victims did not enable him to disentangle the sophistry which
bewildered him or prove to him that he was in the wrong, but
the contrary, however the actual results might occasionally
stagger him: to save was in his mind to destroy, to destroy was
to save; and he remained in all probability as great a contradiction to himself as he has been an anomaly and riddle incapable of solution to others. The fault of such characters is
not the absence of strictness of principle or a sense of duty,
but an excess of these over their natural sensibility or instinctive prejudices, which makes them both dangerous to the
community and hateful in themselves by their obstinate determination to carry into effect any dogma or theory to which
they have made up their minds, be the objections or consequences what they will. Such instruments may indeed be
wanted for great and trying occasions; but their being thrown
into such a situation does not alter the odiousness of their
characters nor the opinion of mankind concerning them. The
action alone is certain; the motive is hid; the future benefit
doubtful. Fame and even virtue are to a certain degree common-
place things! This 'differences' Robespierre* from characters
of mere natural ferocity or from the tyrants of antiquity, who
indulged in the same insatiable barbarity only to pamper their
personal pride and sense of self-importance. Robespierre was
nothing in himself but as the guider of a machine, the mouth-
piece of an abstract proposition; he would hurt no one but
for differing from him in an opinion, which he had worked
himself up to believe was the link that held the world together,

the peg on which the safety of the state hung, the very 'key-stone that made up the arch'* of the social fabric, and that if it was removed, the whole fell together to cureless ruin.

Secondly, let those who deny this view of the subject explain if they can the conduct of religious persecutors and tyrants for conscience' sake. The religious and the political fanatic are one and the same character, and run into the same errors on the same grounds. Nothing can surely surpass the excesses, the horrors, the refinements in cruelty, and the cold-blooded malignity which have been exercised in the name and under the garb of religion. Yet who will say that this strikes at the root of religion itself or that the instigators and perpetrators of these horrors were men without one particle of the goodness and sanctity to which they made such lofty and exclusive pretensions; that they were not many of them patterns of sincerity, piety, and the most disinterested zeal (who were ready to undergo the same fate they inflicted on others); and that in consigning their opponents to the stake, the dagger, or the dungeon, they did not believe they were doing God and man good service? The kindling pile, the paper-caps of the victims at an *auto-da-fé*, the instruments of torture, the solemn hymn, the shout of triumph, the callousness of the executioner, the gravity of the judges are circumstances sufficiently revolting to human nature; but to argue from hence that those who sanctioned or who periodically assisted at such scenes were mere monsters of cruelty and hypocrisy, would be betraying a total ignorance of the contradictions of the human mind. All sects, all religions have retaliated upon one another where they had the power, and some of the best and most enlightened men have been zealots in the cause. We see by this how far an opinion, the conviction of an abstract and contingent good will carry men to violate all their natural feelings and all common ties conscientiously and in the face of day; nor should we imagine that this is confined to religion. I grant that religion being of the highest and least questionable authority has caused more fanaticism and bigotry, more massacres and persecutions than any thing else; but whatever cause, religion, patriotism, freedom, can strongly excite the affections and agitate large masses of men, will produce the same blindfold and headlong zeal, and plead the same excuse for the excesses of its adherents. At the same time I think that those who have been most forward to distinguish themselves as bigots and persecutors have been generally men of austere, vindictive, and narrow minds; and their names are branded in history accordingly.

Thirdly, there is some affinity between foreign and civil war. We pour molten lead on the heads of those who are scaling the walls of a city; but this would be of no use if those within could be found delivering up the keys with impunity. Why then are all our pity and complaints reserved for the evils of civil war, since the passions are as much excited and the danger as great in the one case as in the other? No one will compare Shaw the Life-guards'-man with the celebrated Coup-Tête;* the one was a gallant soldier, the other a sneaking villain; yet the one cut off as many heads in a day as the other; it is not the blood shed then, but the manner and motive; the one braved a formidable enemy in the field, the other gloated over a hapless victim. We distinguish the soldier and the assassin; to be just, we must distinguish between public and private malice. But here comes in the hypocrisy or cowardice of mankind. In war, the enemy is open and challenges your utmost malice; so that there is nothing more to be said. In conspiracy and civil strife, the enemy is either secret and doubtful or lies at your mercy; and after the catastrophe is over, it is pretended that he was both helpless and innocent, entitled to pity in himself and fixing an indelible stain on his dastardly and cruel oppressor. Here then is again required in times of revolution that *moral courage*, which uses a discretionary power and takes an awful responsibility upon itself, going right forward to its object, and setting fastidious scruples, character, and consequences (all but principle and self-preservation) at defiance. What were the leaders of the Revolution to do? Were they to suffer a renewal of the massacres of Ismael and Warsaw,* by those tender preachers of morality and the puling sentimentalists that follow in their train, who think to crush men like worms and complain that they have trod on asps? They not only had these scenes fresh before their eyes, but they were in part the same identical persons who threatened to treat them with a second course of them! 'Rather than so, come Fate into the lists and champion us to the outrance!'*—seems to have been the motto of the Revolutionists and their reply. Were they not to anticipate the ignominious blow prepared for them by their insolent invaders? Or should they spare those who stood gaping by and beckoning others on to their banquet of blood? But the number of these last increased, and made it difficult to know where to strike. It was this very uncertainty that distracted and irritated the government; and in the multitude and concealment of their adversaries, hurried them forward to indiscriminate fury. What the Revolution wanted, and what Robespierre did for it in these circumstances, was to give to the political machine the utmost possible *momentum* and energy of which it was capable; to stagger the presumption and pride of the Coalition by shewing on the opposite side an equally inveterate and intense degree of determined hostility and ruthless vengeance; to out-face, to out-dare; to stand the brunt not only of all the violence but of all the cant, hypocrisy, obloquy and prejudice with which they were assailed; to stamp on the revolution a *practical* character; to wipe out the imputation of visionary and Utopian refinement and consequent imbecility from all plans of reform; to prove that 'brave Sansculottes were no triflers;'* and to enlist all passions, all interests, all classes, and all the resources of the country in the one great object, the defence of the Republic. The decks were cleared as for a battle, all other considerations, scruples, objections were thrown on one side; and the only question being to save the vessel of the state, it was saved. Under this impulse the Revolution went on through all chances and changes, 'like tumbler-pigeons making all sorts of summersaults and evolutions of figure,'* but never losing sight of its goal, and arriving safe at its place of destination. All feelings, all pretensions, all characters, levity, brutality, rage, envy, ambition, self- interest, generosity, refinement, were melted down in the furnace of the Revolution, but all heightened the flame and swelled the torrent of patriotism. The blaze thus kindled threw its glare on all objects, so that the whole passed in a strange, preternatural light, that precluded the discrimination of motives or characters. Nor was it necessary to distinguish to a nicety. The great point was to distinguish friends from foes, and for this purpose they were put to a speedy probation. Otherwise, it was not asked whether a man wore a long beard or a short one, whether he carried an axe or a pike, no attention was paid to the *dramatis personæ* or to costume—but all to the conduct of the fable and to bringing about the catastrophe! Every state contains within itself the means of salvation, if it will look its danger in the face and not shrink from the course actually necessary to save it. But to do this, it must rise to the magnitude of the occasion, above rules and appearances. France, baited, hunted down as she was, had but one resource left to retaliate on her aggressors, to throw aside all self-regards and all regards for others, and in order to escape from the toils spread around, to discard all obligations, and cut asunder the very nerves of humanity. Few persons could be found to help her at this exigency so well as Robespierre. The Brissotins, who were fine gentlemen, would have been entangled in 'the drapery of a moral imagination':* Robespierre, to give no hold to his adversary, fought the battle naked and threw away both shame and fear. When it comes to the abstract choice between slavery or freedom, principles are of more importance than individuals; it is to be apprehended that an energy and pertinacity of character that would not have exceeded the occasion, would not have come up to it; and we see that when the dread of hostile invasion or domestic treachery no longer existed and tyrannised over the minds of men, the reign of terror ceased with the extreme causes that had provoked and alone rendered its continuance endurable.*

CULTURE

ON MODERN COMEDY

...BUT your Correspondent sees nothing in the progress of modern manners and characters but a vague, abstract progression from grossness to refinement, marked on a graduated scale of human perfectibility. This sweeping distinction appears to him to explain satisfactorily the whole difference between all sorts of manners, and all kinds and degrees of dramatic excellence. These two words stand him instead of other ideas on the texture of society, or the nature of the dramatic art. He is not, however, quite consistent on this subject, for in one place he says, that 'the stock of folly in the world is in no danger of being diminished,' and in the next sentence, that there is a progression in society, an age of grossness and an age of refinement, and he only wonders that the progress of the stage does not keep pace with it. Now the reason why I do not share his wonder is, that though I think the quantity of dull, dry, serious, incorrigible folly in the world is in no danger of being diminished, yet I think the stock of lively, dramatic, entertaining, laughable folly is, and necessarily must be, diminished by the progress of that *mechanical* refinement which consists in throwing our follies, as it were, into a common stock, and moulding them in the same general form. Our peculiarities have become insipid sameness; our eccentricity servile imitation; our wit, wisdom at second-hand; our prejudices indifference; our feelings not our own; our distinguishing characteristic the want of all character. We are become a nation of authors and readers, and even this distinction is confounded by the mediation of the reviewers. We all follow the same profession, which is criticism, each individual is every thing but himself, not one but all mankind's epitome,* and the gradations of vice and virtue, of sense and folly, of refinement and grossness of character, seem lost in a kind of intellectual *hermaphroditism.* But on this *tabula rasa,* according to your Correspondent, the most lively and sparkling hues of comedy may be laid. His present reasoning gives

a very different turn to the question he at first proposed. He
appears to have set out with a theory of his own about the
production of comic excellence, in which it was entirely regu-
lated by the state of the market, and to have supposed that as
long as authors continued to write plays, and managers to
accept them, that is, so long as the thing answered in the way
of trade, Comedy would go on pretty much as it had hitherto
done, to the end of the world. But finding that this was not
exactly the case, he takes his stand near the avenues leading
to the manager's door, and happening to see a young man of
worth and talents, with great knowledge of the world, and of
the refinements of polished society, come out with his piece
in his hand, and a face of disappointment, he is no longer at
a loss for the secret of the decline of Comedy among us, and
proceeds cautiously to hint his discovery to the world. But it
being suggested to him that the change of manners, produced
partly by the stage itself, and the total disappearance of the
characters which before formed the very life and soul of
Comedy, might have something to do with the decline of the
Stage, he will not hear a word of it, but says, that this circumstance, so far from shewing why our modern Comedies
are not so good as the old ones, proves that they *ought to be better*;
that the more we are become like one another, or like nothing, the less distinction of character we have, the greater
discrimination must it require to bring it out; that the less
ridiculous our manners become, the more scope do they
afford for art and ingenuity in discovering our weak sides and
shades of infirmity; and that the greatest sameness and monotony must in the end produce the most exquisite variety. For
a plain man, this is very well. It is on the same principle, that
some writers have contended that Scotland is more fertile
than England, the excellence of the crop being in proportion
to the barrenness of the soil. What a pity it is, that so ingenious
a theory should not have the facts on its side; and that the
perfection of satire should not be found to keep pace with
the want of materials. It is rather too much to assume on a
mere hypothesis, that the present manners are equally favourable to the production of the highest comic excellence, till
they do produce it. Even in France, where encouragement is

given to the noblest and most successful exertions of genius by the sure prospect of profit to yourself or your descendants, every time your piece is acted in any corner of the empire, to the latest posterity, we find the best critics going back to the grossness and illiberality of the age of Louis XIV for the production of the best comedies; which is rather extraordinary, considering the infinitely refined state of manners in France, and the infinite encouragement given to dramatic talent. But has it never occurred to your Correspondent, as a solution of this difficulty, that there is a difference between refinement and imbecility, between general knowledge and personal elegance, between metaphysical subtlety and stage-effect? Does he think all manners, all kinds of folly, and all shades of character equally fit for dramatic representation? Does he not perceive that there is a point where minuteness of distinction becomes laborious foolery, and where the slenderness of the materials must baffle the skill and destroy the exertions of the artist? He insists, indeed, on pulling off the mask of folly, by some ingenious device, though she has been stripped of it long ago; and forced to compose her features into a decent appearance of gravity; and he next proceeds to apply a microscope of a new construction, to detect the freckles on her face and inequalities in her skin, in order to communicate his amusing discoveries to the audience, as some philosophical lecturer does the result of his chemical experiments on the decomposition of substances to the admiring circle. There is no end of this. Your Correspondent confesses that 'we are drilled into a sort of stupid decorum and apparent uniformity,' but this he converts into an advantage. His penetrating eye is infinitely delighted with the picturesque appearance of so many imperceptible deviations from a right line, and mathematical inclinations from the perpendicular. The picture of the Flamborough Family,* painted with each an orange in his hand, must have been a masterpiece of nice discrimination and graceful inflection. Upon this principle of going to work the wrong way, and of making something out of nothing, we must reverse all our rules of taste and common sense. No Comedy can be perfect till the *dramatis personæ* might be reversed without creating much confusion: or the ingredients of character ought to be so blended and poured repeatedly from one vessel into another that the difference would be perceptible only to the finest palate. Thus, if Molière had lived in the present day,* he would not have drawn his Avare, his Tartuffe and his Misanthrope with those strong touches and violent contrasts which he has done, but with those delicate traits which are common to human nature in general, that is, his Miser without avarice, his Hypocrite with-out design, and his Misanthrope without disgust at the vices of mankind. Or instead of the heroines of his *School for Women* (Alithea and Miss Peggy, which Wycherley has contrived* to make the English understand) we should have had two sentimental young ladies brought up much in the same way, with nice shades of difference, which we should have been hardly able to distinguish, subscribing to the same circulating library, reading the same novels and poems, one preferring *Gertrude of Wyoming* to *The Lady of the Lake,** and the other *The Lady of the Lake* to *Gertrude of Wyoming,* differing in their opinions on points of taste or systems of mineralogy, and delivering dissertations on the arts with *Corinna of Italy.**

Considering the difficulty of the task which by our author's own account is thus imposed upon modern writers, may we not suppose this very difficulty to have operated to deter them from the pursuit of dramatic excellence. But I suspect that your Correspondent has taken up his complaint of the deficiency of refined Comedy too hastily, and that he need not despair of finding some modelled upon his favourite principles. Guided by his theory he should have sought them out in their remote obscurity, and have obtruded them on the public eye. He might have formed a new era of criticism, and have claimed the same merit as Voltaire, when he discovered that the English had one good Tragedy, *Cato.** Your Correspondent, availing himself of the idea that frivolity, taste, and elegance are the same, might have shewn how much superior *The Heiress* of Burgoyne was to *The Confederacy* or *The Way of the World,* and the *Basil** of Miss Bailey to *Romeo and Juliet.* He would have found ample scope in the blooming desert for endless discoveries—of beauties of the most shadowy kind, of fancies 'wan that hang the pensive head',* of evanescent smiles, and sighs that breathe not, of delicacy that shrinks from the touch, and feebleness that scarce supports itself, an elaborate vacuity of all thought, and an artificial dearth of sense, spirit, wit and character! I can assure your Correspondent, there has been no want of Comedies to his taste; but the taste of the public was not so far advanced. It was found necessary to appeal to something more palpable: and so, in this interval of want of characters in real life, the actors amuse themselves with taking off one another.

But your Correspondent will have it that there are different degrees of refinement in wit and pleasantry, and he seems to suppose that the best of our old Comedies are no better than the coarse jests of a set of country clowns—a sort of *comedies bourgeoises,* compared with the admirable productions which might and ought to be written. Even our modern dramatists, he suspects, are not so familiar with high life as they ought to be. 'They have not seen the Court, and if they have not seen the Court their manner must be damnable.'* Leaving him to settle this last point with the poetical Lords and Ladies of the present day, I am afraid he has himself fallen into the very error he complains of, and would degrade genteel Comedy from a high Court Lady into a literary prostitute. What does he mean by refinement? Does he find none in Millamant, and her morning dreams, in Sir Roger de Coverly* and his widow? Did not Congreve, Wycherley, and Suckling approach tolerably near 'the ring of mimic Statesmen,* and their merry King?' Does he suppose that their fine ladies were mere rustics, because they did not compose metaphysical treatises, or their fine gentlemen inexperienced tyros, because they had not been initiated into the infinitely refined society of Paris and of Baron Grimm?* Is there no distinction between an Angelica and a Miss Prue,* a Valentine, a Tattle, and a Ben? Where in the annals of modern literature will he find anything more refined, more deliberate, more abstracted in vice than the Nobleman in Amelia? Are not the compliments which Pope paid to his friends, to St John, Murray, and Cornbury, equal in taste and elegance to those which passed between the French philosophers and their patrons?—Are there no

traits in Sterne?—Is not Richardson minute enough?—Must
we part with Sophia Western and Clarissa* for the loves of the
plants and the triangles?*—The beauty of these writers in
general was, that they gave every kind and gradation of character, and they did this, because their portraits were taken
from life. They were true to nature, full of meaning, perfectly
understood and executed in every part. Their coarseness was
not mere vulgarity, their refinement was not a mere negation
of precision. They refined *upon* characters, instead of refining
them *away*. Their refinement consisted in working out the
parts, not in leaving a vague outline. They painted human
nature as it was, and as they saw it with individual character
and circumstances, not human nature in general, abstracted
from time, place and circumstance. Strength and refinement
are so far from being incompatible, that they assist each other,
as the hardest bodies admit of the finest touches and the
brightest polish. But there are some minds that never understand any thing, but by a negation of its opposite. There is
a strength without refinement, which is grossness, as there is
a refinement without strength or effect, which is insipidity.
Neither are grossness and refinement of manners inconsistent
with each other in the same period. The grossness of one class
adds to the refinement of another, by circumscribing it, by
rendering the feeling more pointed and exquisite, by irri-
tating our self-love, &c. There can be no great refinement of
character where there is no distinction of persons. The character of a gentleman is a *relative term*. The diffusion of knowledge, of artificial and intellectual equality, tends to level this
distinction, and to confound that nice perception and high
sense of honour, which arises from conspicuousness of situation, and a perpetual attention to personal propriety and the
claims of personal respect. Your Correspondent, I think, mistakes refinement of individual character for general knowledge and intellectual subtlety, with which it has little more to
do than with the dexterity of a rope-dancer or juggler. The
age of chivalry is gone with the improvements in the art of
war, which superseded personal courage, and the character
of a gentleman must disappear with those refinements in
intellect which render the advantages of rank and situation

common almost to any one. The bag-wig and sword followed
the helmet and the spear, when these outward insignia no
longer implied a real superiority, and were a distinction without a difference. Even the grossness of a state of mixed and
various manners receives a degree of refinement from contrast and opposition, by being defined and implicated with
circumstances. The Upholsterer in *The Tatler** is not a mere
vulgar politician. His intense feeling of interest and curiosity
about what does not at all concern him, displays itself in the
smallest things, assumes the most eccentric forms, and the
peculiarity of his absurdity masks itself under various shifts
and evasions, which the same folly, when it becomes epidemic
and universal as it has since done, would not have occasion
to resort to. In general it is only in a state of mere barbarism
or indiscriminate refinement that we are to look for extreme
grossness or complete insipidity. Our modern dramatists indeed have happily contrived to unite both extremes. *Omne
tulit punctum.** On a soft ground of sentiment they have
daubed in the gross absurdities of modern manners void of
character, have blended metaphysical waiting maids with
jockey noblemen, and the humours of the four in hand club,
and fill up the piece by some vile and illiberal caricature of
particular individuals known in the town.

To return once more to your Correspondent, who condemns all this as much as I do. He is for refining Comedy into
a pure intellectual abstraction, the shadow of a shade. Will he
forgive me if I suggest, as an addition to his theory, that the
drama in general might be constructed on the same abstruse
and philosophical principles. As he imagines that the finest
Comedies may be formed without individual character, so the
deepest Tragedies might be composed without real passion.
The slightest and most ridiculous distresses might be improved by the help of art and metaphysical aid, into the most
affecting scenes. A young man might naturally be introduced
as the hero of a philosophic drama, who had lost the gold
medal for a prize poem; or a young lady, whose verses had
been severely criticized in the reviews. Nothing could come
amiss to this rage for speculative refinement; or the actors
might be supposed to come forward, not in any character, but

as a sort of Chorus, reciting speeches on the general miseries
of human life, or reading alternately a passage out of Seneca's
Morals or Voltaire's *Candide*. This might by some be thought
a great improvement on English Tragedy, or even on the
French.

In fact, Sir, the whole of our author's reasoning proceeds
on a total misconception of the nature of the Drama itself. It
confounds philosophy with poetry, laboured analysis with intuitive perception, general truth with individual observation.
He makes the comic muse a dealer in riddles, and an ex-
pounder of hieroglyphics, and a taste for dramatic excellence,
a species of the second sight. He would have the Drama to be
the most remote, and it is the most substantial and real of all
things. It represents not only looks, but motion and speech.
The painter gives only the former, looks without action or
speech, and the mere writer only the latter, words without
looks or action. Its business and its use is to express the
thoughts and character in the most striking and instantaneous
manner, in the manner most like reality. It conveys them in
all their truth 'and subtlety, but in all their force and with all
possible effect. It brings them into action, obtrudes them on
the sight, embodies them in habits, in gestures, in dress, in
circumstances, and in speech. It renders every thing overt and
ostensible, and presents human nature not in its elementary
principles or by general reflections, but exhibits its essential
quality in all their variety of combination, and furnishes subjects for perpetual reflection.

But the instant we begin to refine and generalise beyond a
certain point, we are reduced to abstraction, and compelled
to see things, not as individuals, or as connected with action
and circumstances, but as universal truths, applicable in a
degree to all things, and in their extent to none, which therefore it would be absurd to predicate of individuals, or to
represent to the senses. The habit, too, of detaching these
abstract species and fragments of nature, destroys the power
of combining them in complex characters, in every degree of
force and variety. The concrete and the abstract cannot co-
exist in the same mind. We accordingly find, that to genuine
comedy succeed satire and novels, the one dealing in general

character and description, and the other making out particulars by the assistance of narrative and comment. Afterwards come traits, and collections of anecdotes, bon mots,
topics, and quotations, &c. which are applicable to any one,
and are just as good told of one person as another. Thus the
trio in the Memoirs of M. Grimm,* attributed to three
celebrated characters, on the death of a fourth, might have
the names reversed, and would lose nothing of its effect. In
general these traits, which are so much admired, are a sort of
systematic libels on human nature, which make up, by their
malice and *acuteness*, for their want of wit and sense. . . .

MODERN TRAGEDY

THE poverty of our present dramatic genius cannot be made
appear more fully than by this, that whatever it has to shew of
profound, is of German taste and origin; and that what little it
can boast of *elegant*, though light and vain, is taken from *petite*
pieces of Parisian mould.

We have been long trying to find out the meaning of all
this, and at last we think we have succeeded. The cause of the
evil complained of, like the root of so many other grievances
and complaints, lies in the French Revolution. That event has
rivetted all eyes, and distracted all hearts; and, like people
staring at a comet, in the panic and confusion in which we
have been huddled together, we have not had time to laugh
at one another's defects, or to condole over one another's
misfortunes. We have become a nation of politicians and
newsmongers; our inquiries in the streets are no less than
after the health of Europe; and in men's faces, we may see
strange matters written,—the rise of stocks, the loss of battles,
the fall of kingdoms, and the death of kings. The Muse,
meanwhile, droops in bye-corners of the mind, and is forced
to take up with the refuse of our thoughts. Our attention has
been turned, by the current of events, to the general nature
of men and things; and we cannot call it heartily back to
individual caprices, or head-strong passions, which are the

nerves and sinews of Comedy and Tragedy. What is an individual man to a nation? Or what is a nation to an abstract
principle? The affairs of the world are spread out before us,
as in a map; we sit with the newspaper, and a pair of compasses
in our hand, to measure out provinces, and to dispose of
thrones; we 'look abroad into universality',* feel in circles of
latitude and longitude, and cannot contract the grasp of our
minds to scan with nice scrutiny particular foibles, or to be
engrossed by any single suffering. What we gain in extent, we
lose in force and depth. A general and speculative interest
absorbs the corroding poison, and takes out the sting of our
more circumscribed and fiercer passions. We are become
public creatures; 'are embowelled of our natural entrails, and
stuffed',* as Mr Burke has it in his high-flown phrase, 'with
paltry blurred sheets of paper about the rights of man', or the
rights of legitimacy. We break our sleep to argue a question;
a piece of news spoils our appetite for dinner. We are not so
solicitous after our own success as the success of a cause. Our
thoughts, feelings, distresses, are about what no way concerns
us, more than it concerns any body else, like those of the
Upholsterer, ridiculed as a new species of character in the
Tatler:* but we are become a nation of upholsterers. We par-
ticipate in the general progress of intellect, and the large
vicissitudes of human affairs; but the hugest private sorrow
looks dwarfish and puerile. In the sovereignty of our minds,
we make mankind our quarry; and, in the scope of our ambitious thoughts, hunt for prey through the four quarters of
the world. In a word, literature and civilization have abstracted
man from himself so far, that his existence is no longer
dramatic; and the press has been the ruin of the stage, unless
we are greatly deceived.

If a bias to abstraction is evidently, then, the reigning spirit
of the age, dramatic poetry must be allowed to be most irreconcileable with this spirit; it is essentially individual and
concrete, both in form and in power. It is the closest imitation
of nature; it has a body of truth; it is 'a counterfeit presentment'* of reality; for it brings forward certain characters to
act and speak for themselves, in the most trying and singular
circumstances. It is not enough for them to declaim on certain

general topics, however forcibly or learnedly—this is merely oratory, and this any other characters might do as well, in any other circumstances: nor is it sufficient for the poet to furnish the colours and forms of style and fancy out of his own store, however inexhaustible; for if he merely makes them express his own feelings, and the idle effusions of his own breast, he had better speak in his own person, without any of those troublesome 'interlocutions between Lucius and Caius'.* The tragic poet (to be truly such) can only deliver the sentiments of given persons, placed in given circumstances; and in order to make what so proceeds from their mouths, at once proper to them and interesting to the audience, their characters must be powerfully marked: their passions, which are the subject-matter of which they treat, must be worked up to the highest pitch of intensity; and the circumstances which give force and direction to them must be stamped with the utmost distinct-ness and vividness in every line. Within the circle of dramatic character and natural passion, each individual is to feel as keenly, as profoundly, as rapidly as possible, but he is not to feel beyond it, for others or for the whole. Each character, on the contrary, must be a kind of centre of repulsion to the rest; and it is their hostile interests, brought into collision, that must tug at their heart-strings, and call forth every faculty of thought, of speech, and action. They must not be represented like a set of profiles, looking all the same way, nor with their faces turned round to the audience; but in dire contention with each other: their words, like their swords, must strike fire from one another,—must inflict the wound, and pour in the poison. The poet, to do justice to his undertaking, must not only identify himself with each, but must take part with all by turns, 'to relish all as sharply,* passioned as they';—must feel scorn, pity, love, hate, anger, remorse, revenge, ambition, in their most sudden and fierce extremes,—must not only have these passions rooted in his mind, but must be alive to every circumstance affecting them, to every accident of which ad-vantage can be taken to gratify or exasperate them; a word must kindle the dormant spark into a flame; an unforeseen event must overturn his whole being *in conceipt*; it is from the excess of passion that he must borrow the activity of his imagination; he must mould the sound of his verse to its fluctuations and caprices, and build up the whole superstructure of his fable on the deep and strict foundations of nature. But surely it is hardly to be thought that the poet should feel for others in this way, when they have ceased almost to feel for themselves; when the mind is turned habitually out of itself to general, speculative truth, and possibilities of good, and when, in fact, the processes of the understanding, analytical distinctions, and verbal disputes, have superseded all personal and local attachments and antipathies, and have, in a manner, put a stop to the pulsation of the heart—quenched the fever in the blood—the madness in the brain;—when we are more in love with a theory than a mistress, and would only crush to atoms those who are of an opposite party to ourselves in taste, philosophy, or politics. The folds of self-love, arising out of natural instincts, connections, and circumstances, have not wound themselves exclusively and unconsciously enough round the human mind to furnish the matter of impassioned poetry in real life: much less are we to expect the poet, without observation of its effects on others, or experience of them in himself, to supply the imaginary form out of vague topics, general reflections, far-fetched tropes, affected sentiments, and fine writing. To move the world, he must have a place to fix the levers of invention upon. The poet (let his genius be what it will) can only act by sympathy with the public mind and manners of his age; but these are, at present, not in sympathy, but in opposition to dramatic poetry. Therefore, we have no dramatic poets. It would be strange indeed (under favour be it spoken) if in the same period of time that produced the *Political Justice* or the *Edinburgh Review*, there should be found such an 'unfeathered, two-legged thing'* as a real tragedy poet.

But it may be answered, that the author of the Enquiry concerning *Political Justice*, is himself a writer of romances, and the author of *Caleb Williams*. We hearken to the suggestion, and will take this and one or two other eminent examples, to show how far we fall short of the goal we aim at. 'You may wear your *bays* with a difference.'* Mr Godwin has written an admirable and almost unrivalled novel (nay, more than one)—he has also written two tragedies, and failed. We can hardly think it would have been possible for him to have failed, but on the principle here stated; *viz.* that it was impossible for him to succeed. His genius is wholly adverse to the stage. As an author, as a novel writer, he may be considered as a philosophical recluse, a closet-hero. He cannot be denied to possess the *constructive* organ, to have originality and invention in an extraordinary degree: but he does not construct according to nature; his invention is not dramatic. He takes a character or a passion, and works it out to the utmost possible extravagance, and palliates or urges it on by every resource of the understanding, or by every species of plausible sophistry; but in doing this, he may be said to be only spinning a subtle theory, to be maintaining a wild paradox, as much as when he extends a philosophical and abstract principle into all its ramifications, and builds an entire and exclusive system of feeling and action on a single daring view of human nature. 'He sits in the centre'* of his web, and 'enjoys' not 'bright day', but a kind of gloomy grandeur. His characters stand alone, self-created, and self-supported, without communication with, or reaction upon, any other (except in the single instance of Caleb Williams himself):—the passions are not excited, qualified, or irritated by circumstances, but moulded by the will of the writer, like clay in the hands of the potter. Mr Godwin's imagination works like the power of steam, with inconceivable and incessant expansive force; but it is all in one direction, mechanical and uniform. By its help, he weaves gigantic figures, and unfolds terrific situations; but they are like the cloudy pageantry that hangs over the edge of day, and the prodigious offspring of his brain have neither fellow nor competitor in the scene of his imagination. They require a clear stage to themselves. They do not enter the lists with other men: nor are actuated by the ordinary wheels, pulleys, and machinery of society: they are at issue with themselves, and at war with the nature of things. Falkland, St Leon, Mandeville, are studies for us to contemplate, not men that we can sympathise with. They move in an orbit of their own, urged on by restless thought and morbid sentiment, on which the antagonist powers of sense, habit, circumstances, and opinion have no influence whatever. The arguments addressed to them are idle and ineffectual. You might as well argue with a madman, or talk to the winds. But this is not the nature of dramatic writing. Mr Godwin, to succeed in tragedy, should compose it almost entirely of long and repeated soliloquies, like the Prometheus of Æschylus; and his dialogues, properly translated, would turn out to be monologues, as we see in the *Iron Chest*.

The same, or similar, remarks would apply to Mr Wordsworth's hankering after the drama.* We understand, that, like Mr Godwin, the author of the Lyrical Ballads formerly made the attempt, and did not receive encouragement to proceed. We cannot say positively: but we much suspect that the writer would be for having all the talk to himself. His moody sensibility would eat into the plot like a cancer, and bespeak both sides of the dialogue for its own share. Mr Wordsworth (we are satisfied with him, be it remembered, as he is), is not a man to go out of himself into the feelings of any one else; much less, to act the part of a variety of characters. He is not, like Bottom, ready to play the lady, the lover, and the lion. His poetry is a virtual proscription passed upon the promiscuous nature of the drama. He sees nothing but himself in the universe: or if he leans with a kindly feeling to any thing else, he would impart to the most uninteresting things the fulness of his own sentiments, and elevate the most insignificant characters into the foremost rank,—before kings, or heroes, or lords, or wits,—because they do not interfere with his own sense of self-importance. He has none of the bye-play, the varying points of view, the venturous magnanimity of dramatic fiction. He thinks the opening of the leaves of a daisy, or the perfume of a hedge (not of a garden) rose, matters of consequence enough for him to notice them; but he thinks the 'daily intercourse of all this unintelligible world',* its cares, its crimes, its noise, love, war, ambition (what else?), mere vanity and vexation of spirit, with which a great poet cannot condescend to disturb the bright, serene, and solemn current of his thoughts. This lofty indifference and contempt for his *dramatis personæ* would not be the most likely means to make them interesting to the audience. We fear Mr Wordsworth's poetical egotism would prevent his writing a tragedy. Yet we have above made the dissipation and rarefaction of this spirit in society, the bar to dramatic excellence. Egotism is of different sorts; and he would not compliment the literary and artificial state of manners so much, as to suppose it quite free from this principle. But it is not allied at present to imagination or passion. It is sordid, servile, inert, a compound of dulness, vanity, and interest. That which is the source of dramatic excellence, is like a mountain spring, full of life and impetuosity, sparkling with light, thundering down precipices, winding along narrow defiles; or

> 'Like a wild overflow, that sweeps before him
> A golden stack, and with it shakes down bridges,
> Cracks the strong hearts of pines, whose cable roots
> Held out a thousand storms, a thousand thunders,
> And so, made mightier, takes whole villages
> Upon his back, and, in that heat of pride,
> Charges strong towns, towers, castles, palaces,
> And lays them desolate'.*

The other sort is a stagnant, gilded puddle. Mr Wordsworth has measured it from side to side. ''Tis three feet long and two feet wide.'*—Lord Byron's patrician haughtiness and monastic seclusion are, we think, no less hostile than the levelling spirit of Mr Wordsworth's Muse, to the endless gradations, variety, and complicated ideas or *mixed modes* of this sort of composition. Yet we have read Manfred.

But what shall we say of Mr Coleridge, who is the author not only of a successful but a meritorious tragedy? We may say of him what he has said of Mr Maturin,* that he is of the transcendental German school. He is a florid poet, and an ingenious metaphysician, who mistakes scholastic speculations for the intricate windings of the passions, and assigns possible reasons instead of actual motives for the excesses of his characters. He gives us studied special-pleadings for involuntary bursts of feeling, and the needless strain of tinkling sentiments for the point-blank language of nature. His *Remorse* is a spurious tragedy.* Take the following passage, and then ask, whether the charge of sophistry and paradox, and dangerous morality, to startle the audience, in lieu of more legitimate methods of exciting their sympathy, which he brings against the author of Bertram, may not be retorted on his own head. Ordonio is made to defend the project of murdering his brother by such arguments as the following:

> 'What? if one reptile sting another reptile,
> Where is the crime? The goodly face of nature
> Hath one disfeaturing stain the less upon it.
> Are we not all predestined Transiency,
> And cold Dishonour? Grant it, that this hand
> *Had* given a morsel to the hungry worms
> Somewhat too early—where's the crime of this?
> That this must needs bring on the idiotcy
> Of moist-eyed Penitence—'tis like a dream!
> Say, I had lay'd a body in the sun!
> Well! in a month there swarm forth from the corse
> A thousand, nay, ten thousand sentient beings
> In place of that one man. Say, I had *killed* him!
> Yet who shall tell me that each one and all
> Of these ten thousand lives is not as happy,
> As that one life, which, being push'd aside,
> Made room for these unnumber'd!'*

This is a way in which no one ever justified a murder to his own mind. No one will suspect Mr Southey of writing a tragedy, nor Mr Moore either.* His Muse is light. Walter Scott excels in the grotesque and the romantic. He gives us that which has been preserved of ancient manners and customs, and barbarous times and characters, and which strikes and staggers the mind the more, by the contrast it affords to the present artificial and effeminate state of society. But we do not know that he could write a tragedy: what he has engrafted of his own in this way upon the actual stock and floating materials of history is, we think, inferior to the general texture of his work. See, for instance, the conclusion of the *Black Dwarf,* where the situation of the parties is as dramatic as possible, and the effect is none at all. It is not a sound inference, that, because parts of a novel are dramatic, the author could write a play. The novelist is dramatic only where he can, and where he pleases; the other must be so. The first is a *ride and tye* business,* like a gentleman leading his horse, or walking by the side of a gig down a hill. We shall not, however, insist farther on this topic, because we are not convinced that the author of *Waverley* could not write a first-rate tragedy, as well as so many first-rate novels. If he can, we wish that he would; and not leave it to others to mar what he has sketched so admirably as a ground-work for that purpose.

THE FIGHT

. . .OUR present business was to get beds and a supper at an inn; but this was no easy task. The public-houses were full, and where you saw a light at a private house, and people poking their heads out of the casement to see what was going on, they instantly put them in and shut the window, the moment you seemed advancing with a suspicious overture for accommodation. Our guard and coachman thundered away at the outer gate of the Crown for some time without effect— such was the greater noise within;—and when the doors were unbarred, and we got admittance, we found a party assembled in the kitchen round a good hospitable fire, some sleeping, others drinking, others talking on politics and on the fight. A tall English yeoman (something like Matthews* in the face, and quite as great a wag)—

'A lusty man to ben an abbot able,'*—

was making such a prodigious noise about rent and taxes, and the price of corn now and formerly, that he had prevented us from being heard at the gate. The first thing I heard him say was to a shuffling fellow who wanted to be off a bet for a shilling glass of brandy and water—'Confound it, man, don't be *insipid*!'* Thinks I, that is a good phrase. It was a good omen. He kept it up so all night, nor flinched with the approach of morning. He was a fine fellow, with sense, wit, and spirit, a hearty body and a joyous mind, free-spoken, frank, convivial—one of that true English breed that went with Harry the Fifth to the siege of Harfleur—'standing like grey-

hounds in the slips,'* &c. We ordered tea and eggs (beds were
soon found to be out of the question) and this fellow's conversation was *sauce piquante*. It did one's heart good to see him
brandish his oaken towel* and to hear him talk. He made
mince-meat of a drunken, stupid, red-faced, quarrelsome,
frowsy farmer, whose nose 'he moralised into a thousand
similes,'* making it out a firebrand like Bardolph's. 'I'll tell
you what, my friend,' says he, 'the landlady has only to keep
you here to save fire and candle. If one was to touch your
nose, it would go off like a piece of charcoal.' At this the other
only grinned like an idiot, the sole variety in his purple face
being his little peering grey eyes and yellow teeth; called for
another glass, swore he would not stand it; and after many
attempts to provoke his humorous antagonist to single combat, which the other turned off (after working him up to a
ludicrous pitch of choler) with great adroitness, he fell quietly
asleep with a glass of liquor in his hand, which he could not
lift to his head. His laughing persecutor made a speech over
him, and turning to the opposite side of the room, where they
were all sleeping in the midst of this 'loud and furious fun',*
said, 'There's a scene, by G—d, for Hogarth to paint. I think
he and Shakespeare were our two best men at copying life.'
This confirmed me in my good opinion of him. Hogarth,
Shakespeare, and Nature, were just enough for him (indeed
for any man) to know. I said, 'You read Cobbett, don't you?
At least,' says I, 'you talk just as well as he writes.' He seemed
to doubt this. But I said, 'We have an hour to spare: if you'll
get pen, ink, and paper, and keep on talking, I'll write down
what you say; and if it doesn't make a capital Political Register,
I'll forfeit my head. You have kept me alive to-night, however.
I don't know what I should have done without you.' He did
not dislike this view of the thing, nor my asking if he was not
about the size of Jem Belcher; and told me soon afterwards,
in the confidence of friendship, that 'the circumstance which
had given him nearly the greatest concern in his life, was
Cribb's beating Jem* after he had lost his eye by racket-
playing.'—The morning dawns; that dim but yet clear light
appears, which weighs like solid bars of metal on the sleepless
eyelids; the guests drop down from their chambers one by

one—but it was too late to think of going to bed now (the clock was on the stroke of seven), we had nothing for it but to find a barber's (the pole that glittered in the morning sun lighted us to his shop), and then a nine miles' march to Hungerford. The day was fine, the sky was blue, the mists were retiring from the marshy ground, the path was tolerably dry, the sitting-up all night had not done us much harm—at least the cause was good; we talked of this and that with amicable difference, roving and sipping of many subjects, but still invariably we returned to the fight. At length, a mile to the left of Hungerford, on a gentle eminence, we saw the ring surrounded by covered carts, gigs, and carriages, of which hundreds had passed us on the road; Toms* gave a youthful shout, and we hastened down a narrow lane to the scene of action.

Reader, have you ever seen a fight? If not, you have a pleasure to come, at least if it is a fight like that between the Gas-man and Bill Neate. The crowd was very great when we arrived on the spot; open carriages were coming up, with streamers flying and music playing, and the country-people were pouring in over hedge and ditch in all directions, to see their hero beat or be beaten. The odds were still on Gas, but only about five to four. Gully* had been down to try Neate, and had backed him considerably, which was a damper to the sanguine confidence of the adverse party. About two hundred thousand pounds were pending. The Gas says, he has lost *3000l.* which were promised him by different gentlemen if he had won. He had presumed too much on himself, which had made others presume on him. This spirited and formidable young fellow seems to have taken for his motto the old maxim,* that 'there are three things necessary to success in life—*Impudence! Impudence! Impudence!*' It is so in matters of opinion, but not in the FANCY,* which is the most practical of all things, though even here confidence is half the battle, but only half. Our friend had vapoured and swaggered too much, as if he wanted to grin and bully his adversary out of the fight. 'Alas! the Bristol man was not so tamed!'*—'This is *the grave-digger'* (would Tom Hickman exclaim in the moments of intoxication from gin and success, shewing his tremendous right hand), 'this will send many of them to their long homes;

I haven't done with them yet!' Why should he—though he had licked four of the best men within the hour, yet why should he threaten to inflict dishonourable chastisement on my old master Richmond,* a veteran going off the stage, and who has borne his sable honours meekly? Magnanimity, my dear Tom, and bravery, should be inseparable. Or why should he go up to his antagonist, the first time he ever saw him at the Fives Court, and measuring him from head to foot with a glance of contempt, as Achilles surveyed Hector,* say to him, 'What, are you Bill Neate? I'll knock more blood out of that great carcase of thine, this day fortnight, than you ever knock'd out of a bullock's!' It was not manly, 'twas not fighter-like. If he was sure of the victory (as he was not), the less said about it the better. Modesty should accompany the FANCY as its shadow. The best men were always the best behaved. Jem Belcher, the Game Chicken* (before whom the Gasman could not have lived) were civil, silent men. So is Cribb, so is Tom Belcher, the most elegant of sparrers, and not a man for every one to take by the nose. I enlarged on this topic in the mail (while Turtle* was asleep), and said very wisely (as I thought) that impertinence was a part of no profession. A boxer was bound to beat his man, but not to thrust his fist, either actually or by implication, in every one's face. Even a highwayman, in the way of trade, may blow out your brains, but if he uses foul language at the same time, I should say he was no gentleman. A boxer, I would infer, need not be a blackguard or a cox-comb, more than another. Perhaps I press this point too much on a fallen man—Mr Thomas Hickman has by this time learnt that first of all lessons, 'That man was made to mourn.'* He has lost nothing by the late fight but his presumption; and that every man may do as well without! By an over-display of this quality, however, the public had been prejudiced against him, and the *knowing-ones* were taken in. Few but those who had bet on him wished Gas to win. With my own prepossessions on the subject, the result of the 11th of December appeared to me as fine a piece of poetical justice as I had ever witnessed. The difference of weight between the two combatants (14 stone to 12) was nothing to the sporting men. Great, heavy, clumsy, long-armed Bill Neate kicked the beam in the scale of the Gas-man's vanity. The amateurs were frightened at his big words, and thought that they would make up for the difference of six feet and five feet nine. Truly, the FANCY are not men of imagination. They judge of what has been, and cannot conceive of any thing that is to be. The Gas-man had won hitherto; therefore he must beat a man half as big again as himself—and that to a certainty. Besides, there are as many feuds, factions, prejudices, pedantic notions in the FANCY as in the state or in the schools. Mr Gully is almost the only cool, sensible man among them, who exercises an unbiassed discretion, and is not a slave to his passions in these matters. But enough of reflections, and to our tale. The day, as I have said, was fine for a December morning. The grass was wet, and the ground miry, and ploughed up with multitudinous feet, except that, within the ring itself, there was a spot of virgin-green closed in and unprofaned by vulgar tread, that shone with dazzling brightness in the mid-day sun. For it was now noon, and we had an hour to wait. This is the trying time. It is then the heart sickens, as you think what the two champions are about, and how short a time will determine their fate. After the first blow is struck, there is no opportunity for nervous apprehensions; you are swallowed up in the immediate interest of the scene—but

> 'Between the acting of a dreadful thing
> And the first motion, all the interim is
> Like a phantasma, or a hideous dream.'*

I found it so as I felt the sun's rays clinging to my back, and saw the white wintry clouds sink below the verge of the horizon. 'So,' I thought, 'my fairest hopes* have faded from my sight!—so will the Gas-man's glory, or that of his adversary, vanish in an hour.' The *swells* were parading in their white box-coats, the outer ring was cleared with some bruises on the heads and shins of the rustic assembly (for the *cockneys* had been distanced by the sixty-six miles); the time drew near, I had got a good stand; a bustle, a buzz, ran through the crowd, and from the opposite side entered Neate, between his second and bottle-holder. He rolled along, swathed in his loose great coat, his knock-knees bending under his huge bulk; and, with a modest cheerful air, threw his hat into the ring. He then just looked round, and began quietly to undress; when from the other side there was a similar rush and an opening made, and the Gas-man came forward with a conscious air of anticipated triumph, too much like the cock-of-the-walk. He strutted about more than became a hero, sucked oranges with a supercilious air, and threw away the skin with a toss of his head, and went up and looked at Neate, which was an act of supererogation. The only sensible thing he did was, as he strode away from the modern Ajax, to fling out his arms, as if he wanted to try whether they would do their work that day. By this time they had stripped, and presented a strong contrast in appearance. If Neate was like Ajax, 'with Atlantean shoul-ders,* fit to bear' the pugilistic reputation of all Bristol, Hick-man might be compared to Diomed, light, vigorous, elastic, and his back glistened in the sun, as he moved about, like a panther's hide. There was now a dead pause—attention was awe-struck. Who at that moment, big with a great event, did not draw his breath short—did not feel his heart throb? All was ready. They tossed up for the sun, and the Gas-man won. They were led up to the *scratch*—shook hands, and went at it.

In the first round every one thought it was all over. After making play a short time, the Gas-man flew at his adversary like a tiger, struck five blows in as many seconds, three first, and then following him as he staggered back, two more, right and left, and down he fell, a mighty ruin. There was a shout, and I said, 'There is no standing this.' Neate seemed like a lifeless lump of flesh and bone, round which the Gas-man's blows played with the rapidity of electricity or lightning, and you imagined he would only be lifted up to be knocked down again. It was as if Hickman held a sword or a fire in that right hand of his, and directed it against an unarmed body. They met again, and Neate seemed, not cowed, but particularly cautious. I saw his teeth clenched together and his brows knit close against the sun. He held out both his arms at full length straight before him, like two sledge-hammers, and raised his left an inch or two higher. The Gas-man could not get over this guard—they struck mutually and fell, but without advantage on either side. It was the same in the next round; but the balance of power was thus restored—the fate of the battle was suspended. No one could tell how it would end. This was the only moment in which opinion was divided; for, in the next, the Gas-man aiming a mortal blow at his adversary's neck, with his right hand, and failing from the length he had to reach, the other returned it with his left at full swing, planted a tremendous blow on his cheek-bone and eyebrow, and made a red ruin of that side of his face. The Gas-man went down, and there was another shout—a roar of triumph as the waves of fortune rolled tumultuously from side to side. This was a settler. Hickman got up, and 'grinned horrible a ghastly smile',* yet he was evidently dashed in his opinion of himself; it was the first time he had ever been so punished; all one side of his face was perfect scarlet, and his right eye was closed in dingy blackness, as he advanced to the fight, less confident, but still determined. After one or two rounds, not receiving another such remembrancer, he rallied and went at it with his former impetuosity. But in vain. His strength had been weakened,—his blows could not tell at such a distance,—he was obliged to fling himself at his adversary, and could not strike from his feet; and almost as regularly as he flew at him with his right hand, Neate warded the blow, or drew back out of its reach, and felled him with the return of his left. There was little cautious sparring—no half-hits—no tapping and trifling, none of the *petit-maîtreship* of the art— they were almost all knock-down blows:—the fight was a good stand up fight. The wonder was the half-minute time. If there had been a minute or more allowed between each round, it would have been intelligible how they should by degrees recover strength and resolution; but to see two men smashed to the ground, smeared with gore, stunned, senseless, the breath beaten out of their bodies; and then, before you recover from the shock, to see them rise up with new strength and courage, stand steady to inflict or receive mortal offence, and rush upon each other 'like two clouds over the Caspian'*—this is the most astonishing thing of all:—this is the high and heroic state of man! From this time forward the event became more certain every round; and about the twelfth it seemed as if it must have been over. Hickman generally stood with his back to me; but in the scuffle, he had changed positions, and Neate just then made a tremendous lunge at him, and hit him full in the face. It was doubtful whether he would fall backwards or forwards; he hung suspended for a second or two, and then fell back, throwing his hands in the air, and with his face lifted up to the sky. I never saw any thing more terrific than his aspect just before he fell. All traces of life, of natural expression, were gone from him. His face was like a human skull, a death's head, spouting blood. The eyes were filled with blood, the nose streamed with blood, the mouth gaped blood. He was not like an actual man, but like a preternatural, spectral appearance, or like one of the figures in Dante's *Inferno*. Yet he fought on after this for several rounds, still striking the first desperate blow, and Neate standing on the defensive, and using the same cautious guard to the last, as if he had still all his work to do; and it was not till the Gas-man was so stunned in the seventeenth or eighteenth round, that his senses forsook him, and he could not come to time, that the battle was declared over. Ye who despise the FANCY, do something to shew as much *pluck*, or as much self-possession as this, before you assume a superiority which you have never given a single proof of by any one action in the whole course of your lives!—When the Gas-man came to himself, the first words he uttered were, 'Where am I? What is the matter?' 'Nothing is the matter, Tom,—you have lost the battle, but you are the bravest man alive.' And Jackson* whispered to him, 'I am collecting a purse for you, Tom.'— Vain sounds, and unheard at that moment! Neate instantly went up and shook him cordially by the hand, and seeing some old acquaintance, began to flourish with his fists, calling out, 'Ah, you always said I couldn't fight—What do you think now?' But all in good humour, and without any appearance of arrogance; only it was evident Bill Neate was pleased that he had won the fight. When it was over, I asked Cribb if he did not think it was a good one? He said, '*Pretty well!*' The carrier-pigeons now mounted into the air, and one of them flew with the news of her husband's victory to the bosom of Mrs Neate. Alas, for Mrs Hickman!

Mais au revoir, as Sir Fopling Flutter* says. I went down with Toms; I returned with Jack Pigott,* whom I met on the ground. Toms is a rattle-brain; Pigott is a sentimentalist. Now, under favour, I am a sentimentalist too—therefore I say nothing, but that the interest of the excursion did not flag as I came back. Pigott and I marched along the causeway leading from Hungerford to Newbury, now observing the effect of a brilliant sun on the tawny meads or moss-coloured cottages, now exulting in the fight, now digressing to some topic of general and elegant literature. My friend was dressed in character for the occasion, or like one of the FANCY; that is, with a double portion of great coats, clogs, and overhauls: and just as we had agreed with a couple of country-lads to carry his superfluous wearing-apparel to the next town, we were overtaken by a return post-chaise, into which I got, Pigott preferring a seat on the bar. There were two strangers already in the chaise, and on their observing they supposed I had been to the fight, I said I had, and concluded they had done the same. They appeared, however, a little shy and sore on the subject; and it was not till after several hints dropped, and questions put, that it turned out that they had missed it. One of these friends had undertaken to drive the other there in his gig: they had set out, to make sure work, the day before at three in the afternoon. The owner of the one-horse vehicle scorned to ask his way, and drove right on to Bagshot, instead of turning off at Hounslow: there they stopped all night, and set off the next day across the country to Reading, from whence they took coach, and got down within a mile or two of Hungerford, just half an hour after the fight was over. This might be safely set down as one of the miseries of human life. We parted with these two gentlemen who had been to see the fight, but had returned as they went, at Wolhampton, where we were promised beds (an irresistible temptation, for Pigott had passed the preceding night at Hungerford as we had done at Newbury), and we turned into an old bow-windowed parlour with a carpet and a snug fire; and after devouring a quantity of tea, toast, and eggs, sat down to consider, during an hour of philosophic leisure, what we should have for supper. In the midst of an Epicurean deliberation between a roasted fowl and mutton chops with mashed potatoes, we were interrupted by an inroad of Goths and Vandals—*O procul este profani**—not real flash-men, but interlopers, noisy pretenders, butchers from Tothill-fields, brokers from White-chapel, who called immediately for pipes and tobacco, hoping it would not be disagreeable to the gentlemen, and began to insist that it was *a cross.** Pigott withdrew from the smoke and noise into another room, and left me to dispute the point with them for a couple of hours *sans intermission* by the dial. The next morning we rose refreshed; and on observing that Jack had a pocket volume in his hand, in which he read in the intervals of our discourse, I inquired what it was, and learned to my particular satisfaction that it was a volume of the *New Eloise.** Ladies, after this, will you contend that a love for the FANCY is incompatible with the cultivation of sentiment?—We jogged on as before, my friend setting me up in a genteel drab great coat and green silk handkerchief (which I must say became me exceedingly), and after stretching our legs for a few miles, and seeing Jack Randall, Ned Turner, and Scroggins, pass on the top of one of the Bath coaches, we engaged with the driver of the second to take us to London for the usual fee. I got inside, and found three other passengers. One of them was an old gentleman with an aquiline nose, powdered hair, and a pigtail, and who looked as if he had played many a rubber at the Bath rooms. I said to myself, he is very like Mr Windham;* I wish he would enter into conversation, that I might hear what fine observations would come from those finely-turned features. However, nothing passed, till, stopping to dine at Reading, some inquiry was made by the company about the fight, and I gave (as the reader may believe) an eloquent and animated description of it. When we got into the coach again, the old gentleman, after a graceful exordium, said, he had, when a boy, been to a fight between the famous Broughton and George Stevenson,* who was called the *Fighting Coachman*, in the year 1770, with the late Mr Windham. This beginning flattered the spirit of prophecy within me and rivetted my attention. He went on— 'George Stevenson was coachman to a friend of my father's. He was an old man when I saw him some years afterwards. He took hold of his own arm and said, "there was muscle here once, but now it is no more than this young gentleman's." He added, "Well, no matter; I have been here long, I am willing to go hence, and I hope I have done no more harm than another man." Once', said my unknown companion, 'I asked him if he had ever beat Broughton? He said Yes; that he had fought with him three times, and the last time he fairly beat him, though the world did not allow it. "I'll tell you how it was, master. When the seconds lifted us up in the last round, we were so exhausted that neither of us could stand, and we fell upon one another, and as Master Broughton fell uppermost, the mob gave it in his favour, and he was said to have won the battle. But," says he, "the fact was, that as his second (John Cuthbert) lifted him up, he said to him, 'I'll fight no more, I've had enough;' which", says Stevenson, "you know gave me the victory. And to prove to you that this was the case, when John Cuthbert was on his death-bed, and they asked him if there was any thing on his mind which he wished to confess, he answered, 'Yes, that there was one thing he wished to set right, for that certainly Master Stevenson won that last fight with Master Broughton; for he whispered him as he lifted him up in the last round of all, that he had had enough.' " ' 'This', said the Bath gentleman, 'was a bit of human nature;' and I have written this account of the fight on purpose that it might not be lost to the world. He also stated as a proof of the candour of mind in this class of men, that Stevenson acknowledged that Broughton could have beat him in his best day; but that he (Broughton) was getting old in their last rencounter. When we stopped in Piccadilly, I wanted to ask the gentleman some questions about the late Mr Windham, but had not courage. I got out. resigned my coat and green silk handkerchief to Pigott (loth to part with these ornaments of life), and walked home in high spirits.

P.S. Toms called upon me the next day, to ask me if I did not think the fight was a complete thing? I said I thought it was. I hope he will relish my account of it.

THE INDIAN JUGGLERS

COMING forward and seating himself on the ground in his white dress and tightened turban, the chief of the Indian Jugglers begins with tossing up two brass balls, which is what any of us could do, and concludes with keeping up four at the same time, which is what none of us could do to save our lives, nor if we were to take our whole lives to do it in. Is it then a trifling power we see at work, or is it not something next to miraculous? It is the utmost stretch of human ingenuity, which nothing but the bending the faculties of body and mind to it from the tenderest infancy with incessant, ever-anxious application up to manhood, can accomplish or make even a slight approach to. Man, thou art a wonderful animal, and thy ways past finding out! Thou canst do strange things, but thou turnest them to little account!—To conceive of this effort of extraordinary dexterity distracts the imagination and makes admiration breathless. Yet it costs nothing to the performer, any more than if it were a mere mechanical deception with which he had nothing to do but to watch and laugh at the astonishment of the spectators. A single error of a hair's-breadth, of the smallest conceivable portion of time, would be fatal: the precision of the movements must be like a mathematical truth, their rapidity is like lightning. To catch four balls in succession in less than a second of time, and deliver them back so as to return with seeming consciousness to the hand again, to make them revolve round him at certain intervals, like the planets in their spheres, to make them chase one another like sparkles of fire, or shoot up like flowers or meteors, to throw them behind his back and twine them round his neck like ribbons or like serpents, to do what appears an impossibility, and to do it with all the ease, the grace, the carelessness imaginable, to laugh at, to play with the glittering mockeries, to follow them with his eye as if he could fascinate them with its lambent fire, or as if he had only to see that they kept time with the music on the stage—there is something in all this which he who does not admire may be quite sure he never really admired any thing in the whole course of his life. It is skill surmounting difficulty, and beauty triumphing over skill. It seems as if the difficulty once mastered naturally resolved itself into ease and grace, and as if to be overcome at all, it must be overcome without an effort. The smallest awkwardness or want of pliancy or self-possession would stop the whole process. It is the work of witchcraft, and yet sport for children. Some of the other feats are quite as curious and wonderful, such as the balancing the artificial tree and shooting a bird from each branch through a quill; though none of them have the elegance or facility of the keeping up of the brass balls. You are in pain for the result, and glad when the experiment is over; they are not accompanied with the same unmixed, unchecked delight as the former; and I would not give much to be merely astonished without being pleased at the same time. As to the swallowing of the sword, the police ought to interfere to prevent it. When I saw the Indian Juggler do the same things before, his feet were bare, and he had large rings on the toes, which kept turning round all the time of the performance, as if they moved of themselves.—The hearing a speech in Parliament, drawled or stammered out by the Honourable Member or the Noble Lord, the ringing the changes on their common-places, which any one could repeat after them as well as they, stirs me not a jot, shakes not my good opinion of myself: but the seeing the Indian Jugglers does. It makes me ashamed of myself. I ask what there is that I can do as well as this? Nothing. What have I been doing all my life? Have I been idle, or have I nothing to shew for all my labour and pains? Or have I passed my time in pouring words like water into empty sieves, rolling a stone up a hill and then down again, trying to prove an argument in the teeth of facts, and looking for causes in the dark, and not finding them? Is there no one thing in which I can challenge competition, that I can bring as an instance of exact perfection, in which others cannot find a flaw? The utmost I can pretend to is to write a description of what this fellow can do. I can write a book: so can many others who have not even learned to spell. What abortions are these

Essays! What errors, what ill-pieced transitions, what crooked reasons, what lame conclusions! How little is made out, and that little how ill! Yet they are the best I can do. I endeavour to recollect all I have ever observed or thought upon a subject, and to express it as nearly as I can. Instead of writing on four subjects at a time, it is as much as I can manage to keep the thread of one discourse clear and unentangled. I have also time on my hands to correct my opinions, and polish my periods: but the one I cannot, and the other I will not do. I am fond of arguing: yet with a good deal of pains and practice it is often as much as I can do to beat my man; though he may be a very indifferent hand. A common fencer would disarm his adversary in the twinkling of an eye, unless he were a professor like himself. A stroke of wit will sometimes produce this effect, but there is no such power or superiority in sense or reasoning. There is no complete mastery of execution to be shewn there: and you hardly know the professor from the impudent pretender or the mere clown.

I have always had this feeling of the inefficacy and slow progress of intellectual compared to mechanical excellence, and it has always made me somewhat dissatisfied. It is a great many years since I saw Richer, the famous rope-dancer, perform at Sadler's Wells. He was matchless in his art, and added to his extraordinary skill exquisite ease, and unaffected natural grace. I was at that time employed in copying a half-length picture of Sir Joshua Reynolds's; and it put me out of conceit with it. How ill this part was made out in the drawing! How heavy, how slovenly this other was painted! I could not help saying to myself, 'If the rope-dancer had performed his task in this manner, leaving so many gaps and botches in his work, he would have broke his neck long ago; I should never have seen that vigorous elasticity of nerve and precision of movement!'—Is it then so easy an undertaking (comparatively) to dance on a tight-rope?* Let any one, who thinks so, get up and try. There is the thing. It is that which at first we cannot do at all, which in the end is done to such perfection. To account for this in some degree, I might observe that mechanical dexterity is confined to doing some one particular thing, which you can repeat as often as you please, in which you know whether you succeed or fail, and where the point of perfection consists in succeeding in a given undertaking.— In mechanical efforts, you improve by perpetual practice, and you do so infallibly, because the object to be attained is not a matter of taste or fancy or opinion, but of actual experiment, in which you must either do the thing or not do it. If a man is put to aim at a mark with a bow and arrow, he must hit it or miss it, that's certain. He cannot deceive himself, and go on shooting wide or falling short, and still fancy that he is making progress. The distinction between right and wrong, between true and false, is here palpable; and he must either correct his aim or persevere in his error with his eyes open, for which there is neither excuse nor temptation. If a man is learning to dance on a rope, if he does not mind what he is about, he will break his neck. After that, it will be in vain for him to argue that he did not make a false step. His situation is not like that of Goldsmith's pedagogue.—

'In argument they own'd his wondrous skill,
And e'en though vanquish'd, he could argue still.'*

Danger is a good teacher, and makes apt scholars. So are disgrace, defeat, exposure to immediate scorn and laughter. There is no opportunity in such cases for self-delusion, no idling time away, no being off your guard (or you must take the consequences)—neither is there any room for humour or caprice or prejudice. If the Indian Juggler were to play tricks in throwing up the three case-knives, which keep their positions like the leaves of a crocus in the air, he would cut his fingers. I can make a very bad antithesis without cutting my fingers. The tact of style is more ambiguous than that of double-edged instruments. If the Juggler were told that by flinging himself under the wheels of the Jaggernaut, when the idol issues forth on a gaudy day, he would immediately be transported into Paradise, he might believe it, and nobody could disprove it. So the Brahmins may say what they please on that subject, may build up dogmas and mysteries without end, and not be detected: but their ingenious countryman cannot persuade the frequenters of the Olympic Theatre that he performs a number of astonishing feats without actually giving proofs of what he says.—There is then in this sort of manual dexterity, first a gradual aptitude acquired to a given exertion of muscular power, from constant repetition, and in the next place, an exact knowledge how much is still wanting and necessary to be supplied. The obvious test is to increase the effort or nicety of the operation, and still to find it come true. The muscles ply instinctively to the dictates of habit. Certain movements and impressions of the hand and eye, having been repeated together an infinite number of times, are unconsciously but unavoidably cemented into closer and closer union; the limbs require little more than to be put in motion for them to follow a regular track with ease and certainty; so that the mere intention of the will acts mathematically, like touching the spring of a machine, and you come with Locksley in Ivanhoe, in shooting at a mark, 'to allow for the wind'.*

Farther, what is meant by perfection in mechanical exercises is the performing certain feats to a uniform nicety, that is, in fact, undertaking no more than you can perform. You task yourself, the limit you fix is optional, and no more than human industry and skill can attain to: but you have no abstract, independent standard of difficulty or excellence (other than the extent of your own powers). Thus he who can keep up four brass balls does this *to perfection*; but he cannot keep up five at the same instant, and would fail every time he attempted it. That is, the mechanical performer undertakes to emulate himself, not to equal another. But the artist undertakes to imitate another, or to do what nature has done, and this it appears is more difficult, *viz.* to copy what she has set before us in the face of nature or 'human face divine',* entire and without a blemish, than to keep up four brass balls at the same instant; for the one is done by the power of human skill and industry, and the other never was nor will be. Upon the whole, therefore, I have more respect for Reynolds, than I have for Richer: for, happen how it will, there have been more people in the world who could dance on a rope like the one than who could paint like Sir Joshua. The latter was but a bungler in his profession to the other, it is true; but then he had a harder task-master to obey, whose will was more wayward and obscure, and whose instructions it was more difficult to practise. You can put a child apprentice to a tumbler or rope-dancer with a comfortable prospect of success, if they are but sound of wind and limb: but you cannot do the same thing in painting. The odds are a million to one. You may make indeed as many H——s and H——s,* as you put into that sort of machine, but not one Reynolds amongst them all, with his grace, his grandeur, his blandness of *gusto*,* 'in tones and gestures hit',* unless you could make the man over again. To snatch this grace* beyond the reach of art is then the height of art—where fine art begins, and where mechanical skill ends. The soft suffusion of the soul, the speechless breathing eloquence, the looks 'commercing with the skies',* the ever-shifting forms of an eternal principle, that which is seen but for a moment, but dwells in the heart always, and is only seized as it passes by strong and secret sympathy, must be taught by nature and genius, not by rules or study. It is suggested by feeling, not by laborious microscopic inspection: in seeking for it without, we lose the harmonious clue to it within: and in aiming to grasp the substance, we let the very spirit of art evaporate. In a word, the objects of fine art are not the objects of sight but as these last are the objects of taste and imagination, that is, as they appeal to the sense of beauty, of pleasure, and of power in the human breast, and are explained by that finer sense, and revealed in their inner structure to the eye in return. Nature is also a language. Objects, like words, have a meaning; and the true artist is the interpreter of this language, which he can only do by knowing its application to a thousand other objects in a thousand other situations. Thus the eye is too blind a guide of itself to distinguish between the warm or cold tone of a deep blue sky, but another sense acts as a monitor to it, and does not err. The colour of the leaves in autumn would be nothing without the feeling that accompanies it; but it is that feeling that stamps them on the canvas, faded, seared, blighted, shrinking from the winter's flaw, and makes the sight as true as touch—

> 'And visions, as poetic eyes avow,
> Cling to each leaf and hang on every bough.'*

The more ethereal, evanescent, more refined and sublime part of art is the seeing nature through the medium of sentiment and passion, as each object is a symbol of the affections and a link in the chain of our endless being. But the unravelling this mysterious web of thought and feeling is alone in the Muse's gift, namely, in the power of that trembling sensibility which is awake to every change and every modification of its ever-varying impressions, that,

'Thrills in each nerve, and lives along the line.'*

This power is indifferently called genius, imagination, feeling, taste; but the manner in which it acts upon the mind can neither be defined by abstract rules, as is the case in science, nor verified by continual unvarying experiments, as is the case in mechanical performances. The mechanical excellence of the Dutch painters in colouring and handling is that which comes the nearest in fine art to the perfection of certain manual exhibitions of skill. The truth of the effect and the facility with which it is produced are equally admirable. Up to a certain point, every thing is faultless. The hand and eye have done their part. There is only a want of taste and genius. It is after we enter upon that enchanted ground that the human mind begins to droop and flag as in a strange road, or in a thick mist, benighted and making little way with many attempts and many failures, and that the best of us only escape with half a triumph. The undefined and the imaginary are the regions that we must pass like Satan, difficult and doubtful, 'half flying, half on foot'.* The object in sense is a positive thing, and execution comes with practice.

Cleverness is a certain *knack* or aptitude at doing certain things, which depend more on a particular adroitness and off-hand readiness than on force or perseverance, such as making puns, making epigrams, making extempore verses, mimicking the company, mimicking a style, &c. Cleverness is either liveliness and smartness, or something answering to *sleight of hand*, like letting a glass fall sideways off a table, or else a trick, like knowing the secret spring of a watch. Accomplishments are certain external graces, which are to be learnt from others, and which are easily displayed to the admiration

THE INDIAN JUGGLERS 135

of the beholder, *viz.* dancing, riding, fencing, music, and so on. These ornamental acquirements are only proper to those who are at ease in mind and fortune. I know an individual* who if he had been born to an estate of five thousand a year, would have been the most accomplished gentleman of the age. He would have been the delight and envy of the circle in which he moved—would have graced by his manners the liberality flowing from the openness of his heart, would have laughed with the women, have argued with the men, have said good things and written agreeable ones, have taken a hand at piquet or the lead at the harpsichord, and have set and sung his own verses—*nugæ canoræ**—with tenderness and spirit; a Rochester without the vice, a modern Surrey! As it is, all these capabilities of excellence stand in his way. He is too versatile for a professional man, not dull enough for a political drudge, too gay to be happy, too thoughtless to be rich. He wants the enthusiasm of the poet, the severity of the prose-writer, and the application of the man of business.—Talent is the capacity of doing any thing that depends on application and industry, such as writing a criticism, making a speech, studying the law. Talent differs from genius, as voluntary differs from involuntary power. Ingenuity is genius in trifles, greatness is genius in undertakings of much pith and mo-ment. A clever or ingenious man is one who can do any thing well, whether it is worth doing or not: a great man is one who can do that which when done is of the highest importance. Themistocles* said he could not play on the flute, but that he could make of a small city a great one. This gives one a pretty good idea of the distinction in question.

Greatness is great power, producing great effects. It is not enough that a man has great power in himself, he must shew it to all the world in a way that cannot be hid or gainsaid. He must fill up a certain idea in the public mind. I have no other notion of greatness than this two-fold definition, great results springing from great inherent energy. The great in visible objects has relation to that which extends over space: the great in mental ones has to do with space and time. No man is truly great, who is great only in his life-time. The test of greatness is the page of history. Nothing can be said to be great that has a distinct limit, or that borders on something evidently greater than itself. Besides, what is short-lived and pampered into mere notoriety, is of a gross and vulgar quality in itself. A Lord Mayor is hardly a great man. A city orator or patriot of the day only shew, by reaching the height of their wishes, the distance they are at from any true ambition. Popularity is neither fame nor greatness. A king (as such) is not a great man. He has great power, but it is not his own. He merely wields the lever of the state, which a child, an idiot, or a madman can do. It is the office, not the man we gaze at. Any one else in the same situation would be just as much an object of abject curiosity. We laugh at the country girl who having seen a king expressed her disappointment by saying, 'Why, he is only a man!' Yet, knowing this, we run to see a king as if he was something more than a man.—To display the greatest powers, unless they are applied to great purposes, makes nothing for the character of greatness. To throw a barley-corn through the eye of a needle, to multiply nine figures by nine in the memory, argues infinite dexterity of body and capacity of mind, but nothing comes of either. There is a surprising power at work, but the effects are not proportionate, or such as take hold of the imagination. To impress the idea of power on others, they must be made in some way to feel it. It must be communicated to their understandings in the shape of an increase of knowledge, or it must subdue and overawe them by subjecting their wills. Admiration, to be solid and lasting, must be founded on proofs from which we have no means of escaping; it is neither a slight nor a voluntary gift. A mathe-matician who solves a profound problem, a poet who creates an image of beauty in the mind that was not there before, imparts knowledge and power to others, in which his great-ness and his fame consists, and on which it reposes. Jedediah Buxton will be forgotten; but Napier's bones* will live. Law-givers, philosophers, founders of religion, conquerors and heroes, inventors and great geniuses in arts and sciences, are great men; for they are great public benefactors, or formid-able scourges to mankind. Among ourselves, Shakespeare, Newton, Bacon, Milton, Cromwell, were great men; for they shewed great power by acts and thoughts, which have not yet been consigned to oblivion. They must needs be men of lofty stature, whose shadows lengthen out to remote posterity. A great farce-writer may be a great man; for Moliere was but a great farce-writer. In my mind, the author of *Don Quixote* was a great man. So have there been many others. A great chess-player is not a great man, for he leaves the world as he found it. No act terminating in itself constitutes greatness. This will apply to all displays of power or trials of skill, which are confined to the momentary, individual effort, and construct no permanent image or trophy of themselves without them. Is not an actor then a great man, because 'he dies and leaves the world no copy?'* I must make an exception for Mrs Siddons,* or else give up my definition of greatness for her sake. A man at the top of his profession is not therefore a great man. He is great in his way, but that is all, unless he shews the marks of a great moving intellect, so that we trace the master-mind, and can sympathise with the springs that urge him on. The rest is but a craft or *mystery*. John Hunter* was a great man—*that* any one might see without the smallest skill in surgery. His style and manner shewed the man. He would set about cutting up the carcase of a whale with the same greatness of *gusto* that Michael Angelo would have hewn a block of marble. Lord Nelson was a great naval commander; but for myself, I have not much opinion of a sea-faring life. Sir Humphry Davy is a great chemist, but I am not sure that he is a great man. I am not a bit the wiser for any of his discoveries, nor I never met with any one that was. But it is in the nature of greatness to propagate an idea of itself, as wave impels wave, circle without circle. It is a contradiction in terms for a coxcomb to be a great man. A really great man has always an idea of something greater than himself. I have observed that certain sectaries and polemical writers have no higher compliment to pay their most shining lights than to say that 'Such a one was a considerable man in his day.' Some new elucidation of a text sets aside the authority of the old inter-pretation, and a 'great scholar's memory outlives him half a century,'* at the utmost. A rich man is not a great man, except to his dependants and his steward. A lord is a great man in the idea we have of his ancestry, and probably of himself, if we know nothing of him but his title. I have heard a story of two bishops, one of whom said (speaking of St Peter's at Rome) that when he first entered it, he was rather awe-struck, but that as he walked up it, his mind seemed to swell and dilate with it, and at last to fill the whole building—the other said that as he saw more of it, he appeared to himself to grow less and less every step he took, and in the end to dwindle into nothing. This was in some respects a striking picture of a great and little mind—for greatness sympathises with greatness, and littleness shrinks into itself. The one might have become a Wolsey;* the other was only fit to become a Mendicant Friar—or there might have been court-reasons for making him a bishop. The French have to me a character of littleness in all about them; but they have produced three great men that belong to every country, Molière, Rabelais, and Montaigne.

To return from this digression, and conclude the Essay. A singular instance of manual dexterity was shewn in the person of the late John Cavanagh, whom I have several times seen. His death was celebrated at the time in an article in the *Examiner* newspaper (Feb. 7, 1819), written apparently between jest and earnest: but as it is *pat* to our purpose, and falls in with my own way of considering such subjects, I shall here take leave to quote it.

'Died at his house in Burbage-street, St. Giles's, John Cavanagh, the famous hand fives-player. When a person dies, who does any one thing better than any one else in the world, which so many others are trying to do well, it leaves a gap in society. It is not likely that any one will now see the game of fives played in its perfection for many years to come—for Cavanagh is dead, and has not left his peer behind him. It may be said that there are things of more importance than striking a ball against a wall—there are things indeed which make more noise and do as little good, such as making war and peace, making speeches and answering them, making verses and blotting them; making money and throwing it away. But the game of fives is what no one despises who has ever played at it. It is the finest exercise for the body, and the best relaxation for the mind. The Roman poet* said that "Care

mounted behind the horseman and stuck to his skirts." But
this remark would not have applied to the fives-player. He who
takes to playing at fives is twice young. He feels neither the
past nor future "in the instant". Debts, taxes, "domestic
treason, foreign levy, nothing can touch him further."* He has
no other wish, no other thought, from the moment the game
begins, but that of striking the ball, of placing it, of *making* it!
This Cavanagh was sure to do. Whenever he touched the ball,
there was an end of the chase. His eye was certain, his hand
fatal, his presence of mind complete. He could do what he
pleased, and he always knew exactly what to do. He saw the
whole game, and played it; took instant advantage of his
adversary's weakness, and recovered balls, as if by a miracle
and from sudden thought, that every one gave for lost. He
had equal power and skill, quickness, and judgment. He could
either out-wit his antagonist by finesse, or beat him by main
strength. Sometimes, when he seemed preparing to send the
ball with the full swing of his arm, he would by a slight turn
of his wrist drop it within an inch of the line. In general, the
ball came from his hand, as if from a racket, in a straight
horizontal line; so that it was in vain to attempt to overtake
or stop it. As it was said of a great orator that he never was at
a loss for a word, and for the properest word, so Cavanagh
always could tell the degree of force necessary to be given to
a ball, and the precise direction in which it should be sent.
He did his work with the greatest ease; never took more pains
than was necessary; and while others were fagging themselves
to death, was as cool and collected as if he had just entered
the court. His style of play was as remarkable as his power of
execution. He had no affectation, no trifling. He did not
throw away the game to show off an attitude, or try an experiment. He was a fine, sensible, manly player, who did what he
could, but that was more than any one else could even affect
to do. His blows were not undecided and ineffectual—lum-
bering like Mr. Wordsworth's epic poetry, nor wavering like
Mr. Coleridge's lyric prose, nor short of the mark like Mr.
Brougham's speeches, nor wide of it like Mr. Canning's wit,
nor foul like the *Quarterly*, not *let* balls like the *Edinburgh
Review*. Cobbett and Junius* together would have made a

Cavanagh. He was the best *up-hill* player in the world; even when his adversary was fourteen, he would play on the same or better, and as he never flung away the game through carelessness and conceit, he never gave it up through laziness or want of heart. The only peculiarity of his play was that he never *volleyed*, but let the balls hop; but if they rose an inch from the ground, he never missed having them. There was not only nobody equal, but nobody second to him. It is supposed that he could give any other player half the game, or beat him with his left hand. His service was tremendous. He once played Woodward and Meredith together (two of the best players in England) in the Fives-court, St. Martin's-street, and made seven and twenty aces following by services alone— a thing unheard of. He another time played Peru,* who was considered a first-rate fives-player, a match of the best out of five games, and in the three first games, which of course decided the match, Peru got only one ace. Cavanagh was an Irishman by birth, and a house-painter by profession. He had once laid aside his working-dress, and walked up, in his smartest clothes, to the Rosemary Branch* to have an afternoon's pleasure. A person accosted him, and asked him if he would have a game. So they agreed to play for half-a-crown a game, and a bottle of cider. The first game began—it was seven, eight, ten, thirteen, fourteen, all. Cavanagh won it. The next was the same. They played on, and each game was hardly contested. "There," said the unconscious fives-player, "there was a stroke that Cavanagh could not take: I never played better in my life, and yet I can't win a game. I don't know how it is." However, they played on, Cavanagh winning every game, and the by- standers drinking the cider, and laughing all the time. In the twelfth game, when Cavanagh was only four, and the stranger thirteen, a person came in, and said, "What! are you here, Cavanagh?" The words were no sooner pronounced than the astonished player let the ball drop from his hand, and saying, "What! have I been breaking my heart all this time to beat Cavanagh?" refused to make another effort. "And yet, I give you my word," said Cavanagh, telling the story with some triumph, "I played all the while with my clenched fist."—He used frequently to play matches at Copenhagen-house* for wagers and dinners. The wall against which they play is the same that supports the kitchen-chimney, and when the wall resounded louder than usual, the cooks exclaimed, "Those are the Irishman's balls," and the joints trembled on the spit!—Goldsmith consoled himself that there were places where he too was admired: and Cavanagh was the admiration of all the fives-courts, where he ever played. Mr. Powell, when he played matches in the Court in St. Martin's-street, used to fill his gallery at half a crown a head, with amateurs and admirers of talent in whatever department it is shown. He could not have shown himself in any ground in England, but he would have been immediately surrounded with inquisitive gazers, trying to find out in what part of his frame his un-rivalled skill lay, as politicians wonder to see the balance of Europe suspended in Lord Castlereagh's face, and admire the trophies of the British Navy lurking under Mr. Croker's hang-ing brow.* Now Cavanagh was as good-looking a man as the Noble Lord, and much better looking than the Right Hon. Secretary. He had a clear, open countenance, and did not look sideways or down, like Mr. Murray the bookseller.* He was a young fellow of sense, humour, and courage. He once had a quarrel with a waterman at Hungerford-stairs, and, they say, served him out in great style. In a word, there are hundreds at this day, who cannot mention his name without admiration, as the best fives-player that perhaps ever lived (the greatest excellence of which they have any notion)—and the noisy shout of the ring happily stood him in stead of the unheard voice of posterity!—The only person who seems to have excelled as much in another way as Cavanagh did in his, was the late John Davies, the racket-player. It was remarked of him that he did not seem to follow the ball, but the ball seemed to follow him. Give him a foot of wall, and he was sure to make the ball. The four best racket-players of that day were Jack Spines, Jem Harding, Armitage, and Church. Davies could give any one of these two hands a time, that is, half the game, and each of these, at their best, could give the best player now in London the same odds. Such are the gradations in all exertions of human skill and art. He once played four capital players together, and beat them. He was also a first-rate tennis-player, and an excellent fives-player. In the Fleet or King's Bench,* he would have stood against Powell, who was reckoned the best open-ground player of his time. This last-mentioned player is at present the keeper of the Fives-court, and we might recommend to him for a motto over his door—"Who enters here, forgets himself, his country, and his friends." And the best of it is, that by the calculation of the odds, none of the three are worth remembering!—Cavanagh died from the bursting of a blood-vessel, which prevented him from playing for the last two or three years. This, he was often heard to say, he thought hard upon him. He was fast recovering, however, when he was suddenly carried off, to the regret of all who knew him. As Mr. Peel made it a qualification of the present Speaker, Mr. Manners Sutton,* that he was an excellent moral character, so Jack Cavanagh was a zealous Catholic, and could not be persuaded to eat meat on a Friday, the day on which he died. We have paid this willing tribute to his memory.

> "Let no rude hand deface it,
> And his forlorn '*Hic Jacet*' " '*

ON PUBLIC OPINION

'Scared at the sound itself has made.'*

ONCE asking a friend why he did not bring forward an explanation of a circumstance, in which his conduct had been called in question, he said, 'His friends were satisfied on the subject, and he cared very little about the opinion of the world.' I made answer that I did not consider this a good ground to rest his defence upon, for that a man's friends seldom thought better of him than the world did. I see no reason to alter this opinion. Our friends, indeed, are more apt than a mere stranger to join in with, or be silent under, any imputation thrown out against us, because they are apprehensive they may be indirectly implicated in it, and they are bound to betray us to save their own credit. To judge of our jealousy, our sensibility, our high notions of responsibility on this score, only consider if a single individual lets fall a solitary remark implying a doubt of the wit, the sense, the courage of a friend,—how it staggers us—how it makes us shake with fear—how it makes us call up all our eloquence and airs of self-consequence in his defence, lest our partiality should be supposed to have blinded our perceptions, and we should be regarded as the dupes of a mistaken admiration. We already begin to meditate an escape from a losing cause, and try to find out some other fault in the character under discussion, to show that we are not behind-hand (if the truth must be spoken) in sagacity, and a sense of the ridiculous. If, then, this is the case with the first flaw, the first doubt, the first speck that dims the sun of friendship, so that we are ready to turn our backs on our sworn attachment and well-known professions the instant we have not all the world with us, what must it be when we have all the world against us; when our friend, instead of a single stain, is covered with mud from head to foot; how shall we expect our feeble voices not to be drowned in the general clamour? how shall we dare to oppose our partial and mistimed suffrages to the just indignation of the public? Or if it should not amount to this, how shall we answer the silence and contempt with which his name is received? how shall we animate the great mass of indifference or distrust with our private enthusiasm? how defeat the involuntary smile, or the suppressed sneer, with the burst of generous feeling and the glow of honest conviction? It is a thing not to be thought of, unless we would enter into a crusade against prejudice and malignity, devote ourselves as martyrs to friendship, raise a controversy in every company we go into, quarrel with every person we meet, and after making ourselves and everyone else uncomfortable, leave off, not by clearing our friend's reputation, but by involving our own pretensions to decency and common sense. People will not fail to observe, that a man may have his reasons for his faults or vices; but that for another to volunteer a defence of them, is without excuse. It is, in fact, an attempt to deprive them of the great and only benefit they derive from the supposed errors of their neighbours and contemporaries— the pleasure of backbiting and railing at them, which they call *seeing justice done.* It is not a single breath of rumour or opinion; but the whole atmosphere is infected with a sort of agueish taint of anger and suspicion, that relaxes the nerves of fidelity, and makes our most sanguine resolutions sicken and turn pale; and he who is proof against it, must either be armed with a love of truth, or a contempt for mankind, which place him out of the reach of ordinary rules and calculations. For myself, I do not shrink from defending a cause or a friend *under a cloud*; though in neither case will cheap or common efforts suffice. But, in the first, you merely stand up for your own judgment and principles against fashion and prejudice, and thus assume a sort of manly and heroic attitude of defiance: in the last, (which makes it a matter of greater nicety and nervous sensibility,) you sneak behind another to throw your gauntlet at the whole world, and it requires a double stock of stoical firmness not to be laughed out of your boasted zeal and independence as a romantic and *amiable weakness.*

There is nothing in which all the world agree but in running down some obnoxious individual. It may be supposed, that this is not for nothing, and that they have good reasons for what they do. On the contrary, I will undertake to say, that so far from there being invariably just grounds for such an universal outcry, the universality of the outcry is often the only ground of the opinion; and that it is purposely raised upon this principle, that all other proof or evidence against the person meant to be run down is wanting. Nay, farther, it may happen, while the clamour is at the loudest; while you hear it from all quarters; while it blows a perfect hurricane; while 'the world rings with the vain stir'*—not one of those who are most eager in hearing and echoing it knows what it is about, or is not fully persuaded, that the charge is equally false, malicious, and absurd. It is like the wind, that 'no man knoweth whence it cometh, or whither it goeth.'* It is *vox et praeterea nihil.** What then is it that gives it its confident circulation and its irresistible force? It is the loudness of the organ with which it is pronounced, the stentorian lungs of the multitude; the number of voices that take it up and repeat it, because others have done so; the rapid flight and the impalpable nature of common fame, that makes it a desperate undertaking for any individual to inquire into or arrest the mischief that, in the deafening buzz or loosened roar of laughter or of indignation, renders it impossible for the still small voice of reason to be heard, and leaves no other course to honesty or prudence than to fall flat on the face before it as before the pestilential blast of the Desert, and wait till it has passed over. Thus everyone joins in asserting, propagating, and in outwardly approving what everyone, in his private and unbiassed judgment, believes and knows to be scandalous and untrue. For everyone in such circumstances keeps his own opinion to himself, and only attends to or acts upon that which he conceives to be the opinion of everyone but himself. So that public opinion is not seldom a farce, equal to any acted upon the stage. Not only is it spurious and hollow in the way that Mr Locke points out,* by one man's taking up at second hand the opinion of another, but worse than this, one man takes up what he believes another *will* think and which the latter professes only because he believes it held by the first! All therefore that is necessary, to control public opinion, is, to gain possession of some organ loud and lofty enough to make yourself heard, that has power and interest on its side; and then, no sooner do you blow a blast in this trump of *ill-fame*, like the horn hung up by an old castle-wall, than you are answered, echoed, and accredited on all sides: the gates are thrown open to receive you, and you are admitted into the very heart of the fortress of public opinion, and can assail from the ramparts with every engine of abuse, and with privileged impunity, all those who may come forward to vindicate the truth, or to rescue their good name from the unprincipled keeping of authority, servility, sophistry and venal falsehood! The only thing wanted is to give an alarm—to excite a panic in the public mind of being left *in the lurch*, and the rabble (whether in the ranks of literature or war) will throw away their arms, and surrender at discretion to any bully or impostor who, for a *consideration*, shall choose to try the experiment upon them!

What I have here described is the effect even upon the candid and well-disposed:—what must it be to the malicious and idle, who are eager to believe all the ill they can hear of

everyone; or to the prejudiced and interested, who are determined to credit all the ill they hear against those who are not
of their own side? To these last it is only requisite to be
understood that the butt of ridicule or slander is of an opposite party, and they presently give you *carte blanche* to say what
you please of him. Do they know that it is true? No; but they
believe what all the world says, till they have evidence to the
contrary. Do you prove that it is false? They dare say, that if
not, that something worse remains behind; and they retain
the same opinion as before, for the honour of their party.
They hire someone to pelt you with mud, and then affect to
avoid you in the street as a dirty fellow. They are told that you
have a hump on your back, and then wonder at your assurance
or want of complaisance in walking into a room where they
are, without it. Instead of apologising for the mistake, and,
from finding one aspersion false, doubting all the rest, they
are only more confirmed in the remainder from being deprived of one handle against you, and resent their disappointment, instead of being ashamed of their credulity. People talk
of the bigotry of the Catholics, and treat with contempt the
absurd claim of the Popes to infallibility— I think, with little
right to do so. I walk into a church in Paris, where I am struck
with a number of idle forms and ceremonies, the chaunting
of the service in Latin, the shifting of the surplices, the sprink-
ling of holy-water, the painted windows 'casting a dim religious light',* the wax-tapers, the pealing organ: the common
people seem attentive and devout, and to put entire faith in
all this—Why? Because they imagine others to do so, they see
and hear certain signs and supposed evidences of it, and it
amuses and fills up the void of the mind, the love of the
mysterious and wonderful, to lend their assent to it. They have
assuredly, in general, no better reason—all our Protestant
divines will tell you so. Well, I step out of the church of St
Roche, and drop into an English reading-room hard by: what
am I the better? I see a dozen or a score of my countrymen,
with their faces fixed, and their eyes glued to a newspaper, a
magazine, a review—reading, swallowing, profoundly rumin-
ating on the lie, the cant, the sophism of the day! Why? It
saves them the trouble of thinking; it gratifies their ill-humour,

and keeps off *ennui*! Does any gleam of doubt, an air of ridicule or a glance of impatience pass across their features at the shallow and monstrous things they find? No, it is all passive faith and dull security; they cannot take their eyes from the page, they cannot live without it. They believe in Mr Blackwood, (you see it in their faces) as implicitly as in Sir John Barleycorn; in the *John Bull* as in a sirloin of beef; in the *Quarterly* as assuredly as in quarter-day*—as they hope to receive their rents, or to see old England again! Are not the Popes, the Fathers, the Councils, as good as these oracles, scouts, and champions of theirs? They know that the John Bull, for instance, is a hoax, a humbug, an impudent imposture, got up, week by week, to puff whom it pleases, to bully whom it pleases, to traduce whom it pleases, without any principle but a hint from its patrons, or without a pretence to any other principle. Do they believe in the known lie, the gross ribaldry, the foul calumny, the less on that account? They believe the more in it: because it is got up solely and expressly to serve a cause that needs such support—and they swear by whatever is devoted to this object.

The greater the profligacy, the effrontery, the servility, the greater the faith. Strange! that the British public (whether at home or abroad) should shake their heads at the Lady of Loretto, and repose deliciously on Mr Theodore Hook!* It may be thought that the enlightened part of the British public (persons of family and fortune, and often title, who have had a college-education and received the benefit of foreign travel) see through the quackery, which they encourage only for a political purpose, without being themselves the dupes of it. Suppose an individual of whom it has been repeatedly asserted that he has warts on his nose, were to enter the reading-room aforesaid in the Rue de la Paix—is there a single red-faced country squire who would not be surprised at not finding this part of the story true—would not persuade himself five minutes after that he could not have been seen correctly, or that some art had been used to conceal the defect, or would be led to doubt, from this instance, Mr Blackwood's general candour and veracity? On the contrary, the gentleman would be obliged to disbelieve his senses rather than give

Mr Blackwood the lie, who is read and believed by the whole world. He would have a host of witnesses against him: there is not a reader of Blackwood who would not swear to the fact. Seeing is believing, it is said. Lying is believing, say I. We do not even see with our own eyes, but must 'wink and shut our apprehensions up',* that we may be able to agree to the report of others, as a piece of good manners and point of established etiquette.—Besides, the supposed deformity answered his wishes: the abuse 'fed fat the ancient grudge he owed'* some presumptuous scribbler, for not agreeing in a number of points with his betters: it gave him a personal advantage over one he did not like—and who will give up what tends to strengthen his aversion against another? To Tory prejudice, sore as it is—to English imagination, morbid as it is, a nick-name, a ludicrous epithet, a malignant falsehood (when it has once been propagated and taken to bosoms as a welcome consolation) becomes a precious property, a vested right; and people would as soon give up a sinecure, or a share in a close borough,* as a plenary indulgence (published monthly with the court privilege) to speak and think with contempt of those who would abolish the one or throw open the other.

ON FASHION

'Born of nothing, begot of nothing.'*

'His garment neither was of silk nor say,
But painted plumes in goodly order dight,
Like as the sun-burnt Indians do array
Their tawny bodies in their proudest plight:
As those same plumes, so seem'd he vain and light,
That by his gait might easily appear;
For still he far'd as dancing in delight,
And in his hands a windy fan did bear,
That in the idle air he mov'd still here and there.'*

FASHION is an odd jumble of contradictions, of sympathies and antipathies. It exists only by its being participated among a certain number of persons, and its essence is destroyed by being communicated to a greater number. It is a continual struggle between 'the great vulgar and the small'* to get the start of or keep up with each other in the race of appearances, by an adoption on the part of the one of such external and fantastic symbols as strike the attention and excite the envy or admiration of the beholder, and which are no sooner made known and exposed to public view for this purpose, than they are successfully copied by the multitude, the slavish herd of imitators, who do not wish to be behind-hand with their betters in outward show and pretensions, and which then sink, without any farther notice, into disrepute and contempt. Thus fashion lives only in a perpetual round of giddy innovation and restless vanity. To be old-fashioned is the greatest crime a coat or a hat can be guilty of. To look like nobody else is a sufficiently mortifying reflection; to be in danger of being mistaken for one of the rabble is worse. Fashion constantly begins and ends in the two things it abhors most, singularity and vulgarity. It is the perpetual setting up and disowning a certain standard of taste, elegance, and refinement, which has no other foundation or authority than that it is the prevailing distinction of the moment, which was yesterday ridiculous from its being new, and to-morrow will be odious from its being common. It is one of the most slight and insignificant of all things. It cannot be lasting, for it depends on the constant change and shifting of its own harlequin disguises; it cannot be sterling, for, if it were, it could not depend on the breath of caprice; it must be superficial, to produce its immediate effect on the gaping crowd; and frivolous, to admit of its being assumed at pleasure by the numbers of those who affect, by being in the fashion, to be distinguished from the rest of the world. It is not any thing in itself, nor the sign of any thing but the folly and vanity of those who rely upon it as their greatest pride and ornament. It takes the firmest hold of the most flimsy and narrow minds, of those whose empti-ness conceives of nothing excellent but what is thought so by others, and whose self-conceit makes them willing to confine the opinion of all excellence to themselves and those like them. That which is true or beautiful in itself, is not the less so for standing alone That which is good for any thing, is the better for being more widely diffused. But fashion is the abortive issue of vain ostentation and exclusive egotism: it is haughty, trifling, affected, servile, despotic, mean, and ambitious, precise and fantastical, all in a breath—tied to no rule, and bound to conform to every whim of the minute. 'The fashion of an hour old mocks the wearer.'* It is a sublimated essence of levity, caprice, vanity, extravagance, idleness, and selfishness. It thinks of nothing but not being contaminated by vulgar use, and winds and doubles like a hare, and betakes itself to the most paltry shifts to avoid being overtaken by the common hunt that are always in full chase after it. It contrives to keep up its fastidious pretensions, not by the difficulty of the attainment, but by the rapidity and evanescent nature of the changes. It is a sort of conventional badge, or understood passport into select circles, which must still be varying (like the water-mark in bank notes) not to be counterfeited by those without the pale of fashionable society; for to make the test of admission to all the privileges of that refined and volatile atmosphere depend on any real merit or extraordinary accomplishment, would exclude too many of the pert, the dull, the ignorant, too many shallow, upstart, and self-admiring pretenders, to enable the few that passed muster to keep one another in any tolerable countenance. If it were the fashion, for instance, to be distinguished for virtue, it would be difficult to set or follow the example; but then this would confine the pretension to a small number, (not the most fashionable part of the community), and would carry a very singular air with it. Or if excellence in any art or science were made the standard of fashion, this would also effectually prevent vulgar imitation, but then it would equally prevent fashionable impertinence. There would be an obscure circle of *virtù* as well as virtue,* drawn within the established circle of fashion, a little province of a mighty empire;—the example of honesty would spread slowly, and learning would still have to boast of a respectable minority. But of what use would such uncourtly and out-of-the-way accomplishments be to the great and noble, the rich and the fair, without any of the *éclat*, the noise and nonsense which belong to that which is followed

and admired by all the world alike? The real and solid will
never do for the current coin, the common wear and tear of
foppery and fashion. It must be the meretricious, the showy,
the outwardly fine, and intrinsically worthless—that which lies
within the reach of the most indolent affectation, that which
can be put on or off at the suggestion of the most wilful
caprice, and for which, through all its fluctuations, no mortal
reason can be given, but that it is the newest absurdity in
vogue! The shape of a head-dress, whether flat or piled (curl
on curl) several stories high by the help of pins and pomatum,
the size of a pair of paste buckles, the quantity of gold-lace on
an embroidered waistcoat, the mode of taking a pinch of
snuff, or of pulling out a pocket handkerchief, the lisping and
affected pronunciation of certain words, the saying *Me'm* for
Madam, Lord Foppington's *Tam and 'Paun honour*,* with a
regular set of visiting phrases and insipid sentiments ready
sorted for the day, were what formerly distinguished the mob
of fine gentlemen and ladies from the mob of their inferiors.*
These marks and appendages of gentility had their day, and
were then discarded for others equally peremptory and unequivocal. But in all this chopping and changing, it is generally one folly that drives out another; one trifle that by its
specific levity acquires a momentary and surprising ascend-
ency over the last. There is no striking deformity of appearance or behaviour that has not been made 'the sign of an
inward and invisible grace'.* Accidental imperfections are
laid hold of to hide real defects. Paint, patches, and powder,
were at one time synonymous with health, cleanliness, and
beauty. Obscenity, irreligion, small oaths, tippling, gaming,
effeminacy in the one sex and Amazon airs in the other, any
thing is the fashion while it lasts. In the reign of Charles II,
the profession and practice of every species of extravagance
and debauchery were looked upon as the indispensable marks
of an accomplished cavalier. Since that period the court has
reformed, and has had rather a rustic air. Our belles formerly
overloaded themselves with dress: of late years, they have
affected to go almost naked,—'and are, when unadorned,
adorned the most'.* The women having left off stays, the men
have taken to wear them, if we are to believe the authentic

Memoirs of the Fudge Family.* The Niobe head is at present
buried in the *poke* bonnet, and the French milliners and
marchands des modes have proved themselves an overmatch for
the Greek sculptors, in matters of taste and costume.

A very striking change has, however, taken place in dress of
late years, and some progress has been made in taste and
elegance, from the very circumstance, that, as fashion has
extended its empire in that direction, it has lost its power.
While fashion in dress included what was costly, it was confined to the wealthier classes: even this was an encroachment
on the privileges of rank and birth, which for a long time were
the only things that commanded or pretended to command
respect, and we find Shakespeare complaining that 'the city
madam bears the cost of princes on unworthy shoulders';*
but, when the appearing in the top of the mode no longer
depended on the power of purchasing certain expensive
articles of dress, or the right of wearing them, the rest was so
obvious and easy, that any one who chose might cut as cox-
combical a figure as the best. It became a matter of mere
affectation on the one side, and gradually ceased to be made
a matter of aristocratic assumption on the other. 'In the grand
carnival of this our age',* among other changes this is not the
least remarkable, that the monstrous pretensions to distinctions in dress have dwindled away by tacit consent, and the
simplest and most graceful have been in the same request with
all classes. In this respect, as well as some others, 'the age is
grown so picked, the peasant's toe comes so near the courtier's heel, it galls his kibe;'* a lord is hardly to be distinguished in the street from an attorney's clerk; and a plume
of feathers is no longer mistaken for the highest distinction
in the land! The ideas of natural equality and the Manchester
steam-engines together have, like a double battery, levelled
the high towers and artificial structures of fashion in dress,
and a white muslin gown is now the common costume of the
mistress and the maid, instead of their wearing, as heretofore,
rich silks and satins or coarse linsey-wolsey. It would be
ridiculous (on a similar principle) for the courtier to take the
wall* of the citizen, without having a sword by his side to
maintain his right of precedence; and, from the stricter

notions that have pre-vailed of a man's personal merit and identity, a cane dangling from his arm is the greatest extension of his figure that can be allowed to the modern *petit-maître.*

What shews the worthlessness of mere fashion is, to see how easily this vain and boasted distinction is assumed, when the restraints of decency or circumstances are once removed, by the most uninformed and commonest of the people. I know an undertaker that is the greatest prig in the streets of London, and an Aldermanbury haberdasher, that has the most military strut of any lounger in Bond-street or St James's. We may, at any time, raise a regiment of fops from the same number of fools, who have vanity enough to be intoxicated with the smartness of their appearance, and not sense enough to be ashamed of themselves. Every one remembers the story in *Peregrine Pickle,** of the strolling gipsy that he picked up in spite, had well scoured, and introduced her into genteel company, where she met with great applause, till she got into a passion by seeing a fine lady cheat at cards, rapped out a volley of oaths, and let nature get the better of art. Dress is the great secret of address. Clothes and confidence will set anybody up in the trade of modish accomplishment. Look at the two classes of well-dressed females whom we see at the play-house, in the boxes. Both are equally dressed in the height of the fashion, both are *rouged,* and wear their neck and arms bare,—both have the same conscious, haughty, theatrical air;—the same toss of the head, the same stoop in the shoulders, with all the grace that arises from a perfect freedom from embarrassment, and all the fascination that arises from a systematic disdain of formal prudery,—the same pretence and jargon of fashionable conversation,—the same mimicry of tones and phrases,—the same 'lisping, and ambling, and painting, and nicknaming of Heaven's creatures';* the same every thing but real propriety of behaviour, and real refinement of sentiment. In all the externals, they are as like as the reflection in the looking-glass. The only difference between the woman of fashion and the woman of pleasure is, that the one *is* what the other only *seems to be*; and yet, the victims of dissipation who thus rival and almost outshine women of the first quality in all the blaze, and pride, and glitter of shew and fashion, are, in general, no better than a set of raw, uneducated, inexperienced country girls, or awkward, coarse-fisted servant maids, who require no other apprenticeship or qualification to be on a level with persons of the highest distinction in society, in all the brilliancy and elegance of outward appearance, than that they have forfeited its common privileges, and every title to respect in reality. The truth is, that real virtue, beauty, or understanding, are the same, whether 'in a high or low degree';* and the airs and graces of pretended superiority over these which the highest classes give themselves, from mere frivolous and external accomplishments, are easily imitated, with provoking success, by the lowest, whenever they *dare*.

The two nearest things in the world are gentility and vulgarity—

'And thin partitions do their bounds divide.'*

Where there is much affectation of the one, we may be always sure of meeting with a double share of the other. Those who are conscious to themselves of any real superiority or refinement, are not particularly jealous of the adventitious marks of it. Miss Burney's novels all turn upon this slender distinction. It is the only thing that can be said against them. It is hard to say which she has made out to be the worst; low people always aping gentility, or people in high life always avoiding vulgarity. Mr Smith and the Brangtons were everlastingly trying to do as their fashionable acquaintances did, and these again were always endeavouring *not* to do and say what Mr Smith and the Brangtons did or said. What an instructive game at cross-purposes! 'Kings are naturally lovers of low company,' according to the observation of Mr Burke;* because their rank cannot be called into question by it, and they can only hope to find, in the opposite extreme of natural and artificial inequality, any thing to confirm them in the belief, that their personal pretensions at all answer to the ostensible superiority to which they are raised. By associating only with the worst and weakest, they persuade themselves that they are the best and wisest of mankind.

OUR NATIONAL THEATRES

THE motto of the English nation is 'exclusion'. In this consists our happiness and our pride. If you come to a gentleman's park and pleasure-grounds, you see written up, 'Man-traps and steel-guns set here'—as if he had no pleasure in walking in them, except in the idea of keeping other people out. Having little of the spirit of enjoyment in ourselves, we seek to derive a stupid or sullen satisfaction from the privations and disappointment of others. Everything resolves itself into an idea of *property*, that is, of something that our neighbours dare not touch, and that we have not the heart to enjoy. The invidious distinction of the *private boxes* arose out of this principle; and has done a great deal of harm. Was it to secure the best place for the best company? Are they filled with peers and peeresses eager to see the play, and enjoying it at the height? On the contrary, they are quite empty; or you see nobody there but Madame Vestris and her friends.* But having secured the exclusive privilege, and shut others out, this is all the satisfaction we are capable of. The consequence has been, that the nobility and gentry no longer appearing in the open boxes, they have ceased to be the favourite resort of genteel and fashionable company; people no longer go for the chance of sitting in the next box to a prince or minister of state, of seeing how a courtier smiles on hearing a countess lisp, or with the hope of being mixed up in splendid confusion with the flower of the land. A certain disrepute is thus thrown upon the boxes, which are left to a sort of second city-company. The partitioning off the *stalls* at the Opera is a part of the same wretched system. Before, a seat in the pit of the Opera was a reputable distinction; everyone there was on a footing of equality. This pleasure was envied as getting too common; and to circumscribe it the contrivance of the stalls was invented, by which an implied stigma is thrown on the rest of the pit, and where fine gentlemen and ladies, admitted under lock and key, and sitting at English ease, look back on

the crowd behind them like the footmen behind their chairs.
Whether it is our unsocial temper, or our system of equality
and the dread of encroachment, that produces this exclusive
spirit, we cannot say; but the fruit is most bitter and painful.
The other night an attempt was made to shut out *improper*
people from the theatre; did the *proper* people go the more
the next night? No! their object was to prevent others from
going; and if by this under-hand mode the doors of the theatre
were finally closed, it would afford an additional gratification
to their malice and poverty of imagination. We hope there is
more genuine old English honesty and feeling, and more of
a cordial play-going humour left in the public than to allow
of such a catastrophe. There is no calculating the mischief
that would ensue. There is not a person in this great metropolis who does not rise with a pleasanter feeling in the
morning, and eat his breakfast with a better relish, from a
consciousness (whether adverted to or not) that he may go to
which of the great theatres he pleases in the evening. There
is not a chimney-sweeper who does not get his shilling's worth
of pleasure out of them once a year, which must serve him
the remainder. There is not a young lady who mopes away her
time in the country who does not console herself with the
thought of seeing Mr Charles Kemble* act when she comes
up to town in the winter. The stage is become part of the vital
existence of this civilised country; and our circulation cannot
go on well without it. To the real lover of the drama, to see
the fall of one of our great theatres is like cutting off one of
his hands. Our recollections of the state, of the masterpieces
of wit and pathos that support it, of the proud and happy
names that adorn it, of the Siddonses, the Kembles, the
Jordans, the Lewises, the Quicks, the Mundens, the Cookes,
the Little Simmonses, the Bannisters, the Suetts—what are
they but recollections of ourselves, of our liveliest pleasures,
of our youthful hopes, 'dear as the ruddy drops that visit the
sad heart'?* and shall we close the door on all these bright
visions, and let a noble pile crumble into ruins and bury all
these cherished names in common rubbish, so that we can
never think or speak of them again but with regret and shame,
and not deem it one of the greatest calamities that can happen

to us? Whoever sees a play ought to be better and more sociable for it; for he has something to talk about, some ideas and feelings in common with his neighbours. Even the players, as they pass along the street, glance a light upon the day; and (sports of fortune, puppets of opinion as they are) give us a livelier interest in humanity, of which they are the representatives. If we meet Mrs D——* in Cranbourn-alley, we get up the narrow part of King-street without being jostled by anyone. It would be one of the worst signs of the times to find that Covent-garden was no more; and would be our first approach to the state of those old and once flourishing cities in other parts of the world, where you see the skeletons of mighty theatres still standing as monuments of the past, and the magnificence that raised them mouldering in oblivion.

ENGLISH CHARACTERISTICS

THE English are the only people to whom the term *blackguard* is peculiarly applicable—by which I understand a reference of everything to violence and a contempt for the feelings and opinions of others. It may be affirmed of them, with few exceptions, from the highest to the lowest, whether gentle or simple, they would all rather use *force* to gain their point than have no occasion for it, and regard good-will and complaisance as perfectly insipid and out of character. They think it French grimace and affectation. A common *blackguard* in the street runs up against you if he can, to show he is as good as you; and asks you if you complain, how can you help yourself? And the *fine gentleman* at the play (altering nothing but the name) enters the boxes with a menacing air, as if prepared to force his way through some obstacle, which he habitually anticipates and resents beforehand. A true Englishman, on coming into a coffee-room, looks round to see if the company are good enough for him, to know if his place is not taken, or if he cannot turn others out of theirs, and is not easy unless he can give himself supercilious airs the whole time he is eating his beef-steak, towards someone worse dressed than himself, or else assume a vastly significant and independent spirit in answer to the smallest appearance of advantage over him. There is always much 'internal oath',* preparatory knitting of the brows, implied clenching of the fists, and imaginary shouldering of affronts and grievances going on in the mind of an unsophisticated Englishman. The clown resorts to club-law—it is *a word and a blow* with him; the citizen comforts himself that he has the law on his side, and that the magistrate has a spite at the delinquent. Everything is done *against the grain.* Even the laughter-loving Venuses of our isle would much rather lend their gallants a box on the ear than accept an offer of love or money from them; and it is the prospect of unlimited gin, of calling names, of doing nothing, and thrusting their hard, red hands into white kid gloves, which fills the rank of this profession to the overflowing of our streets and theatres nightly. These half-naked vestals, planted against the pillars in the lobbies, or marching up and down arm-in-arm with *Tom-and-Jerry* admirers,* smart book-keepers, or lawyers' clerks, are the triumphs of English modesty and manners. A peace-officer in this country is the only person who refuses to lift a finger, and proceeds with infinite caution and repugnance in suppressing the natural growth and glory of the soil, *rows* and actions of assault and battery. If a fellow in the street makes an outrageous noise, and threatens to knock anyone down, the watchmen, in pure sympathy and admiration of his prowess, let him pass: if a poor woman falls down in a fit through intoxication or want, they have her to the watch-house* in a moment. They have no compassion for the weak and helpless; their heads are full of blows and bludgeons. Such is our love of liberty; such the spirit of our constitution and our clime! If this subject be harping on a grievance, at least it is not an imaginary one.

BRUMMELLIANA

WE look upon Beau Brummell* as the greatest of small wits. Indeed, he may in this respect be considered, as Cowley says of Pindar,* as 'a species alone', and as forming a class by himself. He has arrived at the very *minimum* of wit, and reduced it, 'by happiness or pains',* to an almost invisible point. All his *bons-mots* turn upon a single circumstance, the exaggerating of the merest trifles into matters of importance, or treating everything else with the utmost *nonchalance* and indifference, as if whatever pretended to pass beyond those limits was a *bore*, and disturbed the serene air of high life. We have heard of

> 'A sound so fine,
> That nothing lived 'twixt it and silence.'*

So we may say of Mr Brummell's jests, that they are of a meaning so attenuated that 'nothing lives 'twixt them and nonsense':—they hover on the very brink of vacancy, and are in their shadowy composition next of kin to nonentities. It is impossible for anyone to go beyond him without falling flat into insignificance and insipidity: he has touched the *ne plus ultra* that divides the dandy from the dunce. But what a fine eye to discriminate: what a sure hand to hit this last and thinnest of all intellectual partitions! *Exempli gratiâ*— for in so new a species, the theory is unintelligible without furnishing the proofs:—

Thus, in the question addressed to a noble person* (which we quoted the other day), 'Do you call that *thing* a coat?' a distinction is taken as nice as it is startling. It seems all at once a vulgar prejudice to suppose that a coat is a coat, the commonest of all common things,—it is here lifted into an ineffable essence, so that a coat is no longer a *thing*; or that it would take infinite gradations of fashion, taste, and refinement, for a *thing* to aspire to the undefined privileges, and mysterious attributes of a coat. Finer 'fooling' than this cannot be imagined. What a cut upon the Duke! The beau becomes an emperor among such insects!

The first anecdote in which Mr Brummell's wit dawned upon us—and it really rises with almost every new instance—was the following: A friend one day called upon him, and found him confined to his room from a lameness in one foot, upon which he expressed his concern at the accident. 'I am sorry for it too,' answered Brummell very gravely, 'particularly as it's *my favourite leg!*' Is not this as if a man of fashion had nothing else to do than to sit and think of which of his legs he liked best; and in the plenitude of his satisfactions, and the absence of all real wants, to pamper this fanciful distinction into a serious sort of *pet* preference? Upon the whole, among so many beauties—*ubi tot nitent*,* I am inclined to give my suffrage in favour of this, as the most classical of all our contemporary's *jeux d'esprit*—there is an Horatian ease and elegance about it—a slippered negligence, a cushioned effeminacy—it would take years of careless study and languid enjoyment to strike out so quaint and ingenious a conceit—

> 'A subtler web Arachne cannot spin;
> Nor the fine nets which oft we woven see
> Of scorched dew, do not in the air more lightly flee!'*

It is truly the art of making something out of nothing.

We shall not go deeply into the common story of Mr Brummell's asking his servant, as he was going out for the evening, 'Where do I dine to-day, John?' This is little more than the common cant of a multiplicity of engagements, so as to make it impossible to bear them all in mind, and of an utter disinclination to all attention to one's own affairs; but the following is brilliant and original. Sitting one day at table between two other persons, Mr Brummell said to his servant, who stood behind his chair—'John!' 'Yes, sir.' 'Who is this at my right hand?' 'If you please, sir, it's the Marquis of Headfort.' 'And who is this at my left hand?' 'It's my Lord Yarmouth.' 'Oh, very well!' and the Beau then proceeded to address himself to the persons who were thus announced to him. Now, this is surely superb, and 'high fantastical'.* No, the smallest fold of that nicely adjusted cravat was not to be deranged, the least deviation from that select posture was not to be supposed possible. Had his head been fastened in a vice, it could not have been more immovably fixed than by the 'great idea in his mind',* of how a coxcomb should sit: the air of fashion and affectation 'bound him with Styx nine times round him';* and the Beau preserved the perfection of an attitude—like a piece of incomprehensible *still-life*,—the whole of dinner-time. The *ideal* is everything, even in frivolity and folly.

It is not one of the least characteristic of our hero's answers to a lady, who asked him if he never tasted vegetables— 'Madam, I once ate a pea!' This was reducing the quantity of offensive grossness to the smallest assignable fraction: anything beyond *that* his imagination was oppressed with; and even this he seemed to confess to, with a kind of remorse, and to hasten from the subject with a certain monosyllabic brevity of style.

I do not like the mere impudence (Mr Theodore Hook,* with his extempore dullness, might do the same thing) of forcing himself into a lady's rout, who had not invited him to her parties, and the gabble about Hopkinses and Tomkinses;* but there is something piquant enough in his answer to a city-fashionable, who asked him if he would dine with him on a certain day—'Yes, if you won't mention it to anyone'; and in an altercation with the same person afterwards, about obligations, the assumption of superiority implied in the appeal—'Do you count my having *borrowed* a thousand pounds of you for nothing?' soars immediately above commonplace.

On one occasion, Mr Brummell falling ill, accounted for it by saying, 'They put me to bed to a damp——!' From what slight causes direst issues spring!* So sensitive and apprehensive a constitution makes one sympathise with its delicate possessor, as much as if he had been shut up in the steam of a laundry, or 'his lodging had been on the cold ground.'* Mr Brummell having been interrogated as to the choice of his present place of residence (Calais) as somewhat dull replied, 'He thought it hard if a gentleman could not pass his time agreeably between London and Paris.'

Some of Brummell's *bons-mots* have been attributed to Sir Lumley Skeffington,* who is even said to have been the first in this minute and tender walk of wit. It is, for instance, reported of him that, being at table and talking of daisies, he should turn round to his valet, and say with sentimental *naïveté* and trivial fondness—'On what day of the month did I first see a daisy, Matthew?' 'On the 1st of February, sir.' There is here a kindred vein; but whoever was the inventor, Brummell has borne away the prize, as Pope eclipsed his master Dryden, and Titian surpassed Giorgione's fame. In fine, it was said, with equal truth and spirit by one of the parties concerned, that 'the year 1815* was fatal to three great men—Byron, Buonaparte, and Brummell!'

THE SELF

SELF-LOVE AND BENEVOLENCE

L. YOU deny, I think, that personal identity, in the qualified way in which you think proper to admit it, is any ground for the doctrine of self-interest?

H.*Yes, in an exclusive and absolute sense I do undoubtedly, that is, in the sense in which it is affirmed by metaphysicians, and ordinarily believed in.

L. Could you not go over the ground briefly, without entering into technicalities?

H. Not easily: but stop me when I entangle myself in difficulties. A person fancies, or feels habitually, that he has a positive, substantial interest in his own welfare, (generally speaking) just as much as he has in any actual sensation that he feels, because he is always and necessarily the same self. What is his interest at one time is therefore equally *his* interest at all other times. This is taken for granted as a self-evident proposition. Say he does not feel a particular benefit or injury at this present moment, yet it is he who is to feel it, which comes to the same thing. Where there is this continued identity of person, there must also be a correspondent identity of interest. I have an abstract, unavoidable interest in whatever can befall myself, which I can have or feel in no other person living, because I am always under every possible circumstance the self-same individual, and not any other individual whatsoever. In short, this word *self* (so closely do a number of associations cling round it and cement it together) is supposed to represent as it were a given concrete substance, as much one thing as any thing in nature can possibly be, and the centre or *substratum* in which the different impressions and ramifications of my being meet and are indissolubly knit together.

A. And you propose then seriously to take 'this one entire and perfect chrysolite',* this self, this 'precious jewel of the soul',* this rock on which mankind have built their faith for ages, and at one blow shatter it to pieces with the sledge-

hammer, or displace it from its hold in the imagination with
the wrenching-irons of metaphysics?

H. I am willing to use my best endeavours for that purpose.

L. You really ought: for you have the prejudices of the whole
world against you.

H. I grant the prejudices are formidable; and I should
despair, did I not think the reasons even stronger. Besides,
without altering the opinions of the whole world, I might be
contented with the suffrages of one or two intelligent people.

L. Nay, you will prevail by flattery, if not by argument.

A. That is something newer than all the rest.

H. 'Plain truth,' dear A——, 'needs no flowers of speech.'*

L. Let me rightly understand you. Do you mean to say that
I am not C. L. and that you are not W. H. or that we shall not
both of us remain so to the end of the chapter, without a
possibility of ever changing places with each other?

H. I am afraid, if you go to that, there is very little chance
that

> '*I* shall be ever mistaken for *you*.'*

But with all this precise individuality and inviolable identity
that you speak of, let me ask, Are you not a little changed (less
so, it is true, than most people) from what you were twenty
years ago? Or do you expect to appear the same that you are
now twenty years hence?

L. 'No more of that if thou lovest me.'* We know what we
are, but we know not what we shall be.

H. A truce then; but be assured that whenever you happen
to fling up your part, there will be no other person found to
attempt it after you.

L. Pray, favour us with your paradox without farther preface.

H. I will then try to match my paradox against your prejudice, which as it is armed all in proof, to make any impression
on it, I must, I suppose, take aim at the rivets; and if I can hit
them, if I do not (round and smooth as it is) cut it into three
pieces, and show that two parts in three are substance and the
third and principal part shadow, never believe me again. Your
real self ends exactly where your pretended self-interest

begins; and in calculating upon this principle as a solid, permanent, absolute, self-evident truth, you are mocked with a name.

L. How so? I hear, but do not see.

H. You must allow that this identical, indivisible, ostensible self is at any rate distinguishable into three parts,—the past, the present, and future?

L. I see no particular harm in that.

H. It is nearly all I ask. Well then, I admit that you have a peculiar, emphatic, incommunicable and exclusive interest or fellow-feeling in the two first of these selves; but I deny resolutely and unequivocally that you have any such natural, absolute, unavoidable, and mechanical interest in the last self, or in your future being, the interest you take in it being necessarily the offspring of understanding and imagination (aided by habit and circumstances), like that which you take in the welfare of others, and yet this last interest is the only one that is ever the object of rational and voluntary pursuit, or that ever comes into competition with the interests of others.

L. I am still to seek for the connecting clue.

H. I am almost ashamed to ask for your attention to a statement so very plain that it seems to border on a truism. I have an interest of a peculiar and limited nature in my present self, inasmuch as I feel my actual sensations not simply in a degree, but in a way and by means of faculties which afford me not the smallest intimation of the sensations of others. I cannot possibly feel the sensations of any one else, nor consequently take the slightest interest in them as such. I have no nerves communicating with another's brain, and transmitting to me either the glow of pleasure or the agony of pain which he may feel at the present moment by means of his senses. So far, therefore, namely, so far as my present self or immediate sensations are concerned, I am cut off from all sympathy with others. I stand alone in the world, a perfectly insulated individual, necessarily and in the most unqualified sense indifferent to all that passes around me, and that does not in the first instance affect myself, for otherwise I neither have nor can have the remotest consciousness of it as a matter of organic sensation, any more than the mole has of light or the deaf adder of sounds.

L. Spoken like an oracle.

H. Again, I have a similar peculiar, mechanical, and untransferable interest in my past self, because I remember and can dwell upon my past sensations (even after the objects are removed) also in a way and by means of faculties which do not give me the smallest insight into or sympathy with the past feelings of others. I may conjecture and fancy what those feelings have been; and so I do. But I have no *memory* or continued consciousness of what either of good or evil may have found a place in their bosoms, no secret spring that touched vibrates to the hopes and wishes that are no more, unlocks the chambers of the past with the same assurance of reality, or identifies my feelings with theirs in the same intimate manner as with those which I have already felt in my own person. Here again, then, there is a real, undoubted, original and positive foundation for the notion of self to rest upon; for in relation to my former self and past feelings, I do possess a faculty which serves to unite me more especially to my own being, and at the same time draws a distinct and impassable line around that being, separating it from every other. A door of communication stands always open between my present consciousness and my past feelings, which is locked and barred by the hand of Nature and the constitution of the human understanding against the intrusion of any straggling impressions from the minds of others. I can only see into their real history darkly and by reflection. To sympathise with their joys or sorrows, and place myself in their situation either now or formerly, I must proceed by guess-work, and borrow the use of the common faculty of imagination. I am ready to acknowledge, then, that in what regards the past as well as the present, there is a strict metaphysical distinction between myself and others, and that my personal identity so far, or in the close, continued, inseparable connection between my past and present impressions, is firmly and irrevocably established.

L. You go on swimmingly. So far all is sufficiently clear.

H. But now comes the rub: for beyond that point I deny that the doctrine of personal identity or self-interest (as a consequence from it) has any foundation to rest upon but a confusion of names and ideas. It has none in the nature of things or of the human mind. For I have no faculty by which I can project myself into the future, or hold the same sort of palpable, tangible, immediate, and exclusive communication with my future feelings, in the same manner as I am made to feel the present moment by means of the senses, or the past moment by means of memory. If I have any such faculty, expressly set apart for the purpose, name it. If I have no such faculty, I can have no such interest. In order that I may possess a proper personal identity so as to live, breathe, and feel along the whole line of my existence in the same intense and intimate mode, it is absolutely necessary to have some general medium or faculty by which my successive impressions are blended and amalgamated together, and to maintain and support this extraordinary interest. But so far from there being any foundation for this merging and incorporating of my future in my present self, there is no link of connection, no sympathy, no reaction, no mutual consciousness between them, nor even a possibility of any thing of the kind, in a mechanical and personal sense. Up to the present point, the spot on which we stand, the doctrine of personal identity holds good; hitherto the proud and exclusive pretensions of self 'come, but no farther'.* The rest is air, is nothing, is a name, or but the common ground of reason and humanity. If I wish to pass beyond this point and look into my own future lot, or anticipate my future weal or woe before it has had an existence, I can do so by means of the same faculties by which I enter into and identify myself with the welfare, the being, and interests of others, but only by these. As I have already said, I have no particular organ or faculty of self-interest, in that case made and provided. I have no sensation of what is to happen to myself in future, no presentiment of it, no instinctive sympathy with it, nor consequently any abstract and unavoidable self-interest in it. Now mark. It is only in regard to my past and present being, that a broad and insurmountable barrier is placed between myself and others: as to future

objects, there is no absolute and fundamental distinction
whatever. But it is only these last that are the objects of any
rational or practical interest. The idea of self properly attaches
to objects of sense or memory, but these can never be the
objects of action or of voluntary pursuit, which must, by the
supposition, have an eye to future events. But with respect to
these the chain of self-interest is dissolved and falls in pieces
by the very necessity of our nature, and our obligations to self
as a blind, mechanical, unsociable principle are lost in the
general law which binds us to the pursuit of good as it comes
within our reach and knowledge.

   A. A most lame and impotent conclusion, I must say. Do you
mean to affirm that you have really the same interest in
another's welfare that you have in your own?

   H. I do not wish to assert any thing without proof. Will you
tell me, if you have this particular interest in yourself, what
faculty is it that gives it you—to what conjuration and what
mighty magic it is owing—or whether it is merely the name
of self that is to be considered as a proof of all the absurdities
and impossibilities that can be drawn from it?

   A. I do not see that you have hitherto pointed out any.

   H. What! not the impossibility that you should be another
being, with whom you have not a particle of fellow-feeling?

   A. Another being! Yes, I know it is always impossible for me
to be another being.

   H. Ay, or yourself either, without such a fellow-feeling, for it
is that which constitutes self. If not, explain to me what you
mean by self. But it is more convenient for you to let that
magical sound lie involved in the obscurity of prejudice and
language. You will please to take notice that it is not I who
commence these hairbreadth distinctions and special-pleading. I take the old ground of common sense and natural
feeling, and maintain that though in a popular, practical sense
mankind are strongly swayed by self-interest, yet in the same
ordinary sense they are also governed by motives of good-
nature, compassion, friendship, virtue, honour, &c. Now all
this is denied by your modern metaphysicians,* who would
reduce every thing to abstract self-interest, and exclude every
other mixed motive or social tie in a strict, philosophical

sense. They would drive me from my ground by scholastic subtleties and newfangled phrases; am I to blame then if I take them at their word, and try to foil them at their own weapons? Either stick to the unpretending *jog-trot* notions on the subject, or if you are determined to refine in analysing words and arguments, do not be angry if I follow the example set me, or even go a little farther to arrive at the truth. Shall we proceed on this understanding?

A. As you please.

H. We have got so far then (if I mistake not, and if there is not some flaw in the argument which I am unable to detect) that the past and present (which alone can appeal to our selfish faculties) are not the objects of action, and that the future (which can alone be the object of practical pursuit) has no particular claim or hold upon self. All action, all passion, all morality and self-interest, is prospective.

A. You have not made that point quite clear. What then is meant by a present interest, by the gratification of the present moment, as opposed to a future one?

H. Nothing, in a strict sense; or rather in common speech, you mean a near one, the interest of the next moment, the next hour, the next day, the next year, as it happens.

A. What! would you have me believe that I snatch my hand out of the flame of a candle from a calculation of future consequences?

L. (*Laughing*). A——had better not meddle with that question. H——is in his element there.* It is his old and favourite illustration.

H. Do you not snatch your hand out of the fire to procure ease from pain?

A. No doubt, I do.

H. And is not this case subsequent to the act, and the act itself to the feeling of pain, which caused it?

A. It may be so; but the interval is so slight that we are not sensible of it.

H. Nature is nicer in her distinctions than we. Thus you could not lift the food to your mouth, but upon the same principle. The viands are indeed tempting, but if it were the sight or smell of these alone that attracted you, you would remain satisfied with them. But you use means to ends, neither of which exist till you employ or produce them, and which would never exist if the understanding which foresees them did not run on before the actual objects and purvey to appetite. If you say it is habit, it is partly so; but that habit would never have been formed, were it not for the connection between cause and effect, which always takes place in the order of time, or of what Hume calls *antecedents* and *consequents*.*

A. I confess I think this a mighty microscopic way of looking at the subject.

H. Yet you object equally to more vague and sweeping generalities. Let me, however, endeavour to draw the knot a little tighter, as it has a considerable weight to bear—no less, in my opinion, than the whole world of moral sentiments. All voluntary action must relate to the future: but the future can only exist or influence the mind as an object of imagination and forethought; therefore the motive to voluntary action, to all that we seek or shun, must be in all cases *ideal* and problematical. The thing itself which is an object of pursuit can never co-exist with the motives which make it an object of pursuit. No one will say that the past can be an object either of prevention or pursuit. It may be a subject of involuntary regrets, or may give rise to the starts and flaws of passion; but we cannot set about seriously recalling or altering it. Neither can that which at present exists, or is an object of sensation, be at the same time an object of action or of volition, since if it *is*, no volition or exertion of mine can for the instant make it to be other than it is. I can make it *cease* to be indeed, but this relates to the future, to the supposed non-existence of the object, and not to its actual impression on me. For a thing to be *willed*, it must necessarily not be. Over my past and present impressions my will has no control: they are placed, according to the poet,* beyond the reach of fate, much more of human means. In order that I may take an effectual and consistent interest in any thing, that it may be an object of hope or fear, of desire or dread, it must be a thing still to come, a thing still in doubt, depending on circumstances and the means used to bring about or avert it. It is my will that determines its existence or the contrary (otherwise there would be no use in troubling oneself about it); it does not itself lay its peremptory, inexorable mandates on my will. For it is as yet (and must be in order to be the rational object of a moment's deliberation) a non-entity, a possibility merely, and it is plain that nothing can be the cause of nothing. That which is not, cannot act, much less can it act mechanically, physically, all-powerfully. So far is it from being true that a real and practical interest in any thing are convertible terms, that a practical interest can never by any possible chance be a real one, that is, excited by the presence of a real object or by mechanical sympathy. I cannot assuredly be induced by a present object to take means to make it exist—it can be no more than present to me—or if it is past, it is too late to think of recovering the occasion or preventing it now. But the future, the future is all our own; or rather it belongs equally to others. The world of action then, of business or pleasure, of self-love or benevolence, is not made up of solid materials, moved by downright, solid springs; it is essentially a void, an unreal mockery, both in regard to ourselves and others, except as it is filled up, animated, and set in motion by human thoughts and purposes. The ingredients of passion, action, and properly of interest are never positive, palpable matters-of-fact, concrete existences, but symbolical representations of events lodged in the bosom of futurity, and teaching us, by timely anticipation and watchful zeal, to build up the fabric of our own or others' future weal.

A. Do we not sometimes plot their woe with at least equal goodwill?

H. Not much oftener than we are accessory to our own.

A. I must say that savours more to me of an antithesis than of an answer.

H. For once, be it so.

A. But surely there is a difference between a real and an imaginary interest? A history is not a romance.

H. Yes; but in this sense the feelings and interests of others are in the end as real, as much matters of fact as mine or yours can be. The history of the world is not a romance, though you and I have had only a small share in it. You would turn every thing into autobiography. The interests of others are no more chimerical, visionary, fantastic than my own, being founded in truth, and both are brought home to my bosom in the same way by the force of imagination and sympathy.

L. But in addition to all this sympathy that you make such a rout about, it is *I* who am to feel a real, downright interest in my own future good, and I shall feel no such interest in another person's. Does not this make a wide, nay a total difference in the case? Am I to have no more affection for my own flesh and blood than for another's?

H. This would indeed make an entire difference in the case, if your interest in your own good were founded in your affection for yourself, and not your affection for yourself in your attachment to your own good. If you were attached to your own good merely because it was *yours,* I do not see why you should not be equally attached to your own ill—both are equally yours! Your own person or that of others would, I take it, be alike indifferent to you, but for the degree of sympathy you have with the feelings of either. Take away the sense or apprehension of pleasure and pain, and you would care no more about yourself than you do about the hair of your head or the paring of your nails, the parting with which gives you no sensible uneasiness at the time or on after-reflection.

L. But up to the present moment you allow that I have a particular interest in my proper self. Where then am I to stop, or how draw the line between my real and my imaginary identity?

H. The line is drawn for you by the nature of things. Or if the difference between reality and imagination is so small that you cannot perceive it, it only shows the strength of the latter. Certain it is that we can no more anticipate our future being than we change places with another individual, except in an *ideal* and figurative sense. But it is just as impossible that I should have an actual sensation of and interest in my future feelings as that I should have an actual sensation of and interest in what another feels at the present instant. An essential and irreconcileable difference in our primary faculties forbids it. The future, were it the next moment, were it an object nearest and dearest to our hearts, is a dull blank,

opaque, impervious to sense as an object close to the eye of
the blind, did not the ray of reason and reflection enlighten
it. We can never say to its fleeting, painted essence, 'Come,
let me clutch thee!'* it is a thing of air, a phantom that flies
before us, and we follow it, and with respect to all but our past
and present sensations, which are no longer any thing to
action, we totter on the brink of nothing. That self which we
project before us into it, that we make our proxy or representative, and empower to embody, and transmit back to us
all our real, substantial interests before they have had an
existence, except in our imaginations, is but a shadow of
ourselves, a bundle of habits, passions, and prejudices, a body
that falls in pieces at the touch of reason or the approach of
inquiry. It is true, we do build up such an imaginary self, and
a proportionable interest in it; we clothe it with the associations of the past and present, we disguise it in the drapery of
language, we add to it the strength of passion and the warmth
of affection, till we at length come to class our whole existence
under one head, and fancy our future history a solid, permanent, and actual continuation of our immediate being, but
all this only proves the force of imagination and habit to build
up such a structure on a merely partial foundation, and does
not alter the true nature and distinction of things. On the
same foundation are built up nearly as high natural affection,
friendship, the love of country, of religion, &c. But of this
presently. What shows that the doctrine of self-interest, however high it may rear its head, or however impregnable it may
seem to attack, is a mere 'contradiction',

'In terms a fallacy, in fact a fiction.'*

is this single consideration, that we never know what is to
happen to us before-hand, no, not even for a moment, and
that we cannot so much as tell whether we shall be alive a year,
a month, or a day hence. We have no presentiment of what
awaits us, making us feel the future in the instant.* Indeed
such an insight into futurity would be inconsistent with itself,
or we must become mere passive instruments in the hands of
fate. A house may fall on my head as I go from this, I may be
crushed to pieces by a carriage running over me, or I may

receive a piece of news that is death to my hopes before another four-and-twenty hours are passed over, and yet I feel nothing of the blow that is thus to stagger and stun me. I laugh and am well. I have no warning given me either of the course or the consequence (in truth if I had, I should, if possible, avoid it). This continued self-interest that watches over all my concerns alike, past, present, and future, and concentrates them all in one powerful and invariable principle of action, is useless here, leaves me at a loss at my greatest need, is torpid, silent, dead, and I have no more consciousness of what so nearly affects me, and no more care about it, (till I find out my danger by other and natural means,) than if no such thing were ever to happen, or were to happen to the Man in the Moon.

> 'And coming events cast their shadows before.'*

This beautiful line is not verified in the ordinary prose of life. That it is not, is a staggering consideration for your fine, practical, instinctive, abstracted, comprehensive, uniform principle of self-interest. Don't you think so, L——?

L. I shall not answer you. Am I to give up my existence for an idle sophism? You heap riddle upon riddle; but I am mystery-proof. I still feel my personal identity as I do the chair I sit on, though I am enveloped in a cloud of smoke and words. Let me have your answer to a plain question.—Suppose I were actually to see a coach coming along and I was in danger of being run over, what I want to know is, should I not try to save myself sooner than any other person?

H. No, you would first try to save a sister, if she were with you.

A. Surely that would be a very rare instance of self, though I do not deny it.

H. I do not think so. I believe there is hardly any one who does not prefer some one to themselves. For example, let us look into Waverley.

A. Ay, that is the way that you take your ideas of philosophy, from novels and romances, as if they were sound evidence.

H. If my conclusions are as true to nature as my premises, I shall be satisfied. Here is the passage* I was going to quote:

'I was only ganging to say, my lord,' said Evan, in what he meant to be an insinuating manner, 'that if your excellent honour and the honourable court would let Vich Ian Vohr go free just this once and let him gae back to France and not trouble King George's government again, that any six o' the very best of his clan will be willing to be justified in his stead; and if you'll just let me gae down to Glennaquoich, I'll fetch them up to ye myself to head or hang, and you may begin with me the very first man.'

A. But such instances as this are the effect of habit and strong prejudice. We can hardly argue from so barbarous a state of society.

H. Excuse me there. I contend that our preference of ourselves is just as much the effect of habit, and very frequently a more unaccountable and unreasonable one than any other.

A. I should like to hear how you can possibly make that out.

H. If you will not condemn me before you hear what I have to say, I will try. You allow that L——, in the case we have been talking of, would perhaps run a little risk for you or me; but if it were a perfect stranger, he would get out of the way as fast as his legs would carry him, and leave the stranger to shift for himself.

A. Yes; and does not that overturn your whole theory?

H. It would if my theory were as devoid of common sense as you are pleased to suppose; that is, if because I deny an original and absolute distinction in nature (where there is no such thing,) it followed that I must deny that circumstances, intimacy, habit, knowledge, or a variety of incidental causes could have any influence on our affections and actions. My inference is just the contrary. For would you not say that L—— cared little about the stranger for this plain reason, that he knew nothing about him?

A. No doubt.

H. And he would care rather more about you and me, because he knows more about us?

A. Why yes, it would seem so.

H. And he would care still more about a sister, (according to the same supposition) because he would be still better acquainted with her, and had been more constantly with her?

A. I will not deny it.

H. And it is on the same principle (generally speaking) that a man cares most of all about himself, because he knows more about himself than about any body else, that he is more in the secret of his own most intimate thoughts and feelings, and more in the habit of providing for his own wants and wishes, which he can anticipate with greater liveliness and certainty than those of others, from being more nearly 'made and moulded of things past'.* The poetical fiction is rendered easier and assisted by my acquaintance with myself, just as it is by the ties of kindred or habits of friendly intercourse. There is no farther approach made to the doctrines of self-love and personal identity.

L. M——, here is H—— trying to persuade me I am not myself.

M. Sometimes you are not.

L. But he says that I never am.—Or is it only that I am not to be so?

H. Nay, I hope 'thou art to continue, thou naughty varlet'—*

'Here and hereafter, if the last may be!'*

You have been yourself (nobody like you) for the last forty years of your life: you would not prematurely stuff the next twenty into the account, till you have had them fairly out?

L. Not for the world, I have too great an affection for them.

H. Yet I think you world have less if you did not look forward to pass them among old books, old friends, old haunts. If you were cut off from all these, you would be less anxious about what was left of yourself.

L. I would rather be the Wandering Jew than not be at all.

H. Or you would not be the person I always took you for.

L. Does not this willingness to be the Wandering Jew rather than nobody, seem to indicate that there is an abstract attachment to self, to the bare idea of existence, independently of circumstances or habit?

H. It must be a very loose and straggling one. You mix up some of your old recollections and favourite notions with your self elect, and indulge them in your new character, or you would trouble yourself very little about it. If you do not come

in in some shape or other, it is merely saying that you would
be sorry if the Wandering Jew were to disappear from the
earth, however strictly he may have hitherto maintained his
incognito.

L. There is something in that; and as well as I remember
there is a curious but exceedingly mystical illustration of this
point in an original Essay of yours* which I have read and
spoken to you about.

H. I believe there is; but A—— is tired of making objections,
and I of answering them to no purpose.

L. I have the book in the closet, and if you like, we will turn
to the place. It is after that burst of enthusiastic recollection
(the only one in the book) that Southey said at the time* was
something between the manner of Milton's prose-works and
Jeremy Taylor.

H. Ah! I as little thought then that I should ever be set down
as a florid prose-writer as that he would become poet-laureat!

J. L. here took the volume from his brother, and read the
following passage from it.

'I do not think I should illustrate the foregoing reasoning so
well by any thing I could add on the subject, as by relating the
manner in which it first struck me. There are moments in the
life of a solitary thinker which are to him what the evening of
some great victory is to the conqueror and hero—milder
triumphs long remembered with truer and deeper delight.
And though the shouts of multitudes do not hail his success—
though gay trophies, though the sounds of music, the glittering of armour, and the neighing of steeds do not mingle with
his joy, yet shall he not want monuments and witnesses of his
glory—the deep forest, the willowy brook, the gathering
clouds of winter, or the silent gloom of his own chamber,
"faithful remembrancers of his high endeavour, and his glad
success",* that, as time passes by him with unreturning wing,
still awaken the consciousness of a spirit patient, indefatigable
in the search of truth, and the hope of surviving in the
thoughts and minds of other men. I remember I had been
reading a speech which Mirabaud (the author of the "System
of Nature")* has put into the mouth of a supposed Atheist at

the last judgment; and was afterwards led on, by some means or other to consider the question, whether it could properly be said to be an act of virtue in any one to sacrifice his own final happiness to that of any other person or number of persons, if it were possible for the one ever to be made the price of the other? Suppose it were my own case—that it were in my power to save twenty other persons by voluntarily consenting to suffer for them: Why should I not do a generous thing, and never trouble myself about what might be the consequence to myself the Lord knows when?

'The reason why a man should prefer his own future welfare to that of others is, that he has a necessary, absolute interest in the one, which he cannot have in the other—and this, again, is a consequence of his being always the same individual, of his continued identity with himself. The difference, I thought, was this, that however insensible I may be to my own interest at any future period, yet when the time comes I shall feel differently about it. I shall then judge of it from the actual impression of the object, that is, truly and certainly; and as I shall still be conscious of my past feelings, and shall bitterly regret my own folly and insensibility, I ought, as a rational agent, to be determined now by what I shall then wish I had done, when I shall feel the consequences of my actions most deeply and sensibly. It is this continued consciousness of my own feelings which gives me an immediate interest in whatever relates to my future welfare, and makes me at all times accountable to myself for my own conduct. As, therefore, this consciousness will be renewed in me after death, if I exist again at all—But stop—as I must be conscious of my past feelings to be myself, and as this conscious being will be myself, how if that consciousness should be transferred to some other being? How am I to know that I am not imposed upon by a false claim of identity? But that is ridiculous, because you will have no other self than that which arises from this very consciousness. Why, then, this self may be multiplied in as many different beings as the Deity may think proper to endue with the same consciousness; which, if it can be renewed at will in any one instance, may clearly be so in a hundred others. Am I to regard all these as equally myself?

Am I equally interested in the fate of all? Of if I must fix upon some one of them in particular as my representative and other self, how am I to be determined in my choice? Here, then, I saw an end put to my speculations about absolute self-interest and personal identity. I saw plainly that the consciousness of my own feelings, which is made the foundation of my continued interest in them, could not extend to what had never been, and might never be; that my identity with myself must be confined to the connection between my past and present being; that with respect to my future feelings or interests, they could have no communication with, or influence over, my present feelings and interests, merely because they were future; that I shall be hereafter affected by the recollection of my past feelings and actions; and my remorse be equally heightened by reflecting on my past folly and late-earned wisdom, whether I am really the same being, or have only the same consciousness renewed in me; but that to suppose that this remorse can re-act in the reverse order on my present feelings, or give me an immediate interest in my future feelings, before they exist, is an express contradiction in terms. It can only affect me as an imaginary idea, or an idea of truth. But so may the interests of others; and the question proposed was, whether I have not some real, necessary, absolute interest in whatever relates to my future being, in consequence of my immediate connection with myself—independently of the general impression which all positive ideas have on my mind. How, then, can this pretended unity of consciousness which is only reflected from the past—which makes me so little acquainted with the future that I cannot even tell for a moment how long it will be continued, whether it will be entirely interrupted by or renewed in me after death, and which might be multiplied in I don't know how many different beings, and prolonged by complicated sufferings, without my being any the wiser for it,—how, I say, can a principle of this sort identify my present with my future interests, and make me as much a participator in what does not at all affect me as if it were actually impressed on my senses? It is plain, as this conscious being may be decompounded, entirely destroyed, renewed again, or multiplied in a great number of beings, and as, whichever of these takes place, it cannot produce the least alteration in my present being—that what I am does not depend on what I am to be, and that there is no communication between my future interests, and the motives by which my present conduct must be governed. This can no more be influenced by what may be my future feelings with respect to it, than it will then be possible for me to alter my past conduct by wishing that I had acted differently. I cannot, therefore, have a principle of active self-interest arising out of the immediate connection between my present and future self, for no such connection exists, or is possible. I am what I am in spite of the future. My feelings, actions, and interests, must be determined by causes already existing and acting, and are absolutely independent of the future. Where there is not an intercommunity of feelings, there can be no identity of interests. My personal interest in any thing must refer either to the interest excited by the actual impression of the object, which cannot be felt before it exists, and can last no longer than while the impression lasts; or it may refer to the particular manner in which I am mechanically affected by the idea of my own impressions in the absence of the object. I can, therefore, have no proper personal interest in my future impressions, since neither my ideas of future objects, nor my feelings with respect to them, can be excited either directly or indirectly by the impressions themselves, or by any ideas or feelings accompanying them, without a complete transposition of the order in which causes and effects follow one another in nature. The only reason for my preferring my future interest to that of others, must arise from my anticipating it with greater warmth of present imagination. It is this greater liveliness and force with which I can enter into my future feelings, that in a manner identifies them with my present being; and this notion of identity being once formed, the mind makes use of it to strengthen its habitual propensity, by giving to personal motives a reality and absolute truth which they can never have. Hence it has been inferred that my real, substantial interest in any thing, must be derived in some indirect manner from the impression of the object itself, as if that could have any sort of communication with my present

feelings, or excite any interest in my mind but by means of
the imagination, which is naturally affected in a certain manner by the prospect of future good or evil.'

    J. L. 'This is the strangest tale that e'er I heard.'
    C. L. 'It is the strangest fellow, brother John!'

MIND AND MOTIVE

THE love of power or action is another independent principle
of the human mind, in the different degrees in which it exists,
and which are not by any means in exact proportion to its
physical sensibility. It seems evidently absurd to suppose that
sensibility to pleasure or pain is the only principle of action.
It is almost too obvious to remark, that sensibility alone, without an active principle in the mind, could never produce
action. The soul might lie dissolved in pleasure, or be agon-
ised with woe; but the impulses of feeling, in order to excite
passion, desire, or will, must be first communicated to some
other faculty. There must be a principle, a fund of activity
somewhere, by and through which our sensibility operates;
and that this active principle owes all its force, its precise
degree and direction, to the sensitive faculty, is neither self-
evident nor true. Strength of will is not always nor generally
in proportion to strength of feeling. There are different degrees of activity as of sensibility in the mind; and our passions,
characters, and pursuits, often depend no less upon the one
than on the other. We continually make a distinction in common discourse between sensibility and irritability, between
passion and feeling, between the nerves and muscles; and we
find that the most voluptuous people are in general the most
indolent. Every one who has looked closely into human
nature must have observed persons who are naturally and
habitually restless in the extreme, but without any extraordinary susceptibility to pleasure or pain, always making or finding excuses to do something,—whose actions constantly
outrun the occasion, and who are eager in the pursuit of the
greatest trifles,—whose impatience of the smallest repose

keeps them always employed about nothing,—and whose whole lives are a continued work of supererogation. There are others again who seem born to act from a spirit of contradiction only, that is, who are ready to act not only without a reason, but against it,—who are ever at cross-purposes with themselves and others,—who are not satisfied unless they are doing two opposite things at a time,—who contradict what you say, and if you assent to them, contradict what they have said,—who regularly leave the pursuit in which they are successful to engage in some other in which they have no chance of success,—who make a point of encountering difficulties and aiming at impossibilities, that there may be no end of their exhaustless task: while there is a third class whose *vis inertiæ** scarcely any motives can overcome,—who are devoured by their feelings, and the slaves of their passions, but who can take no pains and use no means to gratify them,— who, if roused to action by any unforeseen accident, require a continued stimulus to urge them on,—who fluctuate between desire and want of resolution,—whose brightest projects burst like a bubble as soon as formed,—who yield to every obstacle,—who almost sink under the weight of the atmosphere,—who cannot brush aside a cobweb in their path, and are stopped by an insect's wing. Indolence is want of will—the absence or defect of the active principle—a repugnance to motion; and whoever has been much tormented with this passion, must, we are sure, have felt that the inclination to indulge it is something very distinct from the love of pleasure or actual enjoyment. Ambition is the reverse of indolence, and is the love of power or action in great things. Avarice, also, as it relates to the acquisition of riches, is, in a great measure, an active and enterprising feeling; nor does the hoarding of wealth, after it is acquired, seem to have much connection with the love of pleasure. What is called niggardliness, very often, we are convinced from particular instances that we have known, arises less from a selfish principle than from a love of contrivance, from the study of economy as an art, for want of a better, from a pride in making the most of a little, and in not exceeding a certain expense previously determined upon; all which is wilfulness, and is perfectly consistent, as it is frequently found united, with the most lavish expenditure and the utmost disregard for money on other occasions. A miser may in general be looked upon as a particular species of *virtuoso*. The constant desire in the rich to leave wealth in large masses, by aggrandising some branch of their families, or sometimes in such a manner as to accumulate for centuries, shews that the imagination has a considerable share in this passion. Intemperance, debauchery, gluttony, and other vices of that kind, may be attributed to an excess of sensuality or gross sensibility; though even here, we think it evident that habits of intoxication are produced quite as much by the strength as by the agreeableness of the excitement; and with respect to some other vicious habits, curiosity makes many more votaries than inclination. The love of truth, when it predominates, produces inquisitive characters, the whole tribe of gossips, tale-bearers, harmless busy bodies, your blunt honest creatures, who never conceal what they think, and who are the more sure to tell it you the less you want to hear it,—and now and then a philosopher.

Our passions in general are to be traced more immediately to the active part of our nature, to the love of power, or to strength of will. Such are all those which arise out of the difficulty of accomplishment, which become more intense from the efforts made to attain the object, and which derive their strength from opposition. Mr Hobbes says well* on this subject:

'But for an utmost end, in which the ancient philosophers placed felicity, and disputed much concerning the way thereto, there is no such thing in this world nor way to it, than to Utopia; for while we live, we have desires, and desire presupposeth a further end. Seeing all delight is appetite, and desire of something further, there can be no contentment but in proceeding, and therefore we are not to marvel, when we see that as men attain to more riches, honour, or other power, so their appetite continually groweth more and more; and when they are come to the utmost degree of some kind of power, they pursue some other, as long as in any kind they think themselves behind any other. Of those therefore that have attained the highest degree of honour and riches, some have affected mastery in some art, as Nero in music and poetry, Commodus in the art of a gladiator; and such as affect not some such thing, must find diversion and recreation of their thoughts in the contention either of play or business, and men justly complain as of a great grief that they know not what to do. Felicity, therefore, by which we mean continual delight, consists not in having prospered, but in prospering.'

This account of human nature, true as it is, would be a mere romance, if physical sensibility were the only faculty essential to man, that is, if we were the slaves of voluptuous indolence. But our desires are kindled by their own heat, the will is urged on by a restless impulse, and, without action, enjoyment becomes insipid. The passions of men are not in proportion only to their sensibility, or to the desirableness of the object, but to the violence and irritability of their tempers, and the obstacles to their success. Thus an object, to which we were almost indifferent while we thought it in our power, often excites the most ardent pursuit or the most painful regret, as soon as it is placed out of our reach. How eloquently is the contradiction between our desires and our success described in *Don Quixote* where it is said of the lover, that 'he courted a statue, hunted the wind, cried aloud to the desert!'*

The necessity of action to the mind, and the keen edge it gives to our desires, is shewn in the different value we set on past and future objects. It is commonly and we might almost say universally supposed, that there is an essential difference in the two cases. In this instance, however, the strength of our passions has converted an evident absurdity into one of the most inveterate prejudices of the human mind. That the future is really or in itself of more consequence than the past, is what we can neither assent to nor even conceive. It is true, the past has ceased to be and is no longer any thing, except to the mind; but the future is still to come, and has an existence in the mind only. The one is at an end, the other has not even had a beginning; both are purely ideal: so that this argument would prove that the present only is of any real value, and that both past and future objects are equally indifferent, alike nothing. Indeed, the future is, if possible, more imaginary than the past; for the past may in some sense be said to exist in its consequences; it acts still; it is present to us in its effects; the mouldering ruins and broken fragments still remain; but of the future there is no trace. What a blank does the history of the world for the next six thousand years, present to the mind, compared with that of the last! All that strikes the imagination, or excites any interest in the mighty scene, is *what has been.* Neither in reality, then, nor as a subject of general contemplation, has the future any advantage over the past; but with respect to our own passions and pursuits it has. We regret the pleasures we have enjoyed, and eagerly anticipate those which are to come; we dwell with satisfaction on the evils from which we have escaped, and dread future pain. The good that is past is like money that is spent, which is of no use, and about which we give ourselves no farther concern. The good we expect is like a store yet untouched, in the enjoyment of which we promise ourselves infinite gratification. What has happened to us we think of no consequence,—what is to happen to us, of the greatest. Why so? Because the one is in our power, and the other not; because the efforts of the will to bring an object to pass or to avert it strengthen our attachment to or our aversion from that object; because the habitual pursuit of any purpose redoubles the ardour of our pursuit, and converts the speculative and indolent interest we should otherwise take in it into real passion. Our regrets, anxiety, and wishes, are thrown away upon the past, but we encourage our disposition to exaggerate the importance of the future, as of the utmost use in aiding our resolutions and stimulating our exertions.

It in some measure confirms this theory, that men attach more or less importance to past and future events, according as they are more or less engaged in action and the busy scenes of life. Those who have a fortune to make, or are in pursuit of rank and power, are regardless of the past, for it does not contribute to their views: those who have nothing to do but to think, take nearly the same interest in the past as in the future. The contemplation of the one is as delightful and real as of the other. The season of hope comes to an end, but the remembrance of it is left. The past still lives in the memory of those who have leisure to look back upon the way that they have trod, and can from it 'catch glimpses that may make them less forlorn'.* The turbulence of action and uneasiness of desire *must* dwell upon the future; it is only amidst the innocence of shepherds, in the simplicity of the pastoral ages, that a tomb was found with this inscription— 'I ALSO WAS AN ARCADIAN!'*

We feel that some apology is necessary for having thus plunged our readers all at once into the middle of meta-physics. If it should be asked what use such studies are of, we might answer with Hume,* *perhaps of none, except that there are certain persons who find more entertainment in them than in any other.* An account of this matter, with which we were amused ourselves, and which may therefore amuse others, we met with some time ago in a metaphysical allegory,* which begins in this manner:

'In the depth of a forest, in the kingdom of Indostan, lived a monkey, who, before his last step of transmigration, had occupied a human tenement. He had been a Bramin, skilful in theology, and in all abstruse learning. He was wont to hold in admiration the ways of Nature, and delighted to penetrate the mysteries in which she was enrobed; but in pursuing the footsteps of philosophy, he wandered too far from the abode of the social Virtues. In order to pursue his studies, he had retired to a cave on the banks of the Jumna. There he forgot society, and neglected ablution; and therefore his soul was degraded to a condition below humanity. So inveterate were the habits which he had contracted in his human state, that his spirit was still influenced by his passion for abstruse study. He sojourned in this wood from youth to age, regardless of everything, *save cocoa-nuts and metaphysics.*'

For our own part, we should be content to pass our time much in the same way as this learned savage, if we could only find a substitute for his cocoa-nuts! We do not, however, wish to recommend the same pursuit to others, nor to dissuade them from it. It has its pleasures and its pains—its successes and its disappointments. It is neither quite so sublime nor quite so uninteresting as it is sometimes represented. The worst is, that much thought on difficult subjects tends, after a certain time, to destroy the natural gaiety and dancing of the spirits; it deadens the elastic force of the mind, weighs upon the heart, and makes us insensible to the common enjoyments and pursuits of life.

> 'Sithence no fairy lights, no quick'ning ray,
> Nor stir of pulse, nor objects to entice
> Abroad the spirits; but the cloyster'd heart
> Sits squat at home, like pagod in a niche
> Obscure.'*

Metaphysical reasoning is also one branch of the tree of the knowledge of good and evil. The study of man, however, does, perhaps, less harm than a knowledge of the world, though it must be owned that the practical knowledge of vice and misery makes a stronger impression on the mind, when it has imbibed a habit of abstract reasoning. Evil thus becomes embodied in a general principle, and shews its harpy form in all things. It is a fatal, inevitable necessity hanging over us. It follows us wherever we go: if we fly into the uttermost parts of the earth, it is there: whether we turn to the right or the left, we cannot escape from it. This, it is true, is the disease of philosophy; but it is one to which it is liable in minds of a certain cast, after the first order of expectation has been disabused by experience, and the finer feelings have received an irrecoverable shock from the jarring of the world.

Happy are they* who live in the dream of their own existence, and see all things in the light of their own minds; who walk by faith and hope; to whom the guiding star of their youth still shines from afar, and into whom the spirit of the world has not entered! They have not been 'hurt by the archers',* nor has the iron entered their souls. They live in the midst of arrows and of death, unconscious of harm. The evil things come not nigh them. The shafts of ridicule pass unheeded by, and malice loses its sting. The example of vice does not rankle in their breasts, like the poisoned shirt of Nessus. Evil impressions fall off from them like drops of water. The yoke of life is to them light and supportable. The world has no hold on them. They are in it, not of it; and a dream and a glory is ever around them!

ON PERSONAL IDENTITY

'Ha! here be three of us sophisticated.'*—LEAR.

'IF I were not Alexander, I would be Diogenes!' said the Macedonian hero; and the cynic might have retorted the compliment upon the prince by saying, that, 'were he not Diogenes, he would be Alexander!' This is the universal exception, the invariable reservation that our self-love makes, the utmost point at which our admiration or envy ever arrives—to wish, if we were not ourselves, to be some other individual. No one ever wishes to be another, *instead* of himself. We may feel a desire to change places with others—to have one man's fortune—another's health or strength—his wit or learning, or accomplishments of various kinds—

> 'Wishing to be like one more rich in hope,
> Featured like him, like him with friends possessed,
> Desiring this man's art, and that man's scope:'*

but we would still be our selves, to possess and enjoy all these, or we would not give a doit for them. But, on this supposition, what in truth should we be the better for them? It is not we, but another, that would reap the benefit; and what do we care about that other? In that case, the present owner might as well continue to enjoy them. *We* should not be gainers by the change. If the meanest beggar who crouches at a palace-gate, and looks up with awe and suppliant fear to the proud inmate as he passes, could be put in possession of all the finery, the pomp, the luxury, and wealth that he sees and envies on the sole condition of getting rid, together with his rags and misery, of all recollection that there ever was such a wretch as himself, he would reject the proffered boon with scorn. He might be glad to change situations; but he would insist on keeping his own thoughts, to *compare notes,* and point the transition by the force of contrast. He would not, on any account, forego his self-congratulation on the unexpected accession of good fortune, and his escape from past suffering.

All that excites his cupidity, his envy, his repining or despair, is the alternative of some great good to himself; and if, in order to attain that object, he is to part with his own existence to take that of another, he can feel no farther interest in it. This is the language both of passion and reason.

Here lies 'the rub that makes calamity of so long life':* for it is not barely the apprehension of the ills that 'in that sleep of death may come', but also our ignorance and indifference to the promised good, that produces our repugnance and backwardness to quit the present scene. No man, if he had his choice, would be the angel Gabriel to-morrow! What is the angel Gabriel to him but a splendid vision? He might as well have an ambition to be turned into a bright cloud, or a particular star. The interpretation of which is, he can have no sympathy with the angel Gabriel. Before he can be transformed into so bright and ethereal an essence, he must necessarily 'put off this mortal coil'—be divested of all his old habits, passions, thoughts, and feelings—to be endowed with other lofty and beatific attributes, of which he has no notion; and, therefore, he would rather remain a little longer in this mansion of clay, which, with all its flaws, inconveniences, and perplexities, contains all that he has any real knowledge of, or any affection for. When, indeed, he is about to quit it in spite of himself, and has no other chance left to escape the darkness of the tomb, he may then have no objection (making a virtue of necessity) to put on angels' wings, to have radiant locks, to wear a wreath of amaranth, and thus to masquerade it in the skies.

It is an instance of the truth and beauty of the ancient mythology, that the various transmutations it recounts are never voluntary, or of favourable omen, but are interposed as a timely release to those who, driven on by fate, and urged to the last extremity of fear or anguish, are turned into a flower, a plant, an animal, a star, a precious stone, or into some object that may inspire pity or mitigate our regret for their misfortunes. Narcissus was transformed into a flower; Daphne into a laurel; Arethusa into a fountain (by the favour of the gods)—but not till no other remedy was left for their despair.* It is a sort of smiling cheat upon death, and graceful compromise with annihilation. It is better to exist by proxy, in some softened type and soothing allegory, than not at all—to breathe in a flower or shine in a constellation, than to be utterly forgot; but no one would change his natural condition (if he could help it) for that of a bird, an insect, a beast, or a fish, however delightful their mode of existence, or however enviable he might deem their lot compared to his own. Their thoughts are not our thoughts—their happiness is not our happiness; nor can we enter into it except with a passing smile of approbation, or as a refinement of fancy. As the poet sings:

> 'What more felicity can fall to creature
>   Than to enjoy delight with liberty,
> And to be lord of all the works of nature?
>   To reign in the air from earth to highest sky;
> To feed on flowers and weeds of glorious feature;
>   To taste whatever thing doth please the eye?—
> Who rests not pleased with such happiness,
> Well worthy he to taste of wretchedness!'*

This is gorgeous description and fine declamation: yet who would be found to act upon it, even in the forming of a wish; or would not rather be the thrall of wretchedness, than launch out (by the aid of some magic spell) into all the delights of such a butterfly state of existence? The French (if any people can) may be said to enjoy this airy, heedless gaiety and unalloyed exuberance of satisfaction: yet what Englishman would deliberately change with them? We would sooner be miserable after our own fashion than happy after theirs. It is not happiness, then, in the abstract, which we seek, that can be addressed as

> 'That something still that prompts th' eternal sigh,
> For which we wish to live or dare to die.—'*

but a happiness suited to our taste and faculties—that has become a part of ourselves, by habit and enjoyment—that is endeared to us by a thousand recollections, privations, and sufferings. No one, then, would willingly change his country or his kind for the most plausible pretences held out to him. The most humiliating punishment inflicted in ancient fable

is the change of sex: not that it was any degradation in itself—
but that it must occasion a total derangement of the moral
economy and confusion of the sense of personal propriety.
The thing is said to have happened, *au sens contraire*, in our
time. The story is to be met with in 'very choice Italian'; and
Lord D——* tells it in very plain English!

We may often find ourselves envying the possessions of
others, and sometimes inadvertently indulging a wish to
change places with them altogether; but our self-love soon
discovers some excuse to be off the bargain we were ready to
strike, and retracts 'vows made in haste, as violent and void'.*
We might make up our minds to the alteration in every other
particular; but, when it comes to the point, there is sure to be
some trait or feature of character in the object of our admiration to which we cannot reconcile ourselves—some favourite
quality or darling foible of our own, with which we can by no
means resolve to part. The more enviable the situation of
another, the more entirely to our taste, the more reluctant we
are to leave any part of ourselves behind that would be so fully
capable of appreciating all the exquisiteness of its new situation, or not to enter into the possession of such an imaginary
reversion of good fortune with all our previous inclinations
and sentiments. The outward circumstances were fine: they
only wanted a *soul* to enjoy them, and that soul is ours (as the
costly ring wants the peerless jewel to perfect and set it off).
The humble prayer and petition to sneak into visionary felicity
by personal adoption, or the surrender of our own personal
pretensions, always ends in a daring project of usurpation,
and a determination to expel the actual proprietor, and supply his place so much more worthily with our own identity—
not bating a single jot of it. Thus, in passing through a fine
collection of pictures, who has not envied the privilege of
visiting it every day, and wished to be the owner? But the rising
sigh is soon checked, and 'the native hue of emulation is
sicklied o'er with the pale cast of thought,'* when we come
to ask ourselves not merely whether the owner has any taste
at all for these splendid works, and does not look upon them
as so much expensive furniture, like his chairs and tables—but
whether he has the same precise (and only true) taste that we

have—whether he has the very same favourites that we have—whether he may not be so blind as to prefer a Vandyke to a Titian, a Ruysdael to a Claude;—nay, whether he may not have other pursuits and avocations that draw off his attention from the sole objects of our idolatry, and which seem to us mere impertinences and waste of time? In that case, we at once lose all patience, and exclaim indignantly, 'Give us back our taste and keep your pictures!' It is not we who should envy them the possession of the treasure, but they who should envy us the true and exclusive enjoyment of it. A similar train of feeling seems to have dictated Warton's spirited Sonnet* on visiting Wilton-House:

> 'From Pembroke's princely dome, where mimic art
> Decks with a magic hand the dazzling bowers,
> Its living hues where the warm pencil pours,
> And breathing forms the rude marble start,
> How to life's humbler scene can I depart?
> My breast all glowing from those gorgeous towers,
> In my low cell how cheat the sullen hours?
> Vain the complaint! For Fancy can impart
> (To fate superior and to fortune's power)
> Whate'er adorns the stately storied-hall:
> She, mid the dungeon's solitary gloom,
> Can dress the Graces in their attic pall;
> Bid the green landskip's vernal beauty bloom;
> And in bright trophies clothe the twilight wall.'

One sometimes passes by a gentleman's park, an old family-seat, with its moss-grown ruinous paling, its 'glades mild-opening to the genial day',* or embrowned with forest-trees. Here one would be glad to spend one's life, 'shut up in measureless content',* and to grow old beneath ancestral oaks, instead of gaining a precarious, irksome, and despised livelihood, by indulging romantic sentiments, and writing disjointed descriptions of them. The thought has scarcely risen to the lips, when we learn that the owner of so blissful a seclusion is a thorough-bred fox-hunter, a preserver of the game, a brawling electioneerer, a Tory member of parliament, a 'no-Popery' man!—'I'd sooner be a dog, and bay the moon!'* Who would be Sir Thomas Lethbridge for his title and estate?

asks one man. But would not almost any one wish to be Sir
Francis Burdett, the man of the people, the idol of the electors
of Westminster? says another. I can only answer for myself.
Respectable and honest as he is, there is something in his
white boots, and white breeches, and white coat, and white
hair, and red face, and white hat, that I cannot, by any effort
of candour, confound my personal identity with! If Mr Hobhouse* can prevail on Sir Francis to exchange, let him do so
by all means. Perhaps they might contrive to *club* a soul between them! Could I have had my will, I should have been
born a lord: but one would not be a booby lord neither. I am
haunted by an odd fancy of driving down the Great North
Road in a chaise and four, about fifty years ago, and coming
to the inn at Ferry-bridge, with out-riders, white favours, and
a coronet on the panels; and then I choose my companion in
the coach. Really there is a witchcraft in all this that makes it
necessary to turn away from it, lest, in the conflict between
imagination and impossibility, I should grow feverish and
light-headed! But, on the other hand, if one was born a lord,
should one have the same idea (that every one else has) of *a
peeress in her own right?* Is not distance, giddy elevation, mysterious awe, an impossible gulf, necessary to form this idea of
the mind, that fine ligament of 'ethereal braid, sky-woven',*
that lets down heaven upon earth, fair as enchantment, soft
as Berenice's hair, bright and garlanded like Ariadne's
crown;* and is it not better to have had this idea all through
life—to have caught but glimpses of it, to have known it but
in a dream—than to have been born a lord ten times over,
with twenty pampered menials at one's back, and twenty de-
scents to boast of? It is the envy of certain privileges, the sharp
privations we have undergone, the cutting neglect we have
met with from the want of birth or title, that gives its zest to
the distinction: the thing itself may be indifferent or contemptible enough. It is the *becoming* a lord that is to be desired;
but he who becomes a lord in reality is an upstart—a mere
pretender, without the sterling essence; so that all that is of
any worth in this supposed transition is purely imaginary and
impossible. Had I been a lord, I should have married
Miss——, and my life would not have been one long-drawn

sigh, made up of sweet and bitter regret!* Had I been a lord,
I would have been a Popish lord, and then I might also have
been an honest man:—poor, and then I might have been
proud and not vulgar! Kings are so accustomed to look down
on all the rest of the world, that they consider the condition
of mortality as vile and intolerable, if stripped of royal state,
and cry out in the bitterness of their despair, 'Give me a
crown, or a tomb!'* It should seem from this as if all mankind
would change with the first crowned head that could propose
the alternative, or that it would be only the presumption of
the supposition, or a sense of their own unworthiness, that
would deter them. Perhaps there is not a single throne that,
if it was to be filled by this sort of voluntary metempsychosis,
would not remain empty. Many would, no doubt, be glad to
'monarchise, be feared, and kill with looks'* in their own
persons and after their own fashion: but who would be the
double of ———,* or of those shadows of a shade—those 'tenth
transmitters of a foolish face'*—Charles X and Ferdinand
VII?* If monarchs have little sympathy with mankind, mankind have even less with monarchs. They are merely to us a
sort of state-puppets or royal wax-work, which we may gaze at
with superstitious wonder, but have no wish to become; and
he who should meditate such a change must not only feel by
anticipation an utter contempt for the *slough* of humanity
which he is prepared to cast, but must feel an absolute void
and want of attraction in those lofty and incomprehensible
sentiments which are to supply its place. With respect to actual
royalty, the spell is in a great measure broken. But, among
ancient monarchs, there is no one, I think, who envies Darius
or Xerxes. One has a different feeling with respect to
Alexander or Pyrrhus;* but this is because they were great
men as well as great kings, and the soul is up in arms at the
mention of their names as at the sound of a trumpet. But as
to all the rest—those 'in the catalogue who go for kings'*—
the praying, eating, drinking, dressing monarchs of the earth,
in time past or present—one would as soon think of wishing
to personate the Golden Calf, or to turn out with Nebuchad-
nezzar to graze, as to be transformed into one of that 'swinish
multitude'.* There is no point of affinity. The extrinsic

circumstances are imposing: but, within, there is nothing but morbid humours and proud flesh! Some persons might vote for Charlemagne; and there are others who would have no objection to be the modern Charlemagne,* with all he inflicted and suffered, even after the necromantic field of Waterloo, and the bloody wreath on the vacant brow of his conqueror, and that fell jailer* set over him by a craven foe, that 'glared round his soul, and mocked his closing eyelids!'*

It has been remarked, that could we at pleasure change our situation in life, more persons would be found anxious to descend than to ascend in the scale of society. One reason may be, that we have it more in our power to do so; and this encourages the thought, and makes it familiar to us. A second is, that we naturally wish to throw off the cares of state, of fortune or business, that oppress us, and to seek repose before we find it in the grave. A third reason is, that, as we descend to common life, the pleasures are simple, natural, such as all can enter into, and therefore excite a general interest, and combine all suffrages. Of the different occupations of life, none is beheld with a more pleasing emotion, or less aversion to a change of our own, than that of a shepherd tending his flock: the pastoral ages have been the envy and the theme of all succeeding ones; and a beggar with his crutch is more closely allied than the monarch and his crown to the associations of mirth and heart's-ease. On the other hand, it must be admitted that our pride is too apt to prefer grandeur to happiness; and that our passions make us envy great vices oftener than great virtues.

The world shew their sense in nothing more than in a distrust and aversion to those changes of situation which only tend to make the successful candidates ridiculous, and which do not carry along with them a mind adequate to the circumstances. The common people, in this respect, are more shrewd and judicious than their superiors, from feeling their own awkwardness and incapacity, and often decline, with an instinctive modesty, the troublesome honours intended for them. They do not overlook their original defects so readily as others overlook their acquired advantages. It is wonderful, therefore, that opera-singers and dancers refuse, or only *condescend* as it were, to accept lords, though the latter are so often fascinated by them. The fair performer knows (better than her unsuspecting admirer) how little connection there is between the dazzling figure she makes on the stage and that which she may make in private life, and is in no hurry to convert 'the drawing-room into a Green-room.' The nobleman (supposing him not to be very wise) is astonished at the miraculous powers of art in

'The fair, the chaste, the inexpressive *she*;'*

and thinks such a paragon must easily conform to the routine of manners and society which every trifling woman of quality of his acquaintance, from sixteen to sixty, goes through without effort. This is a hasty or a wilful conclusion. Things of habit only come by habit, and inspiration here avails nothing. A man of fortune who marries an actress for her fine performance of tragedy, has been well compared to the person who bought Punch. The lady is not unfrequently aware of the inconsequentiality, and unwilling to be put on the shelf, and hid in the nursery of some musty country-mansion. Servant girls, of any sense and spirit, treat their masters (who make serious love to them) with suitable contempt. What is it but a proposal to drag an unmeaning trollop at his heels through life, to her own annoyance and the ridicule of all his friends? No woman, I suspect, ever forgave a man who raised her from a low condition in life (it is a perpetual obligation and reproach); though, I believe men often feel the most disinterested regard for women under such circumstances. Sancho Panza discovered no less folly in his eagerness to enter upon his new government, than wisdom in quitting it as fast as possible.* Why will Mr Cobbett persist in getting into Parliament?* He would find himself no longer the same man. What member of Parliament, I should like to know, could write his Register? As a popular partisan, he may (for aught I can say) be a match for the whole Honourable House; but, by obtaining a seat in St Stephen's Chapel, he would only be equal to a 576th part of it. It was surely a puerile ambition in Mr Addington to succeed Mr Pitt as prime-minister. The situation was only a foil to his imbecility. Gipsies have a fine faculty of evasion: catch them who can in the same place or story twice! Take them; teach them the comforts of civilisation; confine them in warm rooms, with thick carpets and down beds; and they will fly out of the window—like the bird, described by Chaucer,* out of its golden cage. I maintain that there is no common language or medium of understanding between people of education and without it—between those who judge of things from books or from their senses. Ignorance has so far the advantage over learning; for it can make an appeal to you from what you know; but you cannot re-act upon it through that which it is a perfect stranger to. Ignorance is, therefore, power. This is what foiled Buonaparte in Spain and Russia. The people can only be gained over by informing them, though they may be enslaved by fraud or force. You say there is a common language in nature.* They see nature through their wants, while you look at it for your pleasure. Ask a country lad if he does not like to hear the birds sing in the spring? And he will laugh in your face. 'What is it, then, he does like?'—'Good victuals and drink!' As if you had not these too; but because he has them not, he thinks of nothing else, and laughs at you and your refinements, supposing you to live upon air. To those who are deprived of every other advantage, even nature is a *book sealed*. I have made this capital mistake all my life, in imagining that those objects which lay open to all, and excited an interest merely from the *idea* of them, spoke a common language to all; and that nature was a kind of universal home, where all ages, sexes, classes met. Not so. The vital air, the sky, the woods, the streams—all these go for nothing, except with a favoured few. The poor are taken up with their bodily wants—the rich, with external acquisitions: the one, with the sense of property—the other, of its privation. Both have the same distaste for *sentiment*. The *genteel* are the slaves of appearances—the vulgar, of necessity; and neither has the smallest regard to true worth, refinement, generosity. All savages are irreclaimable. I can understand the Irish character better than the Scotch. I hate the formal crust of circumstances and the mechanism of society. I have been recommended, indeed, to settle down into some respectable profession for life:

'Ah! why so soon the blossom tear?'*

I am 'in no haste to be venerable!'*

  In thinking of those one might wish to have been, many
people will exclaim, 'Surely, you would like to have been
Shakespeare?' Would Garrick have consented to the change?
No, nor should he; for the applause which he received, and
on which he lived, was more adapted to his genius and taste.
If Garrick had agreed to be Shakespeare, he would have made
it a previous condition that he was to be a better player. He
would have insisted on taking some higher part than *Polonius*
or the *Grave-digger*. Ben Jonson and his companions at the
Mermaid would not have known their old friend Will in his
new disguise. The modern Roscius* would have scouted the
halting player. He would have shrunk from the parts of the
inspired poet. If others were unlike us, we feel it as a presumption and an impertinence to usurp their place; if they were
like us, it seems a work of supererogation. We are not to be
cozened out of our existence for nothing. It has been ingeniously urged, as an objection to having been Milton, that 'then
we should not have had the pleasure of reading Paradise Lost.'
Perhaps I should incline to draw lots with Pope, but that he
was deformed, and did not sufficiently relish Milton and
Shakespeare. As it is, we can enjoy his verses and theirs too.
Why, having these, need we ever be dissatisfied with ourselves?
Goldsmith is a person whom I considerably affect, notwithstanding his blunders and his misfortunes. The author of
the *Vicar of Wakefield*, and of *Retaliation*, is one whose temper
must have had something eminently amiable, delightful, gay,
and happy in it.

'A certain tender bloom his fame o'erspreads.'*

But then I could never make up my mind to his preferring
Rowe and Dryden* to the worthies of the Elizabethan age;
nor could I, in like manner, forgive Sir Joshua—whom I number among those whose existence was marked with a *white
stone*, and on whose tomb might be inscribed 'Thrice Fortunate!'—his treating Nicholas Poussin with contempt. Differences in matters of taste and opinion are points of

honour—'stuff o' the conscience'*—stumbling-blocks not to
be got over. Others, we easily grant, may have more wit,
learning, imagination, riches, strength, beauty, which we
should be glad to borrow of them; but that they have sounder
or better views of things, or that we should act wisely in
changing in this respect, is what we can by no means persuade
ourselves. We may not be the lucky possessors of what is best
or most desirable; but our notion of what is best and most
desirable we will give up to no man by choice or compulsion;
and unless others (the greatest wits or brightest geniuses) can
come into our way of thinking, we must humbly beg leave to
remain as we are. A Calvinistic preacher would not relinquish
a single point of faith to be the Pope of Rome; nor would a
strict Unitarian acknowledge the mystery of the Holy Trinity
to have painted Raphael's *Assembly of the Just.** In the range of
ideal excellence, we are distracted by variety and repelled by
differences: the imagination is fickle and fastidious, and requires a combination of all possible qualifications, which
never meet. Habit alone is blind and tenacious of the most
homely advantages; and after running the tempting round of
nature, fame, and fortune, we wrap ourselves up in our
familiar recollections and humble pretensions—as the lark,
after long fluttering on sunny wing, sinks into its lowly bed!

We can have no very importunate craving, nor very great
confidence, in wishing to change characters, except with
those with whom we are intimately acquainted by their works;
and having these by us (which is all we know or covet in them),
what would we have more? We can have *no more of a cat than
her skin*; nor of an author than his brains. By becoming Shakespeare in reality, we cut ourselves out of reading Milton, Pope,
Dryden, and a thousand more—all of whom we have in our
possession, enjoy, and *are*, by turns, in the best part of them,
their thoughts, without any metamorphosis or miracle at all.
What a microcosm is ours! What a Proteus is the human mind!
All that we know, think of, or can admire, in a manner becomes ourselves. We are not (the meanest of us) a volume,
but a whole library! In this calculation of problematical con-
tingencies, the lapse of time makes no difference. One would
as soon have been Raphael as any modern artist. Twenty,

thirty, or forty years of elegant enjoyment and lofty feeling were as great a luxury in the fifteenth as in the nineteenth century. But Raphael did not live to see Claude, nor Titian Rembrandt. Those who found arts and sciences* are not witnesses of their accumulated results and benefits; nor in general do they reap the meed of praise which is their due. We who come after in some 'laggard age',* have more enjoyment of their fame than they had. Who would have missed the sight of the Louvre in all its glory to have been one of those whose works enriched it? Would it not have been giving a certain good for an uncertain advantage? No: I am as sure (if it is not presumption to say so) of what passed through Raphael's mind as of what passes through my own; and I know the difference between seeing (though even that is a rare privilege) and producing such perfection. At one time I was so devoted to Rembrandt, that I think, if the Prince of Darkness had made me the offer in some rash mood, I should have been tempted to close with it, and should have become (in happy hour, and in downright earnest) the great master of light and shade!

I have run myself out of my materials for this Essay, and want a well-turned sentence or two to conclude with; like Benvenuto Cellini,* who complains that, with all the brass, tin, iron, and lead he could muster in the house, his statue of Perseus was left imperfect, with a dent in the heel of it. Once more then—I believe there is one character that all the world would be glad to change with—which is that of a favoured rival.* Even hatred gives way to envy. We would be any thing—a toad in a dungeon—to live upon her smile, which is our all of earthly hope and happiness; nor can we, in our infatuation, conceive that there is any difference of feeling on the subject, or that the pressure of her hand is not in itself divine, making those to whom such bliss is deigned like the Immortal Gods!

CHARACTERISTICS

105. THE error in the reasonings of Mandeville, Rochefoucault, and others,* is this: they first find out that there is

something mixed in the motives of all our actions, and they then proceed to argue, that they must all arise from one motive, *viz.* self-love. They make the exception the rule. It would be easy to reverse the argument, and prove that our most selfish actions are disinterested. There is honour among thieves. Robbers, murderers, &c. do not commit those actions, from a pleasure in pure villainy, or for their own benefit only, but from a mistaken regard to the welfare or good opinion of those with whom they are immediately connected.

106. It is ridiculous to say, that compassion, friendship, &c. are at bottom only selfishness in disguise, because it is *we* who feel pleasure or pain in the good or evil of others; for the meaning of self-love is not that it is I who love, but that I love myself. The motive is no more selfish because it is I who feel it, than the action is selfish because it is I who perform it. To prove a man selfish, it is not surely enough to say, that it is *he who feels* (this is a mere quibble) but to shew that he does not feel *for another*, that is, that the idea of the suffering or welfare of others does not excite any feeling whatever of pleasure or pain in his mind, except from some reference to or reflection on himself. Self-love or the love of self means, that I have an immediate interest in the contemplation of my own good, and that this is a motive to action; and benevolence or the love of others means in like manner, that I have an immediate interest in the idea of the good or evil that may befall them, and a disposition to assist them, in consequence. Self-love, in a word, is sympathy with myself, that is, it is I who feel it, and I who am the object of it: in benevolence or compassion, it is I who still feel sympathy, but another (not myself) is the object of it. If I feel sympathy with others at all, it must be disinterested. The pleasure it may give me is the consequence, not the cause, of my feeling it. To insist that sympathy is self-love because we cannot feel for others, without being ourselves affected pleasurably or painfully, is to make nonsense of the question; for it is to insist that in order to feel for others properly and truly, we must in the first place feel nothing. *C'est une mauvaise plaisanterie.* That the feeling exists in the individual must be granted, and never admitted of a question: the

only question is, how that feeling is caused, and what is its object—and it is to express the two opinions that may be entertained on this subject, that the terms *self-love* and *benevolence* have been appropriated. Any other interpretation of them is an evident abuse of language, and a subterfuge in argument, which, driven from the fair field of fact and observation, takes shelter in verbal sophistry.

159. Our approbation of others has a good deal of selfishness in it. We like those who give us pleasure, however little they may wish for or deserve our esteem in return. We prefer a person with vivacity and high spirits, though bordering upon insolence, to the timid and pusillanimous; we are fonder of wit joined to malice, than of dullness without it. We have no great objection to receive a man who is a villain as our friend, if he has plausible exterior qualities; nay, we often take a pride in our harmless familiarity with him, as we might in keeping a tame panther; but we soon grow weary of the society of a good-natured fool who puts our patience to the test, or of an awkward clown who puts our pride to the blush.

160. We are fonder of visiting our friends in health than in sickness. We judge less favourably of their characters, when any misfortune happens to them; and a lucky hit, either in business or reputation, improves even their personal appearance in our eyes.

161. An heiress, with a large fortune and a moderate share of beauty, easily rises into a reigning toast.

162. One shining quality lends a lustre to another, or hides some glaring defect.

163. We are never so much disposed to quarrel with others as when we are dissatisfied with ourselves.

164. We are never so thoroughly tired of the company of any one else as we sometimes are of our own.

165. People outlive the interest, which, at different periods of their lives, they take in themselves. When we forget old friends, it is a sign we have forgotten ourselves; or despise our former ways and notions, as much as we do their present ones.

166. We fancy ourselves superior to others, because we find that we have improved; and at no time did we think ourselves inferior to them.

167. The notice of others is as necessary to us as the air we breathe. If we cannot gain their good opinion, we change our battery, and strive to provoke their hatred and contempt.

168. Some malefactors, at the point of death, confess crimes of which they have never been guilty, thus to raise our wonder and indignation in the same proportion; or to shew their superiority to vulgar prejudice, and brave that public opinion, of which they are the victims.

169. Others make an ostentatious display of their penitence and remorse, only to invite sympathy, and create a diversion in their own minds from the subject of their impending punishment. So that we excite a strong emotion in the breasts of others, we care little of what kind it is, or by what means we produce it. We have equally the feeling of power. The sense of insignificance or of being an object of perfect indifference to others, is the only one that the mind never covets nor willingly submits to.

170. There are not wanting instances of those, who pass their whole lives in endeavouring to make themselves ridiculous. They only tire of their absurdities when others are tired of talking about and laughing at them, so that they have become a stale jest.

171. People in the grasp of death wish all the evil they have done (as well as all the good) to be known, not to make atonement by confession, but to excite one more strong sensation before they die, and to leave their interests and passions a legacy to posterity, when they themselves are exempt from the consequences.

172. We talk little, if we do not talk about ourselves.

173. We may give more offence by our silence than even by impertinence.

174. Obstinate silence implies either a mean opinion of ourselves or a contempt of our company: and it is the more

provoking, as others do not know to which of these causes to attribute it, whether to humility or pride.

175. Silence proceeds either from want of something to say, or from a phlegmatic indifference which closes up our lips. The sea, or any other striking object, suddenly bursting on a party of mutes in a stage-coach, will occasion a general exclamation of surprise; and the ice being once broken, they may probably be good company for the rest of the journey.

176. We compliment ourselves on our national reserve and taciturnity by abusing the loquacity and frivolity of the French.

177. Nations, not being willing or able to correct their own errors, justify them by the opposite errors of other nations.

178. We easily convert our own vices into virtues, the virtues of others into vices.

179. A person who talks with equal vivacity on every subject, excites no interest in any. *Repose* is as necessary in conversation as in a picture.

180. The best kind of conversation is that which may be called *thinking aloud*. I like very well to speak my mind on any subject (or to hear another do so) and to go into the question according to the degree of interest it naturally inspires, but not to have to get up a thesis upon every topic. There are those, on the other hand, who seem always to be practising on their audience, as if they mistook them for a DEBATING-SOCIETY, or to hold a general retainer, by which they are bound to explain every difficulty, and answer every objection that can be started. This, in private society and among friends, is not desirable. You thus lose the two great ends of conversation, which are to learn the sentiments of others, and see what they think of yours. One of the best talkers I ever knew had this defect—that he evidently seemed to be considering less what he felt on any point than what might be said upon it, and that he listened to you, not to weigh what you said, but to reply to it, like counsel on the other side. This habit gave a brilliant smoothness and polish to his general discourse, but, at the same time, took from its solidity and prominence: it reduced it to a tissue of lively, fluent, ingenious *commonplaces*,

(for original genuine, observations are like 'minute drops from off the eaves', and not an incessant shower) and, though his talent in this way was carried to the very extreme of cleverness, yet I think it seldom, if ever, went beyond it.

181. Intellectual excellence can seldom be a source of much satisfaction to the possessor. In a gross period, or in vulgar society, it is not understood; and among those who are refined enough to appreciate its value, it ceases to be a distinction.

182. There is, I think, an essential difference of character in mankind, between those who wish *to do*, and those who wish to *have* certain things. I observe persons expressing a great desire to possess fine horses, hounds, dress, equipage, &c. and an envy of those who have them. I myself have no such feeling, nor the least ambition to shine, except by doing something better than others. I have the love of power, but not of property. I should like to be able to outstrip a grey-hound in speed; but I should be ashamed to take any merit to myself from possessing the fleetest greyhound in the world. I cannot transfer my personal identity from myself to what I merely call *mine*. The generality of mankind are contented to be estimated by what they possess, instead of what they are.

183. Buonaparte observes, that the diplomatists of the new school were no match for those brought up under the ancient *regime.* The reason probably is, that the modern style of intellect inclines to abstract reasoning and general propositions, and pays less attention to individual character, interests, and circumstances. The moderns have, therefore, less tact in watching the designs of others, and less closeness in hiding their own. They perhaps have a greater knowledge of things, but less of the world. They calculate the force of an argument, and rely on its success, moving *in vacuo*, without sufficiently allowing for the resistance of opinion and prejudice.

HEROES

MY FIRST ACQUAINTANCE WITH POETS

MY father was a Dissenting Minister at W—m* in Shropshire;
and in the year 1798 (the figures that compose that date are
to me like the 'dreaded name of Demogorgon')* Mr
Coleridge came to Shrewsbury, to succeed Mr Rowe in the
spiritual charge of a Unitarian Congregation there. He did
not come till late on the Saturday afternoon before he was to
preach; and Mr Rowe, who himself went down to the coach
in a state of anxiety and expectation, to look for the arrival of
his successor, could find no one at all answering the description but a round-faced man in a short black coat (like a
shooting jacket) which hardly seemed to have been made for
him, but who seemed to be talking at a great rate to his
fellow-passengers. Mr Rowe had scarce returned to give an
account of his disappointment, when the round-faced man in
black entered, and dissipated all doubts on the subject, by
beginning to talk. He did not cease while he staid; nor has he
since, that I know of. He held the good town of Shrewsbury
in delightful suspense for three weeks that he remained there,
'fluttering the *proud Salopians* like an eagle in a dove-cote';*
and the Welch mountains that skirt the horizon with their
tempestuous confusion, agree to have heard no such mystic
sounds since the days of

'High-born Hoel's harp or soft Llewellyn's lay!'*

As we passed along between W—m and Shrewsbury, and I
eyed their blue tops seen through the wintry branches, or the
red rustling leaves of the sturdy oak-trees by the road-side, a
sound was in my ears as of a Siren's song; I was stunned,
startled with it, as from deep sleep; but I had no notion then
that I should ever be able to express my admiration to others
in motley imagery or quaint allusion, till the light of his genius
shone into my soul, like the sun's rays glittering in the puddles
of the road. I was at that time dumb, inarticulate, helpless,
like a worm by the way-side,* crushed, bleeding, lifeless; but
now, bursting from the deadly bands that 'bound them,

'With Styx nine times round them,'*

my ideas float on winged words, and as they expand their plumes, catch the golden light of other years. My soul has indeed remained in its original bondage, dark, obscure, with longings infinite and unsatisfied; my heart, shut up in the prison-house of this rude clay, has never found, nor will it ever find, a heart to speak to; but that my understanding also did not remain dumb and brutish, or at length found a language to express itself, I owe to Coleridge. But this is not to my purpose.

My father lived ten miles from Shrewsbury, and was in the habit of exchanging visits with Mr Rowe, and with Mr Jenkins of Whitchurch (nine miles farther on) according to the custom of Dissenting Ministers in each other's neighbourhood. A line of communication is thus established, by which the flame of civil and religious liberty is kept alive, and nourishes its smouldering fire unquenchable, like the fires in the Agamemnon of Æschylus, placed at different stations, that waited for ten long years to announce with their blazing pyramids the destruction of Troy. Coleridge had agreed to come over to see my father, according to the courtesy of the country, as Mr Rowe's probable successor; but in the meantime I had gone to hear him preach the Sunday after his arrival. A poet and a philosopher getting up into a Unitarian pulpit to preach the Gospel, was a romance in these degenerate days, a sort of revival of the primitive spirit of Christianity, which was not to be resisted.

It was in January, 1798, that I rose one morning before daylight, to walk ten miles in the mud, and went to hear this celebrated person preach. Never, the longest day I have to live, shall I have such another walk as this cold, raw, comfortless one, in the winter of the year 1798. *Il y a des impressions que ni le tems ni les circonstances peuvent effacer. Dusse-je vivre des siècles entiers, le doux tems de ma jeunesse ne peut renaître pour moi, ni s'effacer jamais dans ma mémoire.** When I got there, the organ was playing the 100th psalm, and, when it was done, Mr Coleridge rose and gave out his text, 'And he went up into the mountain to pray, HIMSELF, ALONE.'* As he gave out his text, his voice 'rose like a steam of rich distilled perfumes',* and when he came to the two last words, which he pronounced loud, deep, and distinct, it seemed to me, who was then young, as if the sounds had echoed from the bottom of the human heart, and as if that prayer might have floated in solemn silence through the universe. The idea of St John came into mind, 'of one crying in the wilderness, who had his loins girt about, and whose food was locusts and wild honey'.* The preacher then launched into his subject, like an eagle dallying with the wind. The sermon was upon peace and war; upon church and state—not their alliance, but their separation—on the spirit of the world and the spirit of Christianity, not as the same, but as opposed to one another. He talked of those who had 'inscribed the cross of Christ on banners dripping with human gore'.* He made a poetical and pastoral excursion,—and to shew the fatal effects of war, drew a striking contrast between the simple shepherd boy, driving his team afield, or sitting under the hawthorn, piping to his flock, 'as though he should never be old', and the same poor country-lad, crimped, kidnapped, brought into town, made drunk at an alehouse, turned into a wretched drummer-boy, with his hair sticking on end with powder and pomatum, a long cue at his back, and tricked out in the loathsome finery of the profession of blood.

'Such were the notes our once-lov'd poet sung.'*

And for myself, I could not have been more delighted if I had heard the music of the spheres. Poetry and Philosophy had met together. Truth and Genius had embraced, under the eye and with the sanction of Religion. This was even beyond my hopes. I returned home well satisfied. The sun that was still labouring pale and wan through the sky, obscured by thick mists, seemed an emblem of the *good cause*; and the cold dank drops of dew that hung half melted on the beard of the thistle, had something genial and refreshing in them; for there was a spirit of hope and youth in all nature, that turned every thing into good. The face of nature had not then the brand of JUS DIVINUM* on it:

'Like to that sanguine flower inscrib'd with woe.'*

On the Tuesday following, the half-inspired speaker came. I was called down into the room where he was, and went half-hoping, half-afraid. He received me very graciously, and I listened for a long time without uttering a word. I did not suffer in his opinion by my silence. 'For those two hours,' he afterwards was pleased to say, 'he was conversing with W. H.'s forehead!' His appearance was different from what I had anticipated from seeing him before. At a distance, and in the dim light of the chapel, there was to me a strange wildness in his aspect, a dusky obscurity, and I thought him pitted with the small-pox. His complexion was at that time clear, and even bright—

'As are the children of yon azure sheen.'*

His forehead was broad and high, light as if built of ivory, with large projecting eyebrows, and his eyes rolling beneath them like a sea with darkened lustre. 'A certain tender bloom his face o'erspread,'* a purple tinge as we see it in the pale thoughtful complexions of the Spanish portrait-painters, Murillo and Velasquez. His mouth was gross, voluptuous, open, eloquent; his chin good-humoured and round; but his nose, the rudder of the face, the index of the will, was small, feeble, nothing—like what he has done. It might seem that the genius of his face as from a height surveyed and projected him (with sufficient capacity and huge aspiration) into the world unknown of thought and imagination, with nothing to support or guide his veering purpose, as if Columbus had launched his adventurous course for the New World in a scallop, without oars or compass. So at least I comment on it after the event. Coleridge in his person was rather above the common size, inclining to the corpulent, or like Lord Hamlet, 'somewhat fat and pursy'.* His hair (now, alas! grey) was then black and glossy as the raven's, and fell in smooth masses over his forehead. This long pendulous hair is peculiar to enthu-siasts, to those whose minds tend heavenward; and is tradi-tionally inseparable (though of a different colour) from the pictures of Christ. It ought to belong, as a character, to all who preach *Christ crucified*, and Coleridge was at that time one of those!

It was curious to observe the contrast between him and my father, who was a veteran in the cause, and then declining into the vale of years. He had been a poor Irish lad, carefully brought up by his parents, and sent to the University of Glasgow (where he studied under Adam Smith) to prepare him for his future destination. It was his mother's proudest wish to see her son a Dissenting Minister. So if we look back to past generations (as far as eye can reach) we see the same hopes, fears, wishes, followed by the same disappointments, throbbing in the human heart; and so we may see them (if we look forward) rising up for ever, and disappearing, like vapourish bubbles, in the human breast! After being tossed about from congregation to congregation in the heats of the Unitarian controversy,* and squabbles about the American war, he had been relegated to an obscure village, where he was to spend the last thirty years of his life, far from the only converse that he loved, the talk about disputed texts of Scripture and the cause of civil and religious liberty. Here he passed his days, repining but resigned, in the study of the Bible, and the perusal of the Commentators,—huge folios, not easily got through, one of which would outlast a winter! Why did he pore on these from morn to night (with the exception of a walk in the fields or a turn in the garden to gather broccoli-plants or kidney-beans of his own rearing, with no small degree of pride and pleasure)?—Here were 'no figures nor no fantasies',*—neither poetry nor philosophy—nothing to dazzle, nothing to excite modern curiosity; but to his lack-lustre eyes there appeared, within the pages of the ponderous, unwieldy, neglected tomes, the sacred name of JEHOVAH in Hebrew capitals: pressed down by the weight of the style, worn to the last fading thinness of the understanding, there were glimpses, glimmering notions of the patriarchal wanderings, with palm-trees hovering in the horizon, and processions of camels at the distance of three thousand years; there was Moses with the Burning Bush, the number of the Twelve Tribes, types, shadows, glosses on the law and the prophets; there were discussions (dull enough) on the age of

Methuselah, a mighty speculation! there were outlines, rude
guesses at the shape of Noah's Ark and of the riches of
Solomon's Temple; questions as to the date of the creation,
predictions of the end of all things; the great lapses of time,
the strange mutations of the globe were unfolded with the
voluminous leaf, as it turned over; and though the soul might
slumber with an hieroglyphic veil of inscrutable mysteries
drawn over it, yet it was in a slumber ill-exchanged for all the
sharpened realities of sense, wit, fancy, or reason. My father's
life was comparatively a dream; but it was a dream of infinity
and eternity, of death, the resurrection, and a judgment to
come!

No two individuals were ever more unlike than were the
host and his guest. A poet was to my father a sort of nondescript: yet whatever added grace to the Unitarian cause was
to him welcome. He could hardly have been more surprised
or pleased, if our visitor had worn wings. Indeed, his thoughts
had wings; and as the silken sounds rustled round our little
wainscoted parlour, my father threw back his spectacles over
his forehead, his white hairs mixing with its sanguine hue;
and a smile of delight beamed across his rugged cordial face,
to think that Truth had found a new ally in Fancy! Besides,
Coleridge seemed to take considerable notice of me, and that
of itself was enough. He talked very familiarly, but agreeably,
and glanced over a variety of subjects. At dinner-time he grew
more animated, and dilated in a very edifying manner on
Mary Wolstonecraft and Mackintosh.* The last, he said, he
considered (on my father's speaking of his *Vindiciæ Gallicæ* as
a capital performance) as a clever scholastic man—a master
of the topics,—or as the ready warehouseman of letters, who
knew exactly where to lay his hand on what he wanted, though
the goods were not his own. He thought him no match for
Burke, either in style or matter. Burke was a metaphysician,
Mackintosh a mere logician. Burke was an orator (almost a
poet) who reasoned in figures, because he had an eye for
nature: Mackintosh, on the other hand, was a rhetorician, who
had only an eye to common-places. On this I ventured to say
that I had always entertained a great opinion of Burke, and
that (as far as I could find) the speaking of him with contempt

might be made the test of a vulgar democratical mind. This
was the first observation I ever made to Coleridge, and he said
it was a very just and striking one. I remember the leg of Welsh
mutton and the turnips on the table that day had the finest
flavour imaginable. Coleridge added that Mackintosh and
Tom Wedgwood* (of whom, however, he spoke highly) had
expressed a very indifferent opinion of his friend Mr Wordsworth, on which he remarked to them—'He strides on so far
before you, that he dwindles in the distance!' Godwin had
once boasted* to him of having carried on an argument with
Mackintosh for three hours with dubious success; Coleridge
told him—'If there had been a man of genius in the room,
he would have settled the question in five minutes.' He asked
me if I had ever seen Mary Wolstonecraft, and I said, I had
once for a few moments, and that she seemed to me to turn
off Godwin's objections to something she advanced with quite
a playful, easy air. He replied, that 'this was only one instance
of the ascendancy which people of imagination exercised over
those of mere intellect.' He did not rate Godwin very high
(this was caprice or prejudice, real or affected) but he had a
great idea of Mrs Wolstonecraft's powers of conversation,
none at all of her talent for book-making. We talked a little
about Holcroft.* He had been asked if he was not much struck
with him, and he said, he thought himself in more danger of
being struck *by* him. I complained that he would not let me
get on at all, for he required a definition of every the commonest word, exclaiming, 'What do you mean by a *sensation*,
Sir? What do you mean by an *idea*?' This, Coleridge said, was
barricadoing the road to truth:—it was setting up a turnpike-
gate at every step we took. I forget a great number of things,
many more than I remember; but the day passed off plea-
santly, and the next morning Mr Coleridge was to return to
Shrewsbury. When I came down to breakfast, I found that he
had just received a letter from his friend T. Wedgwood, making him an offer of *150l.* a-year if he chose to wave his present
pursuit, and devote himself entirely to the study of poetry and
philosophy. Coleridge seemed to make up his mind to close
with this proposal in the act of tying on one of his shoes. It
threw an additional damp on his departure. It took the

wayward enthusiast quite from us to cast him into Deva's winding vales,* or by the shores of old romance. Instead of living at ten miles distance, of being the pastor of a Dissenting congregation at Shrewsbury, he was henceforth to inhabit the Hill of Parnassus, to be a shepherd on the Delectable Mountains. Alas! I knew not the way thither, and felt very little gratitude for Mr Wedgwood's bounty. I was presently relieved from this dilemma; for Mr Coleridge, asking for a pen and ink, and going to a table to write something on a bit of card, advanced towards me with undulating step, and giving me the precious document, said that that was his address, *Mr Coleridge, Nether-Stowey, Somersetshire*; and that he should be glad to see me there in a few weeks' time, and, if I chose, would come half-way to meet me. I was not less surprised than the shepherd-boy (this simile is to be found in Cassandra)* when he sees a thunder-bolt fall close at his feet. I stammered out my acknowledgments and acceptance of this offer (I thought Mr Wedgwood's annuity a trifle to it) as well as I could; and this mighty business being settled, the poet-preacher took leave, and I accompanied him six miles on the road. It was a fine morning in the middle of winter, and he talked the whole way. The scholar in Chaucer is described as going

——'Sounding on his way.'*

So Coleridge went on his. In digressing, in dilating, in passing from subject to subject, he appeared to me to float in air, to slide on ice.* He told me in confidence (going along) that he should have preached two sermons before he accepted the situation at Shrewsbury, one on Infant Baptism, the other on the Lord's Supper, shewing that he could not administer either, which would have effectually disqualified him for the object in view. I observed that he continually crossed me on the way by shifting from one side of the foot-path to the other. This struck me as an odd movement; but I did not at that time connect it with any instability of purpose or involuntary change of principle, as I have done since. He seemed unable to keep on in a strait line. He spoke slightingly of Hume* (whose Essay on Miracles he said was stolen from an objection started in one of South's sermons—*Credat Judæus Apella*!)* I was not very much pleased at this account of Hume, for I had just been reading, with infinite relish, that completest of all metaphysical *choke-pears* his *Treatise on Human Nature*, to which the *Essays*, in point of scholastic subtlety and close reasoning, are mere elegant trifling, light summer-reading. Coleridge even denied the excellence of Hume's general style, which I think betrayed a want of taste or candour. He however made me amends by the manner in which he spoke of Berkeley.* He dwelt particularly on his *Essay on Vision* as a masterpiece of analytical reasoning. So it undoubtedly is. He was exceedingly angry with Dr Johnson for striking the stone with his foot, in allusion to this author's Theory of Matter and Spirit, and saying, 'Thus I confute him, Sir.'* Coleridge drew a parallel (I don't know how he brought about the connection) between Bishop Berkeley and Tom Paine.* He said the one was an instance of a subtle, the other of an acute mind, than which no two things could be more distinct. The one was a shop-boy's quality, the other the characteristic of a philosopher. He considered Bishop Butler* as a true philosopher, a profound and conscientious thinker, a genuine reader of nature and of his own mind. He did not speak of his *Analogy*, but of his *Sermons at the Rolls' Chapel*, of which I had never heard. Coleridge somehow always contrived to prefer the *unknown* to the *known*. In this instance he was right. The *Analogy* is a tissue of sophistry, of wire-drawn, theological special-pleading; the *Sermons* (with the Preface to them) are in a fine vein of deep, matured reflection, a candid appeal to our observation of human nature, without pedantry and without bias. I told Coleridge I had written a few remarks,* and was sometimes foolish enough to believe that I had made a discovery on the same subject (the *Natural Disinterestedness of the Human Mind*)—and I tried to explain my view of it to Coleridge, who listened with great willingness, but I did not succeed in making myself understood. I sat down to the task shortly afterwards for the twentieth time, got new pens and paper, determined to make clear work of it, wrote a few meagre sentences in the skeleton-style of a mathematical demonstration, stopped half-way down the second page; and, after trying in vain to pump up any words, images, notions, apprehensions, facts, or observations, from that gulph of abstraction in which I had plunged myself for four or five years preceding, gave up the attempt as labour in vain, and shed tears of helpless despondency on the blank unfinished paper. I can write fast enough now. Am I better than I was then? Oh no! One truth discovered, one pang of regret at not being able to express it, is better than all the fluency and flippancy in the world. Would that I could go back to what I then was! Why can we not revive past times as we can revisit old places? If I had the quaint Muse of Sir Philip Sidney to assist me, I would write a *Sonnet to the Road between W—m and Shrewsbury*, and immortalise every step of it by some fond enigmatical conceit. I would swear that the very milestones had ears, and that Harmer-hill stooped with all its pines, to listen to a poet, as he passed! I remember but one other topic of discourse in this walk. He mentioned Paley,* praised the naturalness and clearness of his style, but condemned his sentiments, thought him a mere time-serving casuist, and said that 'the fact of his work on Moral and Political Philosophy being made a text-book in our Universities was a disgrace to the national character.' We parted at the six-mile stone; and I returned homeward pensive but much pleased. I had met with unexpected notice from a person, whom I believed to have been prejudiced against me. 'Kind and affable to me had been his condescension, and should be honoured ever with suitable regard.'* He was the first poet I had known, and he certainly answered to that inspired name. I had heard a great deal of his powers of conversation, and was not disappointed. In fact, I never met with any thing at all like them, either before or since. I could easily credit the accounts which were circulated of his holding forth to a large party of ladies and gentlemen, an evening or two before, on the Berkeleian Theory, when he made the whole material universe look like a transparency of fine words; and another story (which I believe he has somewhere told himself)* of his being asked to a party at Birmingham, of his smoking tobacco and going to sleep after dinner on a sofa, where the company found him to their no small surprise, which was increased to wonder when he started up of a sudden, and rubbing his eyes, looked about him, and launched into a three-hours' description of the third heaven, of which he had had a dream, very different from Mr Southey's Vision of Judgment, and also from that other Vision of Judgment,* which Mr Murray, the Secretary of the Bridge-street Junto,* has taken into his especial keeping!

On my way back, I had a sound in my ears, it was the voice of Fancy: I had a light before me, it was the face of Poetry. The one still lingers there, the other has not quitted my side! Coleridge in truth met me half-way on the ground of philosophy, or I should not have been won over to his imaginative creed. I had an uneasy, pleasurable sensation all the time, till I was to visit him. During those months the chill breath of winter gave me a welcoming; the vernal air was balm and inspiration to me. The golden sunsets, the silver star of evening, lighted me on my way to new hopes and prospects. *I was to visit Coleridge in the spring*. This circumstance was never absent from my thoughts, and mingled with all my feelings. I wrote to him at the time proposed, and received an answer postponing my intended visit for a week or two, but very cordially urging me to complete my promise then. This delay did not damp, but rather increased my ardour. In the meantime, I went to Llangollen Vale, by way of initiating myself in the mysteries of natural scenery; and I must say I was enchanted with it. I had been reading Coleridge's description of England in his fine *Ode on the Departing Year*,* and I applied it, *con amore*, to the objects before me. That valley was to me (in a manner) the cradle of a new existence: in the river that winds through it, my spirit was baptised in the waters of Helicon!*

I returned home, and soon after set out on my journey with unworn heart and untried feet. My way lay through Worcester and Gloucester, and by Upton, where I thought of Tom Jones and the adventure of the muff.* I remember getting completely wet through one day, and stopping at an inn (I think it was at Tewkesbury) where I sat up all night to read *Paul and Virginia*.* Sweet were the showers in early youth that drenched my body, and sweet the drops of pity that fell upon the books I read! I recollect a remark of Coleridge's upon this very book, that nothing could shew the gross indelicacy of French

manners and the entire corruption of their imagination more
strongly than the behaviour of the heroine in the last fatal
scene, who turns away from a person on board the sinking
vessel, that offers to save her life, because he has thrown off
his clothes to assist him in swimming. Was this a time to think
of such a circumstance? I once hinted to Wordsworth, as we
were sailing in his boat on Grasmere lake, that I thought he
had borrowed the idea of his *Poems on the Naming of Places* from
the local inscriptions of the same kind in *Paul and Virginia.*
He did not own the obligation, and stated some distinction
without a difference, in defence of his claim to originality. Any
the slightest variation would be sufficient for this purpose in
his mind; for whatever *he* added or omitted would inevitably
be worth all that any one else had done, and contain the
marrow of the sentiment. I was still two days before the time
fixed for my arrival, for I had taken care to set out early
enough. I stopped these two days at Bridgewater, and when I
was tired of sauntering on the banks of its muddy river,
returned to the inn, and read *Camilla.** So have I loitered my
life away, reading books, looking at pictures, going to plays,
hearing, thinking, writing on what pleased me best. I have
wanted only one thing to make me happy;* but wanting that,
have wanted everything!

I arrived, and was well received. The country about Nether
Stowey is beautiful, green and hilly, and near the sea-shore. I
saw it but the other day, after an interval of twenty years, from
a hill near Taunton. How was the map of my life spread out
before me, as the map of the country lay at my feet! In the
afternoon, Coleridge took me over to All-Foxden, a romantic
old family-mansion of the St Aubins, where Wordsworth lived.
It was then in the possession of a friend of the poet's who gave
him the free use of it. Somehow that period (the time just
after the French Revolution) was not a time when *nothing was
given for nothing.* The mind opened, and a softness might be
perceived coming over the heart of individuals, beneath 'the
scales that fence'* our self-interest. Wordsworth himself was
from home, but his sister kept house, and set before us a
frugal repast; and we had free access to her brother's poems,
the *Lyrical Ballads,* which were still in manuscript, or in the

form of *Sybilline Leaves*.* I dipped into a few of these with great satisfaction, and with the faith of a novice. I slept that night in an old room with blue hangings, and covered with the round-faced family-portraits of the age of George I and II, and from the wooded declivity of the adjoining park that over-looked my window, at the dawn of day, could

'——hear the loud stag speak.'*

In the outset of life (and particularly at this time I felt it so) our imagination has a body to it. We are in a state between sleeping and waking, and have indistinct but glorious glimpses of strange shapes, and there is always something to come better than what we see. As in our dreams the fulness of the blood gives warmth and reality to the coinage of the brain, so in youth our ideas are clothed, and fed, and pampered with our good spirits; we breathe thick with thoughtless happiness, the weight of future years presses on the strong pulses of the heart, and we repose with undisturbed faith in truth and good. As we advance, we exhaust our fund of enjoyment and of hope. We are no longer wrapped in *lamb's-wool*, lulled in Elysium.* As we taste the pleasures of life, their spirit evapor-ates, the sense palls; and nothing is left but the phantoms, the lifeless shadows of what *has been*!

That morning, as soon as breakfast was over, we strolled out into the park, and seating ourselves on the trunk of an old ash-tree that stretched along the ground, Coleridge read aloud with a sonorous and musical voice, the ballad of *Betty Foy*.* I was not critically or sceptically inclined. I saw touches of truth and nature, and took the rest for granted. But in the *Thorn*, the *Mad Mother*, and the *Complaint of a Poor Indian Woman*, I felt that deeper power and pathos which have been since acknowledged,

'In spite of pride, in erring reason's spite,'*

as the characteristics of this author; and the sense of a new style and a new spirit in poetry came over me. It had to me something of the effect that arises from the turning up of the fresh soil, or of the first welcome breath of Spring,

'While yet the trembling year is unconfirmed.'*

Coleridge and myself walked back to Stowey that evening, and
his voice sounded high

> 'Of Providence, foreknowledge, will, and fate,
> Fix'd fate, free-will, foreknowledge absolute,'*

as we passed through echoing grove, by fairy stream or water-
fall, gleaming in the summer moonlight! He lamented that
Wordsworth was not prone enough to believe in the traditional superstitions of the place, and that there was a something corporeal, a *matter-of-fact-ness*, a clinging to the palpable,
or often to the petty, in his poetry, in consequence. His genius
was not a spirit that descended to him through the air; it
sprung out of the ground like a flower, or unfolded itself from
a green spray, on which the gold-finch sang. He said, however
(if I remember right), that this objection must be confined to
his descriptive pieces, that his philosophic poetry had a grand
and comprehensive spirit in it, so that his soul seemed to
inhabit the universe like a palace, and to discover truth by
intuition, rather than by deduction. The next day Wordsworth
arrived from Bristol at Coleridge's cottage. I think I see him
now. He answered in some degree to his friend's description
of him, but was more gaunt and Don Quixote-like. He was
quaintly dressed (according to the *costume* of that unconstrained period) in a brown fustian jacket and striped pan-
taloons. There was something of a roll, a lounge in his gait,
not unlike his own Peter Bell.* There was a severe, worn
pressure of thought about his temples, a fire in his eye (as if
he saw something in objects more than the outward appearance), an intense high narrow forehead, a Roman nose,
cheeks furrowed by strong purpose and feeling, and a convulsive inclination to laughter about the mouth, a good deal at
variance with the solemn, stately expression of the rest of his
face. Chantry's bust wants the marking traits; but he was
teazed into making it regular and heavy: Haydon's head* of
him, introduced into the *Entrance of Christ into Jerusalem*, is the
most like his drooping weight of thought and expression. He
sat down and talked very naturally and freely, with a mixture

of clear gushing accents in his voice, a deep guttural intonation, and a strong tincture of the northern *burr*, like the crust
on wine. He instantly began to make havoc of the half of a
Cheshire cheese on the table, and said triumphantly that 'his
marriage with experience had not been so unproductive as
Mr Southey's in teaching him a knowledge of the good things
of this life'. He had been to see the *Castle Spectre* by Monk
Lewis,* while at Bristol, and described it very well. He said 'it
fitted the taste of the audience like a glove'. This *ad captandum** merit was however by no means a recommendation of
it, according to the severe principles of the new school, which
reject rather than court popular effect. Wordsworth, looking
out of the low, latticed window, said, 'How beautifully the sun
sets on that yellow bank!' I thought within myself, 'With what
eyes these poets see nature!' and ever after, when I saw the
sun-set stream upon the objects facing it, conceived I had
made a discovery, or thanked Mr Wordsworth for having made
one for me! We went over to All-Foxden again the day following, and Wordsworth read us the story of Peter Bell in the
open air; and the comment made upon it by his face and voice
was very different from that of some later critics! Whatever
might be thought of the poem, 'his face was as a book* where
men might read strange matters', and he announced the fate
of his hero in prophetic tones. There is a *chaunt* in the recita-
tion both of Coleridge and Wordsworth, which acts as a spell
upon the hearer, and disarms the judgment. Perhaps they
have deceived themselves by making habitual use of this
ambiguous accompaniment. Coleridge's manner is more full,
animated, and varied; Wordsworth's more equable, sustained,
and internal. The one might be termed more *dramatic*, the
other more *lyrical*. Coleridge has told me that he himself liked
to compose in walking over uneven ground, or breaking
through the straggling branches of a copse-wood; whereas
Wordsworth always wrote (if he could) walking up and down
a straight gravel-walk, or in some spot where the continuity of
his verse met with no collateral interruption. Returning that
same evening, I got into a metaphysical argument with Wordsworth, while Coleridge was explaining the different notes
of the nightingale to his sister, in which we neither of us

succeeded in making ourselves perfectly clear and intelligible. Thus I passed three weeks at Nether Stowey and in the neighbourhood, generally devoting the afternoons to a delightful chat in an arbour made of bark by the poet's friend Tom Poole,* sitting under two fine elm-trees, and listening to the bees humming round us, while we quaffed our *flip*.* It was agreed, among other things, that we should make a jaunt down the Bristol-Channel, as far as Linton. We set off together on foot, Coleridge, John Chester, and I. This Chester was a native of Nether Stowey, one of those who were attracted to Coleridge's discourse as flies are to honey, or bees in swarming-time to the sound of a brass pan. He 'followed in the chase, like a dog who hunts, not like one that made up the cry'.* He had on a brown cloth coat, boots, and corduroy breeches, was low in stature, bow-legged, had a drag in his walk like a drover, which he assisted by a hazel switch, and kept on a sort of trot by the side of Coleridge, like a running footman by a state coach, that he might not lose a syllable or sound that fell from Coleridge's lips. He told me his private opinion, that Coleridge was a wonderful man. He scarcely opened his lips, much less offered an opinion the whole way: yet of the three, had I to chuse during that journey, I would be John Chester. He afterwards followed Coleridge into Germany, where the Kantean philosophers were puzzled how to bring him under any of their categories. When he sat down at table with his idol, John's felicity was complete; Sir Walter Scott's, or Mr Blackwood's, when they sat down at the same table with the King, was not more so. We passed Dunster on our right, a small town between the brow of a hill and the sea. I remember eyeing it wistfully as it lay below us: contrasted with the woody scene around, it looked as clear, as pure, as *embrowned* and ideal as any landscape I have seen since, of Gaspar Poussin's or Domenichino's. We had a long day's march—(our feet kept time to the echoes of Coleridge's tongue)—through Minehead and by the Blue Anchor, and on to Linton, which we did not reach till near midnight, and where we had some difficulty in making a lodgment. We however knocked the people of the house up at last, and we were repaid for our apprehensions and fatigue by some excellent rashers of fried bacon and eggs. The view in coming along had been splendid. We walked for miles and miles on dark brown heaths overlooking the Channel, with the Welsh hills beyond, and at times descended into little sheltered valleys close by the seaside, with a smuggler's face scowling by us, and then had to ascend conical hills with a path winding up through a coppice to a barren top, like a monk's shaven crown, from one of which I pointed out to Coleridge's notice the bare masts of a vessel on the very edge of the horizon and within the red-orbed disk of the setting sun, like his own spectre-ship in the *Ancient Mariner*. At Linton the character of the sea-coast becomes more marked and rugged. There is a place called the *Valley of Rocks* (I suspect this was only the poetical name for it) bedded among precipices overhanging the sea, with rocky caverns beneath, into which the waves dash, and where the sea-gull for ever wheels its screaming flight. On the tops of these are huge stones thrown transverse, as if an earthquake had tossed them there, and behind these is a fretwork of perpendicular rocks, something like the *Giant's Causeway*. A thunder-storm came on while we were at the inn, and Coleridge was running out bare-headed to enjoy the commotion of the elements in the *Valley of Rocks*, but as if in spite, the clouds only muttered a few angry sounds, and let fall a few refreshing drops. Coleridge told me that he and Wordsworth were to have made this place the scene of a prose-tale, which was to have been in the manner of, but far superior to, the *Death of Abel*,* but they had relinquished the design. In the morning of the second day, we breakfasted luxuriously in an old-fashioned parlour, on tea, toast, eggs, and honey, in the very sight of the bee-hives from which it had been taken, and a garden full of thyme and wild flowers that had produced it. On this occasion Coleridge spoke of Virgil's Georgics, but not well. I do not think he had much feeling for the classical or elegant. It was in this room that we found a little worn-out copy of the *Seasons*, lying in a window-seat, on which Coleridge exclaimed, '*That* is true fame!' He said Thomson was a great poet, rather than a good one; his style was as meretricious as his thoughts were natural. He spoke of Cowper as the best modern poet. He said the *Lyrical*

Ballads were an experiment about to be tried by him and Wordsworth, to see how far the public taste would endure poetry written in a more natural and simple style than had hitherto been attempted; totally discarding the artifices of poetical diction, and making use only of such words as had probably been common in the most ordinary language since the days of Henry II. Some comparison was introduced between Shakespeare and Milton. He said 'he hardly knew which to prefer. Shakespeare appeared to him a mere stripling in the art; he was as tall and as strong, with infinitely more activity than Milton, but he never appeared to have come to man's estate; or if he had, he would not have been a man, but a monster.' He spoke with contempt of Gray, and with intolerance of Pope. He did not like the versification of the latter. He observed that 'the ears of these couplet-writers might be charged with having short memories, that could not retain the harmony of whole passages.' He thought little of Junius as a writer;* he had a dislike of Dr Johnson; and a much higher opinion of Burke as an orator and politician, than of Fox or Pitt. He however thought him very inferior in richness of style and imagery to some of our elder prose-writers, particularly Jeremy Taylor. He liked Richardson, but not Fielding; nor could I get him to enter into the merits of *Caleb Williams.** In short, he was profound and discriminating with respect to those authors whom he liked, and where he gave his judgment fair play; capricious, perverse, and prejudiced in his antipathies and distastes. We loitered on the 'ribbed sea-sands',* in such talk as this, a whole morning, and I recollect met with a curious sea- weed, of which John Chester told us the country name! A fisherman gave Coleridge an account of a boy that had been drowned the day before, and that they had tried to save him at the risk of their own lives. He said 'he did not know how it was that they ventured, but, Sir, we have a *nature* towards one another.' This expression, Coleridge remarked to me, was a fine illustration of that theory of disinterestedness which I (in common with Butler) had adopted. I broached to him an argument of mine to prove that *likeness* was not mere association of ideas. I said that the mark in the sand put one in mind of a man's foot, not because it was part of a former impression of a man's foot (for it was quite new) but because it was like the shape of a man's foot. He assented to the justness of this distinction (which I have explained at length elsewhere,* for the benefit of the curious) and John Chester listened; not from any interest in the subject, but because he was astonished that I should be able to suggest any thing to Coleridge that he did not already know. We returned on the third morning, and Coleridge remarked the silent cottage-smoke curling up the valleys where, a few evenings before, we had seen the lights gleaming through the dark.

In a day or two after we arrived at Stowey, we set out, I on my return home, and he for Germany. It was a Sunday morning, and he was to preach that day for Dr Toulmin of Taunton.* I asked him if he had prepared any thing for the occasion? He said he had not even thought of the text, but should as soon as we parted. I did not go to hear him,—this was a fault,—but we met in the evening at Bridgewater. The next day we had a long day's walk to Bristol, and sat down, I recollect, by a well-side on the road, to cool ourselves and satisfy our thirst, when Coleridge repeated to me some descriptive lines from his tragedy of Remorse;* which I must say became his mouth and that occasion better than they, some years after, did Mr Elliston's and the Drury-lane boards,*—

> 'Oh memory! shield me from the world's poor strife,
> And give those scenes thine everlasting life.'

I saw no more of him for a year or two, during which period he had been wandering in the Hartz Forest in Germany; and his return was cometary, meteorous, unlike his setting out. It was not till some time after that I knew his friends Lamb and Southey. The last always appears to me (as I first saw him) with a common-place book under his arm, and the first with a *bon-mot* in his mouth. It was at Godwin's that I met him with Holcroft and Coleridge, where they were disputing fiercely which was the best—*Man as he was, or man as he is to be.* 'Give me,' says Lamb,* 'man as he is *not* to be.' This saying was the beginning of a friendship between us, which I believe still continues.—Enough of this for the present.

'But there is matter for another rhyme,
And I to this may add a second tale.'*

THE LIFE OF NAPOLEON

I

OF my object in writing the LIFE here offered to the public,
and of the general tone that pervades it, it may be proper that
I should render some account in order to prevent mistakes
and false applications. It is true, I admired the man; but what
chiefly attached me to him, was his being, as he had been long
ago designated, 'the child and champion of the Revolution'.*
Of this character he could not divest himself, even though he
wished it. He was nothing, he could be nothing but what he
owed to himself and to his triumphs over those who claimed
mankind as their inheritance by a divine right; and as long as
he was *a thorn in the side of kings* and kept them at bay, his
cause rose out of the ruins and defeat of their pride and hopes
of revenge. He stood (and he alone stood) between them and
their natural prey. He kept off that last indignity and wrong
offered to a whole people (and through them to the rest of
the world) of being handed over, like a herd of cattle, to a
particular family, and chained to the foot of a legitimate
throne. This was the chief point at issue—this was the great
question, compared with which all others were tame and
insignificant—Whether mankind were, from the beginning to
the end of time, born slaves or not? As long as he remained,
his acts, his very existence gave a proud and full answer to this
question. As long as he interposed a barrier, a gauntlet, and
an arm of steel between us and them who alone could set up
the plea of old, indefeasible right over us, no increase of
power could be too great that tended to shatter this claim to
pieces: even his abuse of power and aping the style and title
of the imaginary Gods of the earth only laughed their pretensions the more to scorn. He did many things wrong and
foolish; but they were individual acts, and recoiled upon the
head of the doer. They stood upon the ground of their own

merits, and could not urge in their vindication 'the right divine of kings to govern wrong;'* they were not precedents; they were not exempt from public censure or opinion; they were not softened by prescription, nor screened by prejudice, nor sanctioned by superstition, nor rendered formidable by a principle that imposed them as sacred obligations on all future generations: either they were state-necessities extorted by the circumstances of the time, or violent acts of the will, that carried their own condemnation in their bosom. Whatever fault might be found with them, they did not proceed upon the avowed principle, that 'millions were made for one,'* but one for millions; and as long as this distinction was kept in view, liberty was saved, and the Revolution was untouched; for it was to establish it that the Revolution was commenced, and to overturn it that the enemies of liberty waded through seas of blood, and at last succeeded. It is the practice of the partisans of the old school to cry *Vive le Roi, quand même!* Why do not the people learn to imitate the example? Till they do, they will be sure to be foiled in the end by their adversaries, since half-measures and principles can never prevail against whole ones. In fact, Buonaparte was not strictly a free agent. He could hardly do otherwise than he did, ambition apart, and merely to preserve himself and the country he ruled. France was in a state of siege; a citadel in which Freedom had hoisted the flag of revolt against the threat of hereditary servitude; and that in the midst of distraction and convulsions consequent on the sentence of ban and anathema passed upon it by the rest of Europe for having engaged in this noble struggle, required a military dictator to repress internal treachery and headstrong factions, and repel external force. Who then shall blame Buonaparte for having taken the reins of government and held them with a tight hand? The English, who having set the example of liberty to the world, did all they could to stifle it? Or the Continental Sovereigns, who were only acquainted with its principles by their fear and hatred of them? Or the Emigrants, traitors to the name of men as well as Frenchmen? Or the Jacobins, who made the tree of liberty spout nothing but blood? Or its *paper* advocates, who reduce it to a harmless theory? Or its true

friends, who would sacrifice all for its sake? The last, who
alone have the right to call him to a severe account, will not;
for they know that, being but a handful or scattered, they had
not the power to effect themselves what they might have
recommended to him; and that there was but one alternative
between him and that slavery, which kills both the bodies and
the souls of men! There were two other feelings that influenced me on this subject; a love of glory, when it did not
interfere with other things, and the wish to see personal merit
prevail over external rank and circumstance. I felt pride (not
envy) to think that there was one reputation in modern times
equal to the ancients, and at seeing one man greater than the
throne he sat upon.

II

. . .Not satisfied with waking the echoes of ancient liberty in
the rocks and valleys of Switzerland, the Directory were determined to bring all the owls and bats about their ears that were
likely to be dislodged from the crumbling ruins of papal
superstition. The court of Rome even after the treaty of
Tolentino, urged on by its disappointments and disregarding
its engagements, still chose to persist in its hostility against the
French name, quarrelled with the Cisalpine Republic, again
placed an Austrian General (Provera) at the head of its troops,
and excited a popular tumult; in attempting to quell which
Duphot,* a young General of the greatest promise, and who
happened to be at this time at Rome on his travels, was
murdered at the gate of the French Ambassador's palace. The
latter withdrew to Florence. Napoleon when consulted replied
that *Events ought not to govern policy, but policy events*; that
however wrong the court of Rome might be, the object was
not to punish its folly or presumption, but to prevent the
recurrence of similar accidents in future; that for this purpose
it would be best not to overturn the Holy See, but to require
that it should make an example of the guilty, send away
Provera, compose its ministry of the most moderate prelates,
and conclude a Concordat with the Cisalpine Republic, which
might prepare men's minds for something like a similar arrangement at a future period with the French Republic.' But

all this, except the last, had been tried before and failed. The Directory therefore (this time led by Lepaux)* determined to give the rein to their resentment and revolutionary zeal, to march against the Pope, and dethrone that idol of slavish superstition. They thought that the words *Roman Republic* would act as a talisman and kindle all Italy into a flame. They did not at all approve of the half-measures suggested and pursued by Napoleon, his neutralising the spirit of liberty and tampering with the remains of antiquated bigotry; and threw out shrewd hints that he might have his private views in all this caution and moderation, and that not only by his considerate behaviour to the Pope, but by his zealous anxiety for the exiled priests, he wished to gain friends (and indeed had done so) among those who were not the friends of the Revolution. The idea that the attack on Rome might bring on a war with Naples they treated as altogether chimerical. Berthier accordingly received orders to march an army on Rome, and to re-establish the old Roman Republic, which was done without delay. The Capitol once more beheld Consuls, a Senate, and a Tribunate. Fourteen Cardinals went in procession to St Peter's to sing *Te Deum* in commemoration of the restoration of the Roman Republic, and the destruction of the throne of St Peter. Really in reading over such accounts as these, one is not surprised at Mr Burke's expression of 'the grand carnival and masquerade of this our age',* applied to the freaks and absurdities of the French Revolution, though no one contributed more to them than he did by impeding its natural and salutary course with the rubbish of mouldering prejudices and venal sophistry. One would suppose from the scene acted on this occasion that states were built up and Republics manufactured on the same principle that children build houses with packs of cards. But revolutions must be accomplished, like other things, according to nature. The fabric of society must grow up from a solid foundation, and its improvements be effected by the wide-spread and gradual triumph of general principles, and not by the sudden changes of scenery or preposterous assumptions of character, that are met with in a pantomime. Power and authority has its date; and different systems and maxims prevail at different periods of the world, and sweep away all traces of those which went before them; but to suppose that we can disarm inveterate bigotry and crimson pride by a few cant-phrases, that we can decompose the texture of men's minds and the inmost passions of their souls by infusing into them our own opinions of yesterday, or that we can get the very props and pillars of an ancient edifice of superstition to become accessary to their own condemnation and to walk in the pageant of their own disgrace, is contrary to all we know of history or human nature. To make an adversary an accomplice in the triumph over him, is a cruel mockery: those on the other hand who suppose that others are sincere converts to a cause that takes all their power and self-consequence from them, or thrusts them out from being installed as the oracles of truth or the vice-gerents of God upon earth, to be a bye-word and a laughing-stock to the world or to depend upon the shout and caprice of a mob, who before scarcely breathed but through their nostrils, are grossly deceived, and will in the end be both the dupes and victims of their own egotism and blindfold presumption.

III

The expedition to Moscow in 1812 arose out of the inability or disinclination of Alexander* to keep the engagements he had entered into at Tilsit and Erfurt. Those stipulations might be hard and galling in their consequences; but they were the penalty of defeat and the price of peace at the time. He had also accepted Finland as an equivalent, and had leave to march upon Turkey unmolested, which opened a different channel for his warlike preparations, if he felt a disposition that way. It was (to be sure) ridiculous to see fifty millions of people prevented from trading with England, because it interfered with the pleasure of a single individual: a prohibition, apparently so arbitrary and so strictly enforced, might be thought to reflect on the spirit and independence of the country, and certainly bore hard upon its interests. But England would not make peace with France, while she had any means left of carrying on war; and there was no mode of

compelling her to a course she abhorred (and the necessity
had been acknowledged by Alexander himself) but by excluding her commerce entirely from the Continent. Whether she
was right in assuming that attitude of bold defiance and inter-
minable war, is another question; but she by that virtually
outlawed France, and Napoleon and his allies (such as he
could make or find) only followed the example she had set,
in adhering in their turn to the Continental System.* It was
however a hopeless case; and it would have been better to
have let go the only hold he had upon England than by
continuing to grasp it (in spite of warning and every day's
experience of its inefficiency and danger) to suffer himself to
be dragged to the edge of a precipice. Alexander gave the
first umbrage in not fulfilling the conditions of his treaties
with Napoleon; and by his want of frankness and candour,
manifested no disposition to come to an explanation or good
understanding. It was a sullen challenge, and Napoleon
thought proper to accept it. Alexander doubtless began to feel
that the other had no immediate claim to dictate a line of
policy to any one with his influence and at the distance at
which he was. This is true: neither would Buonaparte have
had any pretext to do so, had he never come to seek him, and
thus given his rival advantages and laid himself under obligations, not arising out of his natural position nor the real
interests of his country. He had put it in Napoleon's power to
give the law to him by making himself a party to the affairs of
others: he had no consistent right therefore to cancel the
obligations he had thus laid himself under by retiring upon
his own resources, and saying that he was bound by none but
Russian interests. He had come out of his fastnesses into the
common arena, thinking to make a gallant figure and to
throw Russia as a casting-weight into the scale of European
policy; he had no right to say then, 'In Russia I am unassail-
able, I want nothing to do with your quarrels or disputes,'
since in that case he ought to have staid there. To say nothing
of the partition of Poland and the encroachments on Turkey,
Russia had lately appropriated Finland, had thrice gone to
crush France; and yet Alexander talked of nothing but the
honour of sovereigns and the desire of Russia to remain quiet.

The fear that Buonaparte entertained of Russia was affected or chimerical as to practical purposes—her great strength was in the *vis inertiæ** she opposed to foreign blows: his real motive was anger at not having been able to make her come into his schemes either by art of arms, and a determination to let Alexander see that what he had failed in by persuasion, he could make good by force. Still he was sensible of the immense difficulty and hazard of the undertaking; made more careful inquiries, consulted more opinions, and hesitated longer than about any other of his enterprises. This very hesitation might have decided him against it: had there been dishonour or danger in the alternative, he could not have hesitated. In his situation, there were only two motives that should have induced him to undertake new plans, either absolute necessity or the certainty of success. In weighing the objections to the war, Buonaparte did not and would not allow the disproportioned odds, against which he contended. Had he entered the lists as a legitimate sovereign, as a *parchment* Emperor, he might have gone forth and had a tilting-bout with Alexander, either in the Niemen or the Don, in summer or winter, and returned as he came, not much the better or worse, with a battle lost or won, with more or less fame, with so much influence or territory added or taken off; but in his case he never fought but for his existence. *His retreat was*, in technical language, *always cut off.* He should therefore have defied them to catch him at a disadvantage. He did not like to contemplate the lodged hatred and rankling hostility of which he was and must necessarily be the mark. His elevation prevented him from seeing the depth below: yet he trod upon a precipice where any false step was ruinous. The very extent of his power showed the precarious and ungrateful tenure by which he held it; for he could only have attained it by a triumph over the last resources and efforts of his enemies. No ordinary objects of ambition or interest would have brought them to that pass: it was a deadly quarrel which made them risk their last stake before they would give in. But the principle remained unaltered; and however coiled up in its dusky folds or severed into unsightly fragments, would re-unite and spring into action again with the first opportunity of revenge. That

Buonaparte did not dwell on this view of the subject, was but natural: that he ever acted on the contrary one, was inexcusable.

There was another general consideration which Napoleon overlooked: all that related to the statistics of the question he was perfectly master of, population, productions, number of towns, rivers, bridges, extent of country, &c. but it was trying an unknown ground, a new species of warfare. He knew what resistance civilization could make: did he know equally well what resistance barbarism could make? It appears by the result—Not: and yet the burning of Moscow was in this undetermined order of events, to which his failure was properly owing. Notwithstanding the grasp and manly strength of his mind, the air of Paris had perhaps made him lay rather too much stress on artificial advantages; but there is an extreme resource in the very dearth of resources, and a despotic power over mind and matter acquired by the very ignorance, poverty, and subjection of a people.* Buonaparte himself says that 'he had no more right to anticipate the burning of Moscow than he could be required to foretell an earthquake;' and that is true, supposing that capital to have stood anywhere but where it did; but there was something in the idea of its gilded domes rising out of barren boundless wildernesses that placed it out of the routine of ordinary calculation and might have prevented its being counted upon as substantial winter-quarters. These are the only points in which I think Buonaparte erred, in not weighing the consequences if he failed, and not considering the possibility that he might do so from the untrodden path he was about to enter. As to ordinary political or military calculations, I should suppose that he was completely justified; that is, he was prepared to overcome all the obstacles of a kind to be foreseen; and no one else (any more than himself) suspected his defeat till after it happened. It was a thunder-clap to friend and foe alike. Those who at present assert that the enterprise from the first contained the visible seeds of destruction within itself, and that Buonaparte had lost half his army by mismanagement and obstinacy before he had even reached the Russian frontier, will make few converts either to their judgment or veracity. . . .

... The next day at dawn, he appeared on the field of Valoutina.* The soldiers of Ney and those of the division Goudin* (bereaved of their leader) were ranged round the dead bodies of their companions and of the Russians. The battalions of Goudin appeared reduced to mere platoons, but they seemed to feel a pride in the reduction of their numbers. The Emperor could not proceed in front without stepping or trampling upon the bodies of the slain and scattered bayonets absolutely wrenched and twisted by the violence of the conflict. But over these horrors he threw a drapery of glory. His gratitude transformed the field of battle into a field of triumph. He felt that the time was come in which his soldiers required the support of praises and reward. Accordingly, never were his looks more impressive and affectionate. He declared that this battle was the most brilliant exploit in their military history. In his rewards he was magnificent. The 12th, 21st, and 127th of the line and the 7th of the light troops received eighty-seven decorations and promotions. These were the regiments of Goudin. Hitherto the 127th had marched without an eagle, because it had not according to the established rule conquered one on the field of battle. The Emperor delivered one to it with his own hands. He also rewarded and distinguished the corps of Ney. The favours were valuable in themselves and for the mode in which they were conferred. He was surrounded by every regiment in turn as by a family of his own. These cordial manners, which had the effect of making the privates the companions in arms of the master of Europe—forms which brought back the long-regretted usages of the republic—delighted and transported them. He was a monarch, but he was the monarch of the Revolution; and they were devotedly attached to a sovereign who had elevated himself by his own merits and who elevated others in proportion to theirs. In him there was every thing to stimulate zeal and effort, nothing to excite offence or imply reproach.

Never was there a field of battle better employed to stir and exalt the feelings; but when out of the observation of the soldiers, his reflections took a different tone. On his return to Smolensk, every object tended to oppress and deject him.

This city was one vast hospital, and the groans of anguish which issued from it, prevailed over the acclamations of triumph which had been just heard on the field of Valoutina. At Wilna and Witepsk there had been a want of hospitals, but this was not the case at Smolensk. Fifteen large brick-buildings saved from the flames had been set apart for this purpose; and there was plenty of wine, brandy, and medicines. There was only a want of dressings. At the end of the second night, the surgeons who were indefatigable had used up all the linen for bandages or for staunching the wounds; and it was necessary to substitute the paper found in the city-archives. One hospital containing a hundred wounded had been forgotten for three days, and was discovered by Rapp* in the most distressing state: Napoleon immediately ordered his own stock of wine and many pecuniary gratuities to be bestowed on these unfortunate men, whose sufferings had only kept them alive. There was another consideration in addition to the inevitable accidents and evils of war, which now gave the Emperor a good deal of uneasiness. The burning of Smolensk he could no longer believe to be merely casual or even the result of a sudden fit of desperation. It was the effect of cool determination. The Russians had employed the utmost caution and arrangement in this work of destruction, and then (as he learnt from a Greek priest) laid it on the French, whom they represented as bands of incendiaries or legions of demons, headed by Antichrist. The nobles and their slaves fled from their approach like a pestilence. The natives even refused to touch the utensils which the French soldiers had employed. One great fear of the Russians was that their slaves would rise up and throw off their bondage; and it was therefore an object to prevent their having any communication with the French. They made use of the most improbable and disgusting fables to excite their terror and hatred, and of their ignorance and degradation, to perpetuate that ignorance and degradation. It was their dread that the doctrines of the Revolution might loosen their grasp on the wretched serfs who compose the population of the country that first made them send their barbarous hordes against the French territory; the consequences of which now came back to themselves

to their infinite horror and surprise in the shape of an invasion, which might produce the same effects. Buonaparte
should have availed himself of the offers that were made to
him to detach the serf from the proprietor and the soil. But
this was his weak side. He did not understand extreme remedies; and he was fonder of power than of liberty!

IV

. . . All that was human rejoiced; the tyrant and the slave
shrunk back aghast, as the clash of arms was drowned in the
shout of the multitude. This is popularity; not when a thousand persons consult and deliver the result of their decisions
formally and securely, but where each of the thousand does
this (before that of the others can be known) from an uncon-
trollable impulse, and without ever thinking of the consequences. It was the greatest instance ever known of the power
exerted by one man over opinion; nor is this difficult to be
accounted for, since it was one man armed with the rights of
a people against those who had robbed them of all natural
rights and gave them leave to breathe by a charter. Therefore
Buonaparte seemed from his first landing to bestride the
country like a Colossus, for in him rose up once more the
prostrate might and majesty of man; and the Bourbons, like
toads or spiders, got out of the way of the huge shadow of the
Child Roland of the Revolution.* The implied power to serve
and buckler up a state was portentous: if it was fear and
personal awe that threw a spell over them in spite of themselves, and turned aside all opposition, though it might take
from the goodness of the cause, it would not lessen the
prowess and reputation of the man. Even if the French had
forgot themselves and him, would not their former sentiments
be revived in all their force by his present appearance among
them, so full of the bold and marvellous? The very audacity
of the undertaking, as it baffled calculation, baffled resistance
to it, as much as if he had actually returned from the dead.
Its not seeming ridiculous stamped it sublime; any one but he
making such an attempt would have been stopped at the
outset; and this shows that he possessed more influence than
any other human being. It was the admiration inspired by the

person and the enterprise that carried him through, and made all sanguine, anxious, full of interest for him, as for the hero of some lofty poem or high-wrought romance. He dispersed the *Compagnons du Lys*,* as Ulysses slew the suitors. The only pleas I have heard in favour of the popularity of the Bourbons in comparison are, first, that the French dreaded the return of war. If peace is to be purchased at that price, it may always be obtained by setting your enemies on the throne, for they will hardly make war on themselves. The second is like unto the first, and admits the same answer. It is said the army and not the people were favourable to Buonaparte and against the Government. But the army cannot be conceived to be against the government, unless the government has been imposed by foreigners by whom they have been foiled; and in this case, the enthusiasm of the military and the zeal of the people must be supposed to go hand-in-hand. These arguments may therefore be returned on the hands of their original fabricators or more wretched endorsers—Whig orators and parliamentary speakers, whose vanity will not let them remain silent, and who have not courage to speak the truth. The Bourbons had reckoned on the troops to defend them: if the people were for them, why did they not trust their cause to them? They did more wisely in appealing to their old friends and acquaintances, the Allies; who this time forced them back without the formality of asking any questions of the French people. This was so far at least well.

Buonaparte travelled several hours a-head of his army, often without any guard, or attended only by a few Polish lancers. His advanced-guard now regularly consisted of the troops who happened to be before him on the road, and to whom couriers were sent forward to apprise them of his approach. Thus he entered Paris, escorted by the very troops who in the morning had been ordered out to oppose him. Louis XVIII, had left the capital* at one in the morning of the 20th. Marshal Macdonald* had taken the command of the troops at Melun, the last place where they could make a stand. They were drawn up in three lines to receive the Emperor's troops, who were said to be advancing from Fontainebleau. There was a long pause of suspense, which seldom fails to render men

more accessible to strong and sudden emotion. The glades of
the forest and the winding ascent which leads to it were full
in view of the troops, but presented the appearance of a deep
solitude. All was silence, except when the bands played some
old tunes connected with the name and family of the Bourbons. The sounds excited no corresponding sentiment among
the soldiers. At length, in the afternoon, a galloping of horse
was heard. An open carriage appeared, surrounded by a few
hussars, and drawn by four horses. It came on at full speed;
stopped, and Napoleon leaping out of it, was in the midst of
the ranks which had been drawn up to oppose him. His escort
threw themselves from their horses, mingled with their
ancient comrades, and the effect of their exhortations was
instantaneous on men, whose minds were already made up to
the same purpose. There was a general shout of *Vive
l'Empereur!* The last troops of the Bourbons passed over to the
other side, and there was no farther obstacle between
Napoleon and the capital. He arrived at the Thuilleries about
nine o'clock in the evening with an escort of about a hundred
horse. On alighting, he was almost squeezed to death by the
crowd of officers and citizens who thronged about him, and
fairly carried him up-stairs in their arms. . .

EDMUND KEAN

I

I WENT to see him the first night of his appearing in Shylock.
I remember it well. The boxes were empty, and the pit not
half full: 'some quantity of barren spectators* and idle renters
were thinly scattered to make up a show.' The whole presented a dreary, hopeless aspect. I was in considerable apprehension for the result. From the first scene in which Mr Kean
came on, my doubts were at an end. I had been told to give
as favourable an account as I could: I gave a true one. I am
not one of those who, when they see the sun breaking from
behind a cloud, stop to ask others whether it is the moon. Mr
Kean's appearance was the first gleam of genius breaking

athwart the gloom of the Stage, and the public have since gladly basked in its ray, in spite of actors, managers, and critics. I cannot say that my opinion has much changed since that time. Why should it? I had the same eyes to see with that I have now, the same ears to hear with, and the same understanding to judge with. Why then should I not form the same judgment? My opinions have been sometimes called singular: they are merely sincere. I say what I think: I think what I feel. I cannot help receiving certain impressions from things; and I have sufficient courage to declare (somewhat abruptly) what they are. This is the only singularity I am conscious of. I do not shut my eyes to extraordinary merit because I hate it, and refuse to open them till the clamours of others make me, and then affect to wonder extravagantly at what I have before affected hypocritically to despise. I do not make it a common practice, to think nothing of an actor or an author, because all the world have not pronounced in his favour, and after they have, to persist in condemning him, as a proof not of imbecility and ill-nature, but of independence of taste and spirit. Nor do I endeavour to communicate the infection of my own dulness, cowardice, and spleen to others, by chilling the coldness of their constitutions by the poisonous slime of vanity or interest, and setting up my own conscious inability or unwillingness to form an opinion on any one subject, as the height of candour and judgment.—I did not endeavour to persuade Mr Perry* that Mr Kean was an actor that would not last, merely because he had not lasted; nor that Miss Stephens knew nothing of singing, because she had a sweet voice. On the contrary, I did all I could to counteract the effect of these safe, not very sound, insinuations, and 'screw the courage' of one principal organ of public opinion 'to the sticking-place'.* I do not repent of having done so.

With respect to the spirit of partisanship in which the controversy respecting Mr Kean's merits as an actor was carried on, there were two or three things remarkable. One set of persons, out of the excess of their unbounded admiration, furnished him with all sorts of excellences which he did not possess or pretend to, and covered his defects from the wardrobe of their own fancies. With this class of persons,

'Pritchard's genteel, and Garrick's six feet high!'*

I never enlisted in this corps of Swiss bodyguards;* I was even suspected of disloyalty and *leze-majesté*, because I did not cry out—*Quand meme!**—to all Mr Kean's stretches of the prerogatives of genius, and was placed out of the pale of theatrical orthodoxy, for not subscribing implicitly to all the articles of belief imposed upon my senses and understanding. If you had not been to see the little man twenty times in Richard, and did not deny his being hoarse in the last act, or admire him for being so, you were looked on as a lukewarm devotee, or half an infidel. On the other hand, his detractors constantly argued not from what he was, but from what he was not. 'He was not tall. He had not a fine voice. He did not play at Covent-Garden. He was not John Kemble.'* This was all you could get from them, and this they thought quite sufficient to prove that he was not any thing, because he was not something quite different from himself. They did not consider that an actor might have the eye of an eagle with the voice of a raven, a 'pigmy body', and 'a fiery soul that o'er-informed its tenement';* that he might want grace and dignity, and yet have enough nature and passion in his breast to set up a whole corps of regular stagers. They did not enquire whether this was the case with respect to Mr Kean, but took it for granted that it was not, for no other reason, than because the question had not been settled by the critics twenty or thirty years ago, and admitted by the town ever since, that is, before Mr Kean was born. A royal infant may be described as 'un haut et puissant prince, agé d'un jour,'* but a great and powerful actor cannot be known till he arrives at years of discretion, and he must be first a candidate for theatrical reputation before he can be a veteran. This is a truism, but it is one that our prejudices constantly make us not only forget, but frequently combat with all the spirit of martyrdom. I have (as it will be seen in the following pages) all along spoken freely of Mr Kean's faults, or what I considered such, physical as well as intellectual; but the balance inclines decidedly to the favourable side, though not more I think than his merits exceed his defects. It was also the more necessary to dwell on the claims of an actor to public support, in proportion as they were original, and to the illiberal opposition they unhappily had to encounter. I endeavoured to prove (and with some success), that he was not 'the very worst actor in the world'.*

II

A chasm has been produced in the amusements of Drury-Lane Theatre by the accident which has happened to Mr Kean. He was to have played the Duke of Milan on Tuesday, but as he had not come to the Theatre at the time of the drawing up of the curtain, Mr Rae came forward to propose another tragedy, Douglas. To this the audience did not assent, and wished to wait. Mr Kean, however, not appearing, nor any tidings being heard of him, he was at length given up, and two farces substituted in his stead. Conjectures and rumours were afloat; and it was not till the next day that it was discovered that Mr Kean having dined a few miles in the country, and returning at a very quick pace to keep his engagement at the Theatre, was thrown out of his gig, and had his arm dislocated, besides being stunned and very much bruised with the fall. On this accident a grave morning paper is pleased to be facetious. It observes that this is a very *serious* accident; that actors in general are liable to *serious* accidents; that the late Mr Cooke used to meet with *serious* accidents; that it is a sad thing to be in the way of such accidents; and that it is to be hoped that Mr Kean will meet with no more *serious* accidents. It is to be hoped that he will not—nor with any such profound observations upon them, if they should happen. Next to that spirit of bigotry which in a neighbouring country would deny actors Christian burial after death, we hate that cant of criticism, which slurs over their characters while living with a half-witted jest. Actors are accused as a profession of being extravagant and intemperate. While they are said to be so as a piece of common cant, they are likely to continue so. But there is a sentence in Shakespeare which should be stuck as a label in the mouths of the beadles and whippers-in of morality: 'The web of our life is of a mingled yarn: our virtues would be proud if our vices whipped them not, and our faults would despair if they were not cherished by our virtues.'*

   With respect to the extravagance of actors, as a traditional
character, it is not to be wondered at: they live from hand to
mouth; they plunge from want into luxury; they have no
means of making money *breed*, and all professions that do not
live by turning money into money, or have not a certainty of
accumulating it in the end by parsimony, spend it. Uncertain
of the future, they make sure of the present moment. This is
not unwise. Chilled with poverty, steeped in contempt, they
sometimes pass into the sunshine of fortune, and are lifted to
the very pinnacle of public favour, yet even there cannot
calculate on the continuance of success, but are, 'like the
giddy sailor on the mast, ready with every blast to topple down
into the fatal bowels of the deep!'* Besides, if the young
enthusiast who is smitten with the stage, and with the public
as a mistress, were naturally a close *hunks*, he would become
or remain a city clerk, instead of turning player. Again, with
respect to the habit of convivial indulgence, an actor, to be a
good one, must have a great spirit of enjoyment in himself,
strong impulses, strong passions, and a strong sense of pleasure, for it is his business to imitate the passions and to communicate pleasure to others. A man of genius is not a
machine. The neglected actor may be excused if he drinks
oblivion of his disappointments; the successful one, if he
quaffs the applause of the world, and enjoys the friendship of
those who are the friends of the favourites of fortune, in
draughts of nectar. There is no path so steep as that of fame;
no labour so hard as the pursuit of excellence. The intellectual excitement inseparable from those professions which call
forth all our sensibility to pleasure and pain, requires some
corresponding physical excitement to support our failure,
and not a little to allay the ferment of the spirits attendant on
success. If there is any tendency to dissipation beyond this in
the profession of a player, it is owing to the state of public
opinion, which paragraphs like the one we have alluded to
are not calculated to reform; and players are only not so
respectable as a profession as they might be, because their
profession is not *respected* as it ought to be.
   There is something, we fear, impertinent and uncalled for
in these remarks: the more so, as in the present instance the

insinuation which they were meant to repel is wholly unfounded. We have it on very good authority, that Mr Kean,
since his engagement at Drury-Lane, and during his arduous
and uninterrupted exertions in his profession, has never
missed a single rehearsal, nor been absent a minute beyond
the time for beginning his part.

III

Mr Kean's friends felt some unnecessary anxiety with respect
to his reception in the part of Shylock, on Monday night at
Drury-Lane, being his first appearance after his recovery from
his accident, which we are glad to find has not been a very
serious one. On his coming on the stage there was a loud burst
of applause and welcome; but as this was mixed with some
hisses, Mr Kean came forward, and spoke nearly as follows:

> Ladies and Gentlemen, for the first time in my life I have been the
> unfortunate cause of disappointing the public amusement.
> That it is the only time, on these boards, I can appeal to your own
> recollection; and when you take into calculation the 265 times that I
> have had the honour to appear before you, according to the testimony
> of the Manager's books, you will, perhaps, be able to make some
> allowance.
> To your favour I owe all the reputation I enjoy.
> I rely on your candour, that prejudice shall not rob me of what your
> kindness has conferred upon me.

This address was received with cordial cheers, and the play
went forward without interruption. As soon as the curtain
drew up, some persons had absurdly called out 'Kean, Kean',
though Shylock does not appear in the first scenes. This was
construed into a call for 'God save the *King*:' and the Duke
of Gloucester's being in one of the stage-boxes seemed to
account for this sudden effusion of loyalty,—a sentiment indeed always natural in the hearts of Englishmen, but at present not very noisy, and rather 'deep than loud'. For our own
parts, we love the King according to law, but we cannot sing.
Shylock was the part in which Mr Kean first sought the
favour of the town, and in which perhaps he chose for that
reason to be reconciled to it, after the first slight misunder-
standing. We were a little curious on this occasion to see the

progress he has made in public opinion since that time; and
on turning to our theatrical common-place book (there is
nothing like a common-place book after all) found the following account* of his first reception, copied from the most
respectable of the Morning Papers: 'Mr. Kean (of whom
report has spoken so highly) made his appearance at Drury-
Lane in the character of Shylock. For *voice*, eye, action, and
expression, no actor has come out for many years at all equal
to him. The applause, from the first scene to the last, was
general, loud, and uninterrupted. Indeed, the very first scene
in which he comes on with Bassanio and Anthonio, shewed
the master in his art, and at once decided the opinion of the
audience. Perhaps it was the most perfect of any. Notwithstanding the complete success of Mr. Kean in Shylock, we
question whether he will not become a greater favourite in
other parts. There was a lightness and vigour in his tread, a
buoyancy and elasticity of spirit, a fire and animation, which
would accord better with almost any other character than with
the morose, sullen, inward, inveterate, inflexible, malignity of
Shylock. The character of Shylock is that of a man brooding
over one idea, that of its wrongs, and bent on an unalterable
purpose, that of revenge. In conveying a profound impression
of this feeling, or in embodying the general conception of
rigid and uncontroulable self-will, equally proof against every
sentiment of humanity or prejudice of opinion, we have seen
actors more successful than Mr. Kean. But in giving effect to
the conflict of passions arising out of the contrast of situation,
in varied vehemence of declamation, in keenness of sarcasm,
in the rapidity of his transitions from one tone or feeling to
another, in propriety and novelty of action, presenting a succession of striking pictures, and giving perpetually fresh
shocks of delight and surprise, it would be difficult to single
out a competitor. The fault of his acting was (if we may hazard
an objection), an over-display of the resources of the art,
which gave too much relief to the hard, impenetrable, dark
ground-work of the character of Shylock. It would be needless
to point out individual beauties, where almost every passage
was received with equal and deserved applause. His style of
acting is, if we may use the expression, more significant, more

pregnant with meaning, more varied and alive in every part, than any we have almost ever witnessed. The character never stands still; there is no vacant pause in the action: the eye is never silent. It is not saying too much of Mr. Kean, though it is saying a great deal, that he has all that Mr. Kemble *wants* of perfection.'

LIBER AMORIS: CONCLUSION

I DID not sleep a wink all that night; nor did I know till the next day the full meaning of what had happened to me. With the morning's light, conviction glared in upon me that I had not only lost her for ever—but every feeling I had ever had towards her—respect, tenderness, pity—all but my fatal passion, was gone. The whole was a mockery, a frightful illusion. I had embraced the false Florimel instead of the true; or was like the man in the Arabian Nights who had married a *goul.* How different was the idea I once had of her? Was this she,

> —'Who had been beguiled—she who was made
> Within a gentle bosom to be laid—
> To bless and to be blessed—to be heart-bare
> To one who found his bettered likeness there—
> To think for ever with him, like a bride—
> To haunt his eye, like taste personified—
> To double his delight, to share his sorrow,
> And like a morning beam, wake to him every morrow?'*

I saw her pale, cold form glide silent by me, dead to shame as to pity. Still I seemed to clasp this piece of witchcraft to my bosom; this lifeless image, which was all that was left of my love, was the only thing to which my sad heart clung. Were she dead, should I not wish to gaze once more upon her pallid features? She is dead to me; but what she once was to me, can never die! The agony, the conflict of hope and fear, of adoration and jealousy is over; or it would, ere long, have ended with my life. I am no more lifted now to Heaven, and then plunged in the abyss; but I seem to have been thrown from the top of a precipice, and to lie groveling, stunned, and stupefied. I am melancholy, lonesome, and weaker than a child. The worst is, I have no prospect of any alteration for the better: she has cut off all possibility of a reconcilement at any future period. Were she even to return to her former pretended fondness and endearments, I could have no pleas-ure, no confidence in them. I can scarce make out the contradiction to myself. I strive to think she always was what I now know she is; but I have great difficulty in it, and can hardly believe but she still *is* what she so long *seemed.* Poor thing! I am afraid she is little better off herself; nor do I see what is to become of her, unless she throws off the mask at once, and *runs a-muck* at infamy. She is exposed and laid bare to all those whose opinion she set a value upon. Yet she held her head very high, and must feel (if she feels any thing) proportionably mortified. —A more complete experiment on character was never made. If I had not met her lover imme-diately after I parted with her, it would have been nothing. I might have supposed she had changed her mind in my ab-sence, and had given him the preference as soon as she felt it, and even shewn her delicacy in declining any farther intimacy with me. But it comes out that she had gone on in the most forward and familiar way with both at once—(she could not change her mind in passing from one room to another)—told both the same bare-faced and unblushing falsehoods, like the commonest creature; received presents from me to the very last, and wished to keep up the game still longer, either to gratify her humour, her avarice, or her vanity in playing with my passion, or to have me as a *dernier resort,* in case of accidents. Again, it would have been nothing, if she had not come up with her demure, well-composed, wheedling looks that morning, and then met me in the evening in a situation, which (she believed) might kill me on the spot, with no more feeling than a common courtesan shews, who *bilks* a customer,* and passes him, leering up at her bully,* the mo-ment after. If there had been the frailty of passion, it would have been excusable; but it is evident she is a practised, callous jilt,* a regular lodging-house decoy, played off by her mother upon the lodgers, one after another, applying them to her different purposes, laughing at them in turns, and herself the

probable dupe and victim of some favourite gallant in the end.
I know all this; but what do I gain by it, unless I could find
some one with her shape and air, to supply the place of the
lovely apparition? That a professed wanton should come and
sit on a man's knee, and put her arms round his neck, and
caress him, and seem fond of him, means nothing, proves
nothing, no one concludes anything from it; but that a pretty,
reserved, modest, delicate-looking girl should do this, from
the first hour to the last of your being in the house, without
intending anything by it, is new, and, I think, worth explaining. It was, I confess, out of my calculation, and may be out
of that of others. Her unmoved indifference and self-possession all the while, shew that it is her constant practice. Her
look even, if closely examined, bears this interpretation. It is
that of studied hypocrisy or startled guilt, rather than of
refined sensibility or conscious innocence. 'She defied anyone
to read her thoughts,' she once told me. 'Do they then require
concealing?' I imprudently asked her. The command over
herself is surprising. She never once betrays herself by any
momentary forgetfulness, by any appearance of triumph or
superiority to the person who is her dupe, by any levity of
manner in the plenitude of her success; it is one faultless,
undeviating, consistent, consummate piece of acting. Were
she a saint on earth, she could not seem more like one. Her
hypocritical high-flown pretensions, indeed, make her the
worse: but still the ascendancy of her will, her determined
perseverance in what she undertakes to do, has something
admirable in it, approaching to the heroic. She is certainly an
extraordinary girl! Her retired manner, and invariable propriety of behaviour made me think it next to impossible she
could grant the same favours indiscriminately to every one
that she did to me. Yet this now appears to be the fact. She
must have done the very same with C——,* invited him into
the house to carry on a closer intrigue with her, and then
commenced the double game with both together. She always
'despised looks'. This was a favourite phrase with her, and one
of the hooks which she baited for me. Nothing could win her
but a man's behaviour and sentiments. Besides, she could
never like another—she was a martyr to disappointed

affection—and friendship was all she could even extend to any other man. All the time, she was making signals, playing off her pretty person, and having occasional interviews in the street with this very man, whom she could only have taken so sudden and violent a liking to from his looks, his personal appearance, and what she probably conjectured of his circumstances. Her sister had married a counsellor—the Miss F——'s,* who kept the house before, had done so too—and so would she. 'There was a precedent for it.'* Yet if she was so desperately enamoured of this new acquaintance, if he had displaced *the little image** from her breast, if he was become her *second* 'unalterable attachment' (which I would have given my life to have been) why continue the same unwarrantable familiarities with me to the last, and promise that they should be renewed on my return (if I had not unfortunately stumbled upon the truth to her aunt) and yet keep up the same refined cant about her old attachment all the time, as if it was that which stood in the way of my pretensions, and not her faithlessness to it? 'If one swerves from one, one shall swerve from another'—was her excuse for not returning my regard. Yet that which I thought a prophecy, was I suspect a history. She had swerved twice from her vowed engagements, first to me, and then from me to another. If she made a fool of me, what did she make of her lover? I fancy he has put that question to himself. I said nothing to him about the amount of the presents; which is another damning circumstance, that might have opened my eyes long before; but they were shut by my fond affection, which 'turned all to favour and to prettiness'.* She cannot be supposed to have kept up an appearance of old regard to me, from a fear of hurting my feelings by her desertion; for she not only shewed herself indifferent to, but evidently triumphed in my sufferings, and heaped every kind of insult and indignity upon them. I must have incurred her contempt and resentment by my mistaken delicacy at different times; and her manner, when I have hinted at becoming a reformed man in this respect, convinces me of it. 'She hated it!' She always hated whatever she liked most. She 'hated Mr C——'s red slippers', when he first came! One more count finishes the indictment. She not only discovered the most hardened indifference to the feelings of others; she has not shewn the least regard to her own character, or shame when she was detected. When found out, she seemed to say, 'Well, what if I am? I have played the game as long as I could; and if I could keep it up no longer, it was not for want of good will!' Her colouring once or twice is the only sign of grace she has exhibited. Such is the creature on whom I had thrown away my heart and soul—one who was incapable of feeling the commonest emotions of human nature, as they regarded herself or any one else. 'She had no feelings with respect to herself,' she often said. She in fact knows what she is, and recoils from the good opinion or sympathy of others, which she feels to be founded on a deception; so that my overweening opinion of her must have appeared like irony, or direct insult. My seeing her in the street has gone a good way to satisfy me. Her manner there explains her manner in-doors to be conscious and overdone; and besides, she looks but indifferently. She is diminutive in stature, and her measured step and timid air do not suit these public airings. I am afraid she will soon grow common to my imagination, as well as worthless in herself. Her image seems fast 'going into the wastes of time',* like a weed that the wave bears farther and farther from me. Alas! thou poor hapless weed, when I entirely lose sight of thee, and for ever, no flower will ever bloom on earth to glad my heart again!

ART AND LITERATURE

FRAGMENTS ON ART. WHY THE ARTS ARE NOT PROGRESSIVE?

I

IT is often made a subject of complaint and surprise, that the arts in this country, and in modern times, have not kept pace with the general progress of society and civilisation in other respects, and it has been proposed to remedy the deficiency by more carefully availing ourselves of the advantages which time and circumstances have placed within our reach, but which we have hitherto neglected, the study of the antique, the formation of academies, and the distribution of prizes.

First, the complaint itself, that the arts do not attain that progressive degree of perfection which might reasonably be expected from them, proceeds on a false notion, for the analogy appealed to in support of the regular advances of art to higher degrees of excellence, totally fails; it applies to science, not to art. Secondly, the expedients proposed to remedy the evil by adventitious means are only calculated to confirm it. The arts hold immediate communication with nature, and are only derived from that source. When that original impulse no longer exists, when the inspiration of genius is fled, all the attempts to recal it are no better than the tricks of galvanism to restore the dead to life. The arts may be said to resemble Antæus in his struggle with Hercules, who was strangled when he was raised above the ground, and only revived and recovered his strength when he touched his mother earth.

Nothing is more contrary to the fact than the supposition that in what we understand by the *fine arts*, as painting and poetry, relative perfection is only the result of repeated efforts, and that what has been once well done constantly leads to something better. What is mechanical, reducible to rule, or capable of demonstration, is progressive, and admits of gradual improvement: what is not mechanical or definite, but depends on genius, taste, and feeling, very soon becomes stationary or retrograde, and loses more than it gains by transfusion. The contrary opinion is, indeed, a common error, which has grown up, like many others, from transferring an analogy of one kind to something quite distinct, without thinking of the difference in the nature of the things, or attending to the difference of the results. For most persons, finding what wonderful advances have been made in biblical criticism, in chemistry, in mechanics, in geometry, astronomy, &c.—*i.e.* in things depending on mere inquiry and experiment, or on absolute demonstration—have been led hastily to conclude, that there was a general tendency in the efforts of the human intellect to improve by repetition, and in all other arts and institutions to grow perfect and mature by time. We look back upon the theological creed of our ancestors, and their discoveries in natural philosophy, with a smile of pity; science, and the arts connected with it, have all had their infancy, their youth, and manhood, and seem to have in them no principle of limitation or decay; and, inquiring no farther about the matter, we infer, in the height of our self-congratulation, and in the intoxication of our pride, that the same progress has been, and will continue to be, made in all other things which are the work of man. The fact, however, stares us so plainly in the face, that one would think the smallest reflection must suggest the truth, and overturn our sanguine theories. The greatest poets, the ablest orators, the best painters, and the finest sculptors that the world ever saw, appeared soon after the birth of these arts, and lived in a state of society which was, in other respects, comparatively barbarous. Those arts, which depend on individual genius and incommunicable power, have always leaped at once from infancy to manhood, from the first rude dawn of invention to their meridian height and dazzling lustre, and have in general declined ever after. This is the peculiar distinction and privilege of each, of science and of art; of the one, never to attain its utmost summit of perfection, and of the other, to arrive at it almost at once. Homer, Chaucer, Spenser, Shakespeare, Dante, and Ariosto (Milton alone was of a later age, and not the worse for it), Raphael, Titian, Michael Angelo, Correggio,

Cervantes, and Boccaccio—all lived near the beginning of their arts—perfected, and all but created them. These giant sons of genius stand, indeed, upon the earth, but they tower above their fellows, and the long line of their successors does not interpose any thing to obstruct their view, or lessen their brightness. In strength and stature they are unrivalled, in grace and beauty they have never been surpassed. In after-ages, and more refined periods (as they are called), great men have arisen one by one, as it were by throes and at intervals: though in general the best of these cultivated and artificial minds were of an inferior order, as Tasso and Pope among poets, Claude Lorraine and Vandyke among painters. But in the earliest stages of the arts, when the first mechanical difficulties had been got over, and the language as it were acquired, they rose by clusters and in constellations, never to rise again.

II

Science and the mechanic arts depend not on the force with which the mind itself is endued, or with which it contemplates given things (for this is naturally much the same), but on the number of things, successively perceived by the same or different persons, and formally arranged and registered in books or memory, which admits of being varied and augmented indefinitely. The number of objects to which the understanding may be directed is endless, and the results, so far as they are positive, tangible things, may be set down and added one to another, and made use of as occasion requires, without creating any confusion, and so as to produce a perpetual accumulation of useful knowledge. What is once gained is never lost, and may be multiplied daily, because this increase of knowledge does not depend upon increasing the force of the mind, but on directing the same force to different things, all of them in their nature definite, demonstrable, existing to the mind outwardly and by signs, less as the power than as the form of truth, and in which all the difficulty lies in the first invention, not in the subsequent communication. In like manner the mechanic parts of painting for instance, such as the mode of preparing colours, the laws of perspective, &c., which may be taught by rule and method, so that the principle being once known, every one may avail himself of it, these subordinate and instrumental parts of the art admit of uniform excellence, though from accidental causes it has happened otherwise. But it is not so in art itself, in its higher and nobler essence. 'There is no shuffling,' but 'we ourselves compelled to give in evidence even to the teeth and forehead of our faults.'* There is no room for the division of labour—for the accumulation of borrowed advantages; no artificial scale by which *to heaven we may ascend*; because here excellence does not depend on the quantity of representative knowledge, abstracted from a variety of subjects, but on the original force of capacity, and degree of attention, applied to the same given subject, natural feelings and images. To use the distinction of a technical philosophy, science depends on the discursive or *extensive*—art on the intuitive and *intensive* power of the mind.* One chemical or mathematical discovery may be added to another, because the degree and sort of faculty required to apprehend and retain them, are in both cases the same; but no one can voluntarily add the colouring of Rubens to the expression of Raphael, till he has the same eye for colour as Rubens, and for expression as Raphael—that is, the most thorough feeling of what is profound in the one, or splendid in the other—of what no rules can teach, nor words convey—and of what the mind must possess within itself, and by a kind of participation with nature, or remain for ever destitute of it. Titian and Correggio are the only painters who united to perfect colouring a degree of expression, the one in his portraits, and the other in his histories, all but equal, if not equal, to the highest. But this union of different qualities they had from nature, and not by method. In fact, we judge of science by the number of effects produced—of art by the energy which produces them. The one is knowledge—the other power.

The arts of painting and poetry are conversant with the world of thought within us, and with the world of sense without us—with what we know, and see, and feel intimately. They flow from the sacred shrine of our own breasts, and are kindled at the living lamp of nature. The pulse of the passions

assuredly beat as high, the depths and soundings of the
human heart were as well understood three thousand years
ago, as they are at present; the face of nature and 'the human
face divine',* shone as bright then as they have ever done. It
is this light, reflected by true genius on art, that marks out its
path before it, and sheds a glory round the Muses' feet, like
that which 'circled Una's angle face,

'And made a sunshine in the shady place.'*

Nature is the soul of art. There is a strength in the imagination
that reposes entirely on nature, which nothing else can supply.
There is in the old poets and painters a vigour and grasp of
mind, a full possession of their subject, a confidence and firm
faith, a sublime simplicity, an elevation of thought, propor-
tioned to their depth of feeling, an increasing force and
impetus, which moves, penetrates, and kindles all that comes
in contact with it, which seems, not theirs, but given to them.
It is this reliance on the power of nature which has produced
those masterpieces by the Prince of Painters,* in which expression is all in all, where one spirit, that of truth, pervades
every part, brings down heaven to earth, mingles cardinals
and popes with angels and apostles, and yet blends and harmonises the whole by the true touches and intense feeling of
what is beautiful and grand in nature. It was the same trust
in nature that enabled Chaucer to describe the patient sorrow
of Griselda; or the delight of that young beauty in the Flower
and the Leaf,* shrouded in her bower, and listening, in the
morning of the year, to the singing of the nightingale, while
her joy rises with the rising song, and gushes out afresh at
every pause, and is borne along with the full tide of pleasure,
and still increases and repeats and prolongs itself, and knows
no ebb. It is thus that Boccaccio,* in the divine story of the
Hawk, has represented Frederigo Alberigi steadily contem-
plating his favourite Falcon (the wreck and remnant of his
fortune), and glad to see how fat and fair a bird she is, thinking
what a dainty repast she would make for his Mistress, who had
deigned to visit him in his low cell. So Isabella mourns over
her pot of Basile, and never asks for any thing but that. So
Lear calls out for his poor fool, and invokes the heavens, for

they are old like him. So Titian impressed on the countenance of that young Neapolitan nobleman in the Louvre, a look that never passed away. So Nicolas Poussin* describes some shepherds wandering out in a morning of the spring, and coming to a tomb with this inscription, 'I also was an Arcadian.'

What have we left to console us for all this? Why, we have Mr Rogers's 'Pleasures of Memory,' and Mr Campbell's 'Pleasures of Hope'; Mr Westall's pictures, and all West's; Miss Burney's new novel (which is, however, some comfort), Miss Edgeworth's Fashionable Tales, Madame de Staël's next work, whatever it may be, and the praise of it in the *Edinburgh Review,* and Sir James Macintosh's *History.**

WHETHER THE FINE ARTS ARE PROMOTED BY ACADEMIES

... IN general, it must happen in the first stages of the arts, that as none but those who had a natural genius for them would attempt to practise them, so none but those who had a natural taste for them would pretend to judge of or criticise them. This must be an incalculable advantage to the man of true genius; for it is no other than the privilege of being tried by his peers. In an age when connoisseurship had not become a fashion; when religion, war, and intrigue occupied the time and thoughts of the great, only those minds of superior refinement would be led to notice the works of art who had a real sense of their excellence; and, in giving way to the powerful bent of his own genius, the painter was most likely to consult the taste of his judges. He had not to deal with pretenders to taste, through vanity, affectation, and idleness. He had to appeal to the higher faculties of the soul,—to that deep and innate sensibility to truth and beauty, which required only fit objects to have its enthusiasm excited,—and to that independent strength of mind, which, in the midst of ignorance and barbarism, hailed and fostered genius wherever it met with it. Titian was patronised by Charles V. Count Castiglione was the friend of Raphael. These were true patrons and true critics; and, as there were no others (for the world, in general, merely looked on and wondered), there can be little doubt that such a period of dearth of factitious patronage would be most favourable to the full development of the greatest talents, and to the attainment of the highest excellence.

The diffusion of taste is not, then, the same thing as the improvement of taste; but it is only the former of these objects that is promoted by public institutions and other artificial means. Thus the number of candidates for fame, and pretenders to criticism, is increased beyond all calculation, while the quantity of genius and feeling remain much the same as before; with these disadvantages, that the man of original genius is often lost among the crowd of competitors who would never have become such, but from encouragement and example, and that the voice of the few whom nature intended for judges, is apt to be drowned in the noisy and forward suffrages of shallow smatterers in taste. The principle of universal suffrage, however applicable to matters of government, which concern the common feelings and common interests of society, is by no means applicable to matters of taste, which can only be decided upon by the most refined understandings. It is throwing down the barriers which separate knowledge and feeling from ignorance and vulgarity, and proclaiming a Bartholomew-fair-show of the fine arts—

'And fools rush in where angels fear to tread.'*

The public taste is, therefore, necessarily vitiated, in proportion as it is public; it is lowered with every infusion it receives of common opinion. The greater the number of judges, the less capable must they be of judging, for the addition to the number of good ones will always be small, while the multitude of bad ones is endless, and thus the decay of art may be said to be the necessary consequence of its progress.

Can there be a greater confirmation of these remarks than to look at the texture of that assemblage of select critics, who every year visit the exhibition at Somerset-house* from all parts of the metropolis of this united kingdom? Is it at all wonderful that for such a succession of connoisseurs, such a

collection of works of art should be provided; where the eye
in vain seeks relief from the glitter of the frames in the glare
of the pictures; where vermillion cheeks make vermillion lips
look pale; where the merciless splendour of the painter's
pallet puts nature out of countenance; and where the unmeaning grimace of fashion and folly is almost the only variety
in the wide dazzling waste of colour. Indeed, the great error
of British art has hitherto been a desire to produce popular
effect by the cheapest and most obvious means, and at the
expence of every thing else;—to lose all the delicacy and
variety of nature in one undistinguished bloom of florid
health, and all precision, truth, and refinement of character
in the same harmless mould of smiling, self-complacent
insipidity,

'Pleased with itself, that all the world can please.'*

It is probable that in all that stream of idleness and curiosity
which flows in, hour after hour, and day after day, to the richly
hung apartments of Somerset-house, there are not fifty persons to be found who can really distinguish 'a Guido from a
Daub',* or who would recognise a work of the most refined
genius from the most common and everyday performance.
Come, then, ye banks of Wapping, and classic haunts of
Ratcliffe-highway, and join thy fields, blithe Tothill—let the
postchaises, gay with oaken boughs, be put in requisition for
school-boys from Eton and Harrow, and school-girls from
Hackney and Mile-end,—and let a jury be empannelled to
decide on the merits of Raphael, and ——.* The verdict will
be infallible. We remember having been formerly a good deal
amused with seeing a smart, handsome-looking Quaker lad,
standing before a picture of Christ as the saviour of the world,
with a circle of young female friends around him, and a
newspaper in his hand, out of which he read to his admiring
auditors a criticism on the picture ascribing to it every perfection, human and divine.—Now, in truth, the colouring was
any thing but solemn, the drawing any thing but grand, the
expression any thing but sublime. The friendly critic had,
however, bedaubed it so with praise, that it was not easy to
gainsay its wondrous excellence. In fact, one of the worst

consequences of the establishment of academies, &c. is, that the rank and station of the painter throw a lustre round his pictures, which imposes completely on the herd of spectators, and makes it a kind of treason against the art, for any one to speak his mind freely, or detect the imposture. If, indeed, the election to title and academic honours went by merit, this might form a kind of clue or standard for the public to decide justly upon:—but we have heard that genius and taste determine precedence there, almost as little as at court; and that modesty and talent stand very little chance indeed with interest, cabal, impudence, and cunning. The purity or liberality of professional decisions cannot, therefore, in such cases be expected to counteract the tendency which an appeal to the public has to lower the standard of taste. The artist, to succeed, must let himself down to the level of his judges, for he cannot raise them up to his own. The highest efforts of genius, in every walk of art, can never be properly understood by mankind in general: there are numberless beauties and truths which lie far beyond their comprehension. It is only as refinement or sublimity are blended with other qualities of a more obvious and common nature, that they pass current with the world. Common sense, which has been sometimes appealed to as the criterion of taste, is nothing but the common capacity, applied to common facts and feelings; but it neither is, nor pretends to be, the judge of any thing else.—To suppose that it can really appreciate the excellence of works of high art, is as absurd as to suppose that it could produce them.

Taste is the highest degree of sensibility, or the impression made on the most cultivated and sensible of minds, as genius is the result of the highest powers both of feeling and invention. It may be objected, that the public taste is capable of gradual improvement, because, in the end, the public do justice to works of the greatest merit. This is a mistake. The reputation ultimately, and often slowly affixed to works of genius is stamped upon them by authority, not by popular consent or the common sense of the world. We imagine that the admiration of the works of celebrated men has become common, because the admiration of their names has become so. But does not every ignorant connoisseur pretend the same veneration, and talk with the same vapid assurance of Michael Angelo, though he has never seen even a copy of any of his pictures, as if he had studied them accurately,—merely because Sir Joshua Reynolds has praised him? Is Milton more popular now than when the *Paradise Lost* was first published? Or does he not rather owe his reputation to the judgment of a few persons in every successive period, accumulating in his favour, and overpowering by its weight the public indifference? Why is Shakespeare popular? Not from his refinement of character or sentiment, so much as from his power of telling a story, the variety and invention, the tragic catastrophe and broad farce of his plays. Spenser is not yet understood. Does not Boccaccio pass to this day for a writer of ribaldry, because his jests and lascivious tales were all that caught the vulgar ear, while the story of the Falcon* is forgotten!

ON GUSTO

GUSTO in art is power or passion defining any object. It is not so difficult to explain this term in what relates to expression (of which it may be said to be the highest degree) as in what relates to things without expression, to the natural appearances of objects, as mere colour or form. In one sense, however, there is hardly any object entirely devoid of expression, without some character of power belonging to it, some precise association with pleasure or pain: and it is in giving this truth of character from the truth of feeling, whether in the highest or the lowest degree, but always in the highest degree of which the subject is capable, that gusto consists.

There is a gusto in the colouring of Titian. Not only do his heads seem to think—his bodies seem to feel. This is what the Italians mean by the *morbidezza** of his flesh-colour. It seems sensitive and alive all over; not merely to have the look and texture of flesh, but the feeling in itself. For example, the limbs of his female figures have a luxurious softness and delicacy, which appears conscious of the pleasure of the

beholder. As the objects themselves in nature would produce
an impression on the sense, distinct from every other object,
and having something divine in it, which the heart owns and
the imagination consecrates, the objects in the picture preserve the same impression, absolute, unimpaired, stamped
with all the truth of passion, the pride of the eye, and the
charm of beauty. Rubens makes his flesh-colour like flowers;
Albano's is like ivory;* Titian's is like flesh, and like nothing
else. It is as different from that of other painters, as the skin
is from a piece of white or red drapery thrown over it. The
blood circulates here and there, the blue veins just appear,
the rest is distinguished throughout only by that sort of ting-
ling sensation to the eye, which the body feels within itself.
This is gusto. Vandyke's flesh-colour, though it has great truth
and purity, wants gusto. It has not the internal character, the
living principle in it. It is a smooth surface, not a warm,
moving mass. It is painted without passion, with indifference.
The hand only has been concerned. The impression slides off
from the eye, and does not, like the tones of Titian's pencil,
leave a sting behind it in the mind of the spectator. The eye
does not acquire a taste or appetite for what it sees. In a word,
gusto in painting is where the impression made on one sense
excites by affinity those of another.

Michael Angelo's forms are full of gusto. They everywhere
obtrude the sense of power upon the eye. His limbs convey
an idea of muscular strength, of moral grandeur, and even of
intellectual dignity: they are firm, commanding, broad, and
massy, capable of executing with ease the determined purposes of the will. His faces have no other expression than his
figures, conscious power and capacity. They appear only to
think what they shall do, and to know that they can do it. This
is what is meant by saying that his style is hard and masculine.
It is the reverse of Correggio's, which is effeminate. That is,
the gusto of Michael Angelo consists in expressing energy of
will without proportionable sensibility, Correggio's in expressing exquisite sensibility without energy of will. In Correggio's
faces as well as figures we see neither bones nor muscles, but
then what a soul is there, full of sweetness and of grace—pure,
playful, soft, angelical! There is sentiment enough in a hand

painted by Correggio to set up a school of history painters. Whenever we look at the hands of Correggio's women or of Raphael's, we always wish to touch them.

Again, Titian's landscapes have a prodigious gusto, both in the colouring and forms. We shall never forget one that we saw many years ago in the Orleans Gallery* of Acteon hunting. It had a brown, mellow, autumnal look. The sky was of the colour of stone. The winds seemed to sing through the rustling branches of the trees, and already you might hear the twanging of bows resound through the tangled mazes of the wood. Mr West,* we understand, has this landscape. He will know if this description of it is just. The landscape background of the St Peter Martyr* is another well known instance of the power of this great painter to give a romantic interest and an appropriate character to the objects of his pencil, where every circumstance adds to the effect of the scene,—the bold trunks of the tall forest trees, the trailing ground plants, with that tall convent spire rising in the distance, amidst the blue sapphire mountains and the golden sky.

Rubens has a great deal of gusto in his Fauns and Satyrs, and in all that expresses motion, but in nothing else. Rembrandt has it in everything; everything in his pictures has a tangible character. If he puts a diamond in the ear of a burgomaster's wife, it is of the first water; and his furs and stuffs are proof against a Russian winter. Raphael's gusto was only in expression; he had no idea of the character of anything but the human form. The dryness and poverty of his style in other respects is a phenomenon in the art. His trees are like sprigs of grass stuck in a book of botanical specimens. Was it that Raphael never had time to go beyond the walls of Rome? That he was always in the streets, at church, or in the bath? He was not one of the Society of Arcadians.*

Claude's landscapes, perfect as they are, want gusto. This is not easy to explain. They are perfect abstractions of the visible images of things; they speak the visible language of nature truly. They resemble a mirror or a microscope. To the eye only they are more perfect than any other landscapes that ever were or will be painted; they give more of nature, as cognisable by one sense alone; but they lay an equal stress on

all visible impressions. They do not interpret one sense by
another; they do not distinguish the character of different
objects as we are taught, and can only be taught, to distinguish
them by their effect on the different senses. That is, his eye
wanted imagination: it did not strongly sympathise with his
other faculties. He saw the atmosphere, but he did not feel it.
He painted the trunk of a tree or a rock in the foreground as
smooth—with as complete an abstraction of the gross, tangible impression, as any other part of the picture. His trees
are perfectly beautiful, but quite immovable; they have a look
of enchantment. In short, his landscapes are unequalled imitations of nature, released from its subjection to the elements,
as if all objects were become a delightful fairy vision, and the
eye had rarefied and refined away the other senses.

The gusto in the Greek statues is of a very singular kind.
The sense of perfect form nearly occupies the whole mind,
and hardly suffers it to dwell on any other feeling. It seems
enough for them *to be*, without acting or suffering. Their forms
are ideal, spiritual. Their beauty is power. By their beauty they
are raised above the frailties of pain or passion; by their beauty
they are deified.*

The infinite quantity of dramatic invention in Shakespeare
takes from his gusto. The power he delights to show is not
intense, but discursive. He never insists on anything as much
as he might, except a quibble. Milton has great gusto. He
repeats his blows twice; grapples with and exhausts his subject.
His imagination has a double relish of its objects, an inveterate
attachment to the things he describes, and to the words describing them.

> ——'Or where Chineses drive
> With sails and wind their *cany* waggons *light.*'

> .   .   .   .

> 'Wild above rule or art, *enormous* bliss.'*

There is a gusto in Pope's compliments, in Dryden's satires,
and Prior's tales;* and among prose writers Boccaccio and
Rabelais had the most of it. We will only mention one other
work which appears to us to be full of gusto, and that is the

Beggar's Opera. If it is not, we are altogether mistaken in our notions on this delicate subject.

ORIGINALITY

ORIGINALITY is any conception of things, taken immediately from nature, and neither borrowed from, nor common to, others. To deserve this appellation, the copy must be both true and new. But herein lies the difficulty of reconciling a seeming contradiction in the terms of the explanation. For as any thing to be *natural* must be referable to a consistent principle, and as the face of things is open and familiar to all, how can any imitation be new and striking, without being liable to the charge of extravagance, distortion, and singularity? And, on the other hand, if it has no such peculiar and distinguishing characteristic to set it off, it cannot possibly rise above the level of the trite and common-place. This objection would indeed hold good and be unanswerable, if nature were one thing, or if the eye or mind comprehended the whole of it at a single glance; in which case, if an object had been once seen and copied in the most cursory and mechanical way, there could be no farther addition to, or variation from, this idea, without obliquity and affectation; but nature presents an endless variety of aspects, of which the mind seldom takes in more than a part or than one view at a time; and it is in seizing on this unexplored variety, and giving some one of these new but easily recognised features, in its characteristic essence, and according to the peculiar bent and force of the artist's genius, that true originality consists. Romney,* when he was first introduced into Sir Joshua's gallery, said, 'there was something in his portraits which had been never seen in the art before, but which every one must be struck with as true and natural the moment he saw it.' This could not happen if the human face did not admit of being contemplated in several points of view, or if the hand were necessarily faithful to the suggestions of sense. Two things serve to perplex this question; first, the construction of language, from which, as one object is represented by one word, we imagine that it is one thing, and that we can no more conceive differently of the same object than we can pronounce the same word in different ways, without being wrong in all but one of them; secondly, the very nature of our individual impressions puts a deception upon us; for, as we know no more of any given object than we see, we very pardonably conclude that we see the whole of it, and have exhausted inquiry at the first view, since we can never suspect the existence of that which, from our ignorance and incapacity, gives us no intimation of itself. Thus, if we are shown an exact likeness of a face, we give the artist credit chiefly for dexterity of hand; we think that any one who has eyes can *see a face*; that one person sees it just like another, that there can be no mistake about it (as the object and the image are in our notion the same)—and that if there is any departure from our version of it, it must be purely fantastical and arbitrary. *Multum abludit imago.** We do not look beyond the surface; or rather we do not see into the surface, which contains a labyrinth of difficulties and distinctions, that not all the effects of art, of time, patience, and study, can master and unfold. But let us take this *self-evident proposition*, the human face, and examine it a little; and we shall soon be convinced what a Proteus, what an inexplicable riddle it is! Ask any one who thinks he has a perfect idea of the face of his friend, what the shape of his nose or any other feature is, and he will presently find his mistake;—ask a lover to draw his 'mistress' eyebrow',* it is not merely that his hand will fail him, but his memory is at fault both for the form and colour; he may, indeed, dream, and tell you with the poet, that

> 'Grace is in all her steps, heaven in her eye,
> In every gesture, dignity and love':—*

but if he wishes to embody his favourite conceit, and to convince any one else of all this by proof positive, he must borrow the painter's aid. When a young artist first begins to make a study from a head, it is well known that he has soon done, because after he has got in a certain general outline and rude masses, as the forehead, the nose, the mouth, the eyes in a general way, he sees no farther, and is obliged to stop; he feels in truth that he has made a very indifferent copy, but is quite at a loss how to supply the defect—after a few months' or a year or two's practice, if he has a real eye for nature and a turn for his art, he can spend whole days in working up the smallest details, in correcting the proportions, in softening the gradations; and does not know when to leave off, till night closes in upon him, and then he sits musing and gazing in the twilight at what remains for his next day's work. Sir Joshua Reynolds used to say, that if he did not finish any one of his pictures till he saw nothing more to be done to it, he should never leave off. Titian wrote on his pictures, *faciebat**—as much as to say that he was about them, but that it was an endless task. As the mind advances in the knowledge of nature, the horizon of art enlarges and the air refines. Then, in addition to an infinity of details, even in the most common object, there is the variety of form and colour, of light and shade, of character and expression, of the voluptuous, the thoughtful, the grand, the graceful, the grave, the gay, the *I know not what*; which are all to be found (separate or combined) in nature, which sufficiently account for the diversity of art, and to detect and carry off the *spolia opima** of any one of which is the highest praise of human genius and skill—

> 'Whate'er Lorrain light-touch'd with softening hue,
> Or savage Rosa dash'd, or learned Poussin drew.'*

All that we meet with in the master-pieces of taste and genius is to be found in the previous capacity of nature; and man, instead of adding to the store, or *creating* any thing either as to matter or manner, can only draw out a feeble and imperfect transcript, bit by bit, and one appearance after another, according to the peculiar aptitude and affinity that subsists between his mind and some one part. The mind resembles a prism, which untwists the various rays of truth, and displays them by different modes and in several parcels. Enough has been said to vindicate both conditions of originality, which distinguish it from singularity on the one hand and from vulgarity on the other; or to show how a thing may at the same time be both true and new. This novel truth is brought out

when it meets with a strong congenial mind—that is, with a
mind in the highest degree susceptible of a certain class of
impressions, or of a certain kind of beauty or power; and this
peculiar strength, congeniality, truth of imagination, or command over a certain part of nature, is, in other words, what is
meant by *genius*. This will serve to show why original inventors
have in general (and except in what is mechanical), left so
little for their followers to improve upon; for as the original
invention implies the utmost stretch and felicity of thought,
or the greatest strength and sagacity to discover and dig the
ore from the mine of truth, so it is hardly to be expected that
a greater degree of capacity should ever arise (than the
highest), that a greater mastery should be afterwards obtained
in shaping and fashioning the precious materials, than in the
first heat and eagerness of discovery; or that, if the capacity
were equal, the same scope and opportunity would be left for
its exercise in the same field. If the genius were different, it
would then seek different objects and a different vent, and
open new paths to fame and excellence, instead of treading
in old ones. Hence the well-known observation,* that in each
particular style or class of art, the greatest works of genius are
the earliest. Hence, also, the first productions of men of
genius are often their best. What was that *something* that Romney spoke of in Reynolds's pictures that the world had never
seen before, but with which they were enchanted the moment
they beheld it, and which both Hoppner and Jackson,* with
all their merit, have but faintly imitated since? It was a reflection of the artist's mind—an emanation from his character,
transferred to the canvass. It was an ease, an amenity, an
indolent but anxious satisfaction, a graceful playfulness,
belonging to his disposition, and spreading its charm on all
around it, attracting what harmonized with, and softening and
moulding what repelled it, avoiding every thing hard, stiff,
and formal, shrinking from details, reposing on effect, impart-
ing motion to *still life*, viewing all things in their 'gayest,
happiest attitudes',* and infusing his own spirit into nature
as the leaven is kneaded into the dough; but, though the
original bias existed in himself, and was thence stamped upon
his works, yet the character could neither have been formed

without the constant recurrence and pursuit of proper nourishment, nor could it have expressed itself without a reference to those objects, looks, and attitudes in nature, which soothed and assimilated with it. What made Hogarth original and inimitable, but the wonderful redundance, and, as it were, *supererogation* of his genius, which poured the oil of humanity into the wounds and bruises of human nature, redeemed, while it exposed, vice and folly, made deformity pleasing, and turned misfortune into a jest? But could he have done so if there were no enjoyment or wit in a night-cellar, or if the cripple could not dance and sing? No, the *moral* was in nature; but let no one dare to insist upon it after him, in the same language and with the same pretensions! There was Rembrandt—did he invent the extremes of light and shade, or was he only the first that embodied them? He was so only because his eye drank in light and shade more deeply than any one before or since; and, therefore, the sunshine hung in liquid drops from his pencil, and the dungeon's gloom hovered over his canvass. Who can think of Correggio without a swimming of the head—the undulating line, the melting grace, the objects advancing and retiring as in a measured dance or solemn harmony! But all this fulness, roundness, and delicacy, existed before in nature, and only found a fit sanctuary in his mind. The breadth and masses of Michael Angelo were studies from nature, which he selected and cast in the mould of his own manly and comprehensive genius. The landscapes of Claude are in a fixed repose, as if nothing could be moved from its place without a violence to harmony and just proportion: in those of Rubens every thing is flutter-ing and in motion, light and indifferent, as the winds blow where they list. All this is characteristic, original, a different mode of nature, which the artist had the happiness to find out and carry to the utmost point of perfection. It has been laid down that no one paints any thing but his own character, and almost features; and the workman is always to be traced in the work. Mr Fuseli's figures, if they were like nothing else, were like himself, or resembled the contortions of a dream; Wilkie's have a parochial air; Haydon's are heroical; Sir Thomas's* genteel. What Englishman could bear to sit to a

French artist ? What English artist could hope to succeed in a
French coquet? There is not only an individual but a national
bias, which is observable in the different schools and productions of art. *Mannerism* is the bane (though it is the occasional
vice) of genius, and is the worst kind of imitation, for it is a
man's imitating himself. Many artists go on repeating and
caricaturing themselves, till they complain that nature puts
them out. Gross plagiarism may consist with great originality.
Sterne was a notorious plagiarist, but a true genius. His Corporal Trim, his Uncle Toby, and Mr Shandy, are to be found
no where else. If Raphael had done nothing but borrow the
two figures from Masaccio,* it would have been impossible to
say a word in his defence: no one has a right to steal, who is
not rich enough to be robbed by others. So Milton has borrowed more than almost any other writer; but he has uniformly stamped a character of his own upon it. In what relates
to the immediate imitation of nature, people find it difficult
to conceive of an opening for originality, inasmuch as they
think that they themselves see the whole of nature, and that
every other view of it is wrong:—in what relates to the productions of imagination or the discoveries of science, as they
themselves are totally in the dark, they fancy the whole to be
a fabrication, and give the inventor credit for a sort of dealing
with the Devil, or some preternatural kind of talent. Poets lay
a popular and prescriptive claim to inspiration: the astro-
nomer of old was thought able to conjure with the stars; and
the skilful leech, who performed unexpected cures, was condemned for a sorcerer. This is as great an error the other way.
The vulgar think there is nothing in what lies on the surface;
though the learned only see beyond it by stripping off in-
cumbrances and coming to another surface beneath the first.
The difference between art and science is only the difference
between the *clothed* and *naked* figure: but the veil of truth must
be drawn aside before we can distinctly see the face. The
physician is qualified to prescribe remedies because he is
acquainted with the internal structure of the body, and has
studied the symptoms of disorders: the mathematician arrives
at his most surprising conclusions by slow and sure steps; and
where he can add discovery to discovery by the very certainty

of the hold he has of all the previous links. There is no witchcraft in either case. The invention of the poet is little more than the fertility of a teeming brain—that is, than the number and quantity of associations present to his mind, and the various shapes in which he can turn them without being distracted or losing a 'semblable coherence'* of the parts; as the man of observation and reflection strikes out just and unforeseen remarks by taking off the mask of custom and appearances; or by judging for himself of men and things, without taking it for granted that they are what he has hitherto supposed them, or waiting to be told by others what they are. If there were no foundation for an unusual remark in our own consciousness or experience, it would not strike us as a discovery: it would sound like a *jeu-d'esprit*, a whim or oddity, or as flat nonsense. The mere mob, 'the great vulgar and the small',* are not therefore capable of distinguishing between originality and singularity, for they have no idea beyond the *commonplace* of fashion or custom. Prejudice has no ears either for or against itself; it is alike averse to objections and proofs, for both equally disturb its blind implicit notions of things. Originality is, then, 'the strong conception'* of truth and nature 'that the mind groans withal', and of which it cannot stay to be delivered by authority or example. It is feeling the ground sufficiently firm under one's feet to be able to go alone. Truth is its essence; it is the strongest possible feeling of truth; for it is a secret and instinctive yearning after, and approximation towards it, before it is acknowledged by others, and almost before the mind itself knows what it is. Paradox and eccentricity, on the other hand, show a dearth of originality, as bombast and hyperbole show a dearth of imagination; they are the desperate resources of affectation and want of power. Originality is necessary to genius; for when that which, in the first instance, conferred the character, is afterwards done by rule and routine, it ceases to be genius. To conclude, the value of any work of art or science depends chiefly on the quantity of originality contained in it, and which constitutes either the charm of works of fiction or the improvement to be derived from those of progressive information. But it is not so in matters of opinion, where every individual thinks he can judge for himself, and does not wish to be set right. There is, consequently, nothing that the world like better than origin-ality of invention, and nothing that they hate worse than originality of thought. Advances in science were formerly regarded with like jealousy, and stigmatised as dangerous by the friends of religion and the state: Galileo was imprisoned in the same town of Florence, where they now preserve his finger pointing to the skies!

ON THE ELGIN MARBLES

AT the conclusion of a former article on this subject, we ventured to lay down some general principles, which we shall here proceed to elucidate in such manner as we are able.

I. The first was, that art is (*first and last*) *the imitation of nature.*

By nature, we mean actually existing nature, or some one object to be found *in rerum naturâ*,* not an idea of nature existing solely in the mind, got from an infinite number of different objects, but which was never yet embodied in an individual instance. Sir Joshua Reynolds may be ranked* at the head of those who have maintained the supposition that nature (or the universe of things) was indeed the groundwork or foundation on which art rested; but that the superstructure rose above it, that it towered by degrees above the world of realities, and was suspended in the regions of thought alone—that a middle form, a more refined idea, borrowed from the observation of a number of particulars, but unlike any of them, was the standard of truth and beauty, and the glittering phantom that hovered round the head of the genuine artist:

> 'So from the ground
> Springs lighter the green stalk, from thence the leaves
> More airy, last the bright consummate flower!'*

We have no notion of this vague, equivocal theory of art, and contend, on the other hand, that each image in art should have a *tally* or corresponding prototype in some object in nature. Otherwise, we do not see the use of art at all: it is a

mere superfluity, an incumbrance to the mind, a piece of
'laborious foolery'*—for the word, the mere name of any
object or class of objects will convey the general idea, more
free from particular details or defects than any the most
neutral and indefinite representation that can be produced
by forms and colours. The word Man, for instance, conveys a
more filmy, impalpable, abstracted, and (according to this
hypothesis) sublime idea of the species, than Michael
Angelo's Adam, or any real image can possibly do. If this then
is the true object of art, the language of painting, sculpture,
&c. becomes quite supererogatory. Sir Joshua and the rest
contend, that nature (properly speaking) does not express
any single individual, nor the whole mass of things as they
exist, but a general principle, a *something common* to all these,
retaining the perfections, that is, all in which they are alike,
and abstracting the defects, namely, all in which they differ:
so that, out of actual nature, we compound an artificial
nature, never answering to the former in any one part of its
mock- existence, and which last is the true object of imitation
to the aspiring artist. Let us adopt this principle of abstraction
as the rule of perfection, and see what havoc it will make in
all our notions and feelings in such matters. If the *perfect* is
the *intermediate*, why not confound all objects, all forms, all
colours at once? Instead of painting a landscape with blue sky,
or white clouds, or green earth, or grey rocks and towers; what
should we say if the artist (so named) were to treat all these
'fair varieties'* as so many imperfections and mistakes in the
creation, and mass them altogether, by mixing up the colours
on his palette in the same dull, leaden tone, and call this the
true principle of epic landscape-painting? Would not the
thing be abominable, an abortion, and worse than the worst
Dutch picture? Variety then is one principle, one beauty in
external nature, and not an everlasting source of pettiness
and deformity, which must be got rid of at all events, before
taste can set its seal upon the work, or fancy own it. But it may
be said, it is different in things of the same species, and
particularly in man, who is cast in a regular mould, which
mould is one. What then, are we, on this pretext, to confound
the difference of sex in a sort of hermaphrodite softness, as

Mr Westall, Angelica Kauffman,* and others, have done in their effeminate performances? Are we to leave out of the scale of legitimate art, the extremes of infancy and old age, as not *middle terms* in man's life? Are we to strike off from the list of available topics and sources of interest, the varieties of character, of passion, of strength, activity, &c.? Is everything to wear the same form, the same colour, the same unmeaning face? Are we only to repeat the same average idea of perfection, that is, our own want of observation and imagination, for ever, and to melt down the inequalities and excrescences of individual nature in the monotony of abstraction? Oh no! As well might we prefer the cloud to the rainbow; the dead corpse to the living moving body! So Sir Joshua debated upon Rubens's landscapes, and has a whole chapter* to inquire whether *accidents in nature*, that is, rainbows, moonlight, sunsets, clouds and storms, are the proper thing in the classical style of art. Again, it is urged that this is not what is meant, *viz.* to exclude different classes or characters of things, but that there is in each class or character a *middle point*, which is the point of perfection. What middle point? Or how is it ascertained? What is the middle age of childhood? Or are all children to be alike, dark or fair? Some of Titian's children have black hair, and others yellow or auburn: who can tell which is the most beautiful? May not a St John be older than an infant Christ? Must not a Magdalen be different from a Madonna, a Diana from a Venus? Or may not a Venus have more or less gravity, a Diana more or less sweetness? What then becomes of the abstract idea in any of these cases? It varies as it does in nature; that is, there is indeed a general principle or character to be adhered to, but modified everlastingly by various other given or nameless circumstances. The highest art, like nature, is a living spring of unconstrained excellence, and does not produce a continued repetition of itself, like plaster-casts from the same figure. But once more it may be insisted, that in what relates to mere form or organic structure, there is necessarily a middle line or central point, anything short of which is deficiency, and anything beyond it excess, being the average form to which all the other forms included in the same species tend, and approximate more or less. Then this average form as it exists in nature should be taken as the model for art. What occasion to do it out of your own head, when you can bring it under the cognisance of your senses? Suppose a foot of a certain size and shape to be the standard of perfection, or if you will, the *mean proportion* between all other feet. How can you tell this so well as by seeing it? How can you copy it so well as by having it actually before you? But, you will say, there are particular minute defects in the best-shaped actual foot which ought not to be transferred to the imitation. Be it so. But are there not also particular minute beauties in the best, or even the worst shaped actual foot, which you will only discover by ocular inspection, which are reducible to no measurement or pre-cepts, and which in finely-developed nature outweigh the imperfections a thousandfold, the proper general form being contained there also, and these being only the distinctly arti-culated parts of it, with their inflections which no artist can carry in his head alone? For instance, in the bronze monu-ment of Henry VII and his wife, in Westminster Abbey, by the famous Torregiano,* the fingers and finger nails of the woman in particular are made out as minutely, and, at the same time, as beautifully as it is possible to conceive; yet they have exactly the effect that a cast taken from a fine female hand would have, with every natural joint, muscle, and nerve in complete preservation. Does this take from the beauty or magnificence of the whole? No: it aggrandises it. What then does it take from? Nothing but the conceit of the artist that he can paint a hand out of his own head (that is, out of nothing, and by reducing it again as near as can be to nothing, to a mere vague image) that shall be better than any thing in nature. A hand or foot is not *one thing*, because it is *one word* or name; and the painter of mere abstractions had better lay down his pencil at once, and be contented to write the des-criptions or titles under works of art. Lastly, it may be objected that a whole figure can never be found perfect or equal; that the most beautiful arm will not belong to the same figure as the most beautiful leg, and so on. How is this to be remedied? By taking the arm from one, and the leg from the other, and clapping them both on the same body? That will never do;

for however admirable in themselves, they will hardly agree together. One will have a different character from the other; and they will form a sort of natural patchwork. Or, to avoid this, will you take neither from actual models, but derive them from the neutralising medium of your own imagination? Worse and worse. Copy them from the same model, the best in all its parts you can get; so that, if you have to alter, you may alter as little as possible, and retain nearly the whole substance of nature.* You may depend upon it that what is so retained will alone be of any specific value. The rest may have a negative merit, but will be positively good for nothing. It will be to the vital truth and beauty of what is taken from the best nature, like the piecing of an antique statue. It fills a gap, but nothing more. It is, in fact, a mental blank.

2. This leads us to the second point laid down before, which was, that *the highest art is the imitation of the finest nature, or in other words, of that which conveys the strongest sense of pleasure or power, of the sublime or beautiful.*

The artist does not pretend to *invent* an absolutely new class of objects, without any foundation in nature. He does not spread his palette on the canvas, for the mere finery of the thing, and tell us that it makes a brighter show than the rainbow, or even than a bed of tulips. He does not draw airy forms, moving above the earth, 'gay creatures of the element, that play i' th' plighted clouds',* and scorn the mere material existences, the concrete descendants of those that came out of Noah's Ark, and that walk, run, or creep upon it. No, he does not paint only what he has seen *in his mind's eye*, but the common objects that both he and others daily meet—rocks, clouds, trees, men, women, beasts, fishes, birds, or what he calls such. He is then an imitator by profession. He gives the appearances of things that exist outwardly by themselves, and have a distinct and independent nature of their own. But these know their own nature best; and it is by consulting them that he can alone trace it truly, either in the immediate details, or characteristic essences. Nature is consistent, unaffected, powerful, subtle: art is forgetful, apish, feeble, coarse. Nature is the original, and therefore right: art is the copy, and can but tread lamely in the same steps. Nature penetrates into the parts, and moves the whole mass: it acts with diversity, and in necessary connexion; for real causes never forget to operate, and to contribute their portion. Where, therefore, these causes are called into play to the utmost extent that they ever go to, there we shall have a strength and a refinement, that art may imitate but cannot surpass. But it is said that art can surpass this most perfect image in nature by combining others with it. What! by joining to the most perfect in its kind something less perfect? Go to,—this argument will not pass. Suppose you have a goblet of the finest wine that ever was tasted: you will not mend it by pouring into it all sorts of samples of an inferior quality. So the best in nature is the stint and limit of what is best in art: for art can only borrow from nature still; and, moreover, must borrow entire objects, for bits only make patches. We defy any landscape-painter to invent out of his own head, and by jumbling together all the different forms of hills he ever saw, by adding a bit to one, and taking a bit from another, anything equal to Arthur's seat, with the appendage of Salisbury Crags, that overlook Edinburgh. Why so? Because there are no levers in the mind of man equal to those with which nature works at her utmost need. No imagination can toss and tumble about huge heaps of earth as the ocean in its fury can. A volcano is more potent to rend rocks asunder than the most splashing pencil. The convulsions of nature can make a precipice more frightfully, or heave the backs of mountains more proudly, or throw their sides into waving lines more gracefully than all the *beau idéal* of art.* For there is in nature not only greater power and scope, but (so to speak) greater knowledge and unity of purpose. Art is comparatively weak and incongruous, being at once a miniature and caricature of nature. We grant that a tolerable sketch of Arthur's seat, and the adjoining view, is better than Primrose Hill itself, (dear Primrose Hill! ha! faithless pen, canst thou forget its winding slopes, and valleys green, to which all Scotland can bring no parallel?) but no pencil can transform or dandle Primrose Hill (our favourite Primrose Hill!) into a thing of equal character and sublimity with Arthur's seat. It gives us some pain to make this concession; but in doing it, we flatter ourselves that no Scotchman will have the liberality

in any way to return us the compliment. We do not recollect
a more striking illustration of the difference between art and
nature in this respect, than Mr Martin's very singular and, in
some things, very meritorious pictures.* But he strives to
outdo nature. He wants to give more than she does, or than
his subject requires or admits. He sub-divides his groups into
infinite littleness, and exaggerates his scenery into absolute
immensity. His figures are like rows of shiny pins; his mountains are piled up one upon the back of the other, like the
stories of houses. He has no notion of the moral principle in
all art, that a part may be greater than the whole. He reckons
that if one range of lofty square hills is good, another range
above that with clouds between must be better. He thus
wearies the imagination, instead of exciting it. We see no end
of the journey, and turn back in disgust. We are tired of the
effort, we are tired of the monotony of this sort of reduplica-
tion of the same object. We were satisfied before; but it seems
the painter was not, and we naturally sympathise with him.
This craving after quantity is a morbid affection. A landscape
is not an architectural elevation. You may build a house as
high as you can lift up stones with pulleys and levers, but you
cannot raise mountains into the sky merely with the pencil.
They lose probability and effect by striving at too much; and,
with their ceaseless throes, oppress the imagination of the
spectator, and bury the artist's fame under them. The only
error of these pictures is, however, that art here puts on her
seven-league boots, and thinks it possible to steal a march
upon nature. Mr Martin might make Arthur's Seat sublime,
if he chose to take the thing as it is; but he would be for
squaring it according to the mould in his own imagination,
and for clapping another Arthur's Seat on the top of it, to
make the Calton Hill stare! Again, with respect to the human
figure. This has an internal structure, muscles, bones, blood-
vessels, &c. by means of which the external surface is operated
upon according to certain laws. Does the artist, with all his
generalisations, understand these, as well as nature does? Can
he predict, with all his learning, that if a certain muscle is
drawn up in a particular manner, it will present a particular
appearance in a different part of the arm or leg, or bring out

other muscles, which were before hid, with certain modifications? But in nature all this is brought about by necessary laws, and the effect is visible to those, and those only, who look for it in actual objects. This is the great and master-excellence of the Elgin Marbles, that they do not seem to be the outer surface of a hard and immovable block of marble, but to be actuated by an internal machinery, and composed of the same soft and flexible materials as the human body. The skin (or the outside) seems to be protruded or tightened by the natural action of a muscle beneath it. This result is miraculous in art: in nature it is easy and unavoidable. That is to say, art has to imitate or produce certain effects or appearances without the natural causes: but the human understanding can hardly be so true to those causes as the causes to themselves; and hence the necessity (in this sort of *simulated creation*) of recurring at every step to the actual objects and appearances of nature. Having shown so far how indispensable it is for art to identify itself with nature, in order to preserve the truth of imitation, without which it is destitute of value or meaning, it may be said to follow as a necessary consequence, that the only way in which art can rise to greater dignity or excellence is by finding out models of greater dignity and excellence in nature. Will any one, looking at the Theseus, for example, say that it could spring merely from the artist's brain, or that it could be done from a common, ill-made, or stunted body? The fact is, that its superiority consists in this, that it is a perfect combination of art and nature, or an identical, and as it were spontaneous copy of an individual picked out of a finer race of men than generally tread this ball of earth. Could it be made of a Dutchman's trunk-hose? No. Could it be made out of one of Sir Joshua's Discourses on the *middle form*? No. How then? Out of an eye, a head, and hand, with sense, spirit, and energy to follow the finest nature, as it appeared exemplified in sweeping masses, and in subtle details, without pedantry, conceit, cowardice, or affectation! Some one was asking at Mr H—yd—n's* one day, as a few persons were looking at the cast from this figure, why the original might not have been done as a cast from nature. Such a supposition would account at least for what seems otherwise unaccountable—the

incredible labour and finishing bestowed on the back and the
other parts of this figure, placed at a prodigious height against
the walls of a temple, where they could never be seen after
they were once put up there. If they were done by means of
a cast in the first instance, the thing appears intelligible,
otherwise not. Our host stoutly resisted this imputation, which
tended to deprive art of one of its greatest triumphs, and to
make it as mechanical as a shaded profile. So far, so good. But
the reason he gave was bad, *viz.* that the limbs could not
remain in those actions long enough to be cast. Yet surely this
would take a shorter time than if the model sat to the sculptor;
and we all agreed that nothing but actual, continued, and
intense observation of living nature could give the solidity,
complexity, and refinement of imitation which we saw in the
half animated, almost moving figure before us. Be this as it
may, the principle here stated does not reduce art to the
imitation of what is understood by common or low life. It rises
to any point of beauty or sublimity you please, but it rises only
as nature rises exalted with it too. To hear these critics talk,
one would suppose there was nothing in the world really
worth looking at. The Dutch pictures were the best that they
could paint: they had no other landscapes or faces before
them. *Honi soit qui mal y pense.* Yet who is not alarmed at a
Venus by Rembrandt? The Greek statues were (*cum grano
salis*)* Grecian youths and nymphs; and the women in the
streets of Rome (it has been remarked)* look to this hour as
if they had walked out of Raphael's pictures. Nature is always
truth: at its best, it is beauty and sublimity as well; though Sir
Joshua tells us* in one of the papers in the *Idler*, that in itself,
or with reference to individuals, it is a mere tissue of meanness
and deformity. Luckily, the Elgin Marbles say NO to that conclusion: for they are decidedly *part and parcel thereof.* What
constitutes fine nature, we shall inquire under another head.
But we would remark here, that it can hardly be the *middle
form*, since this principle, however it might determine certain
general proportions and outlines, could never be intelligible
in the details of nature, or applicable to those of art. Who will
say that the form of a finger nail is just midway between a
thousand others that he has *not* remarked: we are only struck

with it when it is more than ordinarily beautiful, from symmetry, an oblong shape, &c. The staunch partisans of this
theory, however, get over the difficulty here spoken of, in
practice, by omitting the details altogether, and making their
works sketches, or rather what the French call *ébauches* and
the English *daubs.*

3. *The* IDEAL *is only the selecting a particular form which expresses
most completely the idea of a given character or quality, as of beauty,
strength, activity, voluptuousness, &c. and which preserves that
character with the greatest consistency throughout.*

Instead of its being true in general that the *ideal* is the *middle
point,* it is to be found in the *extremes*; or, it is carrying any *idea*
as far as it will go. Thus, for instance, a Silenus is as much an
ideal thing as an Apollo, as to the principle on which it is done,
viz. giving to every feature, and to the whole form, the utmost
degree of grossness and sensuality that can be imagined, with
this exception (which has nothing to do with the understanding of the question), that the *ideal* means by custom this
extreme on the side of the good and beautiful. With this
reserve, the *ideal* means always the *something more* of anything
which may be anticipated by the fancy, and which must be
found in nature (by looking long enough for it) to be expressed as it ought. Suppose a good heavy Dutch face (we speak
by the proverb)*—this, you will say, is gross; but it is not gross
enough. You have an idea of something grosser, that is, you
have seen something grosser and must seek for it again. When
you meet with it, and have stamped it on the canvas, or carved
it out of the block, this is the true *ideal,* namely, that which
answers to and satisfies a preconceived idea; not that which is
made out of an abstract idea, and answers to nothing. In the
Silenus, also, according to the notion we have of the properties and character of that figure, there must be vivacity, slyness,
wantonness, &c. Not only the image in the mind, but a real
face may express all these combined together; another may
express them more, and another most, which last is the *ideal*;
and when the image in nature coalesces with, and gives a body,
force, and reality to the idea in the mind, then it is that we
see the true perfection of art. The forehead should be
'villainous low';* the eye-brows bent in; the eyes small and

gloating; the nose *pugged*, and pointed at the end, with distended nostrils; the mouth large and shut; the cheeks swollen; the neck thick, &c. There is, in all this process, nothing of softening down, of compromising qualities, of finding out a *mean proportion* between different forms and characters; the sole object is to *intensify* each as much as possible. The only fear is 'to o'erstep the modesty of nature',* and run into caricature. This must be avoided; but the artist is only to stop short of this. He must not outrage probability. We must have seen a class of such faces, or something so nearly approaching, as to prevent the imagination from revolting against them. The forehead must be low, but not so low as to lose the character of humanity in the brute. It would thus lose all its force and meaning. For that which is extreme and ideal in one species is nothing, if, by being pushed too far, it is merged in another. Above all, there should be *keeping* in the whole and every part. In the Pan, the horns and goat's feet, perhaps, warrant the approach to a more *animal* expression than would otherwise be allowable in the human features; but yet this tendency to excess must be restrained within certain limits. If Pan is made into a beast, he will cease to be a God! Let Momus* distend his jaws with laughter, as far as laughter can stretch them, but no farther; or the expression will be that of pain and not of pleasure. Besides, the overcharging the expression or action of any one feature will suspend the action of others. The whole face will no longer laugh. But this universal suffusion of broad mirth and humour over the countenance is very different from a placid smile, midway between grief and joy. Yet a classical Momus, by modern theories of the *ideal*, ought to be such a nonentity in expression. The ancients knew better. They pushed art in such subjects to the verge of 'all we hate',* while they felt the point beyond which it could not be urged with propriety, *i.e.* with truth, consistency, and consequent effect. There is no difference, in philosophical reasoning, between the mode of art here insisted on, and the *ideal* regularity of such figures as the Apollo, the Hercules, the Mercury, the Venus, &c. All these are, as it were, *personifications, essences, abstractions* of certain qualities of virtue in human nature, not of human nature in general, which would make nonsense. Instead of being abstractions of all sorts of qualities jumbled together in a neutral character, they are in the opposite sense *abstractions* of some single quality or customary combination of qualities, leaving out all others as much as possible, and imbuing every part with that one predominant character to the utmost. The Apollo is a representation of graceful dignity and mental power; the Hercules of bodily strength; the Mercury of swiftness; the Venus of female loveliness, and so on. In these, in the Apollo is surely implied and found more grace than usual; in the Hercules more strength than usual; in the Mercury more lightness than usual; in the Venus more softness than usual. Is it not so? What then becomes of the pretended *middle form*? One would think it would be sufficient to prove this, to ask, 'Do not these statues differ from one another? And is this difference a defect?' It would be ridiculous to call them by different names, if they were not supposed to represent different and peculiar characters: sculptors should, in that case, never carve anything but the statue of a *man*, the statue of *a woman*, &c. and this would be the name of perfection. This theory of art is not at any rate justified by the history of art. An extraordinary quantity of bone and muscle is as proper to the Hercules as his club, and it would be strange if the Goddess of Love had not a more delicately rounded form, and a more languishing look withal, than the Goddess of Hunting. That a form combining and blending the properties of both, the downy softness of the one, with the elastic buoyancy of the other, would be more perfect than either, we no more see than that grey is the most perfect of colours. At any rate, this is the march neither of nature nor of art. It is not denied that these antique sculptures are models of the *ideal*; nay, it is on them that this theory boasts of being founded. Yet they give a flat contradiction to its insipid mediocrity. Perhaps some of them have a slight bias to the false *ideal*, to the smooth and uniform, or the negation of nature: any error on this side is, however, happily set right by the Elgin Marbles, which are the paragons of sculpture and the mould of form.—As the *ideal* then requires a difference of character in each figure as a whole, so it expects the same character (or a corresponding one) to be stamped on each part of every figure. As the legs of a Diana should be more muscular and adapted for running, than those of a Venus or a Minerva, so the skin of her face ought to be more tense, bent on her prey, and hardened by being exposed to the winds of heaven. The respective characters of lightness, softness, strength, &c. should pervade each part of the surface of each figure, but still varying according to the texture and functions of the individual part. This can only be learned or practised from the attentive observation of nature in those forms in which any given character or excellence is most strikingly displayed, and which has been selected for imitation and study on that account.—Suppose a dimple in the chin to be a mark of voluptuousness; then the Venus should have a dimple in the chin; and she has one. But this will imply certain corres-pondent indications in other parts of the features, about the corners of the mouth, a gentle undulation and sinking in of the cheek, as if it had just been pinched, and so on: yet so as to be consistent with the other qualities of roundness, smooth-ness, &c. which belong to the idea of the character. Who will get all this and embody it out of the idea of a *middle form*, I cannot say: it may be, and has been, got out of the idea of a number of distinct enchanting graces in the mind, and from some heavenly object unfolded to the sight!

4. *That the historical is nature in action. With regard to the face, it is expression.*

Hogarth's pictures are true history. Every feature, limb, figure, group, is instinct with life and motion. He does not take a subject and place it in a position, like a lay figure, in which it stirs neither limb nor joint. The scene moves before you: the face is like a frame-work of flexible machinery. If the mouth is distorted with laughter, the eyes swim in laughter. If the forehead is knit together, the cheeks are puckered up. If a fellow squints most horribly, the rest of his face is awry. The muscles pull different ways, or the same way, at the same time, on the surface of the picture, as they do in the human body. What you see is the reverse of *still life*. There is a continual and complete action and re-action of one variable part upon another, as there is in the Elgin Marbles. If you pull the string of a bow, the bow itself is bent. So is it in the strings and wires that move the human frame. The action of any one part, the contraction or relaxation of any one muscle, extends more or less perceptibly to every other:

'Thrills in each nerve, and lives along the line.'*

Thus the celebrated Iö of Correggio is imbued, steeped, in a manner in the same voluptuous feeling all over—the same passion languishes in her whole frame, and communicates the infection to the feet, the back, and the reclined position of the head. This is history, not carpenter's work. Some painters fancy that they paint history, if they get the measurement from the foot to the knee and put four bones where there are four bones. This is not our idea of it; but we think it is to show how one part of the body sways another in action and in passion. The last relates chiefly to the expression of the face, though not altogether. Passion may be shown in a clenched fist as well as in clenched teeth. The face, however, is the throne of expression. Character implies the feeling, which is fixed and permanent; expression that which is occasional and momentary, at least, technically speaking. Portrait treats of objects as they are; history of the events and changes to which they are liable. And so far history has a double superiority; or a double difficulty to overcome, *viz.* in the rapid glance over a number of parts subject to the simultaneous action of the same law, and in the scope of feeling required to sympathise with the critical and powerful movements of passion. It requires greater capacity of muscular motion to follow the progress of a carriage in violent motion, than to lean upon it standing still. If, to describe passion, it were merely necessary to observe its outward effects, these, perhaps, in the prominent points, become more visible and more tangible as the passion is more intense. But it is not only necessary to see the effects, but to discern the cause, in order to make the one true to the other. No painter gives more of intellectual or impassioned appearances than he understands or feels. It is an axiom in painting that sympathy is indispensible to truth of expression. Without it, you get only caricatures, which are not the thing. But to sympathise with passion, a greater fund of sensibility is demanded in proportion to the strength or tenderness of the passion. And as he feels most of this whose face expresses most passion, so he also feels most by sympathy whose hand can describe most passion. This amounts nearly, we take it, to a demonstration of an old and very disputed point.* The same reasoning might be applied to poetry, but this is not the place.—Again, it is easier to paint a portrait than an historical face, because the head *sits* for the first, but the expression will hardly *sit* for the last. Perhaps those passions are the best subjects for painting, the expression of which may be retained for some time, so as to be better caught, which throw out a sort of lambent fire, and leave a reflected glory behind them, as we see in Madonnas, Christ's heads, and what is understood by sacred subjects in general. The violences of human passion are too soon over to be copied by the hand, and the mere conception of the internal workings is not here sufficient, as it is in poetry. A portrait is to history what still-life is to portraiture: that is, the whole remains the same while you are doing it; or while you are occupied about each part, the rest wait for you. Yet, what a difference is there between taking an original portrait and making a copy of one! This shows that the face in its most ordinary state is continually varying and in action. So much of history is there in portrait!—No one should pronounce definitively on the superiority of history over portrait, without recollecting Titian's heads. The finest of them are very nearly (say quite) equal to the finest of Raphael's. They have almost the look of *still-life*, yet each part is decidedly influenced by the rest. Everything is *relative* in them. You cannot put any other eye, nose, lip in the same face. As in one part, so is the rest. You cannot fix on any particular beauty; the charm is in the whole. They have least action, and the most expression of any portraits. They are doing nothing, and yet all other business seems insipid in comparison of their thoughts. They are silent, retired, and do not court observation; yet you cannot keep your eyes from them. Some one said, that you would be as cautious of your behaviour in a room where a picture of Titian's was hung, as if there was somebody by—so entirely do they look you through. They are the least tiresome *furniture-company* in the world!

5. *Grandeur consists in connecting a number of parts into a whole, and not leaving out the parts.*

Sir Joshua lays it down that the great style in art consists in the omission of the details. A greater error never man committed. The great style consists in preserving the masses and general proportions; not in omitting the details. Thus, suppose, for illustration's sake, the general form of an eye-brow to be commanding and grand. It is of a certain size, and arched in a particular curve. Now, surely, this general form or outline will be equally preserved, whether the painter daubs it in, in a bold, rough way, as Reynolds or perhaps Rembrandt would, or produces the effect by a number of hair-lines arranged in the same form as Titian sometimes did; and in his best pictures. It will not be denied (for it cannot) that the characteristic form of the eye-brow would be the same, or that the effect of the picture at a small distance would be nearly the same in either case; only in the latter, it would be rather more perfect, as being more like nature. Suppose a strong light to fall on one side of a face, and a deep shadow to involve the whole of the other. This would produce two distinct and large masses in the picture; which answers to the conditions of what is called the grand style of composition. Well, would it destroy these masses to give the smallest veins or variation of colour or surface in the light side, or to shade the other with the most delicate and elaborate *chiaro-scuro*? It is evident not; from common sense, from the practice of the best masters, and, lastly, from the example of nature, which contains both the larger masses, the strongest contrasts, and the highest finishing, within itself. The integrity of the whole, then, is not impaired by the indefinite subdivision and smallness of the parts. The grandeur of the ultimate effects depends entirely on the arrangement of these in a certain form or under certain masses. The Ilissus, or River-god, is floating in his proper element, and is, in appearance, as firm as a rock, as pliable as a wave of the sea. The artist's breath might be said to mould and play upon the undulating surface. The whole is expanded into noble proportions, and heaves with general effect. What then? Are the parts unfinished; or are they not there? No; they are there with the nicest exactness, but in due subordination; that is, they are there as they are found in fine nature; and float upon the general form, like straw or weeds upon the tide of ocean. Once more: in Titian's portraits we perceive a certain character stamped upon the different features. In the Hippolito de Medici the eye-brows are angular, the nose is peaked, the mouth has sharp corners, the face is (so to speak) a pointed oval. The drawing in each of these is as careful and distinct as can be. But the unity of intention in nature, and in the artist, does not the less tend to produce a general grandeur and impressiveness of effect; which at first sight it is not easy to account for. To combine a number of particulars to one end is not to omit them altogether; and is the best way of producing the grand style, because it does this without either affectation or slovenliness.

6. The sixth rule we proposed to lay down was, that *as grandeur is the principle of connexion between different parts; beauty is the principle of affinity between different forms, or their gradual conversion into each other. The one harmonises, the other aggrandises, our impressions of things.*

There is a harmony of colours and a harmony of sounds, unquestionably: why then there should be all this squeamishness* about admitting an original harmony of forms as the principle of beauty and source of pleasure there we cannot understand. It is true, that there is in organised bodies a certain standard of form to which they approximate more or less, and from which they cannot very widely deviate without shocking the sense of custom, or our settled expectations of what they ought to be. And hence it has been pretended that there is in all such cases a *middle central form*, obtained by leaving out the peculiarities of all the others, which alone is the pure standard of truth and beauty. A conformity to custom is, we grant, one condition of beauty or source of satisfaction to the eye, because an abrupt transition shocks; but there is a conformity (or correspondence) of colours, sounds, lines, among themselves, which is soft and pleasing for the same reason. The average or customary form merely determines what is *natural.* A thing cannot please, unless it is to be found in nature; but that which is natural is most pleasing, according

as it has other properties which in themselves please. Thus
the colour of a cheek must be the natural complexion of a
human face;—it would not do to make it the colour of a flower
or a precious stone;—but among complexions ordinarily to
be found in nature, that is most beautiful which would be
thought so abstractedly, or in itself. Yellow hair is not the most
common, nor is it a *mean proportion* between the different
colours of women's hair. Yet, who will say that it is not the
most beautiful? Blue or green hair would be a defect and an
anomaly, not because it is not the *medium* of nature, but
because it is not in nature at all. To say that there is no
difference in the sense of form except from custom, is like
saying that there is no difference in the sensation of smooth
or rough. Judging by analogy, a gradation or symmetry of
form must affect the mind in the same manner as a gradation
of recurrence at given intervals of tones or sounds; and if it
does so in fact, we need not inquire further for the principle.
Sir Joshua (who is the arch-heretic on this subject) makes
grandeur or sublimity consist in the middle form, or abstraction of all peculiarities; which is evidently false, for grandeur
and sublimity arise from extraordinary strength, magnitude,
&c. or in a word, from an excess of power, so as to startle and
overawe the mind. But as sublimity is an excess of power,
beauty is, we conceive, the blending and harmonising different powers or qualities together, so as to produce a soft and
pleasurable sensation. That it is not the middle form of the
species seems proved in various ways. First, because one
species is more beautiful than another, according to common
sense. A rose is the queen of flowers, in poetry at least; but in
this philosophy any other flower is as good. A swan is more
beautiful than a goose; a stag than a goat. Yet if custom were
the test of beauty, either we should give no preference, or our
preference would be reversed. Again, let us go back to the
human face and figure. A straight nose is allowed to be handsome, that is, one that presents nearly a continuation of the
line of the forehead, and the sides of which are nearly parallel.
Now this cannot be the mean proportion of the form of noses.
For, first, most noses are broader at the bottom than at the
top, inclining to the negro head, but none are broader at top

than at the bottom, to produce the Greek form as a balance between both. Almost all noses sink in immediately under the forehead bone, none ever project there; so that the nearly straight line continued from the forehead cannot be a mean proportion struck between the two extremes of convex and concave form in this feature of the face. There must, therefore, be some other principle of symmetry, continuity, &c. to account for the variation from the prescribed rule. Once more (not to multiply instances tediously), a double calf is undoubtedly the perfection of beauty in the form of the leg. But this is a rare thing. Nor is it the medium between two common extremes. For the muscles seldom swell enough to produce this excrescence, if it may be so called, and never run to an excess there, so as, by diminishing the quantity, to subside into proportion and beauty. But this second or lower calf is a connecting link between the upper calf and the small of the leg, and is just like a second chord or half-note in music. We conceive that any one who does not perceive the beauty of the Venus de Medicis, for instance, in this respect, has not the proper perception of form in his mind. As this is the most disputable, or at least the most disputed part of our theory, we may, perhaps, have to recur to it again, and shall leave an opening for that purpose.

7. *That grace is the beautiful or harmonious in what relates to position or motion.*

There needs not much be said on this point; as we apprehend it will be granted that, whatever beauty is as to the form, grace is the same thing in relation to the use that is made of it. Grace, in writing, relates to the transitions that are made from one subject to another, or to the movement that is given to a passage. If one thing leads to another, or an idea or illustration is brought in without effect, or without making a *boggle* in the mind, we call this a graceful style. Transitions must in general be gradual and pieced together. But sometimes the most violent are the most graceful, when the mind is fairly tired out and exhausted with a subject, and is glad to leap to another as a repose and relief from the first. Of these there are frequent instances in Mr Burke's writings, which have something Pindaric in them. That which is not beautiful in itself, or in the mere form, may be made so by position or motion. A figure by no means elegant may be put in an elegant position. Mr Kean's figure is not good; yet we have seen him throw himself into attitudes of infinite spirit, dignity, and grace. John Kemble's figure, on the contrary, is fine in itself; and he has only to show himself to be admired. The direction in which anything is moved has evidently nothing to do with the shape of the thing moved. The one may be a circle and the other a square. Little and deformed people seem to be well aware of this distinction, who, in spite of their unpromising appearance, usually assume the most imposing attitudes, and give themselves the most extraordinary airs imaginable.

8. *Grandeur of motion is unity of motion.*

This principle hardly needs illustration. Awkwardness is contradictory or disjointed motion.

9. *Strength in art is giving the extremes, softness the uniting them.*

There is no incompatibility between strength and softness, as is sometimes supposed by frivolous people. Weakness is not refinement. A shadow may be twice as deep in a finely coloured picture as in another, and yet almost imperceptible, from the gradations that lead to it, and blend it with the light. Correggio had prodigious strength, and greater softness. Nature is strong and soft, beyond the reach of art to imitate. Softness then does not imply the absence of considerable extremes, but it is the interposing a third thing between them, to break the force of the contrast. Guido is more soft than strong. Rembrandt is more strong than soft.

10. And lastly. *That truth is, to a certain degree, beauty* and grandeur, since all things are connected, and all things modify one another in nature. Simplicity is also grand and beautiful for the same reason. Elegance is ease and lightness, with precision.*

This last head appears to contain a number of *gratis dicta*,* got together for the sake of completing a decade of propositions. They have, however, some show of truth, and we should add little clearness to them by any reasoning upon the matter. So we will conclude here for the present.

HOGARTH

WHAT distinguishes his compositions from all others of the same general kind, is, that they are equally remote from caricature, and from mere still life. It of course happens in subjects taken from common life, that the painter can procure real models, and he can get them to sit as long as he pleases. Hence, in general, those attitudes and expressions have been chosen which could be assumed the longest; and in imitating which, the artist by taking pains and time might produce almost as complete *fac-similes* as he could of a flower or a flower-pot, of a damask curtain or a china-vase. The copy was as perfect and as uninteresting in the one case as in the other. On the contrary, subjects of drollery and ridicule affording frequent examples of strange deformity and peculiarity of features, these have been eagerly seized by another class of artists, who, without subjecting themselves to the laborious drudgery of the Dutch school and their imitators, have produced our popular caricatures, by rudely copying or exaggerating the casual irregularities of the human countenance. Hogarth has equally avoided the faults of both these styles: the insipid tameness of the one, and the gross extravagance of the other, so as to give to the productions of his pencil equal solidity and effect. For his faces go to the very verge of caricature, and yet never (I believe in any single instance) go beyond it: they take the very widest latitude, and yet we always see the links which bind them to nature: they bear all the marks, and carry all the conviction of reality with them, as if we had seen the actual faces for the first time, from the precision, consistency, and good sense with which the whole and every part is made out. They exhibit the most uncommon features, with the most uncommon expressions: but which yet are as familiar and intelligible as possible, because with all the boldness, they have all the truth of nature. Hogarth has left behind him as many of these memorable faces, in their memorable moments, as, perhaps, most of us remember in the course of our lives, and has thus doubled the quantity of our experience.

It will assist us in forming a more determinate idea of the peculiar genius of Hogarth, to compare him with a deservedly admired artist in our own times. The highest authority on art in this country,* I understand, has pronounced that Mr Wilkie* united the excellences of Hogarth to those of Teniers.* I demur to this decision in both its branches; but in demurring to authority, it is necessary to give our reasons. I conceive that this ingenious and attentive observer of nature has certain essential, real, and indisputable excellences of his own; and I think it, therefore, the less important to clothe him with any vicarious merits which do not belong to him. Mr Wilkie's pictures, generally speaking, derive almost their whole value from their *reality*, or the truth of the represen-tation. They are works of pure imitative art; and the test of this style of composition is to represent nature faithfully and happily in its simplest combinations. It may be said of an artist like Mr Wilkie, that *nothing human is indifferent to him.* His mind takes an interest in, and it gives an interest to, the most familiar scenes and transactions of life. He professedly gives character, thought, and passion, in their lowest degrees, and in their every-day forms. He selects the commonest events and appearances of nature for his subjects; and trusts to their very commonness for the interest and amusement he is to excite. Mr Wilkie is a serious, prosaic, literal narrator of facts; and his pictures may be considered as diaries, or minutes of what is passing constantly about us. Hogarth, on the contrary, is essentially a comic painter; his pictures are not indifferent, unimpassioned descriptions of human nature, but rich, ex-uberant satires upon it. He is carried away by a passion for the *ridiculous*. His object is 'to shew vice her own feature, scorn her own image'.* He is so far from contenting himself with still-life, that he is always on the verge of caricature, though without ever falling into it. He does not represent folly or vice in its incipient, or dormant, or *grub* state; but full grown, with wings, pampered into all sorts of affectation, airy, ostentatious, and extravagant. Folly is there seen at the height—the moon is at the full; it is 'the very error of the time'.* There is a perpetual collision of eccentricities—a tilt and tournament of absurdities; the prejudices and caprices of mankind are let loose, and set together by the ears, as in a bear-garden. Hogarth paints nothing but comedy, or tragi-comedy. Wilkie paints neither one nor the other. Hogarth never looks at any object but to find out a moral or a ludicrous effect. Wilkie never looks at any object but to see that it is there. Hogarth's pictures are a perfect jest-book, from one end to the other. I do not remember a single joke in Wilkie's, except one very bad one of the boy in the Blind Fiddler, scraping the gridiron, or fire-shovel, I forget which it is. In looking at Hogarth, you are ready to burst your sides with laughing at the unaccountable jumble of odd things which are brought together; you look at Wilkie's pictures with a mingled feeling of curiosity, and admiration at the accuracy of the representation. For instance, there is a most admirable head of a man coughing in the Rent-day; the action, the keeping, the choaked sensation, are inimitable: but there is nothing to laugh at in a man coughing. What strikes the mind is the difficulty of a man's being painted coughing, which here certainly is a masterpiece of art. But turn to the blackguard Cobbler in the Election Dinner, who has been smutting his neighbour's face over, and who is lolling out his tongue at the joke, with a most surprising obliquity of vision; and immediately 'your lungs begin to crow like chanticleer'.* Again, there is the little boy crying in the Cut Finger, who only gives you the idea of a cross, disagreeable, obstinate child in pain: whereas the same face in Hogarth's Noon, from the ridiculous perplexity it is in, and its extravagant, noisy, unfelt distress, at the accident of having let fall the pye-dish, is quite irresistible. Mr Wilkie, in his picture of the Ale-house door, I believe, painted Mr Liston as one of the figures, without any great effect. Hogarth would have given any price for such a subject, and would have made it worth any money. I have never seen anything, in the expression of comic humour, equal to Hogarth's pictures, but Liston's face!

Mr Wilkie paints interiors: but still you generally connect them with the country. Hogarth, even when he paints people in the open air, represents them either as coming from

London, as in the polling for votes at Brentford, or as returning to it, as the dyer and his wife at Bagnigge Wells.* In this
last picture, he has contrived to convert a common rural
image into a type and emblem of city honours. In fact, I know
no one who had a less pastoral imagination than Hogarth. He
delights in the thick of St Giles's or St James's. His pictures
breathe a certain close, greasy, tavern air. The fare he serves
up to us consists of high-seasoned dishes, ragouts and olla
podridas, like the supper in *Gil Blas*,* which it requires a
strong stomach to digest. Mr Wilkie presents us with a sort of
lenten fare, very good and wholesome, but rather insipid than
overpowering! Mr Wilkie's pictures are, in general, much
better painted than Hogarth's; but the Marriage-a-la-Mode is
superior both in colour and execution to any of Wilkie's. . . .

I have promised to say something in this Lecture on the
difference between the grand and familiar style of painting;
and I shall throw out what imperfect hints I have been able
to collect on this subject, so often attempted, and never yet
succeeded in, taking the examples and illustrations from
Hogarth, that is, from what he possessed or wanted in each
kind.

And first, the difference is not that between imitation and
invention: for there is as much of this last quality in Hogarth,
as in any painter or poet whatever. As, for example, to take
two of his pictures only, I mean the Enraged Musician and
the Gin Lane;—in one of which every conceivable variety of
disagreeable and discordant sound—the razor-grinder turning his wheel; the boy with his drum, and the girl with her
rattle momentarily suspended; the pursuivant blowing his
horn; the shrill milkwoman; the inexorable ballad-singer, with
her squalling infant; the pewterer's shop close by; the fish-
women; the chimey-sweepers at the top of a chimney, and the
two cats in melodious concert on the ridge of the tiles; with
the bells ringing in the distance, as we see by the flags flying:—
and in the other, the complicated forms and signs of death
and ruinous decay—the woman on the stairs of the bridge
asleep, letting her child fall over; her ghastly companion
opposite, next to death's door, with hollow, famished cheeks
and staring ribs; the dog fighting with the man for the bare

shin-bone; the man hanging himself in a garret; the female corpse put into a coffin by the parish beadle; the men marching after a funeral, seen through a broken wall in the back ground; and the very houses reeling as if drunk and tumbling about the ears of the infatuated victims below, the pawn-broker's being the only one that stands firm and unimpaired—enforce the moral meant to be conveyed by each of these pieces with a richness and research of combination and artful contrast not easily paralleled in any production of the pencil or the pen. The clock pointing to four in the morning, in Modern Midnight Conversation, just as the immoveable Parson Ford* is filling out another glass from a brimming punch-bowl, while most of his companions, with the exception of the sly Lawyer, are falling around him 'like leaves in October';* and again, the extraordinary mistake of the man leaning against the post, in the Lord Mayor's Procession—shew a mind capable of seizing the most rare and transient coincidences of things, of imagining what either never happened at all, or of instantly fixing on and applying to its purpose what never happened but once. So far, the invention shewn in the great style of painting is poor in the comparison. Indeed, grandeur is supposed (whether rightly or not, I shall not here inquire) to imply a simplicity inconsistent with this inexhaustible variety of incident and circumstantial detail.

Secondly, the difference between the ideal and familiar style is not to be explained by the difference between the genteel and vulgar; for it is evident that Hogarth was almost as much at home in the genteel comedy, as in the broad farce of his pictures. He excelled not only in exhibiting the coarse humours and disgusting incidents of low life, but in exhibiting the vices, follies, and frivolity of the fashionable manners of his time: his fine ladies hardly yield the palm to his waiting-maids, and his lords and his footmen are on a respectable footing of equality. There is no want, for example, in the Marriage-a-la-Mode, or in Taste in High Life, of affectation verging into idiotism, or of languid sensibility, that might—

'Die of a rose in aromatic pain.'*

In short, Hogarth was a painter, not of low but of actual life; and the ridiculous and prominent features of high or low life, of the great vulgar or the small, lay equally open to him. The Country Girl, in the first plate of the Harlot's Progress, coming out of the waggon, is not more simple and ungainly, than the same figure, in the second, is thoroughly initiated into the mysteries of her art, and suddenly accomplished in all the airs and graces of affectation, ease, and impudence. The affected languor and imbecility of the same girl afterwards, when put to beat hemp in Bridewell, is exactly in keeping with the character she has been taught to assume. Sir Joshua could do nothing like it in his line of portrait, which differed chiefly in the back ground. The fine gentleman at his levee, in the Rake's Progress, is also a complete model of a person of rank and fortune, surrounded by needy and worthless adventurers, fiddlers, poetasters and virtuosi, as was the custom in those days. Lord Chesterfield himself* would not have been disgraced by sitting for it. I might multiply examples to shew that Hogarth was not characteristically deficient in that kind of elegance which arises from an habitual attention to external appearance and deportment. I will only add as instances, among his women, the two *elégantes* in the Bedlam scene, which are dressed (allowing for the difference of not quite a century) in the manner of Ackerman's dresses for May;* and among the men, the Lawyer in Modern Midnight Conversation, whose gracious significant leer and sleek lubricated countenance exhibit all the happy finesse of his profession, when a silk gown has been added, or is likely to be added to it; and several figures in the Cockpit, who are evidently, at the first glance, gentlemen of the old school, and where the mixture of the blacklegs with the higher character is a still further test of the discriminating skill of the painter.

Again, Hogarth had not only a perception of fashion, but a sense of natural beauty. There are as many pleasing faces in his pictures as in Sir Joshua. Witness the girl picking the Rake's pocket in the Bagnio scene, whom we might suppose to be 'the Charming Betsy Careless';* the Poet's wife, handsomer than falls to the lot of most poets, who are generally more intent upon the idea in their own minds than on the image before them, and are glad to take up with Dulcineas of their own creating; the theatrical heroine in the Southwark Fair, who would be an accession to either of our play-houses; the girl asleep, ogled by the clerk in church time, and the sweetheart of the Good Apprentice in the reading desk in the second of that series, almost an ideal face and expression; the girl in her cap selected for a partner by the footman in the print of Morning, very handsome; and many others equally so, scattered like 'stray-gifts of love and beauty'* through these pictures. Hogarth was not then exclusively the painter of deformity. He painted beauty or ugliness indifferently, as they came in his way; and was not by nature confined to those faces which are painful and disgusting, as many would have us believe.

Again, neither are we to look for the solution of the difficulty in the difference between the comic and the tragic, between loose laughter and deep passion. For Mr Lamb has shewn* unanswerably that Hogarth is quite at home in scenes of the deepest distress, in the heart-rending calamities of common life, in the expression of ungovernable rage, silent despair, or moody madness, enhanced by the tenderest sympathy, or aggravated by the frightful contrast of the most impenetrable and obdurate insensibility, as we see strikingly exemplified in the latter prints of the Rake's Progress. To the unbeliever in Hogarth's power over the passions and the feelings of the heart, the characters there speak like 'the hand-writing on the wall'.* If Mr Lamb has gone too far in paralleling some of these appalling representations with Shakespeare, he was excusable in being led to set off what may be considered as a staggering paradox against a rooted prejudice. At any rate, the inferiority of Hogarth (be it what it may) did not arise from a want of passion and intense feeling; and in this respect he had the advantage over Fielding, for instance, and others of our comic writers, who excelled only in the light and ludicrous. There is in general a distinction, almost an impassable one, between the power of embodying the serious and the ludicrous; but these contradictory faculties were reconciled in Hogarth, as they were in

Shakespeare, in Chaucer; and as it is said that they were in another extraordinary and later instance, Garrick's acting.*

None of these then will do: neither will the most masterly and entire keeping of character lead us to an explanation of the grand and ideal style; for Hogarth possessed the most complete and absolute mastery over the truth and identity of expression and features in his subjects. Every stroke of his pencil tells according to a preconception in his mind. If the eye squints, the mouth is distorted; every feature acts, and is acted upon by the rest of the face; even the dress and attitude are such as could be proper to no other figure: the whole is under the influence of one impulse, that of truth and nature. Look at the heads in the Cockpit, already mentioned, one of the most masterly of his productions in this way, where the workings of the mind are seen in every muscle of the face; and the same expression, more intense or relaxed, of hope or of fear, is stamped on each of the characters, so that you could no more transpose any part of one countenance to another, than you could change a profile to a front face. Hogarth was, in one sense, strictly an historical painter: that is, he represented the manners and humours of mankind in action, and their characters by varied expression. Every thing in his pictures has life and motion in it. Not only does the business of the scene never stand still, but every feature is put into full play; the exact feeling of the moment is brought out, and carried to its utmost height, and then instantly seized and stamped on the canvass for ever. The expression is always taken *en passant*, in a state of progress or change, and, as it were, at the salient point. Besides the excellence of each individual face, the reflection of the expression from face to face, the contrast and struggle of particular motives and feelings in the different actors in the scene, as of anger, contempt, laughter, compassion, are conveyed in the happiest and most lively manner. His figures are not like the back-ground on which they are painted: even the pictures on the wall have a peculiar look of their own. All this is effected by a few decisive and rapid touches of the pencil, careless in appearance, but infallible in their results; so that one great criterion of the grand style insisted on by Sir Joshua Reynolds,* that of leaving

out the details, and attending to general character and outline, belonged to Hogarth. He did not indeed arrive at middle
forms or neutral expression, which Sir Joshua makes another
test of the ideal; for Hogarth was not insipid. That was the last
fault with which he could be charged. But he had breadth
and boldness of manner, as well as any of them; so that neither
does that constitute the *ideal*.

What then does? We have reduced this to something like
the last remaining quantity in an equation, where all the
others have been ascertained. Hogarth had all the other parts
of an original and accomplished genius except this, but this
he had not. He had an intense feeling and command over
the impressions of sense, of habit, of character, and passion,
the serious and the comic, in a word, of nature, as it fell within
his own observation, or came within the sphere of his actual
experience; but he had little power beyond that sphere, or
sympathy with that which existed only *in idea*. He was 'conformed to this world, not transformed'.* If he attempted to
paint Pharaoh's daughter, and Paul before Felix, he lost himself. His mind had feet and hands, but not wings to fly with.
There is a mighty world of sense, of custom, of every-day
action, of accidents and objects coming home to us, and
interesting because they do so; the gross, material, stirring,
noisy world of common life and selfish passion, of which
Hogarth was absolute lord and master: there is another
mightier world, that which exists only in conception and in
power, the universe of thought and sentiment, that surrounds
and is raised above the ordinary world of reality, as the em-
pyrean surrounds this nether globe, into which few are privileged to soar with mighty wings outspread, and in which, as
power is given them to embody their aspiring fancies, to 'give
to airy nothing a local habitation and a name',* to fill with
imaginary shapes of beauty or sublimity, and make the dark
abyss pregnant, bringing that which is remote home to us,
raising themselves to the lofty, sustaining themselves on the
refined and abstracted, making all things like not what we
know and feel in ourselves, in this 'ignorant present'* time,
but like what they must be in themselves, or in our noblest
idea of them, and stamping that idea with reality, (but chiefly

clothing the best and the highest with grace and grandeur): this is the ideal in art, in poetry, and in painting. There are things which are cognisable only to sense, which interest only our more immediate instincts and passions; the want of food, the loss of a limb, or a sum of money: there are others that appeal to different and nobler faculties; the wants of the mind, the hunger and thirst after truth and beauty; that is, to faculties commensurate with objects greater and of greater refinement, which to be grand must extend beyond ourselves to others, and our interests in which must be refined in proportion as they do so.* The interest in these subjects is in proportion to the power of conceiving them and the power of conceiving them is in proportion to the interest and affection for them, to the innate bias of the mind to elevate itself above every thing low, and purify itself from every thing gross. Hogarth only transcribes or transposes what was tangible and visible, not the abstracted and intelligible. You see in his pictures only the faces which you yourself have seen, or others like them; none of his characters are thinking of any person or thing out of the picture: you are only interested in the objects of their contention or pursuit, because they themselves are interested in them. There is nothing remote in thought, or comprehensive in feeling. The whole is intensely personal and local: but the interest of the ideal and poetical style of art, relates to more permanent and universal objects; and the characters and forms must be such as to correspond with and sustain that interest, and give external grace and dignity to it. Such were the subjects which Raphael chose; faces imbued with unalterable sentiment, and figures, that stand in the eternal silence of thought. He places before you objects of everlasting interest, events of greatest magnitude, and persons in them fit for the scene and action—warriors and kings, princes and nobles, and, greater yet, poets and philosophers; and mightier than these, patriarchs and apostles, prophets and founders of religion, saints and martyrs, angels and the Son of God. We know their importance and their high calling, and we feel that they do not belie it. We see them as they were painted, with the eye of faith. The light which they have kindled in the world, is reflected back upon their faces: the awe and homage which has been paid to them, is seated upon their brow, and encircles them like a glory. All those who come before them, are conscious of a superior presence. For example, the beggars, in the Gate Beautiful, are impressed with this ideal borrowed character. Would not the cripple and the halt feel a difference of sensation, and express it outwardly in such circumstances? And was the painter wrong to transfer this sense of preternatural power and the confidence of a saving faith to his canvass? Hogarth's Pool of Bethesda, on the contrary, is only a collection of common beggars receiving an alms. The waters may be stirred, but the mind is not stirred with them. The fowls, again, in the Miraculous Draught of Fishes,* exult and clap their wings, and seem lifted up with some unusual cause of joy. There is not the same expansive, elevated principle in Hogarth. He has amiable and praise-worthy characters, indeed, among his bad ones. The Master of the Industrious and Idle Apprentice is a good citizen and a virtuous man; but his benevolence is mechanical and confined: it extends only to his shop, or, at most, to his ward. His face is not ruffled by passion, nor is it inspired by thought. To give another instance, the face of the faithful Female, fainting in the prison-scene in the Rake's Progress, is more one of effeminate softness than of distinguished tenderness, or heroic constancy. But in the pictures of the Mother and Child, by Raphael and Leonard da Vinci, we see all the tenderness purified from all the weakness of maternal affection, and exalted by the prospects of religious faith; so that the piety and devotion of future generations seems to add its weight to the expression of feminine sweetness and parental love, to press upon the heart, and breathe in the countenance. This is the *ideal*, passion blended with thought and pointing to distant objects, not debased by grossness, not thwarted by accident, nor weakened by familiarity, but connected with forms and circumstances that give the utmost possible expansion and refinement to the general sentiment. With all my admiration of Hogarth, I cannot think him equal to Raphael. I do not know whether, if the port-folio were opened, I would not as soon look over the prints of Hogarth as those of

Raphael; but, assuredly, if the question were put to me, I would sooner never have seen the prints of Hogarth than never have seen those of Raphael. It is many years ago since I first saw the prints of the Cartoons hanging round the old-fashioned parlour of a little inn in a remote part of the country. I was then young: I had heard of the fame of the Cartoons, but this was the first time I had ever been admitted face to face into the presence of those divine guests. 'How was I then uplifted!'* Prophets and Apostles stood before me as in a dream, and the Saviour of the Christian world, with his attributes of faith and power; miracles were working on the walls; the hand of Raphael was there; and as his pencil traced the lines, I saw godlike spirits and lofty shapes descend and walk visibly the earth, but as if their thoughts still lifted them above the earth. There I saw the figure of St Paul, pointing with noble fervour to 'temples not made with hands, eternal in the heavens';* and that finer one of Christ in the boat, whose whole figure seems sustained by meekness and love; and that of the same person surrounded by his disciples, like a flock of sheep listening to the music of some divine shepherd. I knew not how enough to admire them.—Later in life, I saw other works of this great painter (with more like them) collected in the Louvre: where Art, at that time, lifted up her head, and was seated on her throne, and said, 'All eyes shall see me, and all knees shall bow to me!'* Honour was done to her and all hers. There was her treasure, and there the inventory of all she had. There she had gathered together her pomp, and there was her shrine, and there her votaries came and worshipped as in a temple. The crown she wore was brighter than that of kings. Where the struggles for human liberty had been, there were the triumphs of human genius.

ON POETRY IN GENERAL

THE best general notion which I can give of poetry is, that it is the natural impression of any object or event, by its vivid-ness exciting an involuntary movement of imagination and passion, and producing, by sympathy, a certain modulation of the voice, or sounds, expressing it.

In treating of poetry, I shall speak first of the subject-matter of it, next of the forms of expression to which it gives birth, and afterwards of its connection with harmony of sound.

Poetry is the language of the imagination and the passions. It relates to whatever gives immediate pleasure or pain to the human mind. It comes home to the bosoms and businesses of men;* for nothing but what so comes home to them in the most general and intelligible shape, can be a subject for poetry. Poetry is the universal language which the heart holds with nature and itself. He who has a contempt for poetry, cannot have much respect for himself, or for any thing else. It is not a mere frivolous accomplishment, (as some persons have been led to imagine) the trifling amusement of a few idle readers or leisure hours—it has been the study and delight of mankind in all ages. Many people suppose that poetry is something to be found only in books, contained in lines of ten syllables, with like endings: but wherever there is a sense of beauty, or power, or harmony, as in the motion of a wave of the sea, in the growth of a flower that 'spreads its sweet leaves to the air, and dedicates its beauty to the sun',*— *there* is poetry, in its birth. If history is a grave study, poetry may be said to be a graver: its materials lie deeper, and are spread wider. History treats, for the most part, of the cumbrous and unwieldly masses of things, the empty cases in which the affairs of the world are packed, under the heads of intrigue or war, in different states, and from century to century: but there is no thought or feeling that can have entered into the mind of man, which he would be eager to communicate to others, or which they would listen to with delight, that is not a fit subject for poetry. It is not a branch of authorship: it is 'the stuff of which our life is made.'* The rest is 'mere oblivion',* a dead letter: for all that is worth remembering in life, is the poetry of it. Fear is poetry, hope is poetry, love is poetry, hatred is poetry; contempt, jealousy, remorse, admiration, wonder, pity, despair, or madness, are all poetry. Poetry is that fine particle within us, that expands, rarefies, refines, raises our whole being: without it 'man's life is poor as beast's.'* Man is a poetical animal: and those of us who do not study the principles of poetry, act upon them all our lives, like Molière's *Bourgeois Gentilhomme,** who had always spoken prose without knowing it. The child is a poet in fact, when he first plays at hide-and-seek, or repeats the story of Jack the Giant-killer; the shepherd-boy is a poet, when he first crowns his mistress with a garland of flowers; the countryman, when he stops to look at the rainbow; the city- apprentice, when he gazes after the Lord-Mayor's show; the miser, when he hugs his gold; the courtier, who builds his hopes upon a smile; the savage, who paints his idol with blood; the slave, who worships a tyrant, or the tyrant, who fancies himself a god;—the vain, the ambitious, the proud, the choleric man, the hero and the coward, the beggar and the king, the rich and the poor, the young and the old, all live in a world of their own making; and the poet does no more than describe what all the others think and act. If his art is folly and madness, it is folly and madness at second hand. 'There is warrant for it.'* Poets alone have not 'such seething brains, such shaping fantasies, that apprehend more than cooler reason' can.

> 'The lunatic, the lover, and the poet
> Are of imagination all compact.
> One sees more devils than vast hell can hold;
> The madman. While the lover, all as frantic,
> Sees Helen's beauty in a brow of Egypt.
> The poet's eye in a fine frenzy rolling,
> Doth glance from heav'n to earth, from earth to heav'n;
> And as imagination bodies forth
> The forms of things unknown, the poet's pen
> Turns them to shape, and gives to airy nothing
> A local habitation and a name.
> Such tricks hath strong imagination.'*

If poetry is a dream, the business of life is much the same. If it is a fiction, made up of what we wish things to be, and fancy that they are, because we wish them so, there is no other nor better reality. Ariosto has described the loves of Angelica and Medoro:* but was not Medoro, who carved the name of his mistress on the barks of trees, as much enamoured of her charms as he? Homer has celebrated the anger of Achilles:

but was not the hero as mad as the poet? Plato banished the poets* from his Commonwealth, lest their descriptions of the natural man should spoil his mathematical man, who was to be without passions and affections, who was neither to laugh nor weep, to feel sorrow nor anger, to be cast down nor elated by any thing. This was a chimera, however, which never existed but in the brain of the inventor; and Homer's poetical world has outlived Plato's philosophical Republic.

Poetry then is an imitation of nature, but the imagination and the passions are a part of man's nature. We shape things according to our wishes and fancies, without poetry; but poetry is the most emphatical language that can be found for those creations of the mind 'which ecstacy is very cunning in'.* Neither a mere description of natural objects, nor a mere delineation of natural feelings, however distinct or forcible, constitutes the ultimate end and aim of poetry, without the heightenings of the imagination. The light of poetry is not only a direct but also a reflected light, that while it shews us the object, throws a sparkling radiance on all around it: the flame of the passions, communicated to the imagination, reveals to us, as with a flash of lightning, the inmost recesses of thought, and penetrates our whole being. Poetry represents forms chiefly as they suggest other forms; feelings, as they suggest forms or other feelings. Poetry puts a spirit of life and motion into the universe. It describes the flowing, not the fixed. It does not define the limits of sense, or analyse the distinctions of the understanding, but signifies the excess of the imagination beyond the actual or ordinary impression of any object or feeling. The poetical impression of any object is that uneasy, exquisite sense of beauty or power that cannot be contained within itself; that is impatient of all limit; that (as flame bends to flame) strives to link itself to some other image of kindred beauty or grandeur; to enshrine itself, as it were, in the highest forms of fancy, and to relieve the aching sense of pleasure by expressing it in the boldest manner,* and by the most striking examples of the same quality in other instances. Poetry, according to Lord Bacon,* for this reason, 'has something divine in it, because it raises the mind and hurries it into sublimity, by conforming the shows of things to the desires of the soul, instead of subjecting the soul to external things, as reason and history do.' It is strictly the language of the imagination; and the imagination is that faculty which represents objects, not as they are in themselves, but as they are moulded by other thoughts and feelings, into an infinite variety of shapes and combinations of power. This language is not the less true to nature, because it is false in point of fact; but so much the more true and natural, if it conveys the impression which the object under the influence of passion makes on the mind. Let an object, for instance, be presented to the senses in a state of agitation or fear—and the imagination will distort or magnify the object, and convert it into the likeness of whatever is most proper to encourage the fear. 'Our eyes are made the fools'* of our other faculties. This is the universal law of the imagination,

> 'That if it would but apprehend some joy,
> It comprehends some bringer of that joy:
> Or in the night imagining some fear,
> How easy is each bush suppos'd a bear!'*

When Iachimo says of Imogen,

> '——The flame o' th' taper
> Bows toward her, and would under-peep her lids
> To see the enclosed lights'—*

this passionate interpretation of the motion of the flame to accord with the speaker's own feelings, is true poetry. The lover, equally with the poet, speaks of the auburn tresses of his mistress as locks of shining gold, because the least tinge of yellow in the hair has, from novelty and a sense of personal beauty, a more lustrous effect to the imagination than the purest gold. We compare a man of gigantic stature to a tower: not that he is any thing like so large, but because the excess of his size beyond what we are accustomed to expect, or the usual size of things of the same class, produces by contrast a greater feeling of magnitude and ponderous strength than another object of ten times the same dimensions. The intensity of the feeling makes up for the disproportion of the objects. Things are equal to the imagination, which have the power of affecting the mind with an equal degree of terror, admiration, delight, or love. When Lear calls upon the heavens to avenge his cause, 'for they are old like him,'* there is nothing extravagant or impious in this sublime identification of his age with theirs; for there is no other image which could do justice to the agonising sense of his wrongs and his despair!

Poetry is the high-wrought enthusiasm of fancy and feeling. As describing natural objects, it impregnates sensible impressions with the forms of fancy, so it describes the feelings of pleasure or pain, by blending them with the strongest movements of passion, and the most striking forms of nature. Tragic poetry, which is the most impassioned species of it, strives to carry on the feeling to the utmost point of sublimity or pathos, by all the force of comparison or contrast; loses the sense of present suffering in the imaginary exaggeration of it; exhausts the terror or pity by an unlimited indulgence of it; grapples with impossibilities in its desperate impatience of restraint; throws us back upon the past, forward into the future; brings every moment of our being or object of nature in startling review before us; and in the rapid whirl of events, lifts us from the depths of woe to the highest contemplations on human life. When Lear says of Edgar, 'Nothing but his unkind daughters could have brought him to this;'* what a bewildered amazement, what a wrench of the imagination, that cannot be brought to conceive of any other cause of misery than that which has bowed it down, and absorbs all other sorrow in its own! His sorrow, like a flood, supplies the sources of all other sorrow. Again, when he exclaims in the mad scene, 'The little dogs and all, Tray, Blanche, and Sweetheart, see, they bark at me!'* it is passion lending occasion to imagination to make every creature in league against him, conjuring up ingratitude and insult in their least looked-for and most galling shapes, searching every thread and fibre of his heart, and finding out the last remaining image of respect or attachment in the bottom of his breast, only to torture and kill it! In like manner, the 'So I am'* of Cordelia gushes from her heart like a torrent of tears, relieving it of a weight of love and of supposed ingratitude, which had pressed upon it for years. What a fine return of the passion upon itself is that in Othello—with what a mingled agony of regret and despair he clings to the last traces of departed happiness—when he exclaims,

> ——'Oh now, for ever
> Farewel the tranquil mind. Farewel content;
> Farewel the plumed troops and the big war,
> That make ambition virtue! Oh farewel!
> Farewel the neighing steed, and the shrill trump,
> The spirit-stirring drum, th' ear-piercing fife,
> The royal banner, and all quality,
> Pride, pomp, and circumstance of glorious war:
> And O you mortal engines, whose rude throats
> Th'immortal Jove's dread clamours counterfeit,
> Farewel! Othello's occupation's gone!'*

How his passion lashes itself up and swells and rages like a tide in its sounding course, when in answer to the doubts expressed of his returning love, he says,

> 'Never, Iago. Like to the Pontic sea,
> Whose icy current and compulsive course
> Ne'er feels retiring ebb, but keeps due on
> To the Propontic and the Hellespont:
> Even so my bloody thoughts, with violent pace,
> Shall ne'er look back, ne'er ebb to humble love,
> Till that a capable and wide revenge
> Swallow them up.'—

The climax of his expostulation afterwards with Desdemona is at that line,

> 'But there where I had garner'd up my heart,
> To be discarded thence!'—*

One mode in which the dramatic exhibition of passion excites our sympathy without raising our disgust is, that in proportion as it sharpens the edge of calamity and disappointment, it strengthens the desire of good. It enhances our consciousness of the blessing, by making us sensible of the magnitude of the loss. The storm of passion lays bare and shews us the rich depths of the human soul: the whole of our existence, the sum total of our passions and pursuits, of that which we desire and that which we dread, is brought before us by contrast; the action and re-action are equal; the keenness of immediate suffering only gives us a more intense aspiration after, and a more intimate participation with the antagonist world of good; makes us drink deeper of the cup of human life; tugs at the heartstrings; loosens the pressure about them; and calls the springs of thought and feeling into play with tenfold force.

Impassioned poetry is an emanation of the moral and intellectual part of our nature, as well as of the sensitive—of the desire to know, the will to act, and the power to feel; and ought to appeal to these different parts of our constitution, in order to be perfect. The domestic or prose tragedy, which is thought to be the most natural, is in this sense the least so, because it appeals almost exclusively to one of these faculties, our sensibility. The tragedies of Moore and Lillo,* for this reason, however affecting at the time, oppress and lie like a dead weight upon the mind, a load of misery which it is unable to throw off: the tragedy of Shakespeare, which is true poetry, stirs our inmost affections; abstracts evil from itself by combining it with all the forms of imagination, and with the deepest workings of the heart, and rouses the whole man within us.

The pleasure, however, derived from tragic poetry, is not any thing peculiar to it as poetry, as a fictitious and fanciful thing. It is not an anomaly of the imagination. It has its source and ground-work in the common love of strong excitement. As Mr Burke observes,* people flock to see a tragedy; but if there were a public execution in the next street, the theatre would very soon be empty. It is not then the difference between fiction and reality that solves the difficulty. Children are satisfied with the stories of ghosts and witches in plain prose: nor do the hawkers of full, true, and particular accounts of murders and executions about the streets, find it necessary to have them turned into penny ballads, before they can dispose of these interesting and authentic documents. The grave politician drives a thriving trade of abuse and calumnies poured out against those whom he makes his enemies for no other end than that he may live by them. The popular preacher makes less frequent mention of heaven than of hell. Oaths and nicknames are only a more vulgar sort of poetry or rhetoric. We are as fond of indulging our violent passions as of reading a description of those of others. We are as prone to make a torment of our fears, as to luxuriate in our hopes of good. If it be asked, Why we do so? the best answer will be, Because we cannot help it. The sense of power is as strong a principle in the mind as the love of pleasure. Objects of terror and pity exercise the same despotic control over it as those of love or beauty. It is as natural to hate as to love, to despise as to admire, to express our hatred or contempt, as our love or admiration.

> 'Masterless passion sways us to the mood
> Of what it likes or loathes.'*

Not that we like what we loathe; but we like to indulge our hatred and scorn of it; to dwell upon it, to exasperate our idea of it by every refinement of ingenuity and extravagance of illustration; to make it a bugbear to ourselves, to point it out to others in all the splendour of deformity, to embody it to the senses, to stigmatise it by name, to grapple with it in thought, in action, to sharpen our intellect, to arm our will against it, to know the worst we have to contend with, and to contend with it to the utmost. Poetry is only the highest eloquence of passion, the most vivid form of expression that can be given to our conception of any thing, whether pleasurable or painful, mean or dignified, delightful or distressing. It is the perfect coincidence of the image and the words with the feeling we have, and of which we cannot get rid in any other way, that gives an instant 'satisfaction to the thought'.* This is equally the origin of wit and fancy, of comedy and tragedy, of the sublime and pathetic. When Pope says of the Lord Mayor's shew,—

> 'Now night descending, the proud scene is o'er,
> But lives in Settle's numbers one day more!'*

—when Collins makes Danger, 'with limbs of giant mould,'

——'Throw him on the steep
Of some loose hanging rock asleep:'*

when Lear calls out in extreme anguish,

'Ingratitude, thou marble-hearted fiend,
How much more hideous shew'st in a child
Than the sea-monster!'*

—the passion of contempt in the one case, of terror in the
other, and of indignation in the last, is perfectly satisfied. We
see the thing ourselves, and shew it to others as we feel it to
exist, and as, in spite of ourselves, we are compelled to think
of it. The imagination, by thus embodying and turning them
to shape, gives an obvious relief to the indistinct and importunate cravings of the will.—We do not wish the thing to be
so; but we wish it to appear such as it is. For knowledge is
conscious power; and the mind is no longer, in this case, the
dupe, though it may be the victim of vice or folly.

Poetry is in all its shapes the language of the imagination
and the passions, of fancy and will. Nothing, therefore, can
be more absurd than the outcry which has been sometimes
raised by frigid and pedantic critics, for reducing the language
of poetry to the standard of common sense and reason: for
the end and use of poetry, 'both at the first and now, was and
is to hold the mirror up to nature',* seen through the medium
of passion and imagination, not divested of that medium by
means of literal truth or abstract reason. The painter of history might as well be required to represent the face of a
person who has just trod upon a serpent with the still-life
expression of a common portrait, as the poet to describe the
most striking and vivid impressions which things can be supposed to make upon the mind, in the language of common
conversation. Let who will strip nature of the colours and the
shapes of fancy, the poet is not bound to do so; the impressions of common sense and strong imagination, that is, of
passion and indifference, cannot be the same, and they must
have a separate language to do justice to either. Objects must
strike differently upon the mind, independently of what they
are in themselves, as long as we have a different interest in
them, as we see them in a different point of view, nearer or

at a greater distance (morally or physically speaking) from novelty, from old acquaintance, from our ignorance of them, from our fear of their consequences, from contrast, from unexpected likeness. We can no more take away the faculty of the imagination, than we can see all objects without light or shade. Some things must dazzle us by their preternatural light; others must hold us in suspense, and tempt our curiosity to explore their obscurity. Those who would dispel these various illusions, to give us their drab-coloured creation in their stead, are not very wise. Let the naturalist, if he will, catch the glow-worm, carry it home with him in a box, and find it next morning nothing but a little grey worm; let the poet or the lover of poetry visit it at evening, when beneath the scented hawthorn and the crescent moon it has built itself a palace of emerald light. This is also one part of nature, one appearance which the glow-worm presents, and that not the least interesting; so poetry is one part of the history of the human mind, though it is neither science nor philosophy. It cannot be concealed, however, that the progress of knowledge and refinement has a tendency to circumscribe the limits of the imagination, and to clip the wings of poetry. The province of the imagination is principally visionary, the unknown and undefined: the understanding restores things to their natural boundaries, and strips them of their fanciful pretensions. Hence the history of religious and poetical enthusiasm is much the same; and both have received a sensible shock from the progress of experimental philosophy. It is the undefined and uncommon that gives birth and scope to the imagination; we can only fancy what we do not know. As in looking into the mazes of a tangled wood we fill them with what shapes we please, with ravenous beasts, with caverns vast, and drear enchantments, so in our ignorance of the world about us, we make gods or devils of the first object we see, and set no bounds to the wilful suggestions of our hopes and fears.

> 'And visions, as poetic eyes avow,
> Hang on each leaf and cling to every bough.'*

There can never be another Jacob's dream. Since that time, the heavens have gone farther off, and grown astronomical.

They have become averse to the imagination, nor will they return to us on the squares of the distances, or on Doctor Chalmers's Discourses.* Rembrandt's picture* brings the matter nearer to us.—It is not only the progress of mechanical knowledge, but the necessary advances of civilization that are unfavourable to the spirit of poetry. We not only stand in less awe of the preternatural world, but we can calculate more surely, and look with more indifference, upon the regular routine of this. The heroes of the fabulous ages rid the world of monsters and giants. At present we are less exposed to the vicissitudes of good or evil, to the incursions of wild beasts or 'bandit fierce',* or to the unmitigated fury of the elements. The time has been that 'our fell of hair would at a dismal treatise rouse and stir as life were in it.'* But the police spoils all; and we now hardly so much as dream of a midnight murder. Macbeth is only tolerated in this country for the sake of the music; and in the United States of America, where the philosophical principles of government are carried still farther in theory and practice, we find that the *Beggar's Opera* is hooted from the stage. Society, by degrees, is constructed into a machine that carries us safely and insipidly from one end of life to the other, in a very comfortable prose style.

> 'Obscurity her curtain round them drew,
> And siren Sloth a dull quietus sung.'*

The remarks which have been here made, would, in some measure, lead to a solution of the question of the comparative merits of painting and poetry. I do not mean to give any preference, but it should seem that the argument which has been sometimes set up, that painting must affect the imagination more strongly, because it represents the image more distinctly, is not well founded. We may assume without much temerity, that poetry is more poetical than painting. When artists or connoisseurs talk on stilts about the poetry of painting, they shew that they know little about poetry, and have little love for the art. Painting gives the object itself; poetry what it implies. Painting embodies what a thing contains in itself: poetry suggests what exists out of it, in any manner connected with it. But this last is the proper province of the imagination. Again, as it relates to passion, painting gives the event, poetry the progress of events: but it is during the progress, in the interval of expectation and suspense, while our hopes and fears are strained to the highest pitch of breathless agony, that the pinch of the interest lies.

> 'Between the acting of a dreadful thing
> And the first motion, all the interim is
> Like a phantasma or a hideous dream.
> The mortal instruments are then in council;
> And the state of man, like to a little kingdom,
> Suffers then the nature of an insurrection.'*

But by the time that the picture is painted, all is over. Faces are the best part of a picture; but even faces are not what we chiefly remember in what interests us most.—But it may be asked then, Is there anything better than Claude Lorraine's landscapes, than Titian's portraits, than Raphael's cartoons, or the Greek statues? Of the two first I shall say nothing, as they are evidently picturesque, rather than imaginative. Raphael's cartoons are certainly the finest comments that ever were made on the Scriptures. Would their effect be the same, if we were not acquainted with the text? But the New Testament existed before the cartoons. There is one subject of which there is no cartoon, Christ washing the feet of the disciples the night before his death. But that chapter does not need a commentary! It is for want of some such resting place for the imagination that the Greek statues are little else than specious forms.* They are marble to the touch and to the heart. They have not an informing principle within them. In their faultless excellence they appear sufficient to themselves. By their beauty they are raised above the frailties of passion or suffering. By their beauty they are deified.* But they are not objects of religious faith to us, and their forms are a reproach to common humanity. They seem to have no sympathy with us, and not to want our admiration.

Poetry in its matter and form is natural imagery or feeling, combined with passion and fancy. In its mode of conveyance, it combines the ordinary use of language with musical expression. There is a question of long standing, in what the essence

of poetry consists; or what it is that determines why one set
of ideas should be expressed in prose, another in verse. Milton
has told us his idea of poetry in a single line—

> 'Thoughts that voluntary move
> Harmonious numbers.'*

As there are certain sounds that excite certain movements,
and the song and dance go together, so there are, no doubt,
certain thoughts that lead to certain tones of voice, or modulations of sound, and change 'the words of Mercury into the
songs of Apollo'.* There is a striking instance of this adaptation of the movement of sound and rhythm to the subject, in
Spenser's description of the Satyrs accompanying Una to the
cave of Sylvanus.

> 'So from the ground she fearless doth arise
>   And walketh forth without suspect of crime.
> They, all as glad as birds of joyous prime,
>   Thence lead her forth, about her dancing round,
> Shouting and singing all a shepherd's rhyme;
>   And with green branches strewing all the ground,
> Do worship her as queen with olive garland crown'd.
> And all the way their merry pipes they sound,
>   That all the woods and doubled echoes ring;
> And with their horned feet do wear the ground,
>   Leaping like wanton kids in pleasant spring;
> So towards old Sylvanus they her bring,
>   Who with the noise awaked, cometh out.'*

On the contrary, there is nothing either musical or natural in
the ordinary construction of language. It is a thing altogether
arbitrary and conventional. Neither in the sounds themselves,
which are the voluntary signs of certain ideas, nor in their
grammatical arrangements in common speech, is there any
principle of natural imitation, or correspondence to the individual ideas, or to the tone of feeling with which they are
conveyed to others. The jerks, the breaks, the inequalities,
and harshnesses of prose, are fatal to the flow of a poetical
imagination, as a jolting road or a stumbling horse disturbs
the reverie of an absent man. But poetry makes these odds
all even.* It is the music of language, answering to the music

of the mind, untying as it were 'the secret soul of harmony'.*
Wherever any object takes such a hold of the mind as to make
us dwell upon it, and brood over it, melting the heart in
tenderness, or kindling it to a sentiment of enthusiasm;—
wherever a movement of imagination or passion is impressed
on the mind, by which it seeks to prolong and repeat the
emotion, to bring all other objects into accord with it, and to
give the same movement of harmony, sustained and continuous, or gradually varied according to the occasion, to the
sounds that express it—this is poetry. The musical in sound
is the sustained and continuous; the musical in thought is the
sustained and continuous also. There is a near connection
between music and deep-rooted passion. Mad people sing. As
often as articulation passes naturally into intonation, there
poetry begins. Where one idea gives a tone and colour to
others, where one feeling melts others into it, there can be
no reason why the same principle should not be extended to
the sounds by which the voice utters these emotions of the
soul, and blends syllables and lines into each other. It is to
supply the inherent defect of harmony in the customary
mechanism of language, to make the sound an echo to the
sense, when the sense becomes a sort of echo to itself—to
mingle the tide of verse, 'the golden cadences of poetry',*
with the tide of feeling, flowing and murmuring as it flows—in
short, to take the language of the imagination from off the
ground, and enable it to spread its wings where it may indulge
its own impulses—

> 'Sailing with supreme dominion
> Through the azure deep of air—'*

without being stopped, or fretted, or diverted with the abrupt-
nesses and petty obstacles, and discordant flats and sharps of
prose, that poetry was invented. It is to common language,
what springs are to a carriage, or wings to feet. In ordinary
speech we arrive at a certain harmony by the modulations of
the voice: in poetry the same thing is done systematically by
a regular collocation of syllables. It has been well observed,
that every one who declaims warmly, or grows intent upon a
subject, rises into a sort of blank verse or measured prose. The

merchant, as described in Chaucer, went on his way 'sounding always the increase of his winning'.* Every prose-writer has more or less of rhythmical adaptation, except poets, who, when deprived of the regular mechanism of verse, seem to have no principle of modulation left in their writings.

SHAKESPEARE

THE four greatest names* in English poetry, are almost the four first we come to—Chaucer, Spenser, Shakespeare, and Milton. There are no others that can really be put in competition with these. The two last have had justice done them by the voice of common fame. Their names are blazoned in the very firmament of reputation; while the two first (though 'the fault has been more in their stars than in themselves that they are underlings')* either never emerged far above the horizon, or were too soon involved in the obscurity of time. The three first of these are excluded from Dr Johnson's *Lives of the Poets* (Shakespeare indeed is so from the dramatic form of his compositions): and the fourth, Milton, is admitted with a reluctant and churlish welcome.

In comparing these four writers together, it might be said that Chaucer excels as the poet of manners, or of real life; Spenser, as the poet of romance; Shakespeare as the poet of nature (in the largest use of the term); and Milton, as the poet of morality. Chaucer most frequently describes things as they are; Spenser, as we wish them to be; Shakespeare, as they would be; and Milton as they ought to be. As poets, and as great poets, imagination, that is, the power of feigning things according to nature, was common to them all: but the principle or moving power, to which this faculty was most subservient in Chaucer, was habit, or inveterate prejudice; in Spenser, novelty, and the love of the marvellous; in Shakespeare, it was the force of passion, combined with every variety of possible circumstances; and in Milton, only with the highest. The characteristic of Chaucer is intensity; of Spenser, remoteness; of Milton, elevation; of Shakespeare, every thing.—It has been said by some critic, that Shakespeare was distinguished from the other dramatic writers of his day only by his wit; that they had all his other qualities but that; that one writer had as much sense, another as much fancy, another as much knowledge of character, another the same depth of passion, and another as great a power of language. This statement is not true; nor is the inference from it well-founded, even if it were. This person does not seem to have been aware that, upon his own shewing, the great distinction of Shakespeare's genius was its virtually including the genius of all the great men of his age, and not his differing from them in one accidental particular. But to have done with such minute and literal trifling.

The striking peculiarity of Shakespeare's mind was its generic quality, its power of communication with all other minds—so that it contained a universe of thought and feeling within itself, and had no one peculiar bias, or exclusive excellence more than another. He was just like any other man, but that he was like all other men. He was the least of an egotist that it was possible to be. He was nothing in himself; but he was all that others were, or that they could become. He not only had in himself the germs of every faculty and feeling, but he could follow them by anticipation, intuitively, into all their conceivable ramifications, through every change of fortune or conflict of passion, or turn of thought. He had 'a mind reflecting ages past',* and present:—all the people that ever lived are there. There was no respect of persons with him. His genius shone equally on the evil and on the good, on the wise and the foolish, the monarch and the beggar: 'All corners of the earth, kings, queens, and states, maids, matrons, nay, the secrets of the grave',* are hardly hid from his searching glance. He was like the genius of humanity, changing places with all of us at pleasure, and playing with our purposes as with his own. He turned the globe round for his amusement, and surveyed the generations of men, and the individuals as they passed, with their different concerns, passions, follies, vices, virtues, actions, and motives—as well those that they knew, as those which they did not know, or acknowledge to themselves. The dreams of childhood, the ravings of despair,

were the toys of his fancy. Airy beings waited at his call, and
came at his bidding. Harmless fairies 'nodded to him, and did
him curtesies':* and the night-hag bestrode the blast at the
command of 'his so potent art'.* The world of spirits lay open
to him, like the world of real men and women: and there is
the same truth in his delineations of the one as of the other;
for if the preternatural characters* he describes could be
supposed to exist, they would speak, and feel, and act, as he
makes them. He had only to think of any thing in order to
become that thing, with all the circumstances belonging to it.
When he conceived of a character, whether real or imaginary,
he not only entered into all its thoughts and feelings, but
seemed instantly, and as if by touching a secret spring, to be
surrounded with all the same objects, 'subject to the same
skyey influences',* the same local, outward, and unforeseen
accidents which would occur in reality. Thus the character of
Caliban not only stands before us with a language and manners of its own, but the scenery and situation of the enchanted
island he inhabits, the traditions of the place, its strange
noises, its hidden recesses, 'his frequent haunts and ancient
neighbourhood',* are given with a miraculous truth of nature,
and with all the familiarity of an old recollection. The whole
'coheres semblably together'* in time, place, and circumstance. In reading this author, you do not merely learn what
his characters say,—you see their persons. By something expressed or understood, you are at no loss to decypher their
peculiar physiognomy, the meaning of a look, the grouping,
the bye-play, as we might see it on the stage. A word, an epithet
paints a whole scene, or throws us back whole years in the
history of the person represented. So (as it has been ingeniously remarked)* when Prospero describes himself as left
alone in the boat with his daughter, the epithet which he
applies to her, 'Me and thy *crying* self ',* flings the imagination
instantly back from the grown woman to the helpless condition of infancy, and places the first and most trying scene of
his misfortunes before us, with all that he must have suffered
in the interval. How well the silent anguish of Macduff is
conveyed to the reader, by the friendly expostulation of
Malcolm—'What! man, ne'er pull your hat upon your

brows!'* Again, Hamlet, in the scene with Rosencrans and Guildenstern, somewhat abruptly concludes his fine soliloquy on life by saying, 'Man delights not me, nor woman neither, though by your smiling you seem to say so.'* Which is explained by their answer—'My lord, we had no such stuff in our thoughts. But we smiled to think, if you delight not in man, what lenten entertainment the players shall receive from you, whom we met on the way':—as if while Hamlet was making this speech, his two old schoolfellows from Wittenberg had been really standing by, and he had seen them smiling by stealth, at the idea of the players crossing their minds. It is not 'a combination and a form'* of words, a set speech or two, a preconcerted theory of a character, that will do this: but all the persons concerned must have been present in the poet's imagination, as at a kind of rehearsal; and whatever would have passed through their minds on the occasion, and have been observed by others, passed through his, and is made known to the reader.—I may add in passing, that Shakespeare always gives the best directions for the costume and carriage of his heroes. Thus to take one example, Ophelia gives the following account of Hamlet; and as Ophelia had seen Hamlet, I should think her word ought to be taken against that of any modern authority.

> '*Ophelia.* My lord, as I was reading in my closet,
> Prince Hamlet, with his doublet all unbrac'd,
> No hat upon his head, his stockings loose,
> Ungartred, and down-gyved to his ancle,
> Pale as his shirt, his knees knocking each other,
> And with a look so piteous,
> As if he had been sent from hell
> To speak of horrors, thus he comes before me.
>   *Polonius.* Mad for thy love!
>   *Oph.* My lord, I do not know,
> But truly I do fear it.
>   *Pol.* What said he?
>   *Oph.* He took me by the wrist, and held me hard
> Then goes he to the length of all his arm;
> And with his other hand thus o'er his brow,
> He falls to such perusal of my face,
> As he would draw it: long staid he so;

At last, a little shaking of my arm,
And thrice his head thus waving up and down,
He rais'd a sigh so piteous and profound,
As it did seem to shatter all his bulk,
And end his being. That done, he lets me go,
And with his head over his shoulder turn'd,
He seem'd to find his way without his eyes;
For out of doors he went without their help,
And to the last bended their light on me.'

How after this airy, fantastic idea of irregular grace and bewildered melancholy any one can play Hamlet, as we have seen
it played, with strut, and stare, and antic right-angled sharp-
pointed gestures, it is difficult to say, unless it be that Hamlet
is not bound, by the prompter's cue, to study the part of
Ophelia. The account of Ophelia's death begins thus:

'There is a willow hanging o'er a brook,
That shows its hoary leaves in the glassy stream.'—*

Now this is an instance of the same unconscious power of
mind which is as true to nature as itself. The leaves of the
willow are, in fact, white underneath, and it is this part of
them which would appear 'hoary' in the reflection in the
brook. The same sort of intuitive power, the same faculty of
bringing every object in nature, whether present or absent,
before the mind's eye, is observable in the speech of
Cleopatra, when conjecturing what were the employments of
Antony in his absence:—'He's speaking now, or murmuring,
where's my serpent of old Nile?' How fine to make Cleopatra
have this consciousness of her own character, and to make
her feel that it is this for which Antony is in love with her! She
says, after the battle of Actium, when Antony has resolved to
risk another fight, 'It is my birth-day; I had thought to have
held it poor: but since my lord is Antony again, I will be
Cleopatra.'* What other poet would have thought of such a
casual resource of the imagination, or would have dared to
avail himself of it? The thing happens in the play as it might
have happened in fact.—That which, perhaps, more than
any thing else distinguishes the dramatic productions of
Shakespeare from all others, is this wonderful truth and

individuality of conception. Each of his characters is as much itself, and as absolutely independent of the rest, as well as of the author, as if they were living persons, not fictions of the mind. The poet may be said, for the time, to identify himself with the character he wishes to represent, and to pass from one to another, like the same soul successively animating different bodies. By an art like that of the ventriloquist, he throws his imagination out of himself, and makes every word appear to proceed from the mouth of the person in whose name it is given. His plays alone are properly expressions of the passions, not descriptions of them. His characters are real beings of flesh and blood; they speak like men, not like authors. One might suppose that he had stood by at the time, and overheard what passed. As in our dreams we hold conversations with ourselves, make remarks, or communicate intelligence, and have no idea of the answer which we shall receive, and which we ourselves make, till we hear it: so the dialogues in Shakespeare are carried on without any consciousness of what is to follow, without any appearance of preparation or premeditation. The gusts of passion come and go like sounds of music borne on the wind. Nothing is made out by formal inference and analogy, by climax and antithesis: all comes, or seems to come, immediately from nature. Each object and circum-stance exists in his mind, as it would have existed in reality: each several train of thought and feeling goes on of itself, without confusion or effort. In the world of his imagination, every thing has a life, a place, and being of its own!

Chaucer's characters are sufficiently distinct from one another, but they are too little varied in themselves, too much like identical propositions. They are consistent, but uniform; we get no new idea of them from first to last; they are not placed in different lights, nor are their subordinate *traits* brought out in new situations; they are like portraits or physiognomical studies, with the distinguishing features marked with inconceivable truth and precision, but that preserve the same unaltered air and attitude. Shakespeare's are historical figures, equally true and correct, but put into action, where every nerve and muscle is displayed in the struggle with others, with all the effect of collision and contrast, with every variety of light and shade. Chaucer's characters are narrative, Shakespeare's dramatic, Milton's epic. That is, Chaucer told only as much of his story as he pleased, as was required for a particular purpose. He answered for his characters himself. In Shakespeare they are introduced upon the stage, are liable to be asked all sorts of questions, and are forced to answer for themselves. In Chaucer we perceive a fixed essence of character. In Shakespeare there is a continual composition and decomposition of its elements, a fermentation of every particle in the whole mass, by its alternate affinity or antipathy to other principles which are brought in contact with it. Till the experiment is tried, we do not know the result, the turn which the character will take in its new circumstances. Milton took only a few simple principles of character, and raised them to the utmost conceivable grandeur, and refined them from every base alloy. His imagination, 'nigh sphered in Heaven',* claimed kindred only with what he saw from that height, and could raise to the same elevation with itself. He sat retired and kept his state alone, 'playing with wisdom';* while Shakespeare mingled with the crowd, and played the host, 'to make society the sweeter welcome'.*

The passion in Shakespeare is of the same nature as his delineation of character. It is not some one habitual feeling or sentiment preying upon itself, growing out of itself, and moulding every thing to itself; it is passion modified by passion, by all the other feelings to which the individual is liable, and to which others are liable with him; subject to all the fluctuations of caprice and accident; calling into play all the resources of the understanding and all the energies of the will; irritated by obstacles or yielding to them; rising from small beginnings to its utmost height; now drunk with hope, now stung to madness, now sunk in despair, now blown to air with a breath, now raging like a torrent. The human soul is made the sport of fortune, the prey of adversity: it is stretched on the wheel of destiny, in restless ecstacy. The passions are in a state of projection. Years are melted down to moments, and every instant teems with fate. We know the results, we see the process. Thus after Iago has been boasting to himself of the effect of his poisonous suggestions on the mind of Othello, 'which, with a little act upon the blood, will work like mines of sulphur,' he adds—

> 'Look where he comes! not poppy, nor mandragora,
> Nor all the drowsy syrups of the East,
> Shall ever medicine thee to that sweet sleep
> Which thou ow'dst yesterday.'—*

And he enters at this moment, like the crested serpent, crowned with his wrongs and raging for revenge! The whole depends upon the turn of a thought. A word, a look, blows the spark of jealousy into a flame; and the explosion is immediate and terrible as a volcano. The dialogues in Lear, in Macbeth, that between Brutus and Cassius, and nearly all those in Shakespeare, where the interest is wrought up to its highest pitch, afford examples of this dramatic fluctuation of passion. The interest in Chaucer is quite different; it is like the course of a river, strong, and full, and increasing. In Shakespeare, on the contrary, it is like the sea, agitated this way and that, and loud-lashed by furious storms; while in the still pauses of the blast, we distinguish only the cries of despair, or the silence of death! Milton, on the other hand, takes the imaginative part of passion—that which remains after the event, which the mind reposes on when all is over, which looks upon circumstances from the remotest elevation of thought and fancy, and abstracts them from the world of action to that of contemplation. The objects of dramatic poetry affect us by sympathy, by their nearness to ourselves, as they take us by surprise, or force us upon action, 'while rage with rage doth sympathise';* the objects of epic poetry affect us through the medium of the imagination, by magnitude and distance, by their permanence and universality. The one fill us with terror and pity, the other with admiration and delight. There are certain objects that strike the imagination, and inspire awe in the very idea of them, independently of any dramatic interest, that is, of any connection with the vicissitudes of human life. For instance, we cannot think of the pyramids of Egypt, of a Gothic ruin, or an old Roman encampment, without a certain emotion, a sense of power and sublimity coming over the

mind. The heavenly bodies that hung over our heads wherever we go, and 'in their untroubled element shall shine when
we are laid in dust, and all our cares forgotten',* affect us in
the same way. Thus Satan's address to the Sun* has an epic,
not a dramatic interest; for though the second person in the
dialogue makes no answer and feels no concern, yet the eye
of that vast luminary is upon him, like the eye of heaven, and
seems conscious of what he says, like an universal presence.
Dramatic poetry and epic, in their perfection, indeed,
approximate to and strengthen one another. Dramatic poetry
borrows aid from the dignity of persons and things, as the
heroic does from human passion, but in theory they are
distinct.—When Richard II calls for the looking-glass to contemplate his faded majesty in it, and bursts into that affecting
exclamation: 'Oh, that I were a mockery-king of snow, to melt
away before the sun of Bolingbroke,'* we have here the utmost force of human passion, combined with the ideas of
regal splendour and fallen power. When Milton says of Satan:

> '——His form had not yet lost
> All her original brightness, nor appear'd
> Less than archangel ruin'd, and th' excess
> Of glory obscur'd;'—*

the mixture of beauty, of grandeur, and pathos, from the sense
of irreparable loss, of never-ending, unavailing regret, is
perfect.

The great fault of a modern school of poetry is, that it is an
experiment to reduce poetry to a mere effusion of natural
sensibility; or what is worse, to divest it both of imaginary
splendour and human passion, to surround the meanest objects with the morbid feelings and devouring egotism of the
writers' own minds. Milton and Shakespeare did not so understand poetry. They gave a more liberal interpretation both to
nature and art. They did not do all they could to get rid of
the one and the other, to fill up the dreary void with the
Moods of their own Minds.* They owe their power over the
human mind to their having had a deeper sense than others
of what was grand in the objects of nature, or affecting in the
events of human life. But to the men I speak of there is

nothing interesting, nothing heroical, but themselves. To them the fall of gods or of great men is the same. They do not enter into the feeling. They cannot understand the terms. They are even debarred from the last poor, paltry consolation of an unmanly triumph over fallen greatness; for their minds reject, with a convulsive effort and intolerable loathing, the very idea that there ever was, or was thought to be, any thing superior to themselves. All that has ever excited the attention or admiration of the world, they look upon with the most perfect indifference; and they are surprised to find that the world repays their indifference with scorn. 'With what measure they mete, it has been meted to them again.'*—

Shakespeare's imagination is of the same plastic kind as his conception of character or passion. 'It glances from heaven to earth, from earth to heaven.' Its movement is rapid and devious. It unites the most opposite extremes; or, as Puck says, in boasting of his own feats, 'puts a girdle round about the earth in forty minutes.'* He seems always hurrying from his subject, even while describing it; but the stroke, like the lightning's, is sure as it is sudden. He takes the widest possible range, but from that very range he has his choice of the greatest variety and aptitude of materials. He brings together images the most alike, but placed at the greatest distance from each other; that is, found in circumstances of the greatest dissimilitude. From the remoteness of his combinations, and the celerity with which they are effected, they coalesce the more indissolubly together. The more the thoughts are strangers to each other, and the longer they have been kept asunder, the more intimate does their union seem to become. Their felicity is equal to their force. Their likeness is made more dazzling by their novelty. They startle, and take the fancy prisoner in the same instant. I will mention one or two which are very striking, and not much known, out of *Troilus and Cressida*. Æneas says to Agamemnon,

> 'I ask that I may waken reverence,
> And on the cheek be ready with a blush
> Modest as morning, when she coldly eyes
> The youthful Phœbus.'*

Ulysses urging Achilles to shew himself in the field, says—

> 'No man is the lord of anything,
> Till he communicate his parts to others:
> Nor doth he of himself know them for aught,
> Till he behold them formed in the applause,
> Where they're extended! which like an arch reverberates
> The voice again, or like a gate of steel,
> Fronting the sun, receives and renders back
> Its figure and its heat.'

Patroclus gives the indolent warrior the same advice.

> 'Rouse yourself; and the weak wanton Cupid
> Shall from your neck unloose his amorous fold,
> And like a dew-drop from the lion's mane
> Be shook to air.'

Shakespeare's language and versification are like the rest of him. He has a magic power over words: they come winged at his bidding; and seem to know their places. They are struck out at a heat, on the spur of the occasion, and have all the truth and vividness which arise from an actual impression of the objects. His epithets and single phrases are like sparkles, thrown off from an imagination, fired by the whirling rapidity of its own motion. His language is hieroglyphical. It translates thoughts into visible images. It abounds in sudden transitions and elliptical expressions. This is the source of his mixed metaphors, which are only abbreviated forms of speech. These, however, give no pain from long custom. They have, in fact, become idioms in the language. They are the building, and not the scaffolding to thought. We take the meaning and effect of a well-known passage entire, and no more stop to scan and spell out the particular words and phrases, than the syllables of which they are composed. In trying to recollect any other author, one sometimes stumbles, in case of failure, on a word as good. In Shakespeare, any other word but the true one, is sure to be wrong. If any body, for instance, could not recollect the words of the following description,

> '——Light thickens,
> And the crow makes wing to the rooky wood,'*

he would be greatly at a loss to substitute others for them equally expressive of the feeling. These remarks, however, are strictly applicable only to the impassioned parts of Shakespeare's language, which flowed from the warmth and originality of his imagination, and were his own. The language used for prose conversation and ordinary business is sometimes technical, and involved in the affectation of the time. Compare, for example, Othello's apology to the senate, relating 'his whole course of love', with some of the preceding parts relating to his appointment, and the official dispatches from Cyprus. In this respect, 'the business of the state does him offence.'* His versification is no less powerful, sweet, and varied. It has every occasional excellence, of sullen intricacy, crabbed and perplexed, or of the smoothest and loftiest expansion—from the ease and familiarity of measured conversation to the lyrical sounds

> '——Of ditties highly penned,
> Sung by a fair queen in a summer's bower,
> With ravishing division to her lute.'*

It is the only blank verse in the language, except Milton's, that for itself is readable. It is not stately and uniformly swelling like his, but varied and broken by the inequalities of the ground it has to pass over in its uncertain course,

> 'And so by many winding nooks it strays,
> With willing sport to the wild ocean.'*

It remains to speak of the faults of Shakespeare. They are not so many or so great as they have been represented; what there are, are chiefly owing to the following causes:—The universality of his genius was, perhaps, a disadvantage to his single works; the variety of his resources, sometimes diverting him from applying them to the most effectual purposes. He might be said to combine the powers of Æschylus and Aristophanes, of Dante and Rabelais, in his own mind. If he had been only half what he was, he would perhaps have appeared greater. The natural ease and indifference of his temper made him sometimes less scrupulous than he might have been. He is relaxed and careless in critical places; he is in earnest throughout only in Timon, Macbeth, and Lear. Again, he had no models of acknowledged excellence constantly in view to stimulate his efforts, and by all that appears, no love of fame. He wrote for the 'great vulgar and the small',* in his time, not for posterity. If Queen Elizabeth and the maids of honour laughed heartily at his worst jokes, and the catcalls in the gallery were silent at his best passages, he went home satisfied, and slept the next night well. He did not trouble himself about Voltaire's criticisms.* He was willing to take advantage of the ignorance of the age in many things; and if his plays pleased others, not to quarrel with them himself. His very facility of production would make him set less value on his own excellences, and not care to distinguish nicely between what he did well or ill. His blunders in chronology and geography do not amount to above half a dozen, and they are offences against chronology and geography, not against poetry. As to the unities, he was right in setting them at defiance. He was fonder of puns than became so great a man. His barbarisms were those of his age. His genius was his own. He had no objection to float down with the stream of common taste and opinion: he rose above it by his own buoyancy, and an impulse which he could not keep under, in spite of himself or others, and 'his delights did shew most dolphin-like.'*

He had an equal genius for comedy and tragedy; and his tragedies are better than his comedies, because tragedy is better than comedy. His female characters, which have been found fault with as insipid, are the finest in the world. Lastly, Shakespeare was the least of a coxcomb of any one that ever lived, and much of a gentleman.

MACBETH

'The poet's eye in a fine frenzy rolling
Doth glance from heaven to earth, from earth to heaven;
And as imagination bodies forth
The forms of things unknown, the poet's pen
Turns them to shape, and gives to airy nothing
A local habitation and a name.'*

MACBETH and *Lear, Othello* and *Hamlet,* are usually reckoned
Shakespeare's four principal tragedies. *Lear* stands first for
the profound intensity of the passion; *Macbeth* for the wildness
of the imagination and the rapidity of the action;* *Othello* for
the progressive interest and powerful alternations of feeling;
Hamlet for the refined development of thought and sentiment. If the force of genius shewn in each of these works is
astonishing, their variety is not less so. They are like different
creations of the same mind, not one of which has the slightest
reference to the rest. This distinctness and originality is indeed the necessary consequence of truth and nature. Shakespeare's genius alone appeared to possess the resources of
nature. He is 'your only *tragedy-maker*'.* His plays have the
force of things upon the mind. What he represents is brought
home to the bosom as a part of our experience, implanted in
the memory as if we had known the places, persons, and
things of which he treats. *Macbeth* is like a record of a preternatural and tragical event. It has the rugged severity of an old
chronicle with all that the imagination of the poet can engraft
upon traditional belief. The castle of Macbeth, round which
'the air smells wooingly,'* and where 'the temple-haunting
martlet builds,' has a real subsistence in the mind; the Weïrd
Sisters meet us in person on 'the blasted heath';* the 'air-
drawn dagger'* moves slowly before our eyes; the 'gracious
Duncan',* the 'blood-boultered Banquo'* stand before us; all
that passed through the mind of Macbeth passes, without the
loss of a tittle, through ours. All that could actually take place,
and all that is only possible to be conceived, what was said and
what was done, the workings of passion, the spells of magic,
are brought before us with the same absolute truth and vividness.—Shakespeare excelled in the openings of his plays: that
of Macbeth is the most striking of any. The wildness of the
scenery, the sudden shifting of the situations and characters,
the bustle, the expectations excited, are equally extraordinary. From the first entrance of the Witches and the description
of them when they meet Macbeth,

> ——'What are these
> So wither'd and so wild in their attire,

> That look not like the inhabitants of th' earth
> And yet are on't?'*

the mind is prepared for all that follows.

This tragedy is alike distinguished for the lofty imagination it displays, and for the tumultuous vehemence of the action; and the one is made the moving principle of the other. The overwhelming pressure of preternatural agency urges on the tide of human passion with redoubled force. Macbeth himself appears driven along by the violence of his fate like a vessel drifting before a storm: he reels to and fro like a drunken man; he staggers under the weight of his own purposes and the suggestions of others; he stands at bay with his situation; and from the superstitious awe and breathless suspense into which the communications of the Weïrd Sisters throw him, is hurried on with daring impatience to verify their predictions, and with impious and bloody hand to tear aside the veil which hides the uncertainty of the future. He is not equal to the struggle with fate and conscience. He now 'bends up each corporal instrument to the terrible feat';* at other times his heart misgives him, and he is cowed and abashed by his success. 'The deed, no less than the attempt, confounds him.'* His mind is assailed by the stings of remorse, and full of 'preternatural solicitings'.* His speeches and soliloquies are dark riddles on human life, baffling solution, and entangling him in their labyrinths. In thought he is absent and perplexed, sudden and desperate in act, from a distrust of his own resolution. His energy springs from the anxiety and agitation of his mind. His blindly rushing forward on the objects of his ambition and revenge, or his recoiling from them, equally betrays the harassed state of his feelings.—This part of his character is admirably set off by being brought in connection with that of Lady Macbeth, whose obdurate strength of will and masculine firmness give her the ascendancy over her husband's faultering virtue. She at once seizes on the opportunity that offers for the accomplishment of all their wished-for greatness, and never flinches from her object till all is over. The magnitude of her resolution almost covers the magnitude of her guilt. She is a great bad woman, whom we hate, but whom we fear more than we hate. She does not excite our loathing and abhorrence like Regan and Gonerill. She is only wicked to gain a great end; and is perhaps more distinguished by her commanding presence of mind and inexorable self-will, which do not suffer her to be diverted from a bad purpose, when once formed, by weak and womanly regrets, than by the hardness of her heart or want of natural affections. The impression which her lofty determination of character makes on the mind of Macbeth is well described where he exclaims,

> ——'Bring forth men children only;
> For thy undaunted mettle should compose
> Nothing but males!'*

Nor do the pains she is at to 'screw his courage to the sticking-place',* the reproach to him, not to be 'lost so poorly in himself',* the assurance that 'a little water clears them of this deed,'* show anything but her greater consistency in depravity. Her strong-nerved ambition furnishes ribs of steel to 'the sides of his intent';* and she is herself wound up to the execution of her baneful project with the same unshrinking fortitude in crime, that in other circumstances she would probably have shown patience in suffering. The deliberate sacrifice of all other considerations to the gaining 'for their future days and nights sole sovereign sway and masterdom',* by the murder of Duncan, is gorgeously expressed in her invocation on hearing of 'his fatal entrance under her battlements':*

> ——'Come all you spirits
> That tend on mortal thoughts, unsex me here:
> And fill me, from the crown to th' toe, top-full
> Of direst cruelty; make thick my blood,
> Stop up the access and passage to remorse,
> That no compunctious visitings of nature
> Shake my fell purpose, nor keep peace between
> The effect and it. Come to my woman's breasts,
> And take my milk for gall, you murthering ministers,
> Wherever in your sightless substances
> You wait on nature's mischief. Come, thick night!
> And pall thee in the dunnest smoke of hell,

That my keen knife see not the wound it makes,
Nor heav'n peep through the blanket of the dark,
To cry, hold, hold!'——*

When she first hears that 'Duncan comes there to sleep'* she
is so overcome by the news, which is beyond her utmost
expectations, that she answers the messenger, 'Thou 'rt mad
to say it':* and on receiving her husband's account of the
predictions of the Witches, conscious of his instability of purpose, and that her presence is necessary to goad him on to
the consummation of his promised greatness, she exclaims—

——'Hie thee hither,
That I may pour my spirits in thine ear,
And chastise with the valour of my tongue
All that impedes thee from the golden round,
Which fate and metaphysical aid doth seem
To have thee crowned withal.'*

This swelling exultation and keen spirit of triumph, this uncontroulable eagerness of anticipation, which seems to dilate
her form and take possession of all her faculties, this solid,
substantial flesh and blood display of passion, exhibit a striking contrast to the cold, abstracted, gratuitous, servile malignity of the Witches, who are equally instrumental in urging
Macbeth to his fate for the mere love of mischief, and from
a disinterested delight in deformity and cruelty. They are hags
of mischief, obscene panders to iniquity, malicious from their
impotence of enjoyment, enamoured of destruction, because
they are themselves unreal, abortive, half-existences—who
become sublime from their exemption from all human sympathies and contempt for all human affairs, as Lady Macbeth
does by the force of passion! Her fault seems to have been an
excess of that strong principle of self-interest and family
aggrandisement, not amenable to the common feelings of
compassion and justice, which is so marked a feature in
barbarous nations and times. A passing reflection of this kind,
on the resemblance of the sleeping king to her father, alone
prevents her from slaying Duncan with her own hand.

In speaking of the character of Lady Macbeth, we ought not
to pass over Mrs Siddons's manner* of acting that part. We

can conceive of nothing grander. It was something above nature. It seemed almost as if a being of a superior order had dropped from a higher sphere to awe the world with the majesty of her appearance. Power was seated on her brow, passion emanated from her breast as from a shrine; she was tragedy personified. In coming on in the sleeping-scene, her eyes were open, but their sense was shut. She was like a person bewildered and unconscious of what she did. Her lips moved involuntarily—all her gestures were involuntary and mechanical. She glided on and off the stage like an apparition. To have seen her in that character was an event in every one's life, not to be forgotten.

The dramatic beauty of the character of Duncan, which excites the respect and pity even of his murderers, has been often pointed out. It forms a picture of itself. An instance of the author's power of giving a striking effect to a common reflection, by the manner of introducing it, occurs in a speech of Duncan, complaining of his having been deceived in his opinion of the Thane of Cawdor, at the very moment that he is expressing the most unbounded confidence in the loyalty and services of Macbeth.

> 'There is no art
> To find the mind's construction in the face:
> He was a gentleman, on whom I built
> An absolute trust.
> O worthiest cousin,   (*addressing himself to Macbeth.*)
> The sin of my ingratitude e'en now
> Was great upon me,' etc.*

Another passage to show that Shakespeare lost sight of nothing that could in any way give relief or heightening to his subject, is the conversation which takes place between Banquo and Fleance immediately before the murder-scene of Duncan.

> '*Banquo.* How goes the night, boy?
> *Fleance.* The moon is down: I have not heard the clock.
> *Banquo.* And she goes down at twelve.
> *Fleance.* I take 't, 'tis later, Sir.
> *Banquo.* Hold, take my sword. There's husbandry in heav'n,
> Their candles are all out.—

A heavy summons lies like lead upon me,
And yet I would not sleep: Merciful Powers,
Restrain in me the cursed thoughts that nature
Gives way to in repose.'*

In like manner, a fine idea is given of the gloomy coming on of evening, just as Banquo is going to be assassinated.

'Light thickens and the crow
Makes wing to the rooky wood.'

.   .   .   .   .   .

'Now spurs the lated traveller apace
To gain the timely inn.'*

Macbeth (generally speaking) is done upon a stronger and more systematic principle of contrast than any other of Shakespeare's plays. It moves upon the verge of an abyss, and is a constant struggle between life and death. The action is desperate and the reaction is dreadful. It is a huddling together of fierce extremes, a war of opposite natures which of them shall destroy the other. There is nothing but what has a violent end or violent beginnings. The lights and shades are laid on with a determined hand; the transitions from triumph to despair, from the height of terror to the repose of death, are sudden and startling; every passion brings in its fellow-contrary, and the thoughts pitch and jostle against each other as in the dark. The whole play is an unruly chaos of strange and forbidden things, where the ground rocks under our feet. Shakespeare's genius here took its full swing, and trod upon the farthest bounds of nature and passion. This circumstance will account for the abruptness and violent antitheses of the style, the throes and labour which run through the expression, and from defects will turn them into beauties. 'So fair and foul a day I have not seen,'* etc. 'Such welcome and unwelcome news together'.* 'Men's lives are like the flowers in their caps, dying or ere they sicken.'* 'Look like the innocent flower, but be the serpent under it.'* The scene before the castle-gate follows the appearance of the Witches on the heath, and is followed by a midnight murder. Duncan is cut off betimes by treason leagued with witchcraft, and Macduff is ripped untimely from his mother's womb to avenge his death. Macbeth, after the death of Banquo, wishes for his presence in extravagant terms, 'To him and all we thirst,' and when his ghost appears, cries out, 'Avaunt and quit my sight,'* and being gone, he is 'himself again'.* Macbeth resolves to get rid of Macduff, that 'he may sleep in spite of thunder';* and cheers his wife on the doubtful intelligence of Banquo's taking-off with the encouragement—'Then be thou jocund: ere the bat has flown his cloistered flight; ere to black Hecate's summons the shard-born beetle has rung night's yawning peal, there shall be done—a deed of dreadful note.'* In Lady Macbeth's speech 'Had he not resembled my father as he slept, I had done 't,'* there is murder and filial piety together; and in urging him to fulfil his vengeance against the defence-less king, her thoughts spare the blood neither of infants nor old age. The description of the Witches is full of the same contradictory principle; they 'rejoice when good kings bleed', they are neither of the earth nor the air, but both; 'they should be women, but their beards forbid it';* they take all the pains possible to lead Macbeth on to the height of his ambition, only to betray him 'in deeper consequence',* and after show-ing him all the pomp of their art, discover their malignant delight in his disappointed hopes, by that bitter taunt, 'Why stands Macbeth thus amazedly?'* We might multiply such instances every where.

The leading features in the character of Macbeth are strik-ing enough, and they form what may be thought at first only a bold, rude, Gothic outline. By comparing it with other characters of the same author we shall perceive the absolute truth and identity which is observed in the midst of the giddy whirl and rapid career of events. Macbeth in Shakespeare no more loses his identity of character in the fluctuations of fortune or the storm of passion, than Macbeth in himself would have lost the identity of his person. Thus he is as distinct a being from Richard III* as it is possible to imagine, though these two characters in common hands, and indeed in the hands of any other poet, would have been a repetition of the same general idea, more or less exaggerated. For both are tyrants, usurpers, murderers, both aspiring and ambitious, both courageous, cruel, treacherous. But Richard is cruel

from nature and constitution. Macbeth becomes so from accidental circumstances. Richard is from his birth deformed in
body and mind, and naturally incapable of good. Macbeth is
full of 'the milk of human kindness',* is frank, sociable, generous. He is tempted to the commission of guilt by golden
opportunities, by the instigations of his wife, and by prophetic
warnings. Fate and metaphysical aid conspire against his
virtue and his loyalty. Richard on the contrary needs no
prompter, but wades through a series of crimes to the height
of his ambition from the ungovernable violence of his temper
and a reckless love of mischief. He is never gay but in the
prospect or in the success of his villainies: Macbeth is full of
horror at the thoughts of the murder of Duncan, which he is
with difficulty prevailed on to commit, and of remorse after
its perpetration. Richard has no mixture of common humanity in his composition, no regard to kindred or posterity, he
owns no fellowship with others, he is 'himself alone'.* Macbeth is not destitute of feelings of sympathy, is accessible to
pity, is even made in some measure the dupe of his uxorious-
ness, ranks the loss of friends, of the cordial love of his followers, and of his good name, among the causes which have
made him weary of life, and regrets that he has ever seized
the crown by unjust means, since he cannot transmit it to his
posterity—

> 'For Banquo's issue have I fil'd my mind—
> For them the gracious Duncan have I murther'd,
> To make them kings, the seed of Banquo kings.'*

In the agitation of his mind, he envies those whom he has
sent to peace. 'Duncan is in his grave; after life's fitful fever
he sleeps well.'*—It is true, he becomes more callous as he
plunges deeper in guilt, 'direness is thus rendered familiar to
his slaughterous thoughts,'* and he in the end anticipates his
wife in the boldness and bloodiness of his enterprises, while
she for want of the same stimulus of action, 'is troubled with
thick-coming fancies that rob her of her rest',* goes mad and
dies. Macbeth endeavours to escape from reflection on his
crimes by repelling their consequences, and banishes remorse
for the past by the meditation of future mischief. This is not

the principle of Richard's cruelty, which displays the wanton malice of a fiend as much as the frailty of human passion. Macbeth is goaded on to acts of violence and retaliation by necessity; to Richard, blood is a pastime.—There are other decisive differences inherent in the two characters. Richard may be regarded as a man of the world, a plotting, hardened knave, wholly regardless of every thing but his own ends, and the means to secure them.—Not so Macbeth. The superstitions of the age, the rude state of society, the local scenery and customs, all give a wildness and imaginary grandeur to his character. From the strangeness of the events that surround him, he is full of amazement and fear; and stands in doubt between the world of reality and the world of fancy. He sees sights not shown to mortal eye, and hears unearthly music. All is tumult and disorder within and without his mind; his purposes recoil upon himself, are broken and disjointed; he is the double thrall of his passions and his evil destiny. Richard is not a character either of imagination or pathos, but of pure self-will. There is no conflict of opposite feelings in his breast. The apparitions which he sees only haunt him in his sleep; nor does he live like Macbeth in a waking dream. Macbeth has considerable energy and manliness of character; but then he is 'subject to all the skyey influences'.* He is sure of nothing but the present moment. Richard in the busy turbulence of his projects never loses his self-possession, and makes use of every circumstance that happens as an instrument of his long-reaching designs. In his last extremity we can only regard him as a wild beast taken in the toils: while we never entirely lose our concern for Macbeth; and he calls back all our sympathy by that fine close of thoughtful melancholy—

> 'My way of life is fallen into the sear,
> The yellow leaf; and that which should accompany old age,
> As honour, troops of friends, I must not look to have;
> But in their stead, curses not loud but deep,
> Mouth-honour, breath, which the poor heart
> Would fain deny, and dare not.'*

We can conceive a common actor to play Richard tolerably well; we can conceive no one to play Macbeth properly, or to look like a man that had encountered the Weïrd Sisters. All the actors that we have ever seen, appear as if they had encountered them on the boards of Covent-garden or Drury-lane, but not on the heath at Fores, and as if they did not believe what they had seen. The Witches of *Macbeth* indeed are ridiculous on the modern stage, and we doubt if the Furies of Æschylus would be more respected. The progress of manners* and knowledge has an influence on the stage, and will in time perhaps destroy both tragedy and comedy. . .

CORIOLANUS

SHAKESPEARE has in this play shewn himself well versed in history and state-affairs. *Coriolanus* is a store-house of political common-places. Any one who studies it may save himself the trouble of reading Burke's *Reflections*, or Paine's *Rights of Man*, or the Debates in both Houses of Parliament since the French Revolution or our own.* The arguments for and against aristocracy or democracy, on the privileges of the few and the claims of the many, on liberty and slavery, power and the abuse of it, peace and war, are here very ably handled, with the spirit of a poet and the acuteness of a philosopher. Shakespeare himself seems to have had a leaning to the arbitrary side of the question, perhaps from some feeling of contempt for his own origin; and to have spared no occasion of baiting the rabble. What he says of them is very true: what he says of their betters is also very true, though he dwells less upon it.—The cause of the people is indeed but little calculated as a subject for poetry: it admits of rhetoric, which goes into argument and explanation, but it presents no immediate or distinct images to the mind, 'no jutting frieze, buttress, or coigne of vantage' for poetry 'to make its pendant bed and procreant cradle in.'* The language of poetry naturally falls in with the language of power. The imagination is an exaggerating and exclusive faculty: it takes from one thing to add to another: it accumulates circumstances together to give the greatest possible effect to a favourite object. The understanding is a dividing and measuring faculty: it judges of things not according to their immediate impression on the mind, but according to their relations to one another. The one is a monopolising faculty, which seeks the greatest quantity of present excitement by inequality and disproportion; the other is a distributive faculty, which seeks the greatest quantity of ultimate good, by justice and proportion. The one is an aristocratical, the other a republican faculty. The principle of poetry is a very anti-levelling principle. It aims at effect, it exists by contrast. It admits of no medium. It is every thing by excess. It rises above the ordinary standard of sufferings and crimes. It presents a dazzling appearance. It shows its head turretted, crowned, and crested. Its front is gilt and blood-stained. Before it 'it carries noise,* and behind it leaves tears.' It has its altars and its victims, sacrifices, human sacrifices. Kings, priests, nobles, are its train-bearers, tyrants and slaves its executioners.—'Carnage is its daughter.'*—Poetry is right-royal. It puts the individual for the species, the one above the infinite many, might before right. A lion hunting a flock of sheep or a herd of wild asses is a more poetical object than they; and we even take part with the lordly beast, because our vanity or some other feeling makes us disposed to place ourselves in the situation of the strongest party. So we feel some concern for the poor citizens of Rome when they meet together to compare their wants and grievances, till Coriolanus comes in and with blows and big words drives this set of 'poor rats',* this rascal scum, to their homes and beggary before him. There is nothing heroical in a multitude of miserable rogues not wishing to be starved, or complaining that they are like to be so: but when a single man comes forward to brave their cries and to make them submit to the last indignities, from mere pride and self-will, our admiration of his prowess is immediately converted into contempt for their pusillanimity. The insolence of power is stronger than the plea of necessity. The tame submission to usurped authority or even the natural resistance to it has nothing to excite or flatter the imagination: it is the assumption of a right to insult or oppress others that carries an imposing air of superiority with it. We had rather be the oppressor than the oppressed. The love of power in ourselves and the admiration of it in others are both natural to man: the one makes him a tyrant, the other a slave. Wrong dressed out in pride, pomp, and circumstance, has more attraction than abstract right.

MR WORDSWORTH

MR WORDSWORTH'S genius is a pure emanation of the Spirit of the Age. Had he lived in any other period of the world, he would never have been heard of. As it is, he has some difficulty to contend with the hebetude of his intellect and the meanness of his subject. With him 'lowliness is young ambition's ladder':* but he finds it a toil to climb in this way the steep of Fame. His homely Muse can hardly raise her wing from the ground, nor spread her hidden glories to the sun. He has 'no figures nor no fantasies, which busy *passion* draws in the brains of men':* neither the gorgeous machinery of mythologic lore, nor the splendid colours of poetic diction. His style is vernacular: he delivers household truths. He sees nothing loftier than human hopes, nothing deeper than the human heart. This he probes, this he tampers with, this he poises, with all its incalculable weight of thought and feeling, in his hands, and at the same time calms the throbbing pulses of his own heart by keeping his eye ever fixed on the face of nature. If he can make the life-blood flow from the wounded breast, this is the living colouring with which he paints his verse: if he can assuage the pain or close up the wound with the balm of solitary musing, or the healing power of plants and herbs and 'skyey influences',* this is the sole triumph of his art. He takes the simplest elements of nature and of the human mind, the mere abstract conditions inseparable from our being, and tries to compound a new system of poetry from them; and has perhaps succeeded as well as any one could. '*Nihil humani a me alienum puto*'* is the motto of his works. He thinks nothing low or indifferent of which this can be affirmed: every thing that professes to be more than this, that is not an absolute essence of truth and feeling, he holds to be vitiated, false and spurious. In a word, his poetry is founded on setting up an opposition (and pushing it to the utmost length) between the natural and the artificial, between the spirit of humanity and the spirit of fashion and of the world.

It is one of the innovations of the time. It partakes of, and is carried along with, the revolutionary movement of our age: the political changes of the day were the model on which he formed and conducted his poetical experiments. His Muse (it cannot be denied, and without this we cannot explain its character at all) is a levelling one. It proceeds on a principle of equality, and strives to reduce all things to the same standard. It is distinguished by a proud humility. It relies upon its own resources, and disdains external show and relief. It takes the commonest events and objects, as a test to prove that nature is always interesting from its inherent truth and beauty, without any of the ornaments of dress or pomp of circumstances to set it off. Hence the unaccountable mixture of seeming simplicity and real abstruseness in the *Lyrical Ballads.* Fools have laughed at, wise men scarcely understand, them. He takes a subject or a story merely as pegs or loops to hang thought and feeling on; the incidents are trifling, in proportion to his contempt for imposing appearances; the reflections are profound, according to the gravity and aspiring pretensions of his mind.

His popular, inartificial style gets rid (at a blow) of all the trappings of verse, of all the high places of poetry: 'the cloud-capt towers, the solemn temples, the gorgeous palaces,' are swept to the ground, and 'like the baseless fabric of a vision, leave not a wreck behind.'* All the traditions of learning, all the superstitions of age, are obliterated and effaced. We begin *de novo* on a *tabula rasa* of poetry. The purple pall, the nodding plume of tragedy are exploded as mere pantomime and trick, to return to the simplicity of truth and nature. Kings, queens, priests, nobles, the altar and the throne, the distinctions of rank, birth, wealth, power, 'the judge's robe, the marshal's truncheon, the ceremony that to great ones 'longs',* are not to be found here. The author tramples on the pride of art with greater pride. The Ode and Epode, the Strophe and the Antistrophe, he laughs to scorn. The harp of Homer, the

trump of Pindar and of Alcæus, are still. The decencies of
costume, the decorations of vanity are stripped off without
mercy as barbarous, idle, and Gothic. The jewels in the crisped
hair,* the diadem on the polished brow, are thought meretricious, theatrical, vulgar; and nothing contents his fastidious
taste beyond a simple garland of flowers. Neither does he avail
himself of the advantages which nature or accident holds out
to him. He chooses to have his subject a foil to his invention,
to owe nothing but to himself.

   He gathers manna in the wilderness; he strikes the barren
rock for the gushing moisture. He elevates the mean by the
strength of his own aspirations; he clothes the naked with
beauty and grandeur from the stores of his own recollections.
No cypress grove loads his verse with funeral pomp: but his
imagination lends 'a sense of joy

> 'To the bare trees and mountains bare,
> And grass in the green field.'*

No storm, no shipwreck startles us by its horrors: but the
rainbow lifts its head in the cloud, and the breeze sighs
through the withered fern. No sad vicissitude of fate, no
overwhelming catastrophe in nature deforms his page: but
the dew-drop glitters on the bending flower, the tear collects
in the glistening eye.

> 'Beneath the hills, along the flowery vales,
> The generations are prepared; the pangs,
> The internal pangs are ready; the dread strife
> Of poor humanity's afflicted will,
> Struggling in vain with ruthless destiny.'*

As the lark ascends from its low bed on fluttering wing, and
salutes the morning skies, so Mr Wordsworth's unpretending
Muse in russet guise scales the summits of reflection, while it
makes the round earth its footstool and its home!

   Possibly a good deal of this may be regarded as the effect
of disappointed views and an inverted ambition. Prevented by
native pride and indolence from climbing the ascent of learning or greatness, taught by political opinions to say to the vain
pomp and glory of the world, 'I hate ye,' seeing the path of

classical and artificial poetry blocked up by the cumbrous ornaments of style and turgid *common-places*, so that nothing more could be achieved in that direction but by the most ridiculous bombast or the tamest servility, he has turned back, partly from the bias of his mind, partly perhaps from a judicious policy—has struck into the sequestered vale of humble life, sought out the Muse among sheep-cotes and hamlets, and the peasant's mountain-haunts, has discarded all the tinsel pageantry of verse, and endeavoured (not in vain) to aggrandise the trivial, and add the charm of novelty to the familiar. No one has shown the same imagination in raising trifles into importance: no one has displayed the same pathos in treating of the simplest feelings of the heart. Reserved, yet haughty, having no unruly or violent passions (or those passions having been early suppressed), Mr Wordsworth has passed his life in solitary musing or in daily converse with the face of nature. He exemplifies in an eminent degree the *association*; for his poetry has no other source or character. He has dwelt among pastoral scenes, till each object has become connected with a thousand feelings, a link in the chain of thought, a fibre of his own heart. Every one is by habit and familiarity strongly attached to the place of his birth, or to objects that recal the most pleasing and eventful circumstances of his life.

But to the author of the *Lyrical Ballads* nature is a kind of home; and he may be said to take a personal interest in the universe. There is no image so insignificant that it has not in some mood or other found the way into his heart: no sound that does not awaken the memory of other years.—

> 'To him the meanest flower that blows can give
> Thoughts that do often lie too deep for tears.'*

The daisy looks up to him with sparkling eye as an old acquaintance: the cuckoo haunts him with sounds of early youth not to be expressed: a linnet's nest startles him with boyish delight: an old withered thorn is weighed down with a heap of recollections: a grey cloak, seen on some wild moor, torn by the wind or drenched in the rain, afterwards becomes an object of imagination to him: even the lichens on the rock have a life and being in his thoughts. He has described all these objects in a way and with an intensity of feeling that no one else had done before him, and has given a new view or aspect of nature. He is in this sense the most original poet now living, and the one whose writings could the least be spared: for they have no substitute elsewhere. The vulgar do not read them; the learned, who see all things through books, do not understand them; the great despise. The fashionable may ridicule them: but the author has created himself an interest in the heart of the retired and lonely student of nature, which can never die.

Persons of this class will still continue to feel what he has felt: he has expressed what they might in vain wish to express, except with glistening eye and faltering tongue! There is a lofty philosophic tone, a thoughtful humanity, infused into his pastoral vein. Remote from the passions and events of the great world, he has communicated interest and dignity to the primal movements of the heart of man, and ingrafted his own conscious reflections on the casual thoughts of hinds and shepherds. Nursed amidst the grandeur of mountain scenery, he has stooped to have a nearer view of the daisy under his feet, or plucked a branch of white-thorn from the spray: but, in describing it, his mind seems imbued with the majesty and solemnity of the objects around him. The tall rock lifts its head in the erectness of his spirit; the cataract roars in the sound of his verse; and in its dim and mysterious meaning the mists seem to gather in the hollows of Helvellyn, and the forked Skiddaw hovers in the distance. There is little mention of mountainous scenery in Mr Wordsworth's poetry; but by internal evidence one might be almost sure that it was written in a mountainous country, from its bareness, its simplicity, its loftiness and its depth!

His later philosophic productions have a somewhat different character. They are a departure from, a dereliction of, his first principles. They are classical and courtly. They are polished in style without being gaudy, dignified in subject without affectation. They seem to have been composed not in a cottage at Grasmere, but among the half-inspired groves and stately recollections of Cole-Orton.* We might allude in particular, for examples of what we mean, to the lines on a

Picture by Claude Lorraine and to the exquisite poem, entitled *Laodamia*. The last of these breathes the pure spirit of
the finest fragments of antiquity—the sweetness, the gravity,
the strength, the beauty and the languor of death—

'Calm contemplation and majestic pains.'*

Its glossy brilliancy arises from the perfection of the finishing,
like that of a careful sculpture, not from gaudy colouring. The
texture of the thoughts has the smoothness and solidity of
marble. It is a poem that might be read aloud in Elysium, and
the spirits of departed heroes and sages would gather round
to listen to it!

Mr Wordsworth's philosophic poetry, with a less glowing
aspect and less tumult in the veins than Lord Byron's on
similar occasions, bends a calmer and keener eye on mortality;
the impression, if less vivid, is more pleasing and permanent;
and we confess it (perhaps it is a want of taste and proper
feeling) that there are lines and poems of our author's, that
we think of ten times for once that we recur to any of Lord
Byron's. Or if there are any of the latter's writings, that we can
dwell upon in the same way, that is, as lasting and heart-felt
sentiments, it is when laying aside his usual pomp and pretension, he descends with Mr Wordsworth to the common
ground of a disinterested humanity. It may be considered as
characteristic of our poet's writings, that they either make no
impression on the mind at all, seem mere *nonsense-verses*, or
that they leave a mark behind them that never wears out. They
either

'Fall blunted from the indurated breast'*—

without any perceptible result, or they absorb it like a passion.
To one class of readers he appears sublime, to another (and
we fear the largest) ridiculous. He has probably realised
Milton's wish,—'and fit audience found, though few':* but we
suspect he is not reconciled to the alternative.

There are delightful passages in the *Excursion*, both of
natural description and of inspired reflection (passages of the
latter kind that in the sound of the thoughts and of the
swelling language resemble heavenly symphonies, mournful

requiems over the grave of human hopes); but we must add, in justice and in sincerity, that we think it impossible that this work should ever become popular, even in the same degree as the *Lyrical Ballads*. It affects a system without having any intelligible clue to one, and, instead of unfolding a principle in various and striking lights, repeats the same conclusions till they become flat and insipid. Mr Wordsworth's mind is obtuse, except as it is the organ and the receptacle of accumulated feelings: it is not analytic, but synthetic; it is reflecting, rather than theoretical. The *Excursion*, we believe, fell still-born from the press. There was something abortive, and clumsy, and ill-judged in the attempt. It was long and laboured. The personages, for the most part, were low, the fare rustic; the plan raised expectations which were not fulfilled; and the effect was like being ushered into a stately hall and invited to sit down to a splendid banquet in the company of clowns, and with nothing but successive courses of apple-dumplings served up. It was not even *toujours perdrix*!*

Mr Wordsworth, in his person, is above the middle size, with marked features and an air somewhat stately and quixotic. He reminds one of some of Holbein's heads: grave, saturnine, with a slight indication of sly humour, kept under by the manners of the age or by the pretensions of the person. He has a peculiar sweetness in his smile, and great depth and manliness and a rugged harmony in the tones of his voice. His manner of reading his own poetry is particularly imposing; and in his favourite passages his eye beams with preternatural lustre, and the meaning labours slowly up from his swelling breast. No one who has seen him at these moments could go away with an impression that he was a 'man of no mark or likelihood'.* Perhaps the comment of his face and voice is necessary to convey a full idea of his poetry. His language may not be intelligible; but his manner is not to be mistaken. It is clear that he is either mad or inspired. In company, even in a *tête-à-tête*, Mr Wordsworth is often silent, indolent and reserved. If he is become verbose and oracular of late years, he was not so in his better days. He threw out a bold or an indifferent remark without either effort or pretension, and relapsed into musing again. He shone most (because he seemed most roused and animated) in reciting his own poetry, or in talking about it. He sometimes gave striking views of his feelings and trains of association in composing certain passages; or if one did not always understand his distinctions, still there was no want of interest: there was a latent meaning worth inquiring into, like a vein of ore that one cannot exactly hit upon at the moment, but of which there are sure indications. His standard of poetry is high and severe, almost to exclusiveness. He admits of nothing below, scarcely of anything above, himself. It is fine to hear him talk of the way in which certain subjects should have been treated by eminent poets, according to his notions of the art. Thus he finds fault with Dryden's description of Bacchus in the *Alexander's Feast*, as if he were a mere good-looking youth or boon companion—

> 'Flushed with a purple grace,
> He shows his honest face'*—

instead of representing the God returning from the conquest of India, crowned with vine-leaves and drawn by panthers, and followed by troops of satyrs, of wild men and animals that he had tamed. You would think, in hearing him speak on this subject, that you saw Titian's picture of the meeting of *Bacchus and Ariadne*—so classic were his conceptions, so glowing his style.

Milton is his great idol, and he sometimes dares to compare himself with him. His Sonnets, indeed, have something of the same high-raised tone and prophetic spirit. Chaucer is another prime favourite of his, and he has been at the pains to modernize some of the Canterbury Tales. Those persons, who look upon Mr Wordsworth as a merely puerile writer, must be rather at a loss to account for his strong predilection for such geniuses as Dante and Michael Angelo. We do not think our author has any very cordial sympathy with Shakespeare. How should he? Shakespeare was the least of an egotist of any body in the world. He does not much relish the variety and scope of dramatic composition. 'He hates those interlocutions between Lucius and Caius.'* Yet Mr Wordsworth himself wrote a tragedy* when he was young; and we have heard the following energetic lines quoted from it, as put into the mouth of a person smit with remorse for some rash crime:

> '——Action is momentary,
> The motion of a muscle this way or that;
> Suffering is long, obscure and infinite!'*

Perhaps for want of light and shade, and the unshackled spirit of the drama, this performance was never brought forward. Our critic has a great dislike to Gray, and a fondness for Thomson and Collins. It is mortifying to hear him speak of Pope and Dryden whom, because they have been supposed to have all the possible excellences of poetry, he will allow to have none.

Nothing, however, can be fairer, or more amusing than the way in which he sometimes exposes the unmeaning verbiage of modern poetry. Thus, in the beginning of Dr Johnson's *Vanity of Human Wishes*—

> 'Let observation with extensive view
> Survey mankind from China to Peru'*—

he says there is a total want of imagination accompanying the words; the same idea is repeated three times under the disguise of a different phraseology. It comes to this: '*let observation* with extensive *observation observe* mankind'; or take away the first line, and the second,

> 'Survey mankind from China to Peru,'

literally conveys the whole. Mr Wordsworth is, we must say, a perfect Drawcansir* as to prose writers. He complains of the dry reasoners and matter-of-fact people for their want of *passion*; and he is jealous of the rhetorical declaimers and rhapsodists as trenching on the province of poetry. He condemns all French writers (as well of poetry as prose) in the lump. His list in this way is indeed small. He approves of Walton's Angler, Paley,* and some other writers of an inoffensive modesty of pretension. He also likes books of voyages and travels, and Robinson Crusoe. In art, he greatly esteems Bewick's woodcuts and Waterloo's sylvan etchings.* But he sometimes takes a higher tone, and gives his mind fair play. We have known him enlarge with a noble intelligence and enthusiasm on Nicolas Poussin's fine landscape-compositions, pointing out the unity of design that pervades them, the superintending mind, the imaginative principle that brings all to bear on the same end; and declaring he would not give a rush for any landscape that did not express the time of day, the climate, the period of the world it was meant to illustrate, or had not this character of *wholeness* in it.

His eye also does justice to Rembrandt's fine and masterly effects. In the way in which that artist works something out of nothing, and transforms the stump of a tree, a common figure, into an *ideal* object by the gorgeous light and shade thrown upon it, he perceives an analogy to his own mode of investing the minute details of nature with an atmosphere of sentiment, and in pronouncing Rembrandt to be a man of genius, feels that he strengthens his own claim to the title. It has been said* of Mr Wordsworth, that 'he hates conchology, that he hates the Venus of Medicis.' But these, we hope, are mere epigrams and *jeux-d'esprit*, as far from truth as they are free from malice: a sort of running satire or critical clenches—

'Where one for sense and one for rhyme
Is quite sufficient at one time.'*

We think, however, that if Mr Wordsworth had been a more liberal and candid critic, he would have been a more sterling writer. If a greater number of sources of pleasure had been open to him, he would have communicated pleasure to the world more frequently. Had he been less fastidious in pronouncing sentence on the works of others, his own would have been received more favourably, and treated more leniently. The current of his feelings is deep, but narrow; the range of his understanding is lofty and aspiring rather than discursive. The force, the originality, the absolute truth and identity, with which he feels some things, makes him indifferent to so many others. The simplicity and enthusiasm of his feelings, with respect to nature, render him bigoted and intolerant in his judgments of men and things. But it happens to him, as to others, that his strength lies in his weakness; and perhaps we have no right to complain. We might get rid of the cynic and the egotist, and find in his stead a common-place man. We should 'take the good the Gods provide us':* a fine and original vein of poetry is not one of their most contemptible gifts; and the rest is scarcely worth thinking of, except as it may be a mortification to those who expect per-fection from human nature, or who have been idle enough at some period of their lives to deify men of genius as possess-ing claims above it. But this is a chord that jars, and we shall not dwell upon it.

Lord Byron we have called, according to the old proverb, 'the spoiled child of fortune': Mr Wordsworth might plead, in mitigation of some peculiarities, that he is 'the spoiled child of disappointment'. We are convinced, if he had been early a popular poet, he would have borne his honours meekly, and would have been a person of great *bonhomie* and frankness of disposition. But the sense of injustice and of undeserved ridicule sours the temper and narrows the views. To have produced works of genius, and to find them neglected or treated with scorn, is one of the heaviest trials of human patience. We exaggerate our own merits when they are denied by others, and are apt to grudge and cavil at every particle of praise bestowed on those to whom we feel a conscious superi-ority. In mere self-defence we turn against the world when it turns against us, brood over the undeserved slights we receive; and thus the genial current of the soul is stopped, or vents itself in effusions of petulance and self-conceit. Mr Wordsworth has thought too much of contemporary critics and criticism, and less than he ought of the award of posterity and of the opinion, we do not say of private friends, but of those who were made so by their admiration of his genius.

He did not court popularity by a conformity to established models, and he ought not to have been surprised that his originality was not understood as a matter of course. He has *gnawed too much on the bridle*, and has often thrown out crusts to the critics, in mere defiance or as a point of honour when he was challenged, which otherwise his own good sense would have withheld. We suspect that Mr Wordsworth's feelings are a little morbid in this respect, or that he resents censure more than he is gratified by praise. Otherwise, the tide has turned much in his favour of late years. He has a large body of determined partisans, and is at present sufficiently in request with the public to save or relieve him from the last necessity to which a man of genius can be reduced—that of becoming the God of his own idolatry!

EXPLANATORY NOTES

3 First published in the *Champion* on 12, 19, and 26 October 1817 and republished in the *Yellow Dwarf* on 7 and 14 March the following year.

'*a vile jelly*': cf. *King Lear*, III. vii. 83.

Legitimacy: 'the principle of lineal succession to the throne as a political doctrine' (*NED*). The term appears to have been put into circulation in 1817, as part of the defence of monarchy after the defeat of Napoleon and the restoration of the Bourbons to the throne of France. For English radical writers it represented an attempt to re-assert the divine right of monarchs to their power, threatening the idea that the ultimate power of the monarch resided in popular consent to his or her rule.

'*the unbought grace of life*': the quotation comes from Burke's *Reflections on the Revolution in France* (1790). It is one example of a texture of ironic allusion to Burke's writing that runs through *What is the People?*

4 '*Fine word, Legitimate*': *King Lear*, I. ii. 18.

the Right-Liners . . . Sir Robert Filmer's: Sir Robert Filmer (died 1653), a strong royalist in the English Civil War. His most famous work, *Patriarcha*, is a defence of absolute royal authority, and the target for John Locke's criticism in the first of his *Two Treatises on Civil Government*, published in 1690.

Latter Lammas: 'a day that will never come' (*NED*).

5 '*Miraturque . . . poma*': Virgil, *Georgics*, ii. 82, translated as 'marvels at its strange leafage and fruits not its own' (Loeb edn., trans. H. R. Fairclough).

a certain author: John Stoddart, a leader writer and editor of *The Times*, Hazlitt's brother-in-law, later referred to as 'the professional gentleman'.

6 *though a libel on our own Government*: the phrase is a sign of the times. Hazlitt is awkwardly defending himself against the possibility of arrest for seditious libel by appearing to exempt the

Government of the day from criticism, although his disclaimer
can obviously be read ironically.

7 *the Delphin edition of Ovid's Metamorphoses*: the Delphin edition
was a collection of classical authors, issued by A. & J. Velpey;
160 volumes were published between 1819 and 1830; they were
noted for their gaudy covers.

'*Gods to punish*'. . . '*men of our infirmity*': cf. *Coriolanus*, III. i. 81.

In spite of Mr Malthus: an ironic allusion to Malthus's theory
that there is an in-built tendency for population to grow faster
than the food supply. For Hazlitt's more detailed criticism of
Malthus, see below pp. 67–83.

8 (*compagnons du lys*): a sound pun between English and French.
The Compagnons du Lys was an order whose members supported the restored Bourbon monarchy; their emblem was the
fleur-du-lys. The French pronunciation of the phrase makes it
sound like the English 'companions of Ulysses', the men who
were turned into swine by Circe. The story can be found in
Homer, *Odyssey*, x. Hazlitt is invoking a tradition of interpretation which read the transformation of the men into swine as
an allegory of moral and intellectual corruption.

'*Why, what a fool was I . . . God!*': cf. *The Tempest*, V. i. 295.

'*Because men suffer it, their toy, the world*': Cowper, *The Task*, v.
192.

9 *by-word*: used here in the sense given by the *NED*, 'an object
of scorn or contempt'.

'*cribbed, confined, and cabin'd in*': cf. *Macbeth*, III. iv. 24.

'*the right divine of Kings to govern wrong*': Pope, *The Dunciad*, iv.
188.

'*broad and casing as the general air . . . rock*': cf. *Macbeth*, II. iv. 22.

'*Like the rainbow's lovely form . . . ever*': Burns, *Tam O'Shanter*, ii.
61–6.

'*enthroned in the hearts of Kings*': *The Merchant of Venice*, IV. i. 189.

10 '*and levy cruel wars, wasting the earth*': Milton, *Paradise Lost*, ii.
501–2.

'*steeped in poverty to the very lips*': cf. *Othello*, IV. ii. 50.

'*punish the last successful example of a democratic rebellion*': according to a note Hazlitt wrote to one of his articles on *The Times*
newspaper, the phrase is Stoddart's.

'*large heart*' . . . '*confined in too narrow room*': unidentified in Howe's edition, but there may be an echo of Chapman, *Bussy D'Ambois*, I. ii. 153 and following.

Ferdinand VII: King of Spain in 1808 and, again, from 1813 to 1833. He abdicated the throne in 1808 and was replaced by Joseph Bonaparte. In 1813, with the defeat of Napoleon in Spain, Ferdinand was restored. As a restored monarch, Ferdinand is a sign of the times for Hazlitt.

11 *un peuple serf, corveable . . . misericorde*: roughly translated as 'a servile people, liable to forced labour and exploitation, at the mercy of others'.

lettres de cachet: according to Mme de Staël *lettres de cachet* 'permitted the royal, and consequently the ministerial, power to exile, to deport, or to imprison for his entire life, without trial, any man whatsoever'. They were also used to exempt the French nobility from the process of law.

corvées: a rent payed by labour which a French peasant owed to his or her lord.

menus plaisirs: pocket money or 'perks'.

12 *Mr C——or Lord C——*: Mr Canning (1770–1827); Foreign Secretary 1807–9, 1822–7. Lord Castlereagh (1769–1822); Chief Secretary to Ireland, then Secretary for War and Colonies in the period of the Napoleonic War, and from 1812 Foreign Secretary until his death by suicide in 1822. A notoriously boring and obscure parliamentary orator, his name was linked with Canning's when the two men fought a duel. Both politicians were associated with the repressive measures of Lord Liverpool's ministry.

Count Fathom or Jonathan Wild: Count Fathom is the villainous, gothic hero of a novel by Smollett, published in 1753. Jonathan Wild is a celebrated eighteenth-century criminal and the subject of a book by Henry Fielding, *The Life of Mr. Jonathan Wild the Great*, published in 1743.

'*O silly sheep. . . . *': unidentified.

'*any faction . . . hands*': Hazlitt rewrites a sentence from Burke's *Appeal from the New to the Old Whigs*.

13 *Vox populi vox Dei*: the voice of the people is the voice of God.

. . . *liberties of a country*: the first instalment of the essay published in the *Yellow Dwarf* on 7 March 1818 ended here. The next instalment was published in the issue of 14 March 1818.

14 *Lord Bacon*: Francis Bacon (1561–1626), essayist, philosopher, politician, and an early advocate of scientific method.

15 '*If they had not ploughed. . . . riddle*': Judges 14: 18.

Catholic Claims: Hazlitt alludes to the struggle by Catholics to abolish the laws excluding them from political office and education at Oxford and Cambridge. The outcome was the Catholic Emancipation Act of 1827.

16 *for recommending the dagger*: see Coleridge's 'Friend', no. 15 for the relevant text.

John Gifford . . . William Gifford: the two men were not related by blood but by politics. Both were prominent anti-radical writers of the period. William Gifford (1756–1826) edited the *Anti-Jacobin and Weekly Examiner* between 1797–8 and then in 1809 became editor of the Tory journal the *Quarterly Review*, where he published a savage attack on Keats's poem *Endymion*. Hazlitt launched a counter-attack with *A Letter to William Gifford*, published in 1819. John Gifford (1758–1818) was a miscellaneous writer who took over the Anti-Jacobin title when he launched the *Anti-Jacobin Review* in 1798. The *Anti-Jacobin Review* outlived Gifford by three years, ceasing publication in 1821.

17 '*universal Spanish nation*': the phrase is Canning's.

'*make him a willow cabin at its gate . . . night!*': cf. *Twelfth Night*, I. v. 253.

He indeed assures us . . . an article of 55 pages: see Southey's essay 'On Political Reform' in his *Essays, Moral and Political*, collected by the author I. 420–1.

Mr Locke has observed: the observation is in Locke's *Essay on Human Understanding*, IV. xx. 18.

19 *like Orlando's eldest brother*: cf. *As You Like It*, I. i. 8.

Bell and Lancaster's plans, Cheap Tract Societies: Hazlitt is referring to various early nineteenth-century schemes for popular education. What they had in common was an intention to resist the spread of radical ideas.

Mr Vansittart . . . 'Change-alley: Vansittart (1766–1851) was Chancellor of the Exchequer 1812–22. Hazlitt is probably referring in this passage to an episode in 1816 when Vansittart had been forced to raise revenue through borrowing after Parliament had denied him various forms of taxation.

Joanna Southcott: Joanna Southcott was born in 1750; a religious prophet, she became the centre of a millenarian cult which aroused considerable excitement. Her prophetic writings were sealed until such time as her prophecies came true. She claimed to be a harbinger of Christ's Second Coming. She died in 1814.

'*When the sky falls*': cf. Rabelais, *Gargantua and Pantagruel*, I. xi.

20 *Mr Kean*: Kean (1787–1833) was one of the most celebrated actors of his day. His passionate and expressive style was admired by Hazlitt, who promoted Kean's career in his theatre reviews.

'*hold a barren sceptre*': cf. *Macbeth*, III. i. 61.

'*for the Son to tread . . . steps*': Southey, *The Dream*, stanza 32.

21 *two Ferdinands*: Ferdinand I of Naples and Ferdinand VII of Spain.

a swinish multitude: Burke's notorious phrase from *Reflections on the Revolution in France*. The phrase was taken up by numerous writers, including Coleridge.

'*that complex constable*': unidentified.

Milton only spoke . . . Anglicano: the passage from Milton's *Defence of the People of England* (published 1658) translates 'I should say that a people which has felt the weight of slavery's yoke on its neck may be wise, learned, and noble enough to know what should be done with its own tyrant, without asking the advice of foreigners or pedagogues.' For the translation, see *Complete Prose Works of John Milton*, ed. Don M. Wolfe, iv. 338.

22 *Mr Burke's Sublime and Beautiful*: Hazlitt is referring to Burke's influential work on aesthetics, *A Philosophical Enquiry into the Origin of our Ideas of the Sublime and the Beautiful*, published in 1756.

poor Evans: Thomas Evans was librarian to the radical group, the Society of Spencean Philanthropists. He had been imprisoned on suspicion under the terms of the Habeus Corpus Suspension Act. In July 1817, a petition was presented on his behalf to Parliament. Amongst other things it set forth a set of objections to the conditions of Evans's imprisonment. These included a complaint about the refusal to allow Evans to have his flute with him while in prison. Hiley Addington, brother of Lord Sidmouth, the Home Secretary, replied to the petition on behalf of the Government. In his reply he conceded that Evans be allowed his flute on condition that he did not play it. Hence Hazlitt's ironic references to flute playing. For the text of the debate, see *Hansard* for 2 July 1817.

23 *his Lisbon Job*: according to Howe 'Canning had gone to Lisbon in 1814, and had been appointed ambassador extraordinary, at a salary of £14,000, to receive the King of Portugal on his return from Brazil. The king did not return after all, and Canning's appointment was represented by the Opposition as a job. A vote of censure was moved in the House of Commons on May 6th, 1817, and defeated by a majority of 174.'

'*duller than the fat weed . . . wharf*': cf. *Hamlet*, I. v. 32–4.

24 '*the dim suffusion*' . . . '. . . *find no dawn*': cf. Milton, *Paradise Lost*, iii. 22–6.

'*making Ossa like a wart*': cf. *Hamlet*, v. i. 277.

'*as gross as ignorance made drunk*': cf. *Othello*, III. iii. 408–9.

25 *Wat Tyler*: a leader of the Peasant's Revolt, who was killed in 1381 at a meeting in Smithfields, London, by supporters of Richard II. Southey had written a verse play in 1794 with the title *Wat Tyler*. The play was firmly on the side of the rebels and written as a critique of inequality. Southey did not publish the play in 1794, but in 1817 it was published, without the author's permission, in what proved to be a successful attempt to embarrass the now conservative Poet Laureate with his radical past.

26 '*a necessity that is not chosen, but chuses . . . anarchy*': from Burke's *Reflections on the Revolution in France*.

'*too foolish fond and pitiful*': cf. *King Lear*, IV. vii. 60.

John Ball's: priest and, with Wat Tyler, a leader of the Peasants' Revolt. He was executed in 1381. Like Tyler, he was an important symbolic figure in the English radical tradition.

27 '*did never wrong but with just cause*': cf. *Julius Caesar*, III. i. 47.

Carlton House: located in Pall Mall, and from 1783, after it had been redesigned as a palace, the residence of the Prince of Wales. Hazlitt is referring to a plan developed by the Prince of Wales, now Prince Regent, and Nash to develop the area of London around Carlton House. The scheme was started in 1811. One of its consequences was Regent Street; another, ironically, was the demolition of Carlton House in 1826 to carry on with the redevelopment.

28 *Exit by Mistake*: a comedy by the little-known writer, Jameson, which was produced at the Haymarket in July 1816. Hazlitt had written a mildly favourable notice of the play in the *Examiner* where he first makes the comparison between 'the late Mr Burke' and the character of Crockery as both admirers of 'the good old times'.

ON CONSISTENCY OF OPINION

29 First published in the London Magazine, November 1821. The essay is reprinted here with a minor omission.

'*Servetur ad imum . . . constet*': from Horace, *Ars Poetica*, ll. 126–7 translated as 'have it kept to the end even as it came forth at the first, and have it self-consistent' (Loeb edn., trans. H. R. Fairclough).

'*It is the eye of childhood . . . devil*': *Macbeth*, II. ii. 54.

'*Where the treasure is . . . also*': cf. Matt. 6:21.

'*to be wise were to be obstinate*': echoes *Coriolanus*, V. iii. 26.

30 *Mr —— . . . Catalogue Raisonnée*: refers to the artist, James Northcote RA (1746–1831). Northcote and Hazlitt had a long acquaintance. Their conversations formed the basis for Hazlitt's *Conversations of James Northcote*, published in 1830; 'the *Catalogue Raisonnée*': literally 'descriptive catalogue'. In this context it refers to the catalogues of pictures exhibited each year at the British Institution. As such the *catalogue raisonnée* would constitute a statement of the artistic values of the Royal Academy, a body that Hazlitt loathed. For the argument, see the excerpts from *Why the Arts are not Progressive* and *Whether the Fine Arts are Promoted by Academies* in this volume. See below, pp. 257–66.

sympathising beforehand . . . afterwards: the passage provides a brief sketch of what Hazlitt means by disinterestedness and its relation to belief and commitment; cf. the writings collected on The Self, pp. 165–207 below.

31 *bye-word*: cf. above, *What is the People*, note to p. 9.

32 '*sots, and knaves, and cowards*': cf. Pope, *An Essay on Man*, iv. 215.

'*I had rather hear my mother's cat mew . . . metre-ballad-mongers*': cf. *1 Henry IV*, III. i. 131.

33 '*amazed the very faculties . . . ears*': cf. *Hamlet*, II. ii. 558–9.

33 '*so small a drop of pity*': cf. *Cymbeline*, v. ii. 304.

he disfranchises the whole rustic population: Hazlitt probably has in mind Wordsworth's arguments in his *Two Addresses to the Freeholders of Westmorland*, published in 1818.

34 *Pantisocratist or Constitutional Association-monger*: Pantisocracy was the name given by Southey for a society in which private property would be abolished. In the early 1790s, in collaboration with Coleridge, he planned to found a model Pantisocracy in the United States. The plan was never realized. The Constitutional Association was founded in 1821 'to support the laws for suppressing seditious publications, and for defending the country from the fatal influence of disloyalty and sedition'. The juxtaposition of the two supports Hazlitt's argument about the identity of seemingly opposed political projects.

A gentleman . . . A romantic acquaintance: the gentleman is Charles Lloyd, Hazlitt's informant; the romantic acquaintance is Wordsworth.

35 *Mr Coleridge, indeed, sets down . . . sympathy*: cf. Coleridge's account of Wordsworth in ch. 22 of *Biographia Literaria*, first published in 1817.

Contra audentior ito: Vergil, *Aeneid*, iv. 195. This Latin tag is excerpted from a line whose translation reads 'Yield not thou to ills, but go forth to face them more boldly that thy fortune shall allow thee' (Loeb edn., trans. H. R. Fairclough).

36 *public opinion*: the passage is one example of Hazlitt's argument with himself. Contrast the favourable view of public opinion in *What is the People?*

'*whose genius . . . manna*': cf. Cowper, *The Task*, Bk. III. 255–6.

'*Like a worm . . . way*': cf. Chaucer, 'The Clerk's Tale', l. 880.

'*There's sympathy.*': *The Merry Wives of Windsor*, II. i. 7.

the gardens of Alcinous: the reference is to the story in Homer, *Odyssey*, vi.

'*ancestral voices*': Coleridge, 'Kubla Khan', l. 29.

37 '*I've heard of hearts unkind . . . mourning*': Wordsworth, *Simon Lee*, ll. 93–6.

cried up to the top of the compass: cf. *Hamlet*, III. ii. 359.

Burke: the quotation comes from Burke's *Speech on Economical Reform*. For the text of the speech, see *The Works of the Right*

Honourable Edmund Burke, with an Introduction by F. W. Raffety (Oxford University Press, 1906), ii. 303–85.

38 '*To have done . . . mockery*'; '*with one consent . . .*'; '*Like a fashionable host . . .*': all taken from Ulysses' speech in *Troilus and Cressida*, III. iii. 145–89.

'*noise and inexplicable dumb show*': cf. *Hamlet*, III. ii. 14.

39 '*Tell me your company . . . opinions*': cf. Cervantes, *Don Quixote*, Part 2, ch. 23.

West . . . Stothard: Benjamin West (1738–1820), American-born painter who became President of the Royal Academy in 1792. His paintings were admired by many of his contemporaries, but less so by Hazlitt. See below in the part on Art and Literature. Thomas Stothard (1773–1834) was a painter and book-illustrator, fellow of the Royal Academy from 1794.

40 *Hogarth's Rules of Perspective*: Hazlitt is probably making an ironic reference to the arguments in Hogarth's *Analysis of Beauty*, first published in 1753; see, in particular, chs. 3 and 12.

'*Linked each to each . . . piety*': echoes a line from Wordsworth's lyric 'My heart leaps up . . .' and illustrates one of Hazlitt's strategies for quotation: to turn an author's words ironically against him.

ILLUSTRATIONS OF 'THE TIMES' NEWSPAPER: ON MODERN LAWYERS AND POETS

41 Hazlitt published a series of four articles on *The Times* newspaper in the *Examiner* between 1 December 1816 and 12 January 1817. The last three of these had the title *Illustrations of 'The Times' Newspaper* and it was these three pieces that Hazlitt reprinted in his *Political Essays* of 1819. Excerpts from the second and third of the *Illustrations* are printed in this selection.

'*Facilis descensus Averni . . . . est*': Virgil, *Aeneid*, vi. 126–9; translated as 'Easy is the descent to Avernus: night and day the door to gloomy Dis stands open; but to recall thy steps and to pass out to the upper air, this is the task, this is the toil . . .' (Loeb ed., trans. H. R. Fairclough).

'*Let no man go about to cozen honesty*': cf. *The Merchant of Venice*, II. ix. 37.

41 *He has nothing to support him*: this is one of the occasions in Hazlitt's work when he seems to be writing a disguised self-portrait, and one which takes a characteristically self-mocking turn, as Hazlitt detects the connection between political conviction and theatrical pose.

Sam Sharpset: character in Thomas Morton's comedy *The Slave*, first performed at Covent Garden in November 1816.

42 '*the Devil is very potent . . . them*': cf. *Hamlet*, II. ii. 598–9.

The poet-laureate: Robert Southey, whose poem *Carmen Nuptiale* supplies the quotation beginning 'Britain's warriors . . .'; see *Carmen Nuptiale*, the Dream, stanza 16.

Mr Croker's: John Wilson Croker (1780–1857), writer and politician. He was MP for a number of constituencies, and held office as the chief secretary for Ireland in 1808 and, in the following year, became secretary of the Admiralty. He was a regular contributor to the Quarterly Review, where he attacked the work of Leigh Hunt, Shelley, and Keats, most notably through a review of Keats's *Endymion*, published in September 1818. He was a political and cultural ally of the conservative Southey.

43 '*Our's is an honest employment*': cf. John Gay, *The Beggar's Opera*, I. i. Peachum is a criminal, whose opening song in the Opera establishes the similarities between his profession and the apparently respectables ones.

Lord Ellenborough: Edward Law (1750–1818) Lord Chief Justice of England from 1802, and before then one of the prosecuting counsels in the trials in 1794 of Hardy, Horne Tooke, and others, which were undertaken by the Government in an attempt to suppress the activities of the London Corresponding Society and the Society for Constitutional Information. Ellenborough presided at the trials of Hazlitt's friends, John and Leigh Hunt, when they were prosecuted first for publishing an article in the *Examiner* condemning excessive flogging in the army, and secondly, in 1812, for libelling the Prince of Wales.

'*look on both indifferently*': cf. *Julius Caesar*, I. ii. 87.

44 *Garrow*: Sir William Garrow (1760–1840), Solicitor-General 1812–13, and Attorney-General 1813–17.

Lord Castlereagh: see note above to p. 12.

45 '*the tried wisdom of parliament*': an ironic echo of a phrase from the Prince Regent's reply in 1816 to the Address of the Corporation of London on the subject of the national distress and 'the approaching hard season'.

Such a person: John Stoddart, see note above to p. 5. Stoddart's proposals in various *Times* editorials are referred to in what follows.

'*the lodged hatred*': cf. *The Merchant of Venice*, IV. i. 60.

Marshall Ney: Ney (1769–1815) was one of Napoleon's principal military leaders; he was executed on 7 December 1815 because he went over to Napoleon's side after the latter's return from Elba.

46 *the declaration of the 25th of March*: in fact the Declaration of the Allied Powers of 13 March 1815 which stated that, as a result of his return from Elba, Bonaparte had 'placed himself without the pale of civil and social relations'.

'*with famine, sword, and fire . . . hounds*': cf. *Henry V*, Prologue, ll. 7–8.

'*My soul, turn from them . . . survey*': cf. Goldsmith, *The Traveller*, l. 165.

'*Carnage was the daughter of Humanity*': cf. Wordsworth, *Ode, 1815*.

47 *Pantisocracy's*: see note above to p. 34.

49 '*I've heard of hearts unkind . . . mourning*': Wordsworth, *Simon Lee* ll. 93–6. In the edition of the *Political Essays* Hazlitt adds the following note to this quotation: '*Simon Lee, the old Huntsman*, a tale by Mr. Wordsworth, of which he himself says "It is no tale, but if you think | Perhaps a tale you'll make it." In this view it is a tale indeed, not "of other times", but of these.' This is a coded reference to what Hazlitt regarded as Wordsworth's unjustified hostility towards him.

51 '*Of whatsoever race his godhead be, . . . gold*': Dryden, *Absalom and Achitophel*, ll. 100–103.

Louis XVIII: Louis (1755–1824) was restored to the throne of France after the first defeat of Napoleon. The brother of Louis XVI, he was King from 1814 until his death.

omne tulit punctum: Horace, *Ars Poetica*, l. 343; translated as 'He has won every vote' (Loeb ed., trans. H. R. Fairclough).

52 *just failed it*: Stoddart was dismissed from *The Times* at the end of 1816.

'*in contempt of the will of the people*': Burke, *Reflections on the Revolution in France*.

a true Jacobin: again Hazlitt seems to be describing himself without being explicit about it.

Odia in longum jaciens . . . promeret: Tacitus, *Annals*, i. 69; in its original context the quotation is translated as 'kept sowing the seeds of future hatreds, grievances for the emperor to store away and produce some day with increase' (Loeb edn., trans. J. Jackson).

53 '*three poets in a dream*': the three poets are Wordsworth (the receipt stamp is an ironical reference to his sinecure as Distributor of Stamps for Westmorland); Southey (wearing the laurels of the Poet Laureate); and Coleridge (the 'symbol' alludes to the obscurity of Coleridge's writing).

CHARACTER OF MR BURKE

54 I have selected two pieces about Edmund Burke. The first is excerpted from an essay written by Hazlitt in 1807 as part of his editorial material for a collection of parliamentary speeches, *The Eloquence of the British Senate*. The second character was published in 1817, originally forming part of an article, *Coleridge's Literary Life*, in the *Edinburgh Review*. Hazlitt republished both pieces in his *Political Essays* of 1819. For this volume he added a footnote to the 1807 character: 'This character was written in a fit of extravagant candour, at a time when I thought I could do justice, or more than justice, to an enemy, without betraying a cause.'

'*Alas! Leviathan was not so tamed!*': Cowper, *The Task*, ii. 322.

The corner stone . . . to the Jews: Hazlitt links together two Biblical allusions. One is from Psalm 118: 22; the other comes from 1 Corinthians 1: 23.

59 '*How charming is divine philosophy . . . lute!*': Milton, *Comus*, ll. 476–9.

'*Lady's Magazine*': *The Lady's Magazine or entertaining Companion for the fair sex* was published between 1770 and 1818. Hazlitt is happy to endorse here the pejorative attitudes towards women current at the time.

61 *in the following extracts*: Hazlitt did not bother to edit out reminders of the original provenance of this character when he republished the piece in the *Political Essays* of 1819.

62 *Mr Burke, the opponent of the American war*: Hazlitt is replying to Coleridge's argument in ch. 10 of *Biographia Literaria* that Burke's defence of the American Revolution was consistent with his attack on the French Revolution.

65 *his speech on the Begum's affair . . . Warren Hastings*: Warren Hastings (1732–1818) played a prominent role in Britain's commercial exploitation of India and in the establishment of British political rule there. He worked in India from 1750 to 1785 and was, for a period, governor-general. In 1788 there was a move to impeach Hastings because of what was held to be his corrupt administration of the sub-continent. Burke was one of Hasting's main opponents and waxed eloquent against him. Hastings was finally acquitted in 1795 after a protracted trial, but he was left with enormous costs to pay. One of the occasions of Burke's rhetoric was what Hazlitt refers to as 'the Begum's affair'. A begum is a Mohammedan lady of high rank. One of the accusations against Hastings was that he had been instrumental in the forcible appropriation of property owned by two begums, the mother and grandmother of the Nawab of Oudh.

an interpretation on the word abdication: the interpretation of the political consequences of the abdication of James II in 1688 was a source of controversy between conservatives and radicals. The radical view, maintained by Hazlitt, was that it had created a precedent for the people to dismiss unjust rulers. Burke's argument, put forward in *Reflections on the Revolution in France*, was that 1688 was 'a parent of settlement, and not a nursery of future revolutions'; its purpose 'to render it almost impracticable for any future sovereign to compel the states of the kingdom to have recourse to those violent remedies.' The violent remedy, according to Burke, was abdication.

Beggar's Opera: a highly successful comic opera, set in Newgate Prison, written by John Gay (1685–1732) and first performed in 1728.

Salvator Rosa: Rosa (1615–73) was an Italian painter who was noted in late eighteenth-century England for his wild and savage landscape paintings.

65 *which Mr Coleridge thinks . . . philosophy*: cf. *Biographia Literaria*, ch. 10.

66 *'Never so sure . . . hate'*: cf. Pope, *Moral Essays*, ii. 51–2.

MALTHUS

67 Two excerpts from Hazlitt's writings on Malthus are printed here. Both were originally part of Hazlitt's *Reply to Malthus* first published in 1807. He republished them amongst other writings on Malthus in the *Political Essays* of 1819. The first went under the title, *On the Principle of Population as Affecting the Schemes of Utopian Improvement*; the second under the title, *On the Application of Mr. Malthus's Principle to the Poor Laws*.

'*A swaggering paradox . . . common-place*': unidentified.

Essay on Population: Malthus (1766–1834) wrote and had published anonymously an *Essay on the Principle of Population as it affects the Future Improvement of Society* in 1798. As its full title implies the essay was written as a polemical response to the utopian radicalism of Condorcet and Godwin. Godwin anticipated a society in which 'There will be no war, no crimes, no administration of justice . . . and no government. Beside this, there will be neither disease, anguish, melancholy, nor resentment.' Malthus argued that suffering was an inexorable feature of social existence given the tendency of population to outstrip the available food supply.

68 *a large quarto*: refers to the extensively revised 1803 edition of the essay which Malthus published under his own name.

69 *the Reply of the author of political Justice*: William Godwin (1756–1836): Godwin's main work of political and social theory, *Political Justice*, was published in 1793, and, in the following year, he published a novel, *Caleb Williams*. Godwin's reputation was considerable during the 1790s, but declined during the period of conservative reaction in English culture and politics. Theoretically radical but practically cautious, Godwin was an anarchist who believed that political institutions corrupted the human capacity to live in a society ordered by reason, benevolence, and moral and intellectual happiness. Godwin's circle included, at various times, Wordsworth, Coleridge, Lamb, Shelley, and Hazlitt himself. The reply Hazlitt refers to is *Godwin's Thoughts on Dr. Parr's Spital Sermon*, published in 1801.

70 *Condorcet*: Condorcet (1743–94) was a French mathematician, political economist, and anti-clerical thinker. He believed that gradual social and political reform would bring about a society based on the acknowledgement of human rights. He was a supporter of the French Revolution during its early years, associated with the moderate Girondins. In 1793 he was accused of betraying the revolution by the radical revolutionary, Chabot. He fled Paris, but was recognized and arrested. He poisoned himself and died in a prison cell on 29 March 1794.

'false, sophistical, unfounded in the extreme'.... "exuberant strength of my argument": Hazlitt draws these quotations from Malthus's *Essay on Population*.

Wallace: Robert Wallace (1697–1771), who published two works on population: *A Dissertation on the Numbers of Mankind in Ancient and Modern Times* (1753) and *Various Prospects of Mankind, Nature and Providence* (1761). Wallace's work is difficult to classify, moving between theology, metaphysics, and political economy. Hazlitt was amongst those who claimed that Malthus's main theory on population was borrowed from Wallace.

71 *'What conjuration ... magic'*: *Othello*, I. iii. 92.

72 *'as one picks pears ... loathe'*: unidentified.

73 *Trim ... uncle Toby's*: characters in Laurence Sterne, *The Life and Opinions of Tristram Shandy* (1759–67). Hazlitt refers to an episode in Bk. VI, ch. 23 of the novel.

74 *'These three bear record ... population'*: cf. 1 John 5: 7.

stage-maxim: cf. Buckingham, *The Rehearsal* (1671), I. i.

75 *''Tis as easy as lying ... stops'*: cf. *Hamlet*, III. ii. 348.

Mr Whitbread's Poor Bill: Samuel Whitbread (1758–1815), politician, and vigorous opponent of the Pitt administration in the 1790s. In 1807 Whitbread proposed a complicated bill for the regulation of the poor. It recommended a free education system, an equalization of country rates, and badges to distinguish the deserving from the undeserving poor. Malthus was amongst those who attacked Whitbread's Poor Bill, which was never enacted.

76 *'To this end ... gratitude'*: another quotation from Malthus, in this case from the second edition of the *Essay on Population*.

76 *well answered by Mr Cobbett*: the answer came in the *Political Register* for May 1819 when Cobbett addressed a letter to Parson Malthus, beginning abruptly 'Parson'.

77 *in a separate work*: Hazlitt's *Reply to Malthus* of 1807.

79 *these paper bullets of the brain*: *Much Ado About Nothing*, II. iii. 216.

81 *"would submit to the sufferings . . . Christian"*: Malthus, *Essay on Population* (2nd edn.).

"the interests of humanity": ibid.

Autos-da-fé: literally 'Acts of Faith'. The phrase also refers to the ceremonies accompanying the delivery of judgement by the Inquisition. Now generally taken to refer to the burning of a heretic.

"the strict line of duty . . . man": Malthus, *Essay on Population* (2nd edn.).

82 *curtain lecture*: private lecture given by a wife to her husband.

gravelled: according to the *OED* 'to set fast, confound, embarrass, non-plus, perplex, puzzle'.

THE FRENCH REVOLUTION

84 The French Revolution was the decisive political event of Hazlitt's lifetime, and he frequently recurred to it in his writing. The texts selected here are taken from Hazlitt's *Life of Napoleon*, initially published in four volumes from 1828 to 1830. This work was the occasion of Hazlitt's fullest analysis of the causes and consequences of the Revolution. The first extract is taken from ch. 3, *The French Revolution—Preliminary Remarks*, and the second from ch. 6, *The National Convention*.

the great organ of intellectual improvement and civilisation: Hazlitt added the following footnote: 'The free states of antiquity, or the republics in the middle ages, were single cities, where the spirit of liberty and independence was called forth, and strengthened by personal intercourse and communication. The towns in different parts of Europe, on the same principle, obtained several immunities before the *villains* or country people thought of throwing off their yoke. In Spain the cities are ripe for a revolution, while the peasantry are averse to any change.'

'*they pull down the house . . . nuisance*': adaptation of a sentence from Edmund Burke's 'On Economical Reform'. The original reads 'They go to work by the shortest way—they abate the nuisance, they pull down the house.'

88 *the Tartuffe*: a comedy by the French playwright, Molière (1622–73). The play, an attack on religious hypocrisy, was first performed in 1664. The directness of its attack led to the play's suppression, and it was not performed again until 1667 under another title, *L'Imposteur*.

But books anticipate and conform . . . philosophy: note the contrast between Hazlitt's account of the effects of reading here and his account in *On Modern Comedy* (see below pp. 101–9).

89 *mild, paternal sway*: an ironic echo of Burke's phraseology in his *Reflections on the Revolution in France*.

90 *Magna est veritas, et prevalebit*: truth is great and will prevail.

92 *lettre-de-cachet*: see above note to *What is the People?*, p. 11.

Mr Burke . . . 'king's castle!': see Burke's *Reflections on the Revolution in France* .

93 *The nation, in the language of the day, . . . wanted to be something*: 'the language of the day' is a translation of the opening of Abbe Sieyes's pamphlet, *Qu'est-ce que le Tiers-État* first published in 1789. Sieyes had advanced the claims of the Third Estate in a rhetorical sequence of questions and answers: 'Qu'est-ce que le Tiers-État? Tout. Qu'a-t-il été jusqu'à present dans l'ordre politique? Rien. Que demande-t-il? A être quelque chose.' (What is the Third Estate? Everything. What has it been up till now in the political order? Nothing. What does it ask for? To be something.)

Sieyes (1748–1836) was a Catholic priest who came to prominence as a leader in the early days of the French Revolution. In addition to his activities as a pamphleteer, he proposed in 1789 that the Third Estate should meet as the National Assembly. Later he became a supporter of Napoleon and went into exile in Belgium when the French monarchy was restored in 1814, but returned to France in 1830, under the July Monarchy.

Hazlitt identifies the Third Estate with the nation and, therefore, echoes Sieyes's universalizing claim that it is 'everything'. It would be more accurate to see the term as referring to the French middle class who emerged as an economic and then political force in the eighteenth century and distinguished themselves from the other two 'estates', the nobility and the clergy.

94 *This 'differences' Robespierre*: Hazlitt follows a usage of Sir Thomas Browne's; see *Religio Medici*, Part 1.

95 *'keystone that made up the arch'*: cf. Ps. 118: 22.

96 *Shaw the Life-guards'-man . . . Coup-Tête*: Shaw was a well-known boxer, who was killed at Waterloo, and commemorated in Tom Moore's *Epistle from Tom Crib to Big Ben*, a comic poem, published in 1815, sympathetic to the defeated and exiled Napoleon. 'Coup-Tête' (literally translated as Cut-Head) was the nickname given to Matthew Jourdan, instigator of the massacres at Avignon in 1791.

the massacres of Ismael and Warsaw: in 1794 Kosciusko, the Polish leader, organized an uprising against the partition of Poland. The uprising was defeated and ruthlessly punished by the Russians and the Prussians. Warsaw capitulated in 1794 after the Russian army massacred thousands of the inhabitants of Praga, a suburb of the city, and Hazlitt probably refers to this episode here. The Poles had looked unsuccessfully for support from revolutionary France. Ismael is a city in the Odessa region of the Ukraine. I have not been able to trace the exact episode that concerns Hazlitt, but the city was taken by the Russians in 1770, and it may have been caught up in the Polish uprising.

97 *'Rather than so, . . . outrance'*: cf. *Macbeth*, III. i. 70.

'brave Sansculottes were no triflers': unidentified.

'like tumbler-pigeons . . . figure': unidentified.

98 *'the drapery of a moral imagination'*: echoes Burke's *Reflections* where Burke writes of 'The decent drapery of life . . . the wardrobe of a moral imagination'.

rendered its continuance endurable: Hazlitt added the following footnote in the *Life of Napoleon*: 'I have not tantalised the reader by making it a question whether the dramatic interest which Robespierre's system excited in Paris or the newspaper interest it excited through Europe was not a set-off to the actual sufferings of the individuals who came within its grasp, as some writers have alleged in extenuation of the hardships of the subjects of despotic governments who have not a house over their heads or a rag to cover them, that they have at least the pleasure of seeing the fine palaces and fine liveries of the great. I would only observe that Legitimacy is come to a fine pass, when instead of the *Jus Divinum* and the absolute will of the sovereign, all that its ablest defenders can say in its behalf is reduced to the pleasure which the people have in looking at it as a raree-shew.'

ON MODERN COMEDY

101 The excerpt is taken from the second of two letters written by Hazlitt to the *Morning Chronicle* in October 1813. The first of the two letters was republished as an essay in Hazlitt's 1817 collection, *The Round Table*. The correspondent Hazlitt refers to is William Mudford, who was at the time drama critic of the *Morning Chronicle*.

not one but all mankind's epitome: cf. Dryden, *Absalom and Achitophel*, i. 546.

103 *The picture of the Flamborough Family*: see Oliver Goldsmith's novel, *The Vicar of Wakefield*, ch. 16.

104 *if Molière had lived . . . day*: see note to p. 88 above.

the heroines . . . which Wycherley has contrived: Molière's play *The School for Women* was first performed in 1662. The Restoration dramatist, Sir William Wycherley (1640–1716), was strongly influenced by Molière's play when he wrote *The Country Wife*, first performed in 1675. Alithea and Mrs Peggy are characters in Wycherley's play, which, like Molière's, is a comedy about marriage and the control of women.

Gertrude of Wyoming to The Lady of the Lake: *Gertrude of Wyoming* is a sentimental narrative poem, published in 1809 by Thomas Campbell. *The Lady of the Lake* is a narrative poem on sentimental and romantic themes, written by Sir Walter Scott, and first published in 1810.

Corinna of Italy: refers to a romantic novel by Madame de Staël, published in 1807, containing descriptions of Italian art and manners.

Voltaire . . . Cato: Voltaire had praised Addison's *Cato* in his *Discourse on Tragedy* (1731) where, commenting on English tragedy, he refers to it as 'the only well-written tragedy in the entire nation'. Addison (1672–1719) was a poet, moralist, and dramatist. *Cato* was first performed in 1717.

The Heiress . . . Basil: *The Heiress* was a comedy written by Sir John Burgoyne (1722–92), first produced in 1786; *The Confederacy* was written by Sir John Vanbrugh (1664–1726). The play, a free translation of Dancourt's *Les Bourgeoises à la Mode*, was first performed in 1705. *The Way of the World* by Congreve (1670–1729) was first performed in 1700; *Count Basil* was written by Joanna Baillie (1762–1851) as one of a sequence of *Plays of the Passions*, written and produced between 1798–1802.

105 *'wan that hang the pensive head'*: Milton, *Lycidas*, l. 147.

'They have not seen the court . . . damnable': cf. *As You Like It*, III. ii. 37–40.

Millamant . . . Sir Roger de Coverly: Millamant is the heroine in Congreve's *Way of the World*; Sir Roger de Coverley was an imaginary character invented by Addison as one of the members of the club who supposedly wrote the *Spectator*. He became an emblem of the perfect English gentleman.

'the ring of mimic Statesmen': cf. Pope, *Moral Essays*, Epistle to Bathurst, ll. 309–10.

Baron Grimm: Friedrich Melchior, Baron Grimm (1723–1807); he lived in Paris from 1749 to 1790, where he was a close associate of the 'philosophes', including Diderot; in 1753 he started a critical review, the Correspondance Littéraire, which was circulated amongst a small, cosmopolitan and aristocratic audience. The Correspondance had been published in a more accessible form between 1812 and 1814. As Hazlitt implies, Grimm was thought of as the epitome of the urbane, elegant intellectual, and viewed with some suspicion in England as a result.

Angelica and a Miss Prue: Hazlitt refers to a number of characters in Congreve's play, *Love for Love*, first staged in 1695.

106 *Amelia . . . Clarissa*: heroines of eighteenth-century English fiction: Amelia is the eponymous heroine of Fielding's last novel, published in 1751; Sophia Western is the heroine of Fielding's *Tom Jones*, published in 1749, and Clarissa is the heroine of Richardson's novel, published 1747–8.

loves of the plants and the triangles: an allusion to the poet, philosopher, and scientist Erasmus Darwin (1731–1802). Darwin was a cult figure in the 1790s and, for a while, his work was much admired by Wordsworth and Coleridge. Darwin drew on Linnaeus's theories about the sexuality of plants in his witty poem, *The Loves of Plants*, published in 1789, as the second part of *The Botanic Garden*, intended as a comprehensive poem about the natural world. By the time Hazlitt was writing Darwin's reputation had gone into decline, partly as the result of a satire on his evolutionary ideas, *The Loves of the Triangles*, published in 1798, and co-authored by the Government minister, George Canning.

107 *The Upholsterer in The Tatler*: a character, in Steele's magazine, who follows the news obsessively; see e.g. *The Tatler*, nos. 155, 160, 178.

Omne tulit punctum: Horace, *Ars Poetica*, l. 343: translated as 'he has won every vote'. See also above note to p. 51.

109 *the trio in the Memoirs of M. Grimm*: untraced.

MODERN TRAGEDY

109 First published under the title *The Drama: No. IV* in the *London Magazine* for April 1820 as one of a series of pieces assessing the state of the contemporary theatre. An excerpt from the article of April 1820 is printed here.

110 '*look abroad into universality*': Bacon, *The Advancement of Learning*, bk. I, section 3, para. 6.

'*are embowelled . . . and stuffed*': Burke, *Reflections on the Revolution in France*.

the Upholsterer . . . in the Tatler: see above note to p. 107.

'*a counterfeit presentment*': *Hamlet*, III. iv. 54.

111 '*interlocutions between Lucius and Caius*': Hazlitt is quoting himself. He used the formula on a number of occasions when referring to Wordsworth's dislike of Shakespeare. In his *Reply to Z*, an unpublished riposte to the attack on him in *Blackwood's Magazine*, Hazlitt had written about Wordsworth: 'There was something in Shakespeare that he could not make up his mind to, for he hated those interlocutions between Lucius and Caius.' As Howe points out there is no dialogue between Lucius and Caius in *Julius Caesar*. Hazlitt has either misremembered the play, or he is ironically pointing out that Wordsworth read Shakespeare with little attention.

'*to relish all as sharply*': cf. *The Tempest*, V. i. 23–4.

112 '*unfeathered, two-legged thing*': Dryden, *Absalom and Achitophel*, l. 170.

'*You may wear . . . difference*': cf. *Hamlet*, IV. v. 179.

113 '*He sits in the centre*': cf. Milton, *Comus*, ll. 382–3.

114 *Mr Wordsworth's hankering after the drama*: in 1795–6 Wordsworth had written a tragedy, *The Borderers*, which had been

refused by the Covent Garden management. Hazlitt had either read the play in manuscript, or heard it alluded to in conversation with Wordsworth.

114 '*daily intercourse of all this unintelligible world*': cf. Wordsworth, *Tintern Abbey*, ll. 40–1.

115 '*Like a wild overflow . . . desolate*': Beaumont and Fletcher, *Philaster*, v. ii. 74–81.

' '*Tis three feet long . . . wide*': Wordsworth, *The Thorn*, l. 33.

he has said of Mr Maturin: see Coleridge, *Biographia Literaria*, ch. 23. Charles Maturin (1782–1824) is best remembered for his Gothic novel, *Melmoth the Wanderer*, first published in 1820. In 1816 his tragedy, *Bertram*, was performed at Drury Lane in a production by Edmund Kean.

His Remorse *is a spurious tragedy*: Coleridge's play was first performed on 23 January 1813, at the Drury Lane Theatre and had a run of twenty nights.

116 '*What? if one reptile . . . unnumber'd!*': Coleridge, *Remorse*, III. ii. 96–104 and 107–14. Hazlitt omits Valdez's reply to the first part of Ordonio's speech.

nor Mr Moore either: Thomas Moore (1779–1852), born in Dublin, a prolific poet whose work includes *Lalla Rookh*, published in 1817, and a satirical poem, *The Fudge Family in Paris*, published in 1818 and admired by Hazlitt.

the conclusion of the Black Dwarf: *The Black Dwarf* is one of the shorter of Scott's Waverley Novels and was first published in 1816.

117 *a ride and tye business*: 'of two (or three) persons: to travel with one horse by alternately riding and walking, each one riding ahead for some distance and tying up the horse for the one who comes behind' (*OED*).

THE FIGHT

117 First published in the *New Monthly Magazine* for February 1822. The essay was nearly turned down for publication as 'a very vulgar thing'. The fight Hazlitt writes about was between Tom Hickman, nicknamed the 'gas-man' and Bill Neate. It took place at Hungerford in Berkshire on 11 December 1821. The excerpt printed here begins with Hazlitt's arrival at a coaching inn in Newbury.

something like Matthews: Charles Matthews (1776–1835), an actor and entertainer, celebrated for his powers as a mimic.

'*A lusty man . . . able*': cf. Chaucer, *The Canterbury Tales*, General Prologue, l. 167.

'*confound . . . don't be insipid!*': 'insipid' is one of Hazlitt's favourite terms of disapproval. It indicates a lack of energy and commitment, a defensive conformity. See above p. 106.

118 '*standing like greyhounds in the slips*': cf. *Henry V*, III. i. 31.

oaken towel: slang word for stick or cudgel.

'*he moralised into a thousand similies*': cf. *As You Like It*, II. i. 44–5.

'*loud and furious fun*': cf. Burns, *Tam O' Shanter*, l. 145.

Jem Belcher . . . 'Cribb's beating Jem': Belcher and Cribb were two well-known prize-fighters; Cribb defeated Belcher twice in 1807 and 1809.

119 *Toms*: a fictional name Hazlitt gives to Joseph Parkes (1796– 1865). Apart from being a friend of Hazlitt, Parkes was a lawyer and a follower of Bentham.

Gully: prize-fighter who retired from professional boxing in 1808.

the old maxim: Hazlitt alludes to a speech given in 1792 by the revolutionary leader, Danton. The maxim translates as 'Audacity, more audacity, always audacity, and France is saved.'

the FANCY: the nickname given to prize-fighters and those who follow them. For more on the culture, see Pierce Egan's *Boxiana*, published in 1818.

'*Alas! . . . tamed!*': cf. Cowper, *The Task*, ii. 322.

120 *my old master Richmond*: a boxer who may have taught Hazlitt to fight.

Achilles surveyed Hector: Homer, *Iliad*, xx.

the Game Chicken: nickname of Henry Pearce (1777–1809), one of the celebrated prize-fighters of the period.

Turtle: nickname for John Thirtell (1794–1824), trainer and fight promoter who was executed for murder in 1824.

'*That man was made to mourn*': cf. Prior, *Solomon on the Vanity of the World*, iii. 240 and Burns's poem, 'That man was made to mourn'.

121 '*Between the acting . . . dream*': *Julius Caesar*, II. i. 63–5.

121 '*my fairest hopes*': alludes to the failure of Hazlitt's love affair with Sarah Walker.

122 '*with-Atlantean shoulders*': Milton, *Paradise Lost*, ii. 306.

the scratch: 'line drawn across a ring to which boxers are brought for an encounter' (*OED*).

123 '*grinned horrible . . . smile*': Milton, *Paradise Lost*, ii. 846.

'*like two clouds . . . Caspian*': cf. *Paradise Lost*, ii. 714–16.

124 *Jackson*: John Jackson (1769–1845), a prize-fighter who had retired by the time of the fight that Hazlitt writes about.

125 *Sir Fopling Flutter*: comic character in *The Man of Mode* by Sir George Etherege (1634?–1691). The play was first staged in 1676.

Jack Pigott: fictional name for P. G. Patmore (1786–1855), a friend of Hazlitt. Patmore wrote about Hazlitt in his memoir, *My Friends and Acquaintances*, published in 1854.

126 *O procul este profani*: Virgil, *Aeneid*, vi. 258: translated as 'away unhallowed ones' (Loeb edn., trans. H. R. Fairclough).

a cross: slang for something that is fixed, dishonest, or fraudulent. The 'interlopers' are claiming that the fight has been rigged.

the New Eloise: *La Nouvelle Héloïse* was published in 1761 and was one of Rousseau's most influential works. Rousseau was a formative author for Hazlitt.

very like Mr Windham: William Windham (1750–1810) was a politician and member of a wealthy landed family based in Felbrigg Hall, Norfolk. He was a supporter of Fox and of Cobbett; briefly secretary for war and colonies in Lord Grenville's administration, he was well known at the time for his good looks and strength. Boxing was amongst his many sporting interests.

the famous Broughton and George Stephenson: Hazlitt and his interlocutor have got their dates mixed up. The fight took place in 1741, not 1770.

THE INDIAN JUGGLERS

128 The essay first appeared in *Table Talk; or, Original Essays*, published in two volumes between 1821 and 1822. The conclusion of the essay reprints Hazlitt's obituary tribute to the fives player, John Cavenagh, which had been printed in the

Examiner for 7 February 1819. The Indian Jugglers had performed at the Olympic New Theatre, Newcastle Street, The Strand in the winter of 1815.

130 *to dance on a tight-rope*: according to Sheridan Knowles, Hazlitt had trained as a tight-rope walker.

131 '*In argument they own'd . . . argue still*': Goldsmith, *The Deserted Village*, ll. 211–12.

132 '*to allow for the wind*': the quotation comes from Scott, *Ivanhoe*, ch. 13.

'*human face divine*': Milton, *Paradise Lost*, iii. 44.

133 *H——s and H——s*: refers to Hayman, Highmore, and Hudson, three portrait painters who were contemporaries of Sir Joshua Reynolds.

his blandness of gusto: for Gusto, see below pp. 266–70.

'*in tones and gestures hit*': cf. Milton, *Paradise Regained*, iv. 255.

To snatch this grace: Hazlitt is repeating Pope, *Essay on Criticism*, l. 153.

'*commercing with the skies*': Milton, *Il Penseroso*, l. 39.

'*And visions, . . . every bough*': from Gray's letter to Horace Walpole, ll. 7–8.

134 '*Thrills . . . the line*': rephrases lines from Addison, *Milton's Style Imitated*, ll. 123–4.

'*half flying, half on foot*': cf. Milton, *Paradise Lost*, ii. 941–2.

135 *I know an individual*: the individual is Leigh Hunt, poet, essayist, and for some years editor of the *Examiner*. Hunt was a friend and literary associate of Hazlitt.

nugæ canoræ: from Horace, *Ars Poetica*, l. 322: properly the phrase is 'nugaeque canorae' and translates as 'sonorous trifles' (Loeb edn., trans. H. R. Fairclough).

Themistocles: Themistocles (528–462 BC) was an Athenian statesman and naval commander. Hazlitt probably found the statement attributed to Themistocles in Bacon, *Advancement of Learning*, bk. I.

136 *Jedediah Buxton . . . Napier's bones*: Buxton (1707–72) was a farm labourer and an arithmetical genius. Napier's bones is a nickname for a calculator devised by the mathematician John Napier (1550–1617), the inventor of logarithms.

137 '*he dies . . . no copy*': cf. *Twelfth Night*, I. v. 226–7.

137 *Mrs Siddons*: Sarah Siddons (1755–1831), a celebrated actress, noted especially for her performances in tragic roles.

John Hunter: surgeon (1728–93); presumably Hazlitt had seen him at work.

'*great scholar's . . . century*': cf. *Hamlet*, III. ii. 127.

138 *become a Wolsey*: Thomas Wolsey (1475–1530), cardinal and statesman in the reigns of Henry VII and Henry VIII.

'*The Roman Poet*': Horace, and the quotation comes from his *Odes*, iii. 40.

139 '*in the instant . . . domestic treason . . . further*': cf. *Macbeth*, I. iv. 54 and III. ii. 25.

'*Junius*': popularly identified as Sir Philip Francis (1740–1818). Hazlitt was an admirer of Junius's *Letters* on political subjects.

140 '*Woodward and Meredith . . . Peru*': I have been unable to find information on these.

'*Rosemary Branch*': a pub at Peckham.

'*Copenhagen-house*': pub and tea-house in North London, located on what is now the Caledonian Market.

141 '*Lord Castlereagh's face, . . . Mr. Croker's hanging brow*': for Castlereagh and Croker, see notes to pp. 12 and 42 above.

'*Mr. Murray the bookseller*': John Murray (1778–1843), publisher, notably of Byron. Hazlitt's comment may have something to do with the fact that Murray lost the sight of one eye as a child.

142 '*the Fleet or King's Bench*': sites of open-air rackets courts in what were once prisons: the Fleet in Farringdon Street and the King's Bench in Southwark.

'*Mr. Manners Sutton*': Charles Manners Sutton (1780–1845), first Viscount of Canterbury, elected speaker of the House of Commons in 1817.

'*Let no rude hand . . . Jacet*': cf. Wordsworth, *Ellen Irwin*, ll. 155–6.

ON PUBLIC OPINION

142 First published in the *London Weekly Review*, 19 January 1828. The essay presents a marked contrast to the account of public opinion Hazlitt had given in his writings on the French Revolution; see above pp. 86–9.

'*Scared at the sound . . . made*': cf. Collins, *Ode, The Passions*, l. 20.

144 '*the world rings with the vain stir*': Cowper, *The Task*, iii. 129–30.

'*no man knoweth . . . goeth*': cf. John 3: 8.

vox et praeterea nihil: 'a voice and nothing more'.

145 *Mr Locke points out*: see Locke, *Essay on Human Understanding*, bk. 1, ch. 3, para. 24.

146 '*casting a dim religious light*': Milton, *Il Penseroso*, l. 160.

147 *Mr Blackwood . . . Sir John Barleycorn . . . the John Bull . . . the Quarterly . . . quarter-day*: William Blackwood (1776–1834), publisher and founder of *Blackwood's Magazine* in 1817. In 1818 the magazine had published a libellous attack on Hazlitt. Sir John Barleycorn is 'the personification of barley, as the grain from which malt liquor is made' (*Oxford Companion to English Literature*). The *John Bull* was founded in 1820 to oppose the popular enthusiasm for Queen Caroline. It was another periodical which Hazlitt had reason to dislike. In May 1823, after the anonymous publication of *Liber Amoris*, it had published one of Hazlitt's love-letters to Sarah Walker. The *Quarterly Review* was a Tory periodical, see above note to p. 16. A quarter-day is 'one of the four days fixed by custom as marking off the quarters of the year, on which the tenancy of houses usually begins or ends, and the payment of rent and other quarterly charges falls due' (*OED*).

Lady of Loretto . . . Mr Theodore Hook: the Lady of Loreto's shrine, near Ancona in Italy, was a place of popular pilgrimage. Theodore Hook (1788–1841) was a novelist and journalist; as editor of *John Bull*, he had attached Hazlitt over the publication of *Liber Amoris*. Hook was nicknamed 'Humbug Theodore' because of the self-righteous tone of his journalism.

148 '*wink and shut our apprehensions up*': one of Hazlitt's favourite quotations echoes the Prologue to Marston's play, *Antonio's Revenge*.

'*fed fat . . . he owed*': cf. *The Merchant of Venice*, I. iii. 48.

close borough: 'a borough owned by some person who controls the return of the Member of Parliament' (*OED*).

ON FASHION

148 First published in the *Edinburgh Magazine* for September 1818.

148 '*Born of nothing, begot of nothing*': cf. *Othello*, III. iv. 161–2.

'*His garment . . . there*': Spenser, *Faerie Queene*, III. xii, stanza 8.

149 '*the great vulgar and the small*': another of Hazlitt's favourite quotations, from Cowley, *Horace's Odes*, III. i.

150 '*The fashion of an hour old mocks the wearer*': unidentified.

an obscure circle of virtù as well as virtue: Hazlitt is playing off the conventional moral sense of virtue against the Italian word 'virtù', meaning a love and knowledge of the fine arts.

151 *Lord Foppington's . . . honour*: Lord Foppington is a character in Vanbrugh's play *The Relapse*, first performed in 1696.

mob of their inferiors: cf. Hazlitt's definition of a mob in the preface to his *Political Essays*:

> Talk of mobs as we will, the only true mob is that incorrigible mass of knaves and fools in every country, who never think at all, and who never feel for anyone but themselves. I call any assembly of people a mob (be it the House of Lords or House of Commons) where each person's opinion on any question is governed by what others say of it, and by what he can get by it.

'*the sign of an inward and invisible grace*': ironic citation of part of the Catechism in the *Book of Common Prayer*.

'*and are, . . . the most*': Thompson, *The Seasons*, Autumn, l. 206.

152 *authentic Memoirs of the Fudge Family*: refers to Thomas More's popular satirical poem, *The Fudge Family in Paris*, published in 1818.

'*the city madam . . . unworthy shoulders*': cf. *As You Like It*, II. vii. 75–6.

'*In the grand carnival of this our age*': from Burke, *A Letter to a Noble Lord*, published in 1796.

'*the age . . . his kibe*': cf. *Hamlet*, v. i. 135.

to take the wall: i.e. pass on the inside of the pavement, furthest from the road.

153 *the story in Peregrine Pickle*: the story can be found in Smollett, *Peregrine Pickle*, ch. 87.

'*lisping and ambling . . . creatures*': cf. *Hamlet*, III. i. 144–6.

154 '*in a high or low degree*': cf. Pope, *Epilogue to the Satires*, dialogue 1, l. 137.

'*And thin partitions . . . divide*': Dryden, *Absalom and Achitophel*, i. 164.

the observation of Mr Burke: the observation can be found in Burke's *Speech on Economical Reform*, published in 1780.

OUR NATIONAL THEATRES

155 First published in the *Atlas* for 11 October 1829.

Madame Vestris and her friends: Madame Vestris (1797–1856) was an actress who had a distinguished career on the English stage as a singer and a comedy actress. In the latter part of her career she became a theatre owner and manager.

156 *Mr Charles Kemble*: Charles Kemble (1775–1854), an English actor-manager, noted for his abilities in comedy.

'*dear as . . . sad heart*': *Julius Caesar*, II. i. 289.

157 *Mrs D——*: probably Mrs Davenport (1765–1843), an English actress whom Hazlitt had written about in his *View of the English Stage*. Hazlitt's compliment to her here may be due to the fact that her last season on the English stage was in 1829.

ENGLISH CHARACTERISTICS

157 First published in the *Atlas* for 5 July 1829.

158 '*internal oath*': unidentified.

Tom-and-Jerry admirers: Corinthian Tom and Jerry Hawthorn, popularly known as Tom-and-Jerry, were the two street dandy heroes in Pierce Egan's verse story *Life in London*, first published in 1821.

the watch-house: 'a house used as a station for the municipal night-watchmen, in which the chief constable of the night sits to receive and detain till the morning any disorderly persons brought in by the watchmen' (*OED*).

BRUMMELLIANA

158 First published in the *London Weekly Review* for 2 February 1828.

Beau Brummell: George Bryan Brummell (1778–1840), a famous dandy of the period, and confidant of the Prince Regent.

159 *Cowley says of Pindar*: the reference is to Cowley's poem, *The Praise of Pindar*.

159 '*by happiness or pains*': cf. Pope, *Epistle to Mr. Jervas,* 68.

'*A sound so fine . . . silence*': from James Sheridan Knowles's (1784–1862) *Virginius,* a tragedy first performed in 1820: see v. ii. 90–1.

Exempli gratia: 'for the sake of example', usually compressed to e.g.

a noble person: the Duke of Leicester.

160 *ubi tot nitent*: echoes Horace, *Ars Poetica,* l. 351: '*verum ubi plura nitent in carmine*' translated as 'But when the beauties in a poem are more in number . . .' (Loeb edn., trans. H. R. Fairclough).

'*A subtler web . . . lightly flee!*': cf. Spenser, *Faerie Queene,* ii. II. xii, stanza 77.

'*high fantastical*': *Twelfth Night,* I. i. 15.

'*great idea in his mind*': cf. Thomson, *Castle of Indolence,* I, stanza 59.

'*bound him . . . round him*': cf. Pope, *Ode for Musick, on St. Cecilia's Day,* ll.90–1.

161 *Mr Theodore Hook*: see above note to p. 147.

Hopkinses and Tomkinses: unidentified.

From what slight causes . . . spring: echoes the first line of Pope's *Rape of the Lock.*

'*his lodging had been on the cold ground*': from *The Rivals,* a play by Sir William Davenant (1606–68), playwright and theatre manager, rumoured to be the illegitimate child of Shakespeare.

Sir Lumley Skeffington: playwright and dandy (1771–1850).

162 '*the year 1815*': in 1815 Byron had married; Bonaparte had been defeated at the battle of Waterloo; and Brummell had fallen out of favour with the Prince Regent.

SELF-LOVE AND BENEVOLENCE

165 First published in the *New Monthly Magazine* for October and December 1828. The dialogue published in the December issue is reprinted here, as amended by Howe who restores the initials of the participants in the dialogue as they had appeared in Hazlitt's manuscript.

L . . . H.: 'L' is based on Charles Lamb and 'H' is, of course, based on Hazlitt. The other speakers marked as 'A', 'M', and 'JL' stand for William Ayrton, Martin Burney, and John Lamb, Charles's eldest brother. They were all members of a circle of friends who met regularly at Charles Lamb's house.

'*this one entire and perfect chrysolite*': cf. *Othello*, v. ii. 148.

'*precious jewel of the soul*': cf. *As You Like It*, II. i. 14.

166 '*Plain truth . . . speech*': cf. Pope, *Imitations of Horace, The Sixth Epistle of the First Book*, l.3.

'*I shall . . . for you*': cf. 'And that I may never be mistaken for U', Garrick's epigram in reply to Dr J. Hill's pamphlet, *Petition from the Letters I & U to David Garrick Esq.*

'*No more . . . lovest me*': cf. *1 Henry IV*, II. iv. 274.

169 '*come, but no farther*': Job 37: 11.

170 *denied by your modern metaphysicians*: these would include Hobbes (1588–1679), Mandeville (1670–1733), Condillac (1715–80), and Helvetius (1715–71) who all made self-interest or a utilitarian pursuit of pleasure and avoidance of pain fundamental to their analysis of human action.

171 *H——is in his element there*: Lamb is alluding to the 'illustration' in Hazlitt's *Essay on the Principles of Human Action*, where the hand and the candle is used in a lengthy analysis of the nature of pain.

172 *what Hume calls antecedents and consequents*: unidentified.

according to the poet: unidentified.

175 '*Come, let me clutch thee!*': *Macbeth*, II. i. 34.

'*In terms a fallacy . . . fiction*': unidentified.

making us feel the future in the instant: cf. *Macbeth*, I. v. 54.

176 '*And coming events . . . before*': Thomas Campbell (1777–1844), *Lochiel's Warning*, l. 56.

Here is the passage: the passage is from ch. 68 of Sir Walter Scott's *Waverley*, first published in 1814.

178 '*made and moulded of things past*': *Troilus and Cressida*, III. iii. 177.

'*thou art to continue . . . varlet*': cf. *Measure for Measure*, II. i. 181.

'*Here and hereafter . . . be!*': Byron, *Sardanapalus*, IV. i.

179 *in an original Essay of yours*: refers to Hazlitt's *Essay on the Principles of Human Action*.

179 *Southey said at the time*: Southey is likely to have read Hazlitt's *Essay* in 1806 from the copy that Lamb had sent to Southey's neighbour in the Lake District, Wordsworth.

    "faithful remembrancers . . . success": conflates two lines from separate poems by Cowper: *On the Receipt of My Mother's Picture*, l.1 and *The Task*, v. 901.

    '*Mirabaud (the author of the "System of Nature")*': the author of the *System of Nature* was in fact Baron d'Holbach. The book was first published in 1770 when it caused controversy for its uncompromising arguments in favour of a materialist atheism.

MIND AND MOTIVE

183 First published in the *Examiner* for 26 February and 9 April 1815. The second instalment from 9 April is printed here.

184 *vis inertiæ*: the power of inertia.

185 *Mr Hobbes says well*; the passage Hazlitt quotes comes from Hobbes, *Human Nature.* (first published 1650), paras. 5 and 6.

186 '*he courted a statue . . . desert!*': Hazlitt adapts *Don Quixote*, Part 1, Bk. II, ch. 12.

188 '*catch glimpses that may make them less forlorn*': cf. Wordsworth's sonnet, 'The world is too much with us; late and soon', l. 12.

    '*I ALSO WAS AN ARCADIAN!*': another of Hazlitt's favourite quotations, which he also uses in its Latin form '*et ego in Arcadia*'.

    we might answer with Hume: see Hume, *Enquiry Concerning Human Understanding.*

    in a metaphysical allegory: according to Crabb Robinson, Hazlitt had used this 'metaphysical allegory' in the last of his series of *Lectures on English Philosophy*, given in 1812. See the entry for 27 April 1812 in *The Diary of Henry Crabb Robinson*, ed. T. Sadler, i. 380.

189 '*Sithence no fairy lights, . . . Obscure*': see Sneyd Davies 'To the Honourable and Reverend F. C.' See also below note to p. 319.

    Happy are they: repeats a passage that had been first published in Hazlitt's *Reply to Malthus*, first published in 1807. Evidence from Hazlitt's essay *My First Acquaintance with the Poets* suggests that he has his father in mind as one of those 'who live in a dream of their own existence'.

    '*hurt by the archers*': Cowper, *The Task*, iii. 113.

ON PERSONAL IDENTITY

190 First published in the *Monthly Magazine* for January 1828.

'*Ha! here be three of us sophisticated*': cf. *Lear*, III. iv. 106.

'*Wishing to be . . . scope*': cf. Shakespeare, *Sonnet 34*.

191 '*the rub that makes calamity of so long life*': this initiates a series of quotations, some of them approximate, from *Hamlet*, III. i. 65–70.

'*Narcissus was transformed . . . no other remedy for their despair*': all the transformations alluded to can be found in Ovid, *Metamorphoses*.

192 '*What more felicity . . . wretchedness!*': Spenser, *Muiopotmos*, ll. 209–16.

'*That something . . . to die—*': cf. Pope, *An Essay on Man*, Epistle 4, ll.3–4.

193 in '*very choice Italian*'; *and Lord D——*: the quotation is from *Hamlet*, III. ii. 257. 'Lord D——' is Lord Dillon (1777–1832). Hazlitt had met him in Florence on a visit to Italy in 1825. The story Hazlitt refers to is to be found in Dillon's novel, *Sir Richard Maltravers*, first published in 1822.

'*vows made . . . void*': cf. Milton, *Paradise Lost*, iv. 97.

'*the native hue . . . thought*': cf. *Hamlet*, III. i. 84–5.

194 *Warton's spirited Sonnet*: Thomas Warton (1728–90), professor of poetry at Oxford (1757–67), poet laureate 1785; helped revive interest in the sonnet form, and became influential through his three-volume *History of English Poetry* (1774–81).

'*glades mild-opening to the genial day*': unidentified.

'*shut up in measureless content*': *Macbeth*, II. i. 16–17.

'*I'd sooner be a dog . . . moon*': cf. *Julius Caesar*, IV. iii. 27.

195 *Sir Thomas Lethbridge . . . Sir Francis Burdett . . . Mr Hobhouse*: Lethbridge (1778–1849) was Tory MP for Somerset from 1806–12 and 1820–30; Burdett (1770–1844), energetic reforming politician, and from 1807–37 MP for Westminster: John Cam Hobhouse (1786–1869) reforming politician, close friend of Byron. In 1820 Hobhouse joined Burdett as one of the two MPs for Westminster.

'*ethereal braid, sky woven*': cf. Collins, *Ode to Evening*, l. 7.

Berenice's hair . . . Ariadne's crown: two figures from classical history and mythology. Berenice married Ptolemy III in 247

BC, and according to Catullus, he named a star 'The Lock of Berenice' in her honour. Ariadne, daughter of Minos, King of Crete, helped Theseus out of the Cretan labyrinth with a ball of thread. The Cretan version of her name means 'she who shines in splendour' and, according to one legend, her crown was fixed as a constellation in the heavens by Zeus.

196 *made up of sweet and bitter regret!*: possibly another allusion to Hazlitt's failed love affair with Sarah Walker, but Howe conjectures that it may also refer to an earlier abortive affair in 1818–19, possibly with Miss Windham, 'heiress of Norman Court'. Hazlitt has a footnote: 'When Lord Byron was cut by the great, on account of his quarrel with his wife, he stood leaning on a marble slab at the entrance of a room, while troops of duchesses and countesses passed out. One little, pert, red-haired girl staid a few paces behind the rest; and, as she passed him, said with a nod, 'Aye, you should have married me, and then all this wouldn't have happened to you!'

'*Give me a crown, or a tomb!*': cf. *3 Henry VI*, I. iv. 16.

'*monarchise, be feared, and kill with looks*': *Richard II*, III. ii. 165.

the double of ——: George IV may be the omitted name.

'*tenth transmitters of a foolish face*': Richard Savage (1697?–1743), *The Bastard*, l.8. The poem was first published in 1728.

Charles X and Ferdinand VII: Charles X was the brother of Louis XVIII and succeeded him to the French throne in 1824; a notorious reactionary, he was deposed in the July revolution of 1830. For Ferdinand VII, see above note to p. 10.

Darius or Xerxes. . . Alexander or Pyrrhus: Darius (521–486 BC) and Xerxes (486–465 BC) were both Persian rulers who tried unsuccessfully to conquer Greece. Alexander the Great (356–323 BC) was King of Macedonia, and a notable general who for a brief period ruled much of the Middle East. Pyrrhus (319–272 BC) was King of Epirus, and a military leader who, amongst his numerous campaigns, won the original 'pyrrhic' victory in a battle against the Romans at Heraclea in 280 BC.

'*in the catalogue . . . kings*': cf. *Macbeth*, III. i. 91.

'*swinish multitude*': Burke's phrase again from *Reflections on the Revolution in France*. Characteristically Hazlitt reverses Burke's intended meaning by making the phrase refer to kings.

197 *the modern Charlemagne*: Napoleon.

that fell jailer: Sir Hudson Lowe (1769–1844), Governor of St Helena from 1815–21, and therefore responsible for superintending Napoleon's exile on the island.

'*glared round his soul . . . eyelids!*': unidentified.

198 '*The fair, the chaste, the inexpressive she*': cf. *As You Like It*, III. ii. 10.

Sancho Panza . . . possible: cf. *Don Quixote*, Part 2, Bk. II, chs. 43 and 53.

Why will Mr Cobbett . . . Parliament?: in 1826 Cobbett had been an unsuccessful candidate in the parliamentary election for Preston.

199 *like the bird, described by Chaucer*: see two of *The Canterbury Tales*: 'The Manciple's Tale', l. 59 and following; 'The Squire's Tale', l. 603 and following.

a common language in nature: Hazlitt is disagreeing with Wordsworth's view as set out in the Preface to the 1800 edition of the *Lyrical Ballads*.

200 '*Ah! why so soon the blossom tear?*': unidentified.

'*in no haste to be venerable!*': unidentified.

The modern Roscius: Quintus Roscius (died 62 BC) was the most celebrated Roman actor of his day and his name became proverbial subsequently for other well-known actors. The 'modern Roscius' is evidently Garrick.

'*A certain tender bloom . . . o'erspreads*': Thomson, *The Castle of Indolence*, canto 1, stanza 57.

his preferring Rowe and Dryden: see Goldsmith, *The Vicar of Wakefield* (first published 1766), ch. 18.

201 '*stuff o' the conscience*': cf. *Othello*, I. ii. 2.

Raphael's Assembly of the Just: Hazlitt is probably referring to one of Raphael's frescoes in the Vatican, *The Convocation of the Saints*.

202 *Those who found arts and sciences*: cf. the argument in *Why the Arts are not Progressive*, pp. 257–62 below. Hazlitt suggests here one of the compensations for what he regarded as the historical tendency for the arts to decline in power.

'*laggard age*': Collins, *Ode, The Passions*, l. 112.

202 *like Benvenuto Cellini*: Hazlitt would have read the story about Cellini's statue in chs. 41 and 43 of Roscoe's 1822 translation of Cellini's *Memoirs*.

of a favoured rival: another allusion to Hazlitt's affair with Sarah Walker.

CHARACTERISTICS

202 *Characteristics*: *In the Manner of Rochefoucault's Maxims* was published anonymously in 1823. In a Preface to the book Hazlitt wrote:

> The following work was suggested by a perusal of Rochefoucault's *Maxims & Moral Reflections*. I was so struck with the force and beauty of the style and matter, that I felt an earnest ambition to embody some occasional thoughts of my own in the same form. . . . There is a peculiar *stimulus*, and at the same time a freedom from all anxiety in this mode of writing. A thought must tell at once or not at all . . . . Each Maxim should contain the essence or ground-work of a separate Essay, but so developed as of itself to suggest a whole train of reflections to the reader. . . . There is only one point in which I dare even allude to a comparison with Rochefoucault—*I have had no theory to maintain*; and have endeavoured to set down each thought as it occurred to me, without bias or prejudice of any sort.

Two sequences from the original work are printed here. The first, Maxims 105 and 106, returns to Hazlitt's preoccupation with refuting self-interest as the basic motive for human action. The second and longer sequence, Maxims 159–83, shows something of the movement of Hazlitt's thinking in *Characteristics*. Starting with a set of reflections on the relation between self and other, Hazlitt develops these into observations on the nature of silence and conversation, on the relation of thinking to conversation, and on the superiority of conversational thinking over theoretical. The structure is analogous to a piece of music which sets out a theme and then moves to a series of variations on it.

Mandeville, Rochefoucault, and others: for Mandeville see above note to p. 170. Rochefoucault or Rochefoucauld (1613–80) was a French aristocrat who involved himself in political intrigue during the minority of Louis XIV. This culminated in his participation in the first of a series of insurrections against

the French Government, known as *Les Frondes*. Rochefoucauld was on the losing side and was not allowed to return to
Paris until 1659, on condition that he took no active part in
political life. It was from this period that he began to compose
The Maxims and Moral Reflections that were to become his best-
known published work. A first edition came out in 1664, and
five subsequent editions were published before 1700. *The Maxims* presents a pessimistic and worldly account of human nature, in which self-interest rather than moral virtue is the
primary motive for action.

MY FIRST ACQUAINTANCE WITH POETS

211 The essay first appeared in the *Liberal*, no. 3., April 1823,
although some passages in it had appeared in Hazlitt's letter
to the *Examiner* of 12 January 1817.

W—m: Wem.

'dreaded name of Demogorgon': Milton, *Paradise Lost*, ii. 964–5.

'fluttering the proud Salopians . . . dove-cote': adapts *Coriolanus*, v.
vi. 115–16.

'High-born Hoel's harp . . . lay!': Gray, *The Bard*, l. 28.

like a worm by the way-side: echoes Chaucer's description of
Griselda in 'The Clerk's Tale'; see *The Canterbury Tales*, 'The
Clerk's Tale', l. 880.

212 *'With Styx . . . them'*: Pope, *Ode for Music, on St. Cecilia's Day*,
ll. 90–1.

'Il y a des impressions. . . . mémoire': Rousseau, *Julie ou La Nouvelle
Héloïse*, first published in 1761: translated as 'There are im-
pressions which neither time nor circumstances can erase.
Should I live for centuries, the sweet period of my youth would
not be reborn, nor ever effaced from my memory'; another of
Hazlitt's favourite quotations.

'And he went . . . ALONE': Coleridge's text comes from John 6:
15.

213 *'rose like a steam of rich distilled perfumes'*: Milton, *Comus*, l. 556.

'of one crying . . . honey': Matt. 3: 3–4.

'inscribed the cross . . . gore': this quotation and the one that
follows are presumably from Coleridge's sermon.

'Such were the notes . . . sung': cf. Pope, *Epistle to Robert, Earl of
Oxford*, l. 1.

213 *'Jus Divinum'*: divine justice.

214 *'Like to that sanguine flower . . . woe'*: Milton, *Lycidas*, l. 106.

    'As are the children . . . sheen': Thomson, *The Castle of Indolence*, canto 2, stanza 33.

    'A certain tender bloom . . . o'erspread': Hazlitt often and apparently deliberately misquoted *The Castle of Indolence*, canto 1, stanza 57, 'A certain tender gloom o'erspread his face.' Cf. note to p. 200 above.

    'somewhat fat and pursy': conflates *Hamlet*, III. iv. 153 and V. ii. 279.

215 *the heats of the Unitarian controversy*: probably refers to the argument over the exact status of Christ in the Unitarian religion. Hazlitt's father had been involved in controversies within the Unitarian Church during his period in the United States.

    'no figures nor no fantasies': *Julius Caesar*, II. i. 231.

216 *on Mary Wolstonecraft and Mackintosh*: Mary Wolstonecraft or Wollstonecraft (1759–97) was the author of *The Vindication of the Rights of Woman*, first published in 1792. She wrote novels and political works during her life and the context, linking her name with Mackintosh suggests that Coleridge was probably referring to her *Vindication of the Rights of Men*, first published in 1790 as a critique of Burke's *Reflection on the Revolution in France*. Sir James Mackintosh wrote his *Vindiciae Gallicae* in 1790. Like Wollstonecraft's *Vindication* this was a critique of Burke's interpretation of the French Revolution. Mackintosh later retracted his support for the Revolution, much to Hazlitt's disgust.

217 *Tom Wedgwood*: Thomas Wedgwood (1771–1805) was the son of the famous potter Josiah Wedgwood. He was one of Coleridge's patrons.

    Godwin had once boasted: William Godwin (1756–1836) was a philosopher, novelist, and political radical. In 1793 he published his *Enquiry Concerning Political Justice*, which set out to justify his belief in the possibility of human perfectibility. He was briefly married to Mary Wollstonecraft in the last year of her life. See also the note below on *Caleb Williams* p. 228, and cf. note to p. 69 above.

    Holcroft: Thomas Holcroft (1745–1809) was a political radical and an atheist. In 1794 he was tried for high treason and acquitted. His *Memoirs* were edited and completed by Hazlitt.

218 *Deva's winding vales*: cf. Southey, *Roderick*, xvi. 58–9.

this simile is to be found in Cassandra: Cassandra was a romance novel written by the French author La Calprenede (1614–63) and published in ten volumes between 1644 and 1650. The simile can be found in Part 2, Bk. V.

'*Sounding on his way*': conflates two sources in Chaucer, *The Canterbury Tales*, General Prologue, l. 275 and l. 307.

to float in air, to slide on ice: Hazlitt describes Coleridge in terms close to the latter's poem 'Kubla Khan'; cf. ll.31–6 of the poem.

Hume: David Hume (1711–76), philosopher whose sceptical views were developed in his *Treatise on Human Nature*, first published in 1739.

South's sermons—Credat Judæus Apella!: Robert South (1634–1716), preacher in the court of Charles II, noted for the wit and sarcasm of his sermons, and for his attacks upon religious dissenters. *Credat Judæus Apella* is from Horace, *Satires*, I.V. 100–1. The full line reads '*Credat Judaeus Apella, non ego*', translated as 'Apella the Jew may believe it, not I' (Loeb edn., trans. H. R. Fairclough).

219 *Berkeley*: George Berkeley (1685–1753), philosopher and Bishop of Cloyne; his *Essay towards a New Theory of Vision* was first published in 1709, and *A Treatise Concerning the Principles of Human Knowledge* in 1710. Berkeley, an opponent of Locke's version of mind and knowledge, argues that the existence of objects depends upon our perception of them.

'*Thus I confute him, Sir*': for this famous story see Boswell, *Life of Johnson*, ed. G. B. Hill, i. 471.

Tom Paine: Tom Paine (1737–1809) was a political radical, and author of *The Rights of Man*, published 1791–2. The book was one of the most widely read and actively suppressed books of the period.

Bishop Butler: Joseph Butler (1692–1752) became Bishop of Durham in 1750. In various theological works and collections of sermons he argued against Deism and insisted on the power of conscience in determining moral choice. Butler's *Analogy of Religion* was published in 1736.

I had written a few remarks: Hazlitt is referring to the arguments in his first published work, *An Essay on the Principles of Human Action*, 1805.

220 *He mentioned Paley*: see below note to p. 355.

'Kind and affable . . . regard': cf. Milton, *Paradise Lost*, viii. 648–50.

he has somewhere told himself: Coleridge told the story in ch. 10 of his *Biographia Literaria*, first published in 1817.

221 *that other Vision of Judgment*: Byron was the author of this 'other Vision', a parody of Southey's poem and a satire on its author. Southey's poem was published in 1821, Byron's one year after in the *Liberal*, whose editor, John Hunt, was subsequently prosecuted for libel because of its publication.

Mr Murray, the Secretary of the Bridge-street Junto: see above note to p. 141.

Ode on the Departing Year: Coleridge's description can be found in the 7th stanza of the poem, which was first published in 1796.

the waters of Helicon!: in Greek mythology, Helicon is the river that flows from Mount Parnassus, the home of the muses.

Tom Jones and the adventure of the muff: the adventure can be found in Bk. 10, ch. 5, of Fielding's *Tom Jones*, first published in 1749.

Paul and Virginia: refers to a translation of the sentimental Rousseauist romance *Paul et Virginie*, written by Bernardin de St Pierre (1737–1814) and first published in 1787. The story enjoyed a considerable vogue and was widely translated.

222 *Camilla*: novel by Fanny Burney (1752–1840), first published in 1796. Her two other best-known works were *Evelina* (1778) and *Cecilia* (1782).

I have wanted only one thing . . . happy: an indirect reference to Hazlitt's failed love affair with Sarah Walker.

'the scales that fence': quotation unidentified. The sentence in which this quotation occurs is closely paralleled by one in Hazlitt's *Life of Napoleon*, first published between 1828 and 1830, where the context is an attack by Hazlitt on racial prejudice.

223 *the form of Sybilline Leaves*: Hazlitt is presumably referring to poems by Coleridge which were to be published in 1817 under the title *Sybilline Leaves*.

'——— *hear the loud stag speak'*: Ben Jonson, *To Sir Robert Wroth*, l. 22.

lulled in Elysium: from Greek mythology; Elysium is the paradise for heroes.

ballad of Betty Foy: Hazlitt's name for 'The Idiot Boy', one of a list of titles of poems in the *Lyrical Ballads* that follow this quotation.

'In spite of pride . . . spite': cf. Pope, *An Essay on Man*, Epistle 1, l. 293.

224 *'While yet . . . unconfirmed'*: Thompson, *The Seasons*, Spring, l. 18.

'Of Providence, . . . foreknowledge absolute': Milton, *Paradise Lost*, ii. 559–60.

his own Peter Bell: Wordsworth wrote this narrative poem in 1798, although it was not published until 1819.

Chantry's bust . . . Haydon's head: Sir Francis Chantry (1781–1841), sculptor, who had made a bust of Wordsworth in 1820. For Haydon, see below note to p. 284. Haydon put the heads of Keats and Hazlitt in his picture as well as Wordsworth's. *Christ's Entry into Jerusalem* was first exhibited in 1820, when Hazlitt gave it a favourable review.

225 *Castle Spectre by Monk Lewis*: *Castle Spectre* was first performed at Drury Lane in December 1797. Matthew Gregory Lewis (1775–1817) was nicknamed 'Monk' after the success of his Gothic novel, *The Monk*, first published in 1796.

ad captandum: in full 'ad captandam vulgus', translated as 'to catch the rabble' or 'to tickle the ears of the mob'.

'his face was as a book': cf. *Macbeth*, I. v. 59.

226 *Tom Poole*: Thomas Poole (1765–1837) was a friend and neighbour of Coleridge at Nether Stowey in Somerset.

we quaffed our flip: flip is 'a mixture of beer and spirit sweetened with sugar and heated with a hot iron'(*OED*).

'followed in the chase . . . up the cry': cf. *Othello*, II. iii. 352–4.

227 *scene of a prose-tale . . . the Death of Abel*: the prose tale is probably *The Wanderings of Cain*, left uncomplete and not published until 1828. The *Death of Abel* is a work by the German writer Solomon Gessner, first published in 1758.

228 *Junius as a writer*: for Junius, see above note to p. 139.

the merits of Caleb Williams: *Things as They Are: or, the Adventures of Caleb Williams*, written by William Godwin, first published in

1794, a novel which explores the psychology and effects of tyranny.

228 *'ribbed sea-sands'*: cf. Coleridge, *The Ancient Mariner*, iv. 227.

229 *which I have explained at length elsewhere*: Hazlitt is referring to his *Remarks on the System of Hartley and Helvetius*, published in 1805 as an accompaniment to his *Essay on the Principles of Human Action*.

Dr Toulmin of Taunton: Joshua Toulmin (1740–1815) was a notable religious dissenter and political radical who was sympathetic to the views of Tom Paine. He worked for a long period as minister to the General Baptist Chapel in Taunton.

his tragedy of Remorse: Coleridge wrote a first version of this tragedy in the summer and autumn of 1797 and it was first performed at Drury Lane in January 1813.

Mr Elliston's and the Drury-lane boards: Robert Elliston (1774–1831) was a popular actor at Drury Lane. In 1819 he became the manager of the theatre there. Elliston played the part of Alvar in Coleridge's play. The quotation beginning 'Oh memory! . . .' is unidentified.

says Lamb: Charles Lamb (1775–1834), essayist and co-author with his sister, Mary, of *Tales from Shakespeare*, first published in 1807. He was a close friend of Hazlitt.

230 *'But there is matter . . . second tale'*: cf. Wordsworth, *Hart-Leap Well*, ll. 95–6.

THE LIFE OF NAPOLEON

230 Hazlitt wrote a substantial portion of his *Life of Napoleon* between 1826–7 during the course of a lengthy stay in Paris. A complete version of the Life was not published until 1830 when it appeared in a four-volume edition published jointly by Effingham Wilson and Chapman and Hall. The first half of the work had been published in 1828 by Charles Cowden Clarke and Henry Leigh Hunt. They rejected the Preface, one of the four excerpts from the Life printed here, because of its politically controversial nature. This is one indication of the difficult task that Hazlitt undertook in writing about Napoleon as someone worthy of sympathy and respect as well as criticism.

I. Preface

'the child and champion of the Revolution': the original formulation was by Pitt the Younger in a parliamentary speech made in February 1800:

How or where did the honourable gentleman discover that the jacobinism of Robespierre, the jacobinism of the Triumvirate, the jacobinism of the Five Directors, which he acknowledged to be real, has all vanished and disappeared, because it has all been centered and condensed into one man who was reared and nursed in its bosom, whose celebrity was gained under its auspices, who was at once the child and champion of all its atrocities and horrors?.

a thorn in the side of kings: cf. 2 Corinthians 12: 7.

231 *'the right divine of kings to govern wrong'*: Pope, *The Dunciad*, iv. 188.

'millions were made for one': unidentified.

Vive le Roi, quand même!: 'long live the King, whatever!'

II. Napoleon and the Nature of Revolutions

232 The immediate historical context of this passage is Napoleon's return to Paris in 1797 after his Italian campaign and his opposition to the French Directory's decision to invade the Papal States in 1798.

Duphot: Mathurin-Leonard Duphot (1769–1797), a successful general in the post-Revolutionary French army and highly regarded by Napoleon. He was assassinated in Rome on 27 December 1797.

233 *led by Lepaux*: I have found no information on Lepaux.

'the grand carnival and masquerade of this our age': cf. Burke, *A Letter to a Noble Lord*, 'In the masquerades of the grand carnival of our age, whimsical adventures happen.'

III. Napoleon and the Invasion of Russia

234 *the inability or disinclination of Alexander*: Alexander (1777–1825) was Tsar of Russia from 1801, after he colluded in the murder of his father, Paul. Napoleon had defeated Alexander's army at the Battle of Friedland in 1807 and in the same year, at Tilsit, treaties were signed between them. Amongst the terms of these treaties was an agreement that Russia should join the Continental System if they failed to persuade Britain to make peace with France. The agreements made at Tilsit collapsed by 1810 when Russian commerce was suffering from the Continental System.

235 *to the Continental System*: through the Berlin decree of 1806, Napoleon attempted a form of economic warfare with Britain

by denying British commerce access to European ports. The increasing unpopularity of the arrangement with French merchants as well as the success of a number of countries in avoiding the attempted embargo, meant that the Continental System had effectively collapsed by 1809.

236 *vis inertiæ*: literally 'the force of inertness'.

237 *and subjection of a people*: Hazlitt supplied the following footnote at this point, 'Civilization gives hostages: barbarism has none.'

238 *the field of Valoutina*: an indecisive battle between the French and Russian armies in August 1812.

Ney . . . Goudin: Michel Ney (1769–1815), created a Marshal in the French Army in 1806. After his courage at the battle of Borodino, Napoleon gave him the title Prince of Moscow. He was executed in 1815 for supporting Napoleon after the latter's return from Elba. I have no information on Goudin other than that given by Hazlitt.

239 *discovered by Rapp*: Rapp was an aide-de-camp to Napoleon. He distinguished himself at the battle of Austerlitz in 1805 when he was appointed a general in the French army.

IV. Napoleon and the Return from Elba

240 Napoleon had been exiled on the island of Elba early in 1814. He returned to France in 1815 and conducted a campaign to regain power which ended with his defeat at the battle of Waterloo. He was then exiled to the island of St Helena where he died in 1821.

the Child Roland of the Revolution: Hazlitt may be referring to the courtly medieval hero of the old Scottish ballad *Childe Roland* or to the early medieval French poem *The Song of Roland*, whose legendary hero was celebrated as a defender of Christian Europe.

241 *He dispersed the Compagnons du Lys*: see above note to p. 8.

Louis XVIII had left the capital: Louis XVIII (1755–1824) became King of France in 1814 when Napoleon ceased to be emperor. He was a liberal monarch who tried to contain the excesses of the reactionary terror after Napoleon's final defeat at the battle of Waterloo.

Marshal Macdonald: Macdonald was the son of a Jacobite exile who was created a Marshal of the French Army by Napoleon. After

Napoleon's return from Elba, the Marshal tried unsuccessfully to organize military opposition to his former commander.

EDMUND KEAN

242 As a theatre reviewer Hazlitt wrote frequently about Kean and was a persistent and articulate defender of his acting style. Edmund Kean (1787?–1833) was a deviant figure by the social and moral standards of his time. He was born the illegitimate child of Aaron Kean (possibly) and Anne Carey (definitely). As a child he was both a vagabond and a theatrical prodigy who acquired most of his education through the stage. His first performance of Shylock, which Hazlitt writes about in one of the excerpts printed here, challenged conventional interpretations of the role. Kean dispensed with the red beard and wig, props which a well-established acting tradition had used to signify the jewishness of Shylock. He gave a new aura of excitement and attraction to a repertoire of evil or deviant characters, including Shylock, Iago, Richard III, Macbeth, and Othello. His acting style was a sustained challenge to both genteel and aristocratic convention. Hazlitt no doubt found in Kean the actor who most closely corresponded to his own radical sensibility. The excerpts printed here are taken from Hazlitt's collection of his theatre reviews, *A View of the English Stage*, first published in 1818.

I

242 From the Preface to *A View of the English Stage*.

'*some quantity of barren spectators*': conflates *Romeo and Juliet*, v. i. 48 and *Hamlet*, III. iii. 40.

243 *to persuade Mr Perry*: James Perry (1756–1821) was the owner and editor of the *Morning Chronicle*. Hazlitt was working for Perry as a theatre reviewer when he first saw Kean's performance of Shylock in January 1814.

'*screw the courage . . . to the sticking place*': cf. *Macbeth*, I. vii. 60.

244 '*Pritchard's genteel, and Garrick's six feet high!*': Charles Churchill (1731–64), *The Rosciad*, l. 852. Churchill's poem was published in 1763 and is a satire on the contemporary acting profession. The joke in the line Hazlitt quotes is on the physical appearance of the actors because Pritchard became increasingly stout as she grew older, and Garrick was short in height.

Hannah Pritchard (1711–68) played the heroine in the first performance of Johnson's play *Irene*. Her acting style was regarded as mannered and old-fashioned and therefore would contrast with Kean's manner.

David Garrick (1717–79) is acknowledged as one of the finest and most influential English actors. He was responsible for many changes in acting style, stage design, and management, including, for example, the introduction on to the English stage of concealed lighting.

244 *this corps of Swiss bodyguards*: the Swiss Guard was constituted in 1616 to guard the French monarch.

leze-majesté . . . Quand meme!: *lèze-* or *lèse-majesté*, literally 'hurt-majesty', i.e. 'any offence against sovereign authority' *(OED)*; for '*quand meme*' see above note to p. 231.

'*He was not John Kemble*': John Kemble (1757–1823) a member of then famous acting family; he was trained for the Catholic priesthood but chose acting as a career instead. Hazlitt admired his work, although his formal style of acting was very unlike Kean's.

'*pigmy body*' . . . '*a fiery soul . . . tenement*': Dryden, *Absolom and Achitophel*, ll. 157–8.

'*un haut et puissant . . . jour*': 'a high and mighty prince, one day old'.

245 '*the very worst actor in the world*': unidentified.

II

245 Originally published in the *Examiner* for 31 March 1816.

'*The web of our life . . . virtues*': cf. *All's Well That Ends Well*, IV. iii. 67–9.

246 '*like the giddy sailor . . . the deep!*': cf. *Richard III*, III. iv. 101–3.

III

247 Originally published in the *Examiner* for 7 April 1816.

248 *found the following account*: the account is Hazlitt's own and is taken from his first review of Kean's Shylock published in the *Morning Chronicle* for 27 January 1814.

LIBER AMORIS: CONCLUSION

249 One process at work in Hazlitt's writing is the emergence and the disintegration of ideal images, and Hazlitt's effort to localize and stabilize these images in the real world. The creation of hero-figures is one aspect of this process, but the most

Liber Amoris, first published anonymously in 1823, but immediately recognized as Hazlitt's work. The book gives a thinly fictionalized account of Hazlitt's love affair with Sarah Walker, an affair which began in 1820, led Hazlitt to divorce his wife and ended wretchedly for him in 1822. Although not strictly speaking a hero, in terms either of gender or of access to the public sphere, it seems appropriate to include Sarah Walker in this section as she became, quite unwittingly, the most powerful and contradictory image in Hazlitt's imagination. The final letter, To J. S. K., is printed here. Hazlitt simply put into his book a letter that he had written in 1822 to his friend, James Sheridan Knowles.

'*Who had been beguiled . . . morrow?*': Leigh Hunt, *The Story of Rimini*, iii. 205–12.

250 *who bilks a customer*: to bilk is 'to cheat, deceive, betray' (*OED*).

Leering up at her bully: a bully is a pimp or 'The "gallant" or protector of a prostitute; one who lives by protecting prostitutes' (*OED*).

callous jilt: a jilt is 'a woman who has lost her chastity; a harlot or strumpet; a kept mistress' and 'one who capriciously casts off a lover after giving him encouragement' (*OED*).

251 *the very same with C ——*: 'C ——' was in fact Mr Tomkins, Hazlitt's rival in his affair with Sarah.

252 *the Miss F——s*: unidentified.

'*There was a precedent for it*': cf. *1 Henry IV*, ii. iv. 31.

displaced the little image: Hazlitt had given Sarah an image of Napoleon because she detected a resemblance between it and a former lover.

'*turned all to favour and to prettiness*': cf. *Hamlet*, iv. v. 185.

253 '*going into the wastes of time*': cf. Shakespeare, *Sonnet 12*, l. 10, 'That thou among the wastes of time must goe'.

FRAGMENTS ON ART. WHY THE ARTS ARE NOT PROGRESSIVE?

257 First printed as two articles in the *Morning Chronicle* for 11 and 15 January 1814. Revised and reprinted as part of *The Round Table*, published in 1817. The text of the *Morning Chronicle* articles is printed here.

II

260 '*There is no shuffling . . . faults*': cf. *Hamlet*, III. iii. 61–4.

To use the distinction . . . the mind: the 'technical philosophy' refers to the *Port Royal Logic*, published in 1662, where the distinction between extension and intension is elaborated. The distinction has been the subject of a complex and ambiguous philosophical discussion, which cannot be summarized here, but, roughly, the extension of a concept is concerned with its truth-value, the intension with its range of meanings. In another formulation extensions concern 'objective' descriptions of the world, intensions concern the way we look at it. It is along these lines that Hazlitt makes use of the distinction.

261 '*human face divine*': Milton, *Paradise Lost*, iii. 44.

'*And made a sunshine in the shady place*': Spenser, *Faerie Queene*, I. iii. stanza 4.

the Prince of Painters: either Raphael or Titian.

patient sorrow of Griselda . . . the Flower and the Leaf: for Griselda, see Chaucer's 'The Clerk's Tale' in *The Canterbury Tales*. *The Flower and the Leaf* is a medieval poem no longer attributed to Chaucer.

It is thus that Boccaccio: the stories Hazlitt refers to come from Boccaccio's *Decameron*; the story of the hawk from the Fifth Day, Novel 10, of Isabella from the Fourth Day, Novel 5.

261–262 *So Lear. . . . So Titian. . . . So Nicolas Poussin*: see *King Lear*, II. iv. 187 and following; the painting by Titian is *Young Man with a Glove*; the painting by Poussin is *Et in Arcadia Ego*.

Mr Rogers's 'Pleasures of Memory' . . . History: Hazlitt refers here to a list of contemporary literature and art. The technique of ironic citation parallels that in *On Modern Comedy* see above pp. 104–5.

WHETHER THE FINE ARTS ARE PROMOTED BY ACADEMIES

262 Hazlitt published a series of articles under this title in the *Champion* for August, September, and October of 1814. What is printed here is an excerpt from the second article. One interest of the piece is that it shows the democratic Hazlitt arguing against institutional efforts to make works of art available to a wider audience.

263 '*And fools rush in . . . tread*': cf. Pope, *An Essay on Criticism*, l. 625.

visit the exhibition at Somerset-house: from 1780–1837 Somerset House was the location of the Schools and the annual Exhibition of the Royal Academy of the Arts.

264 '*Pleased with itself . . . please*': Goldsmith, *The Traveller*, l. 42.

'*a Guido from a Daub*': Guido is Guido da Siena, a thirteenth-century painter, who is sometimes identified as one of the earliest to make use, in a rudimentary way, of perspective and other naturalistic effects. I have not been able to identify the quotation.

Raphael and ——: the unnamed painter is probably Benjamin West (1738–1820). West was born in the United States and in 1792 succeeded Reynolds as President of the Royal Academy. He was famous for his historical and religious paintings. He also developed an apocalyptic and melodramatic style, typified in his painting *Death on a Pale Horse* of 1802. Not one of Hazlitt's favourite painters.

266 *the story of the Falcon*: see the reference to Boccaccio above note to p. 261.

ON GUSTO

266 First published in the *Examiner* for 26 May 1816 and reprinted by Hazlitt as one of the essays in *The Round Table*, published in 1817. *The Round Table* essay is printed here.

morbidezza: from the Italian word for delicacy or softness. 'The rendering of flesh tints in the painting with softness and delicacy' (*The Oxford Companion to Art*).

267 *Albano's is like ivory*: Francesco Albano (1578–1660), painter of the Bolognese School, famous for his altar-pieces, allegorical and landscape paintings. His work was admired by connoisseurs in late eighteenth-century England.

268 *Orleans Gallery*: not, as might be thought, a gallery in Orléans, but the name given to an exhibition of Italian old masters which was placed on sale in London in December 1798. The collection had belonged to the Regent Orléans in Paris. Hazlitt saw the collection sometime between December 1798 and July 1799.

Mr West: see above note to p. 264.

St Peter Martyr: the painting was destroyed by fire in 1867. Hazlitt had first seen it during his 1802 visit to the Louvre.

268 *Society of Arcadians*: an imaginary society of landscape and pastoral painters. Hazlitt has a footnote: 'Raphael not only could not paint a landscape; he could not paint people in a landscape. He could not have painted the heads or the figures, or even the dresses, of the St Peter Martyr. His figures have always an *in-door* look, that is, a set, determined, voluntary, dramatic character, arising from their own passions, or a watchfulness of those others, and want that wild uncertainty of expression, which is connected with the accidents of nature and the changes of the elements. He has nothing *romantic* about him.'

269 *by their beauty they are deified*: echoes and changes Wordsworth's *Resolution and Independence*, stanza 7, l. 5. Hazlitt could have read the poem in Wordsworth's 1807 collection, *Poems in Two Volumes*.

'*Or where Chineses drive . . . bliss*: Milton, *Paradise Lost*, iii. 438–9, and v. 297.

Prior's tales: Matthew Prior (1664–1721), poet and diplomat. Hazlitt is probably referring to poems such as *Hans Carvel* (1701), *The Ladle* (1718), and *Henry and Emma* (1709).

ORIGINALITY

270 First printed in the *Atlas* for 3 January 1830 as part of a series 'Specimens of a Dictionary of Definitions'.

Romney: George Romney (1734–1802), portrait painter whose work was strongly influenced by Italian neo-classicism. The quotation may have come from a conversation with Hazlitt.

271 *Multum abludit imago*: cf. Horace, *Satires*, ii. 3. 320. The line in Horace is '*haec a te non multum abludit imago*': 'Not badly does the picture hit you off' (Loeb edn., trans. H. R. Fairclough).

'*mistress' eyebrow*': *As You Like It*, ii. vii. 149.

'*Grace is in . . . love*': cf. Milton, *Paradise Lost*, viii. 488–9.

272 *faciebat*: literally, 'he was making'.

spolia opima: 'the choicest spoils'.

'*Whate'er Lorrain . . . Poussin drew*': Thomson, *The Castle of Indolence*, canto 1, stanza 38.

273 *Hence the well-known observation*: cf. *Why the Arts are not Progressive*, see above pp. 257–62.

both Hoppner and Jackson: John Hoppner (1758–1810), portrait painter; in 1789 appointed portrait painter to the Prince of Wales; imitator first of Reynolds and then of Lawrence. John Jackson (1778–1831), also a portrait painter.

'gayest, happiest attitudes': cf. Akenside, *Pleasures of Imagination,* Bk. I. 30.

274 *Mr Fuseli's . . . Wilkie's . . . Haydon's . . . Sir Thomas's*: Henry Fuseli (1741–1825), Swiss-born, moved to London in 1765. He was strongly attracted to sublime and horrific subjects in his paintings which were expressionist in character. Sir David Wilkie (1785–1841), painter, much influenced by seventeenth-century Dutch and Flemish realism; celebrated for his anecdotal paintings, his work was highly regarded in the first half of the nineteenth century. Haydon, see below note to p. 284. Sir Thomas Lawrence (1769–1830) became England's leading portrait painter after 1810 and succeeded West as President of the Royal Academy in 1820.

275 *two figures from Masaccio*: Tommaso Masaccio (1401–28), one of the leading painters of the Italian Renaissance. Hazlitt would have discovered in Vasari about Raphael's study of Masaccio. Raphael's *Expulsion from Paradise* in the Vatican is the work that borrows two figures from Masaccio's fresco in the Carmelite Church in Florence.

276 *'semblable coherence'*: 2 *Henry IV,* v. i. 73.

'the great vulgar and the small': see above note to p. 149.

'the strong conception': cf. *Othello,* v. ii. 58–9.

ON THE ELGIN MARBLES

277 First published in the *London Magazine* for February and May 1822. Hazlitt had written a much shorter piece on the same topic for the *Examiner* for 16 June 1816. The second of the two articles for the *London Magazine* is printed here. The Elgin Marbles, a collection of sculpture from the Parthenon in Athens, had been sold to the nation by Lord Elgin in 1816 for £35,000. The collection was exhibited in London where it made original Greek sculpture of the classic period more widely accessible than ever before. Its initial impact on thinking about art was considerable.

in rerum naturâ: 'in the nature of things'.

Sir Joshua Reynolds may be ranked: Sir Joshua Reynolds (1723–1792), a major eighteenth-century painter and theoretician, first President of the Royal Academy. The arguments Hazlitt refers to can be found in the third and fourth of Reynolds's *Discourses on Art*. The *Discourses* were initially given as a series of lectures to students at the Royal Academy between 1769 and 1790. They were included in the 1797 edition of Reynolds's *Works*.

277 '*So from the ground . . . flower!*': Milton, *Paradise Lost*, v. 481–3.

278 '*laborious foolery*': unidentified.

'*fair varieties*': cf. Akenside, *Pleasures of Imagination*, Bk. I.

279 *Mr Westall, Angelica Kauffman*: Richard Westall (1765–1836), genre painter and illustrator of poetry; Angelica Kauffman (1740–1807), Swiss painter whose painting was influenced by neo-classical style; she lived for a period in London and worked as a decorative artist for houses designed by the brothers Adam.

So Sir Joshua debated . . . and has a whole chapter: the chapter can be found at the end of Reynolds's *Journey to Flanders and Holland* and see also his discussion of Claude Lorrain in the fourth of the *Discourses*.

280 *Torregiano*: Torregiano (1472–1582), an Italian sculptor, commissioned to make the tomb of Henry VII and his wife in Westminster Abbey.

281 *the whole substance of nature*: Hazlitt supplied the following footnote at this point: 'I believe this rule will apply to all except grotesques, which are evidently taken from opposite natures.'

'*gay creatures . . . clouds*': cf. Milton, *Comus*, ll. 299–301.

282 *beau idéal of art*: equivalent to the English phrase 'grand style'; for a discussion of this, see the third of Reynolds's *Discourses*.

283 *Mr Martin's . . . pictures*: John Martin (1789–1854) was a painter of visionary and apocalyptic landscapes whose work enjoyed a considerable reputation here and in Europe; one of the founders of the British Society of Artists.

284 *Mr H–yd–n's*: Benjamin Robert Haydon (1786–1846), English painter who attempted to rediscover the grand style in his treatment of religious and historical subjects; an acquaintance of Hazlitt, whose face is taken as a model for one of the crowd in Haydon's *Christ's Entry into Jerusalem*.

285 (*cum grano salis*): 'with a grain of salt'.

(*it has been remarked*): according to Hazlitt the remark comes from Coleridge in conversation.

though Sir Joshua tells us: Reynolds's argument can be found in the *Idler*, nos. 76 and 82.

286 (*we speak by the proverb*): unidentified, unless Hazlitt is misremembering the proverb 'The Irishman for his hand, the Welshman for a leg, the Englishman for a face, the Dutchman for a beard.'

'*villainous low*': *The Tempest*, IV. i. 248.

287 '*to o'erstep the modesty of nature*': cf. *Hamlet*, III. ii. 21.

Momus: Momus is a figure from ancient Greek mythology; the god of satire and the satirist of the gods, his capacity for fault-finding and mockery eventually led to him being cast out of Olympus.

'*all we hate*': Pope, *Moral Essays*, 2: Epistle to a Lady, l. 52.

290 '*Thrills in each nerve, and lives along the line*': cf. Addison, *Milton's Style Imitated*, ll. 123–4.

291 *to a demonstration of an old and very disputed point*: the dispute was about the capacity for a purely visual representation to express character or feeling. The argument goes back to classical antiquity: in Xenophon, *Memorabilia*, III. x. 3, Socrates argues that the face is expressive of emotion without the intermediary of verbal language, and, therefore, a visual representation can be expressive. Aristotle in the *Politics*, $1340^{a}35$ argues that visual images cannot be richly expressive, and that speech and melody are the fullest expression of character and emotion.

293 *why then there should be all this squeamishness*: the 'squeamishness' has to do with an an argument over the merits of a psychological as opposed to a proportional aesthetic. The psychological view stresses that 'beauty is in the eye of the beholder'; the proportional view that it consists in the harmony and proportion of the beautiful object. For the latter view, see Burke, *A Philosophical Enquiry into the Origin of our Ideas of the Sublime and the Beautiful* (1757–9); for the former, see Richard Payne Knight, *An Analytical Enquiry into the Principles of Taste* (1805).

296 *That truth is, to a certain degree, beauty*: the echoing of the last line of Keats's 'Ode on a Grecian Urn' is one indication of the dialogue between Hazlitt and Keats. Hazlitt had met Keats

early in 1817. Keats attended some of Hazlitt's *Lectures on the English Poets* in 1818, and wrote enthusiastically about them in a letter to George and Tom Keats written in the February of that year.

296 *gratis dicta*: mere assertions.

HOGARTH

297 Hazlitt regarded Hogarth as the outstanding modern English painter, and often wrote directly about his work or alluded to it. Like Charles Lamb, Hazlitt compared Hogarth's paintings to literature: 'Other pictures we see, Hogarth's we read.' It is not surprising, then, that Hogarth figured in Hazlitt's series of *Lectures on the English Comic Writers*. Hazlitt gave these lectures in 1818 at the Surrey Institution, and they were published in book form the following year. An excerpt from the lecture on Hogarth is printed here.

298 *highest authority on art in this country*: probably Sir George Beaumont (1753–1827), collector of paintings, patron of the arts, and portrait painter. Beaumont was a friend and patron of Wordsworth and Coleridge. Regarded as an arbiter of taste, he built up an extensive collection of paintings, including pictures by Wilkie. He was one of the founders the National Gallery.

Mr Wilkie: see above note to p. 274.

Teniers: David Teniers the Younger (1785–1841), Flemish painter, noted for his genre paintings. Teniers also worked as a curator, and as an avid copyist of Venetian Renaissance painting.

'*to shew . . . image*': cf. *Hamlet*, III. ii. 27.

'*the very error of the time*': cf. *Othello*, V. ii. 112.

299 '*your lungs . . . chanticleer*': cf. *As You Like It*, II. vii. 30.

300 *Bagnigge Wells*: now Sadler's Wells.

like the supper in Gil Blas: *Gil Blas*, a picaresque novel, set in Spain, published between 1715–35, and written by the French writer Alain Le Sage (1688–1747). Hazlitt might have read the novel in Smollett's translation of 1749. The supper is in Bk. I, ch. 2.

301 *immoveable Parson Ford*: in *Modern Midnight Conversation* Hogarth had depicted Samuel Johnson's cousin, Parson Ford,

who, according to Boswell was 'a man in whom both talents and good dispositions were disgraced by licentiousness' (Boswell, *Life of Johnson*, ed. G. Hill, i. 47).

'*like leaves in October*': Beaumont and Fletcher, *The Bloody Brother*, ii. ii, from 'The Drinking Song'.

'*Die of a rose in aromatic pain*': Pope, *Essay on Man*, Epistle 1, l. 200.

302 *Lord Chesterfield himself*: otherwise Philip Stanhope (1694–1773), politician, gambler, and letter-writer, noted for his letters of advice to his son on the education and behaviour of a gentleman.

in the manner of Ackerman's dresses for May: Hazlitt is in fact quoting the last line of Tom Moore's comic translation, *Horace Ode X Lib 11. Freely translated by the Pr—ce R–g—t*. Rudolph Ackermann (1764–1834) was a German-born inventor, designer, lithographer, and publisher who lived and worked in London from 1795 until his death. *His Repository of Arts, Literature, Fashions etc.* included illustrations of fashionable clothes.

'*the Charming Betsy Careless*': a detail in the last of Hogarth's *Rake's Progress* series. In the picture the name 'the Charming Betsy Careless' is scratched on a bannister by one of the inmates of Bedlam.

303 '*stray-gifts of love and beauty*': cf. Wordsworth, *Stray Pleasures*, l. 28.

For Mr Lamb has shewn: see Charles Lamb's *Essay on the Genius & Character of Hogarth.*

'*the hand-writing on the wall*': cf. Daniel 5: 5.

304 *Garrick's acting*: see above note to p. 244.

insisted on by Sir Joshua Reynolds: see the third of Reynold's *Discourses on Art.*

305 '*conformed . . . not transformed*': cf. Romans 12: 2.

'*to give to airy nothing . . . name*': cf. *A Midsummer Night's Dream*, v. i. 16–17.

'*ignorant present*': *Macbeth*, i. iv. 54.

306 *as they do so*: Hazlitt supplied the following footnote at this point, citing a character in Scott's *Guy Mannering*: When Meg Merrilies says in her dying moments—"Nay, nay, lay my head to the East," what was the East to her? Not a reality but an idea

of distant time and the land of her forefathers; the last, the strongest, and the best that occurred to her in this world. Her gipsy slang and dress were quaint and grotesque; her attachment to the Kaim of Derncleugh and the wood of Warrock was romantic; her worship of the East was *ideal*.'

307 *Gate Beautiful . . . Miraculous Draught of Fishes*: two cartoons by Raphael. Hazlitt saw them at Hampton Court.

308 '*How was I then uplifted!* ': cf. *Troilus and Cressida*, III. ii. 164.

'*temples . . . heavens*': cf. 2 Cor. 5: 1.

'*All eyes . . . bow to me!*': cf. Rom. 14: 11

ON POETRY IN GENERAL

308 The initial form of the text printed here was as part of a lecture in a series given by Hazlitt on the English Poets at the Surrey Institution in 1818. Keats was amongst the audience. The lectures were published in the same year and reprinted in a corrected form in 1819. The excerpt printed here is taken from this corrected edition.

309 *It comes home . . . men*: an unacknowledged quotation from the Dedication to Bacon's *Essays*.

'*spreads its sweet leaves*': cf. *Romeo and Juliet*, I. i. 150–1.

'*the stuff of which our life is made*': a distant echo of *The Tempest*, IV. i. 156–8.

'*mere oblivion*': *As You Like It*, II. vii. 165.

310 '*man's life is poor as beast's*': cf. *Lear*, II. iv. 266.

like Molière's Bourgeois Gentilhomme: for the comic discovery about speaking prose, see *Le Bourgeois Gentilhomme*, II. vi.

'*There is warrant for it*': cf. *Macbeth*, II. iii. 144.

'*such seething brains . . . reason*'. . . . '*The lunatic, . . . imagination*': *A Midsummer Night's Dream*, V. i. 4–18.

Angelica and Medoro: both characters from Ariosto's epic poem *Orlando Furioso*, published in 1532.

311 *Plato banished the poets*: see *The Republic*, X.

'*which ecstacy is very cunning in*': cf. *Hamlet*, III. iv. 138.

'*to relieve the aching sense of pleasure . . . manner*': cf. the echo of this sentence in Keats's line, 'and aching Pleasure nigh', from his 'Ode on Melancholy', written about twelve months after he heard Hazlitt lecture, and just one indication of the effect on him of Hazlitt's sense of poetry.

according to Lord Bacon: see *The Advancement of Learning*, Bk. II, ch. 4, para. 2.

312 *'Our eyes are made the fools'*: cf. *Macbeth*, II. i. 44.

'That if it would but apprehend some joy . . . bear': continues the earlier quotation from *A Midsummer Night's Dream*, V. i. 19–22.

'The flame o' th' taper . . . lights': *Cymbeline*, II. ii. 19–21.

313 *'for they are old like him'*: cf. *Lear*, II. iv. 189–91.

'Nothing but . . . this': cf. *Lear*, III. iv. 69–70.

'The little dogs and all . . . me': *Lear*, III. vi. 61–2.

'So I am': *Lear*, IV. vii. 70.

314 *'Oh now, for ever . . . gone'*: *Othello*, III. iii. 351–61.

'Never Iago. . . . thence!': *Othello*, III. iii. 457–64; cf. *Othello*, IV. ii. 58–61.

315 *Moore and Lillo*: Edward Moore (1712–57) wrote two sentimental tragedies, *The Foundling* (1747) and *The Gamester* (1753); George Lillo (1693–1739) preceded Moore in the same vein with his play *The London Merchant* (1731), warmly praised by Alexander Pope.

As Mr Burke observes: in his *Philosophical Enquiry into the Origin of our Ideas of the Sublime and Beautiful* (1757–9), Part 1, para. 15.

316 *'Masterless passion sways . . . loathes'*: cf. *The Merchant of Venice*, IV. i. 51–2.

'satisfaction to the thought': cf. *Othello*, III. iii. 98.

'Now night descending . . . more!': cf. Pope, *The Dunciad*, i. 87–8.

316–317 *'with limbs of giant mould' . . . 'Throw him on the steep . . . asleep'*: Collins, *Ode to Fear*, ll. 10, 11. 14–15.

317 *'Ingratitude, . . . sea-monster!'*: cf. *Lear*, I. iv. 259–61.

'both at the first and now . . . nature': *Hamlet*, III. ii. 25.

318 *'And visions, . . . bough'*: Gray to Horace Walpole.

319 *Doctor Chalmers's Discourses*: Thomas Chalmers (1780–1847) published in 1817 *A Series of Discourses on the Christian Revelation, viewed in connection with Modern Astronomy*; one of many nineteenth-century attempts to square the evidence of science with Christian doctrine.

319 *Rembrandt's picture*: Rembrandt did an etching of Jacob's Dream in 1655, but it is possible the reference is to another of Rembrandt's pictures drawn from an episode in Jacob's life, *Jacob Wrestling with the Angel*, painted in 1659.

'*bandit fierce*': cf. Milton, *Comus*, l. 426.

'*our fell of hair . . . in it*': cf. *Macbeth*, v. v. 11–12.

'*Obscurity her curtain . . . sung*': from *To the Honourable and Reverend F. C.* by Sneyd Davies (1709–69) in vol. 6 of Dodsley's *Collection of Poems* (1758). F. C. is Frederick Cornwallis, Archbishop of Canterbury.

320 '*Between the acting . . . insurrection*': cf. *Julius Caesar*, ii. i. 63–9.

Greek statues are little else than specious forms: contrast Hazlitt's account in *On the Elgin Marbles*, pp. 284–6 above.

By their beauty they are deified: echoes and rewrites Wordsworth, *Resolution and Independence*, l. 47.

321 '*Thoughts . . . numbers*': Milton, *Paradise Lost*, iii. 37–8.

'*the words of Mercury . . . Apollo*': cf. *Love's Labour's Lost*, v. ii. 917–18.

'*So from the ground . . . cometh out*': Spenser, *Faerie Queene*, i. vi, stanzas 13–14.

But poetry makes these odds all even: cf. *Measure for Measure*, iii. i. 41.

322 '*the secret soul of harmony*': cf. Milton, *L'Allegro*, l. 144.

'*the golden cadences of poetry*': cf. *Love's Labour's Lost*, iv. ii. 116.

'*Sailing with supreme dominion . . . air*': Gray, *Progress of Poesy*, A Pindaric Ode, Pt. III, stanza 3, ll. 116–17.

323 '*sounding always the increase of his winning*': Chaucer, *The Canterbury Tales*, General Prologue, l. 275.

SHAKESPEARE

323 As with the preceding piece, *On Poetry in General*, the following excerpt had its initial form as a lecture on Shakespeare and Milton that Hazlitt delivered at the Surrey Institution as part of his series on the English Poets. The text printed here is taken from the corrected 1819 publication of the lectures.

The four greatest names: cf. Hazlitt's argument in *Why the Arts are not Progressive*, pp. 257–62 above.

'*the fault has been . . . underlings*': cf. *Julius Caesar*, I. ii. 140.

324 '*a mind reflecting ages past*': drawn from the opening line of the poem celebrating Shakespeare which prefaces the Second Folio edition of his works, published in 1632.

'*All corners of the earth . . . grave*': cf. *Cymbeline*, III. iv. 35–6.

325 '*nodded to him . . . curtesies*': cf. *A Midsummer Night's Dream*, III. i. 160.

'*his so potent art*': cf. *The Tempest*, V. i. 50.

for if the preternatural characters: cf. Coleridge's account of the composition of his mystery poems. The account is in *Biographia Literaria*, ch. 14, first published in 1817.

'*subject to the same skyey influences*': cf. *Measure for Measure*, III. i. 9.

'*his frequent haunts . . . neighbourhood*': cf. Milton, *Comus*, l. 314.

'*coheres semblably together*': cf. *2 Henry IV*, V. i. 64.

as it has been ingeniously remarked: by Coleridge in his lecture, 'On Shakespeare and Milton', given in a series delivered in 1811–12.

'*Me and thy crying self*': *The Tempest*, I. ii. 132.

326 '*What! man . . . brows*': *Macbeth*, IV. iii. 208.

'*Man delights . . . say so*': *Hamlet*, III. ii. 309, and for the reply of Rosencrantz and Guildenstern, see the lines immediately following.

'*a combination and a form*': *Hamlet*, III. iv. 60.

326–327 '*Ophelia. My lord. . . . glassy stream*': cf. *Hamlet*, II. i. 77–100; *Hamlet*, IV. vii. 167–8.

327 '*He's speaking now . . . Nile?*' . . . '*It is my birth-day . . . Cleopatra*': *Antony and Cleopatra*, I. v. 24–5; III. xiii. 185–7.

329 '*nigh sphered in Heaven*': Collins, *Ode to the Poetical Character*, l. 66.

'*playing with wisdom*': cf. Milton, *Paradise Lost*, vii. 9–11.

'*to make society the sweeter welcome*': *Macbeth*, III. i. 41–2.

330 '*which, with a little act . . . yesterday*': cf. *Othello*, III. iii. 332–6.

'*while rage . . . sympathise*': cf. *Troilus and Cressida*, I. iii. 52.

331 '*in their untroubled element . . . forgotten*': a prose reworking of lines 763–6 in Bk. 6 of Wordsworth's *Excursion*.

331 *Satan's address to the Sun*: Milton, *Paradise Lost*, iv. 32–113.

'*Oh, that I were a mockery-king . . . Bolingbroke*': cf. *Richard II*, IV. i. 260–2.

'*His form had not yet lost . . . obscur'd*': Milton, *Paradise Lost*, i. 591–4.

with the Moods of their own Minds: Wordsworth had classified some of the poems in the two-volume collection of 1807 as 'Moods of my own Mind'. Wordsworth is, of course, the exemplar for Hazlitt of the 'modern school of poetry' and its 'devouring egotism'.

332 '*With what measure they mete . . . again*': Mark 4: 4; Luke 6: 38.

'*It glances from heaven. . . . minutes*': cf. *A Midsummer Night's Dream*, V. i. 13; II. i. 175.

'*I ask that I may awaken reverence . . . Phoebus*': this and the following two quotations come from *Troilus and Cressida*, I. iii. 227–30; III. iii. 115–23, with the omission of line 116; III. iii. 222–5.

333 '*Light thickens . . . wood*': *Macbeth*, III. ii. 50–1.

334 '*his whole course of love*'. . . . '*the business . . . offence*': cf. *Othello*, I. iii. 91; IV. ii. 166.

'*Of ditties highly penned . . . lute*': cf. *1 Henry IV*, III. i. 208–10.

'*And so by many winding nooks . . . ocean*': cf. *The Two Gentlemen of Verona*, II. vii. 31–2.

335 '*great vulgar and the small*': cf. Horace, *Odes* III. i.

Voltaire's criticism: for Voltaire's criticism, see above *On Modern Comedy*, note to p. 104.

'*his delights did shew most dolphin-like*': cf. *Antony and Cleopatra*, v. ii. 88–9.

MACBETH

335 Taken from *Characters of Shakespeare's Plays* first published in 1817. A second edition was published in 1818 to coincide with the appearance in book form of Hazlitt's *Lectures on the English Poets*. It is likely that some of Hazlitt's quotations from Shakespeare come from memory. If he is quoting directly from a text, scholars have not yet been able to establish its identity. As elsewhere in this volume, references are given to Professor Alexander's edition of *The Complete Works of William Shakespeare*. The usual procedure is adopted for indicating a dis-

crepancy between Hazlitt's quotations and the text established by Alexander. As there is extensive quotation from Macbeth in what follows, I have not given the play's title in the references.

'*The poet's eye . . . name*': as will be evident by now, one of Hazlitt's favourite quotations from *A Midsummer Night's Dream*, v. i. 12–17.

336 '*the rapidity of action*': cf. Coleridge's comparison between *Hamlet* and *Macbeth*, 'The one [Hamlet] proceeds with the utmost slowness, the other [Macbeth] with a crowded and breathless rapidity.'

'*your only tragedy-maker*': cf. *Hamlet*, III. ii. 120.

'*the air smells wooingly*': cf. I. vi. 4–6 for this and 'the temple-haunting martlet builds'.

'*the blasted heath*': cf. I. iii. 77.

'*air-drawn dagger*': III. iv. 62.

'*gracious Duncan*': III. i. 65

'*blood-boultered Banquo*': IV. i. 123.

336–337 '*What are these . . . are on't*': I. iii. 39–42.

337 '*bends up each corporal instrument . . . feat*': cf. I. vii. 79–80.

'*The deed, . . . confounds him*': cf. II. ii. 10–11.

'*preternatural solicitings*': cf. I. iii. 130.

338 '*Bring forth men children . . . males*': I. vii. 72–4.

'*screw his courage to the sticking-place*': cf. I. vii. 60.

'*lost so poorly in himself*': cf. II. ii. 71–2.

'*a little water . . . deed*': cf. II. ii. 67.

'*the sides of his intent*': cf. I. vii. 26.

'*for their future days and nights . . . masterdom*': cf. I. v. 66–7.

'*his fatal entrance . . . battlements*': cf. I. v. 36–7.

339 '*Come all you spirits . . . hold!*': I. v. 36–51, although modern editions agree in omitting 'all' from the first line.

'*Duncan comes there to sleep*': cf. I. v. 27.

'*Thou 'rt mad to say it*': I. ii. 28.

'*Hie thee hither . . . withal*': I. ii. 23–7.

Mrs Siddons's manner: see above note to p. 137.

340 *'There is no art . . . upon me, etc.'*: cf. I. iv. 11–16.

341 *'How goes the night . . . repose'*: II. i. 1–9, with the omission of a half-line at line 5.

'Light thickens. . . . inn': III. ii. 50–1; III. iii. 6–7.

'So fair and foul . . . seen': I. iii. 38.

'Such welcome and unwelcome news together': cf. IV. iii. 138.

'Men's lives . . . sickens': cf. IV. iii. 171–3.

'Look like . . . under it.': I. iv. 62–3.

342 *'To him and all . . . Avaunt and quit my sight'*: cf. III. iv. 91 and 93.

'himself again': cf. III. iv. 108.

'he may sleep . . . thunder': cf. IV. i. 86.

'Then be thou jocund . . . note': III. iii. 40–4.

'Had he not resembled . . . done 't': II. ii. 12–13.

'rejoice . . . bleed' . . . 'they should be women . . . forbid it': cf. I. iii. 45–7.

'in deeper consequence': cf. I. iii. 126.

'Why stands Macbeth thus amazedly?': IV. i. 125–6.

as distinct a being from Richard III: the comparison between Richard and Macbeth was a staple of eighteenth-century Shakespearian criticism. See for example J. P. Kemble, *Macbeth and King Richard III, an Essay*, first published in 1786.

343 *'the milk of human kindness'*: I. v. 14.

'himself alone': cf. *3 Henry VI*, V. vi. 83, where Gloucester declares 'I am myself alone'. Cibber placed the line in the last act of *Richard III* and this was the version acted by Edmund Kean.

'For Banquo's issue . . . kings': the quotation conflates lines from III. i. 64–5, and 69.

'Duncan is in his grave . . . sleeps well': III. ii. 22–3.

'direness . . . slaughterous thoughts': V. v. 14.

'is troubled . . . rest': V. iii. 38.

344 *'subject to all the skyey influences'*: cf. *Measure for Measure*, III. i. 9.

'My way of life . . . dare not': cf. V. iii. 22–8.

345 '*The progress of manners*': see above *On Modern Comedy* and *On Modern Tragedy*.

345 The passage printed here is excerpted from *The Characters of Shakespeare's Plays*. For publication details of that volume, see the notes to Hazlitt's essay on *Macbeth* above p. 418. The essay on *Coriolanus* was first published in the *Examiner* for 15 December 1816.

345 *since the French Revolution or our own*: 'our own' revolution is the so-called 'Glorious Revolution' of 1688 when the Catholic monarch, James II was replaced by the Protestant rule of William and Mary.

'*no jutting frieze . . . to make its pendant bed . . . in*: cf. *Macbeth*, I. vi. 6–8.

346 '*it carries noise*': cf. *Coriolanus*, II. i. 150.

'*Carnage is its daughter*': cf. Wordsworth, *Ode, 1815.*

'*poor rats*': cf. *Coriolanus*, I. i. 248.

347 Hazlitt's essay on Wordsworth was first printed in *The Spirit of the Age*, published in 1825.

'*lowliness is young ambition's ladder*': *Julius Caesar*, II. i. 22.

'*no figures nor no fantasies . . . men*': cf. *Julius Caesar*, II. i. 231–2.

'*skyey influences*': *Measure for Measure*, III. i. 9.

'*Nihil humani . . . puto*': from Terence, *Heautontimorumenos* (usually translated as 'The Self- Hater'), I. i. 77. The original reads '*humani nil a me alienum puto*', translated as 'I hold that what affects another man affects me' (Loeb edn. trans. J. Saurgeant).

348 '*the cloud-capt towers . . . like the baseless fabric . . . behind*': cf. *The Tempest*, IV. i. 150–6.

'*the judge's robe . . . 'longs*': cf. *Measure for Measure*, II. ii. 59–60.

349 *The jewels in the crisped hair*: cf. Collins, *The Manners. An Ode*, l. 53.

'*a sense of joy . . . field*': Wordsworth, *To my Sister.*

'*Beneath the hills . . . destiny*': cf. Wordsworth, *The Excursion*, vi. 552–7.

350 '*To him the meanest flower . . . tears*': cf. Wordsworth, *Ode on the Intimations of Immortality.*

351 *a cottage at Grasmere . . . recollections of Cole-Orton*: Wordsworth had lived at Dove Cottage in Grasmere from 1799–1808. Cole-Orton was the name of the country house belonging to Wordsworth's friend and patron, Sir George Beaumont. Wordsworth was a frequent visitor there.

352 '*Calm contemplation . . . pains*': cf. Wordsworth, *Laodamia.*

'*Fall blunted . . . breast*': cf. Goldsmith, *The Traveller.*

'*and fit audience . . . few*': cf. Milton, *Paradise Lost*, vii. 31.

353 *toujours perdrix!*: literally translated as 'always partridge'; proverbially the phrase means 'Always the same old tale'. The comment was originally made by the confessor to the French King, Henry VI, when the latter illustrated the idea that variety is the source of happiness by ordering partridge for every course at dinner.

'*man of no mark or likelihood*': cf. *1 Henry IV*, III. ii. 45.

354 '*Flushed with a purple grace . . . face*': cf. Dryden, *Alexander's Feast*, iii. 51–2.

'*He hates . . . Caius*': Hazlitt quotes from his own conversation with Wordsworth.

Mr Wordsworth himself wrote a tragedy: the tragedy is *The Borderers*, written between 1795–6.

355 '*Action is momentary . . . infinite!*': cf. Wordsworth, *The Borderers*, III. 1539–43.

'*Let observation . . . Peru*': Hazlitt first attributed this analysis of Johnson's poem to Wordsworth in a conversation with John Payne Collier in 1811. The analysis became something of a standard critical turn in the period. Coleridge commented along similar lines to his nephew in April 1811, and the analysis surfaced again in the sixth of his series of Lectures on Shakespeare and Milton, delivered in 1811–12 (see Coleridge, *Collected Works*, vol. 5, Bk. 1. 292–3).

a perfect Drawcansir: 'name of a blustering, bragging character in Villiers's burlesque "The Rehearsal", who in the last scene is made to enter a battle and kill all the combatants on both sides, hence allusively . . .' (*OED*). George Villiers, Duke of Buckingham (1628–87), was a playwright and politician who wrote *The Rehearsal* in 1671.

Walton's Angler, Paley: Izaak Walton (1593–1683) first published *The Compleat Angler* in 1653, and then substantially rewrote it for a second publication in 1655. William Paley (1743–1808) was a theologian who argued in his *Evidences of Christianity* (1794) and in *Natural Theology* (1802) that the evidences of design in nature proved the existence of God.

Bewick's woodcuts and Waterloo's sylvan etchings: Thomas Bewick (1755–1828) was a noted wood-engraver and book illustrator. Antoine Waterloo (1609–76?) was a Belgian-born engraver and painter, noted for the delicacy of his style.

356 *It has been said*: by Hazlitt himself in his 'Lecture on the Living Poets', part of the 1818 series *Lectures on the English Poets*.

'*Where one for sense . . . time*': cf. Butler, *Hudibras*, II. i. 29–30.

357 '*take the good the Gods provide us*': translated from Plautus, *Rudens*, IV. vii. 1229.

American Literature

British and Irish Literature

Children's Literature

Classics and Ancient Literature

Colonial Literature

Eastern Literature

European Literature

Gothic Literature

History

Medieval Literature

Oxford English Drama

Poetry

Philosophy

Politics

Religion

The Oxford Shakespeare

A complete list of Oxford World's Classics, including Authors in Context, Oxford English Drama, and the Oxford Shakespeare, is available in the UK from the Marketing Services Department, Oxford University Press, Great Clarendon Street, Oxford OX2 6DP, or visit the website at www.oup.com/uk/worldsclassics.

In the USA, visit www.oup.com/us/owc for a complete title list.

Oxford World's Classics are available from all good bookshops. In case of difficulty, customers in the UK should contact Oxford University Press Bookshop, 116 High Street, Oxford OX1 4BR.

A SELECTION OF **OXFORD WORLD'S CLASSICS**

JANE AUSTEN

Emma
Mansfield Park
Persuasion
Pride and Prejudice
Sense and Sensibility

MRS BEETON

Book of Household Management

LADY ELIZABETH
BRADDON

Lady Audley's Secret

ANNE BRONTË

The Tenant of Wildfell Hall

CHARLOTTE BRONTË

Jane Eyre
Shirley
Villette

EMILY BRONTË

Wuthering Heights

SAMUEL TAYLOR
COLERIDGE

The Major Works

WILKIE COLLINS

The Moonstone
No Name
The Woman in White

CHARLES DARWIN

The Origin of Species

CHARLES DICKENS

The Adventures of Oliver Twist
Bleak House
David Copperfield
Great Expectations
Nicholas Nickleby
The Old Curiosity Shop
Our Mutual Friend
The Pickwick Papers
A Tale of Two Cities

GEORGE DU MAURIER

Trilby

MARIA EDGEWORTH

Castle Rackrent

A SELECTION OF   **OXFORD WORLD'S CLASSICS**

ROBERT LOUIS   **Kidnapped** and **Catriona**
STEVENSON   **The Strange Case of Dr Jekyll and**
                          Mr Hyde and **Weir of Hermiston**
                      Treasure Island

BRAM STOKER   **Dracula**

WILLIAM MAKEPEACE   **Vanity Fair**
THACKERAY

OSCAR WILDE   **Complete Shorter Fiction**
                      The Major Works
                      The Picture of Dorian Gray

DOROTHY WORDSWORTH   **The Grasmere and Alfoxden Journals**

WILLIAM WORDSWORTH   **The Major Works**

ANTHONY TROLLOPE

An Autobiography
The American Senator
Barchester Towers
Can You Forgive Her?
The Claverings
Cousin Henry
Doctor Thorne
The Duke's Children
The Eustace Diamonds
Framley Parsonage
He Knew He Was Right
Lady Anna
The Last Chronicle of Barset
Orley Farm
Phineas Finn
Phineas Redux
The Prime Minister
Rachel Ray
The Small House at Allington
The Warden
The Way We Live Now

A SELECTION OF   **OXFORD WORLD'S CLASSICS**

HANS CHRISTIAN ANDERSEN   Fairy Tales

J. M. BARRIE   Peter Pan in Kensington Gardens and Peter and Wendy

L. FRANK BAUM   The Wonderful Wizard of Oz

FRANCES HODGSON BURNETT   The Secret Garden

LEWIS CARROLL   Alice's Adventures in Wonderland and Through the Looking-Glass

CARLO COLLODI   The Adventures of Pinocchio

KENNETH GRAHAME   The Wind in the Willows

ANTHONY HOPE   The Prisoner of Zenda

THOMAS HUGHES   Tom Brown's Schooldays

A SELECTION OF **OXFORD WORLD'S CLASSICS**

	Six French Poets of the Nineteenth Century
HONORÉ DE BALZAC	**Cousin Bette** **Eugénie Grandet** **Père Goriot**
CHARLES BAUDELAIRE	**The Flowers of Evil** **The Prose Poems** and **Fanfarlo**
BENJAMIN CONSTANT	**Adolphe**
DENIS DIDEROT	**Jacques the Fatalist**
ALEXANDRE DUMAS (PÈRE)	**The Black Tulip** **The Count of Monte Cristo** **Louise de la Vallière** **The Man in the Iron Mask** **La Reine Margot** **The Three Musketeers** **Twenty Years After** **The Vicomte de Bragelonne**
ALEXANDRE DUMAS (FILS)	**La Dame aux Camélias**
GUSTAVE FLAUBERT	**Madame Bovary** **A Sentimental Education** **Three Tales**
VICTOR HUGO	**Notre-Dame de Paris**
J.-K. HUYSMANS	**Against Nature**
PIERRE CHODERLOS DE LACLOS	**Les Liaisons dangereuses**
MME DE LAFAYETTE	**The Princesse de Clèves**
GUILLAUME DU LORRIS and JEAN DE MEUN	**The Romance of the Rose**

A SELECTION OF   **OXFORD WORLD'S CLASSICS**

GUY DE MAUPASSANT	**A Day in the Country and Other Stories**
	A Life
	Bel-Ami
	Mademoiselle Fifi and Other Stories
	Pierre et Jean
PROSPER MÉRIMÉE	**Carmen and Other Stories**
MOLIÈRE	**Don Juan and Other Plays**
	The Misanthrope, Tartuffe, and Other Plays
BLAISE PASCAL	**Pensées and Other Writings**
JEAN RACINE	**Britannicus, Phaedra, and Athaliah**
ARTHUR RIMBAUD	**Collected Poems**
EDMOND ROSTAND	**Cyrano de Bergerac**
MARQUIS DE SADE	**The Misfortunes of Virtue and Other Early Tales**
GEORGE SAND	**Indiana**
MME DE STAËL	**Corinne**
STENDHAL	**The Red and the Black**
	The Charterhouse of Parma
PAUL VERLAINE	**Selected Poems**
JULES VERNE	**Around the World in Eighty Days**
	Journey to the Centre of the Earth
	Twenty Thousand Leagues under the Seas
VOLTAIRE	**Candide and Other Stories**
	Letters concerning the English Nation

ÉMILE ZOLA

L'Assommoir
The Attack on the Mill
La Bête humaine
La Débâcle
Germinal
The Ladies' Paradise
The Masterpiece
Nana
Pot Luck
Thérèse Raquin